TRAGIC HEROINES IN ANCIENT GREEK DRAMA

Also available from Bloomsbury

ORIENTALISM AND THE RECEPTION OF POWERFUL WOMEN FROM THE ANCIENT WORLD
edited by Filippo Carlà-Uhink and Anja Wieber

WOMEN IN ANCIENT GREECE
by Bonnie MacLachlan

WOMEN IN GREEK MYTH
by Mary R. Lefkowitz

TRAGIC HEROINES IN ANCIENT GREEK DRAMA

Hanna M. Roisman

BLOOMSBURY ACADEMIC
LONDON • NEW YORK • OXFORD • NEW DELHI • SYDNEY

BLOOMSBURY ACADEMIC
Bloomsbury Publishing Plc
50 Bedford Square, London, WC1B 3DP, UK
1385 Broadway, New York, NY 10018, USA

BLOOMSBURY, BLOOMSBURY ACADEMIC and the Diana logo are trademarks
of Bloomsbury Publishing Plc

First published in Great Britain 2021

Copyright © Hanna M. Roisman 2021

Hanna M. Roisman has asserted her right under the Copyright, Designs and Patents Act,
1988, to be identified as Author of this work.

For legal purposes the Acknowledgements on p. viii constitute an extension of this copyright page.

Cover design: Terry Woodley
Cover image: The Caryatids of the Erechtheion, Athens, Greece.
Andronosh / Alamy Stock Photo

All rights reserved. No part of this publication may be reproduced or transmitted in any form or by any
means, electronic or mechanical, including photocopying, recording, or any information storage or
retrieval system, without prior permission in writing from the publishers.

Bloomsbury Publishing Plc does not have any control over, or responsibility for, any third-party
websites referred to or in this book. All internet addresses given in this book were correct at the
time of going to press. The author and publisher regret any inconvenience caused if addresses have
changed or sites have ceased to exist, but can accept no responsibility for any such changes.

A catalogue record for this book is available from the British Library.

Library of Congress Cataloging-in-Publication Data

Names: Roisman, Hanna, author.
Title: Tragic heroines in ancient Greek drama / by Hanna M. Roisman.
Description: London : Bloomsbury Academic, 2021. | Includes bibliographical references and index. |
Summary: "The heroines of Greek tragedy presented in the plays by Aeschylus, Sophocles and Euripides have
long captivated audiences and critics. In this volume each of the eleven chapters discusses one of the heroines:
Clytemnestra, Hecuba, Medea, Iphigenia, Alcestis, Antigone Electra, Deianeira, Phaedra, Creusa and Helen.
The book focuses on characterisation and the motivations of the women, as well as on those of the male
playwrights, and offers multiple viewpoints and critiques that enable readers to understand the context of each
play and form their own views. Four core themes bridge the depictions of the heroines: the socio-political
dynamic of ancient Greek expectations of women and their roles in society, the conflict of masculinity versus
femininity, the alternation of defiance and submission, and the interplay between deceit and rhetoric. Each
chapter offers clear descriptions of plot and mythical background, and builds on the text of the plays to enable
reflections on language and performance. All technical terms are explained and key topics or references are
pulled out into box features that provide further background information. Discussion points at the ends of
chapters enable readers to explore various topics more deeply"– Provided by publisher.
Identifiers: LCCN 2020040454 (print) | LCCN 2020040455 (ebook) | ISBN 9781350103993 (paperback) |
ISBN 9781350103986 (hardback) | ISBN 9781350104006 (epub) | ISBN 9781350104013 (ebook)
Subjects: LCSH: Greek drama (Tragedy)–History and criticism. | Heroines in literature. | Women in literature. |
Mythology in literature.
Classification: LCC PA3136 .R59 2021 (print) | LCC PA3136 (ebook) | DDC 882/.01093522—dc23
LC record available at https://lccn.loc.gov/2020040454
LC ebook record available at https://lccn.loc.gov/2020040455

ISBN:	HB:	978-1-3501-0398-6
	PB:	978-1-3501-0399-3
	ePDF:	978-1-3501-0401-3
	eBook:	978-1-3501-0400-6

Typeset by RefineCatch Limited, Bungay, Suffolk

To find out more about our authors and books visit www.bloomsbury.com
and sign up for our newsletters.

For
Yossi,
Elad and Helaina
and my granddaughters
Talia and Yael
and for Shalev and Diana
and my granddaughters
Noa and Esti

CONTENTS

Acknowledgments		viii
Map		ix
Alphabetical List of the Tragedies Discussed		x
Introduction		1
1	**Clytemnestra**	15
2	**Electra**	59
3	**Iphigenia**	93
4	**Antigone**	119
5	**Helen**	137
6	**Hecuba**	167
7	**Alcestis**	179
8	**Deianeira**	193
9	**Medea**	209
10	**Creusa**	231
11	**Phaedra**	247
	Conclusion	267
Notes		277
Glossary of Names and Terms		291
Bibliography		293
Index		305

ACKNOWLEDGMENTS

First and foremost, I offer fond thanks to the many generations of students who have studied Greek Drama with me at Tel Aviv University, Colby College, Cornell University, and American University. Their interest, insights, and questions have spurred me to revisit and rethink many of my views about tragedy, especially about the characterizations of the tragic heroines. The questions of those reading Greek tragedy for the first time have brought a refreshing vigor to my own lifelong examination of the genre, encouraged new thoughts, and provided many welcome occasions for me to reconsider long-held opinions. I am grateful for all the inspirations granted to me by my students, one of the most significant audiences for whom we write and work.

I also owe special gratitude to a group of people who came to my aid while writing this book. Special thanks are owed to my good friend Dr. Jill Yonassi for her stalwart support in recent years: for her insights, questions, comments, and inspiration, as well as for making this manuscript more readable. Karen Gillum saved me from many referencing pitfalls and gave me very helpful comments. To Dr. Julie Brown many thanks for reading through early drafts. I am more than indebted to Alice Wright for her good will, encouragement, facilitation, and for having found time in a very hectic period of her life to carefully inspect the submitted manuscript. The project would not have been possible without her. To Lily Mac Mahon many thanks for the expert advice and help with the maps and the book cover. Over my long career I have also benefited from the useful suggestions of many referees.

To my beloved family: Yossi, Elad, Shalev, Helaina, Diana, Talia, Noa, Yael, and Esti, thank you for being there for me. None of this would be possible without you!

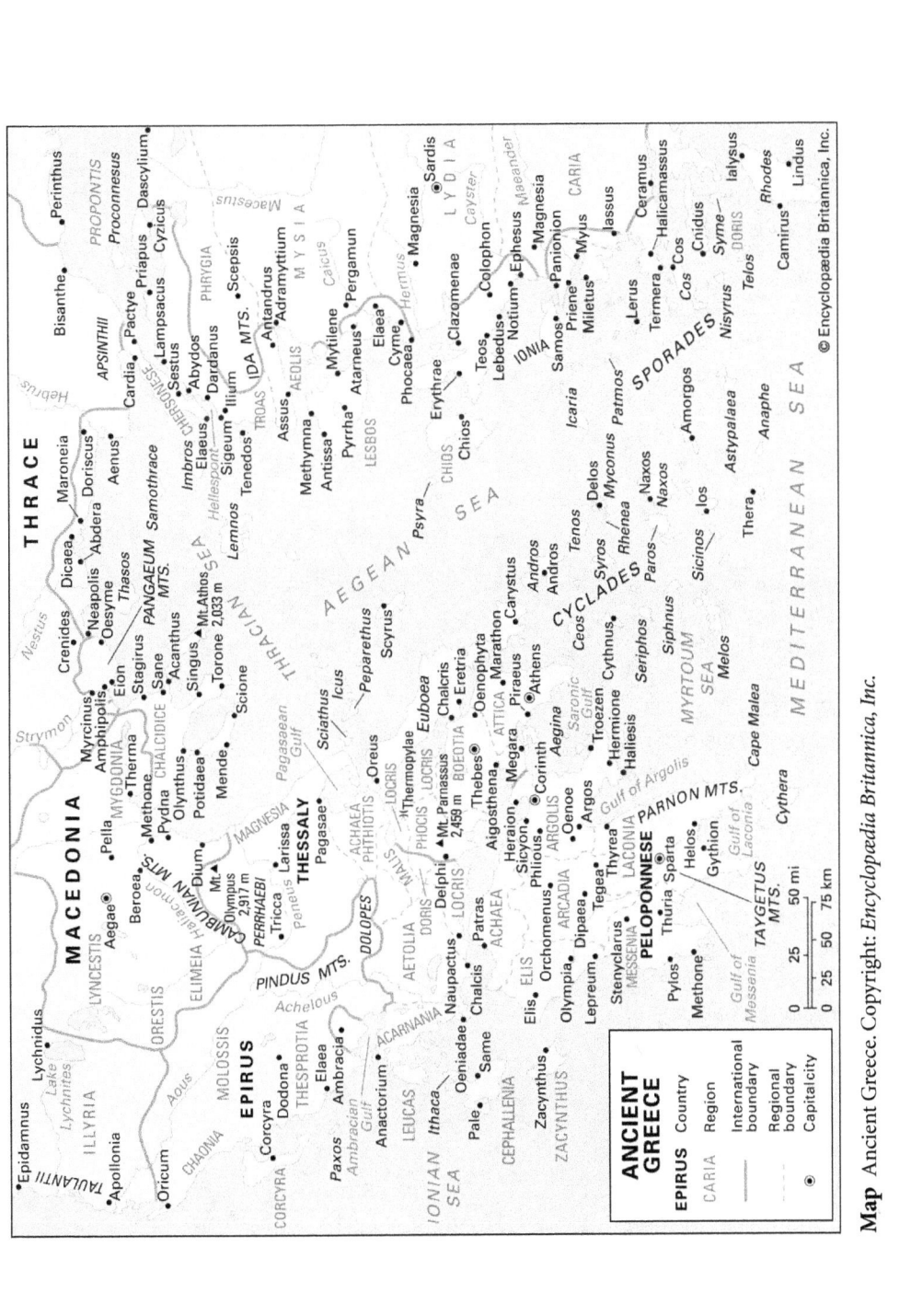

Map Ancient Greece. Copyright: *Encyclopædia Britannica, Inc.*

ALPHABETICAL LIST OF DISCUSSED TRAGEDIES

AESCHYLUS
(ca. 525–456 BCE)

Oresteia 458
    Agamemnon
    Libation Bearers
    Eumenides
Seven against Thebes 467

SOPHOCLES
(ca. 496/5–406/5 BCE)

Antigone
Electra 418–410
Oedipus at Colonus 401
Women of Trachis

EURIPIDES
(ca. 485/80–406 BCE)

Alcestis 438
Electra 422–417 or 415–413
Hecuba
Helen 412
Hippolytus 428
Ion
Iphigenia among the Taurians 414–412
Iphigenia at Aulis 405?
Medea 431
Orestes 408
Phoenician Women 411–409
Trojan Women 415

INTRODUCTION

This book addresses eleven prominent female heroines in extant Greek tragedy: Clytemnestra, Electra, Iphigenia, Antigone, Helen, Hecuba, Alcestis, Deianeira, Medea, Creusa, and Phaedra. The aim is to help students gain a more thorough understanding of the heroines' personalities, roles, and agendas through a close inspection of the texts. The emphasis is on the characters of the heroines and on their relationships, allowing a vivid picture to be formed in the readers' minds. However, the discussion also looks at how the tragedians created their dramatic heroines, through use of language and plot. Bearing in mind that many readers may not be familiar with Greek, the analysis attempts to offer an appreciation of some aspects of the tragedians' use of language in an accessible way. Where Greek terms are introduced they are always transliterated and accompanied by translations. In this way some of the poetry and dramatic effects of the texts may be presented, without presupposing any knowledge of Greek. Tinted boxes at the start of chapters offer brief explanations of the myths and plays the heroine appears in, while those occasionally appearing in the middle or at the end of chapters present usually but not always short snippets of information about topics associated with the heroine. Each heroine will be addressed in a separate chapter, all of which close with discussion topics. Several chapters will not only include the portrayal of the heroines by more than one tragedian but also comparisons of the fluid portrayals of heroines reappearing within a single author such as Helen, Hecuba, and Electra by Euripides.

One of the reasons that the Greek tragedies have become increasingly popular over the last hundred years is that many of their themes are almost shockingly modern. The fictional heroines are depicted as living in a mythic era, several hundred years prior to the lives of the tragedies' Athenian audiences, and some thousands of years before the modern era, yet many of the issues they deal with remain current. Of the eleven heroines that I explore, most appear in Euripides' plays, so the discussions will naturally focus more on his treatment of the female characters. This is in tune with the fact that it is Euripides more than his two counterparts who offers in his plays "the full potential of the female pattern of experience" (Lefkowitz 1981: 5). Electra, Clytemnestra, and Antigone are the only heroines who also appear in Aeschylus, while Deianeira is the only character whose sole appearance is in Sophocles' work.

The heroines faced a plethora of dilemmas touching upon almost every aspect of life, and often had to devise ways to defend not only themselves but also those who were dear to them. Many of the heroines are victims of war, even when they are on the more powerful, victorious side. Others have to cope with the stigma of being a foreigner, who has arrived in a strange land either following a man or as the result of divine intervention. The heroines are presented within their family environments as wives, mothers, daughters, and sisters coping with issues women have faced throughout history. There are love triangles where husbands threaten to bring younger women, often trophies of war, into the marital home. There are loyal loving wives and vengeful ones; principled daughters and sisters to a degree of extreme obstinacy and intransigence; there are devoted mothers desperate to save their children, and monstrous ones who are at best indifferent to their offspring and at worst murder them. Tragedy as a genre, however, overstates each and every one of these characteristics and posits them in exaggerated circumstances that life, it is to be hoped, rarely presents.

The different ways the tragedians choose to represent their approaches to the women and the issues they face present fascinating insights not only into the characters but also into their interpretations. Within patriarchal societies women's roles and powers have traditionally been limited, and before embarking upon discussions of the heroines' characters we must acknowledge that they were indisputably created within a male-dominated society. However, within the given constraints, each heroine finds a unique way of expressing herself and making her mark, with a variety of results.

The discussion of the heroines is followed by a glossary of names and terms, as well as by an index.

Pervasive Themes

Several pervasive themes should be borne in mind throughout the book. The "socio-political" themes serve as background information that provide a backdrop for all the heroines and are not repeated but assumed in all of the chapters. The next four themes, which relate to the characterization of the heroines, provide a framework within which each of the heroines may be considered.

Socio-Political Themes External to the Plot

Societal Expectations of Women in Fifth-Century Athens Even though the tragedies portrayed the mythic heroic period, audience expectations were partially formulated by fifth-century Athenian culture, within which women's roles were mainly limited to functions within the home. The notable exception was that they could conduct and participate in religious rites, including burial rituals, though by the fifth century their functions in public funerals had been curtailed. Women were considered to represent the polar opposite to men, functioning to some extent as the "other" by which man could be defined, the counterpoint in a series of dichotomies. Men, capable of objective rational thought, could be trusted with important public matters. Women, by default, being the opposite to men, could not be trusted. The limits imposed by men on female conduct were thus justified by the supposedly inferior nature of women. The epitome of masculinity in Greek culture was the hero figure, who displayed courage, rational thought, and rhetorical acumen (Moss 1985). By contrast, the ideal female's main attributes were passive subservience and loyalty to her man.

Introduction

Heroines written and acted by men, in a patriarchal society The tragedies were created within an indisputably male dominant society, and were written, produced and acted by men in front of predominantly male audiences. We might therefore consider that we are actually reading about male images found within the women. Women in general would have been perceived through a societal prism that refracts the female character into one not only inferior in physical strength and social status but also in character (e.g. "everywhere we women are in second place, always at a distance from men," or "The man who will stop speaking ill of a woman will in fact be called a wretch and short of understanding," Kannicht 2004: vol. 5.1, frag. 319, 36). That being said, the tragedies still present us with a full-blooded cast of heroines, whose enduring popularity attests both to the skill with which they were crafted, and to the power of the timeless messages they convey to readers, audiences, and playwrights for whom they continue to provide inspiration in the twenty-first century.

When considering the characterizations of the tragic heroines, it is important to remember that they were written by men, which may lead to doubts about their authenticity. However, many memorable heroines have been convincingly created by male authors throughout history, including Ibsen's Nora, Chekov's *Three Sisters*, Tolstoy's *Anna Karenina*, Defoe's *Moll Flanders*, Flaubert's *Madame Bovary*, Forster's Lucy Honeychurch, D. H. Lawrence's Lady Chatterley, and Truman Capote's Holly Golightly. The tragic heroines shared certain features with the women of Athens, including their assumed inferior physical strength and social status in comparison to men. Their physical weakness is clearly noted in Chrysothemis' statement to Electra: "You were born a woman, not a man; physically, you're not as strong as your enemies" (Soph. *El.* 997–98).

Themes Relating to the Characters

The Masculine–Feminine Dichotomy: Femininity Versus Masculinity

The masculine–feminine dichotomy is the first of several mutually exclusive and antithetical polarities which defined characters. In fifth-century Athens, complex ideological constructions of male and female natures were presented as being opposite to each other, but also hierarchically related. However, in tragedy, many of the heroines display some character traits more usually associated with their male counterparts, including courage, e.g. Iphigenia and Antigone, leadership, e.g. Clytemnestra and Hecuba, assertiveness, e.g. Electra and Medea, honor, e.g. Medea and Deianeira, rational thought and rhetorical acumen, e.g. Clytemnestra and Hecuba. This could be perceived as posing a threat to the rigid societal structure and paternalistic hierarchy of the time. Female characters who have a propensity for deeds and values associated mainly with the opposite gender often carry out violent acts with tragic ends. We cannot be certain whether this was to mollify outraged audiences or as an expression of the tragedians' own disquiet about potentially challenging established societal order. However, what clearly can be seen is that the tragedians excel at creating intensely dramatic repercussions for instances where this rigid classification is broken with female characters displaying male traits. (For unacceptability of gender role reversal, see for example, frag. 522 of Euripides: "if men concerned themselves with the labor of weaving and women were overcome by the joys of armed fighting, cast out of their proper sphere of knowledge, they would be good for nothing, and so would we" (Kannicht 2004: vol. 5.1, trans. Collard and Cropp).

The heroines who display predominantly feminine characteristics, especially unquestioning loyalty to their husbands whatever the situation or circumstances, such as Deianeira and Alcestis suffer at the hands of others, through deception or male egocentricity.

Defiance Versus Submission

While bearing in mind the imbalance of power between the sexes, and the constraints limiting the actions of women, the second dichotomy to be considered addresses those women who defy societal norms and display independence of thought and action as opposed to those who passively submit to the roles assigned to them. The discussions also highlight the way in which these "active" and "passive" traits dovetail with the masculinity/femininity of the female characters in that masculine traits are often to be found in the depiction of the tragic heroines who are most independently active in their thoughts, words and deeds (Moss 1988).

Two of Sophocles' heroines, Antigone and Electra, famously defy the wishes of those around them, exhibiting stubbornness unparalleled in any male character (maybe with the exception of Philoctetes). The two young women differ considerably from one another, with Antigone impulsively deciding to take action by herself, while Electra excels in her mourning, but exhibits more of a passive resistance to those around her. By contrast, Euripides' Alcestis, wife of Admetus, takes submission to her husband's wishes to the extreme of being willing to die for him. However, even in her willingness to sacrifice her life, Alcestis finds one small avenue of defiance, in requesting that her husband never take another legitimate wife, whose children may supplant her own as masters of the house.

Deceit

With many avenues of action open to men being far beyond the reach of women, the heroines of Greek tragedy need to find alternatives. Their use of deceit is the third character theme we can identify. Their physical and societal disadvantages often lead them to employ guile or to deceitfully resort to using indirect methods such as poison rather than opting for direct confrontation when they are hostile or angry. However, deception is not a trait of all tragic heroines, and of those that do use deception, some have good intentions, and do not cause harm.

Ample scholarly observations, both of the tragedies and of the behavior of Athenian women, point to numerous associations between "femininity" and deceit, as well as to the anxiety that women's purported deceitfulness aroused in men.[1] Constructing women as *a priori* deceptive would obviously make them appear unreliable and, by extension, necessitate their restriction to the home where their actions may be supervised. After all, as some fragments attest, when hostility motivates a woman to act, her weakness compels her to act by guile or poison (*pharmaka*), avoiding a direct trial of strength.

In discussing the heroines' use of deceit, it is important to remember that deception is not only a ploy used by women. Deceit is used in general wherever characters are faced with a major imbalance of power and need to find a means to redress the disparity. In Greek literature, Odysseus is the best example of a male character associated with deception. When the Greek armies laying siege to Troy were at a disadvantage, and despaired of ever breaching the walls by conventional military means, Odysseus came up with the plan of using the "Trojan Horse" and the Greeks gained victory through deceit. In Sophocles' tragedy *Philoctetes*, Odysseus tries to trick Philoctetes out of his magic bow, while in a lost play by Euripides, he frames Palamedes by planting a pot of gold in Palamedes' tent claiming it was a bribe given him by the Trojans. Other male characters also make use of deceit. Menelaus deceives Andromache in Euripides' play about her, and Agamemnon deceives Clytemnestra in Euripides' *Iphigenia at Aulis*. While deception is therefore not exclusively a feminine tool, and not all tragic heroines employ deception, there is also no clear-cut divide between characters using deceptions and those deceived.

It is also interesting to note that feminine guile and the heroines' use of deceit is not always regarded as negative, in particular if it is motivated by the wish to protect a man. In *Helen* for example, the eponymous heroine successfully tricks Theoclymenus in order to save Menelaus' life. While cunning tricks used by men, and by Odysseus in particular, are also lauded as attesting to heroic acumen and resourcefulness, many heroines are portrayed as lacking the wherewithal that may enable them to complete successfully artful deeds or deceptions that would save themselves or those dear to them. Thus, in the case of Deianeira her plan, motivated by the wish to regain her husband's affections, backfires in the most appalling way, resulting not only in her death but in that of Heracles too. We may easily conclude that Deianeira is more deceived than deceiving.

The Heroines' Use of Rhetoric

Several heroines including Clytemnestra, Hecuba, Medea, and Phaedra make admirable use of rhetoric. It may be observed, however, that rhetoric alone is never allowed to resolve any of the heroines' plights and predicaments. Clytemnestra's early speeches in *Agamemnon* are ignored or misunderstood by the Chorus. Later, she persuades Agamemnon to enter the palace, but takes her revenge and removes him from her life through the use of physical violence. Likewise, Medea uses rhetoric to persuade Creon to grant her an extra day in Corinth and to gain the sympathy of the Chorus, but ultimately resorts to the use of poison and physical violence to exact her revenge on Jason. Alcestis demands one favor from Admetus, but despite his apparent wish to fulfill her last request, we may understand his actions of taking a "strange woman" into his bedroom as breaking his promise on the day it was made. Hecuba wins her *agon* (formal debate) with Helen in *Trojan Women*, but ultimately gains nothing from this purely rhetorical victory. In *Hecuba* she also initially uses rhetoric to persuade Polymestor to enter into the tent where the Trojan women are waiting, but exacts her revenge using violence. Perhaps the failure of the tragic heroines' rhetoric is an example of the tragedians matching negative outcomes to transgressions of societal norms.

The Interaction of the Above Themes in the Heroines' Characterizations

The characterizations of the heroines include the polarized traits that typify the dichotomies found in Greek literature (femininity versus masculinity and defiance versus submission) together with the other themes discussed above, portraying how the heroines make adept use rhetoric and deceit. The variations of these themes and their interactions create a fascinating and varied cast of characters, each one uniquely presented. It is interesting to note that those heroines who are prepared to take action in order to achieve their goals, and who display astonishingly developed rhetorical skills when plying their actions, are often considered to be those displaying the most masculine characteristics. But these same "active" or defiant heroines are also those associated with using deceit and trickery, which have been considered feminine devices. Active heroines who use trickery and deceit, also commit deeds of repellent violence. Conversely, deception is never a feature of the more feminine heroines. Those characters displaying the supposedly feminine trait of passive subservience to their male counterparts, are depicted as the ideal women, and as such are devoid of negative qualities, as in the case of Deianeira.

The characterization of Medea exemplifies the interaction of rhetoric, "feminine" deceit, and independent proactive "masculine" behavior. She exhibits all the qualities of a Homeric hero when she not only eloquently expresses her distress over Jason's behavior, which showed a complete lack of gratitude and respect while wounding her honor, but also actively devises and executes her own shocking revenge, the first part of which hinges upon deceit. However, the association between rhetorical acumen, masculinity, and deceit in a character's portrayal may be both fluid and complex. In the characterization of Clytemnestra, as her skills at rhetorical and strategic thought fade in Sophocles' and Euripides' *Electra* plays, her masculinity also disappears. Set at an earlier stage in her life, Clytemnestra as described in the later play *Iphigenia at Aulis* is a woman who was tricked by her husband Agamemnon into bringing her daughter for sacrifice under the pretext of a wedding to Achilles. This may have been considered a formative event in the heroine's character.

In congruence with the idea that the heroines have been skillfully crafted to express unexpected and divergent characteristics, in-depth discussions throughout the book address the complexity and multifaceted nature of the tragedians' characterizations of their heroines. To achieve this, each chapter not only quotes from the heroines' thoughts expressed in monologues, and their interactions with other characters, but also comments upon textual references within the plays. The rich pictures presented of each heroine also result from insights gained following the author's careful examination of the precise wording used in the Greek texts. This allows both original ideas and those previously presented by other scholars to be considered through discussions firmly grounded in the texts, although philological insights are shared without presuming any familiarity with ancient Greek. Finally, the enduring popularity of the works of the tragedians and the continued authenticity of their heroines may be considered proof of the quality of their characterization.

Aristotle's Theory of Character

Aristotle (382–322 BCE), considered by many to be the "father of western philosophy," who wrote widely on theater as well as on rhetoric, linguistics, logic, physics, metaphysics and many other topics, laid down the foundations of the classical approach to these disciplines. So what is the ancient theoretical view, namely Aristotle's view, of what makes for good characterization?[2] According to Aristotle, character is one of the six constituent parts of tragedy upon which its quality depends: plot-structure (*mythos*), character (*ēthos*), diction or style (*lexis*), thought expressed in rhetoric through which a character expresses his/her *ēthos* (*dianoia*), spectacle (*opsis*), song (*melopoiia*) (*Poet.* 1450a 9–15; cf. Mossman 1995: 139–41). He ranks its importance second only to that of plot, and points out that it is character that makes the dramatic figures what they are and drives their actions (*Poet.* 1450a 19–20). Although the playwright's main purpose is not to elucidate or develop the character or personality traits of his dramatic personae, Aristotle insists that the playwright must have a good understanding of human character so as to create dramatic personae whose choices lead them to the actions they take. That understanding, Aristotle maintains, is acquired by prior study of human nature.

Although Aristotle's judgment is somewhat removed in time from the fifth-century tragedians, and thus not necessarily authoritative in all respects, he is much closer to them than we are and is thus an important source. Aristotle discusses characterization in chapters 6 and 13 of his *Poetics*. For him, characterization involves showing the person making choices that reveal his/her ethical purpose and disposition. He is not interested in the intricacies of personality, in consciousness, or in personal idiosyncrasies, which modern psychology and views of personality associate with the term "character." As Halliwell puts it: "Aristotle regards the fundamental question about character not to be 'in what does the distinctiveness or even uniqueness of this person consist', but rather 'what ethical virtues or vices are embodied in his active life?'" (1987: 140–41).

Aristotle sees a reciprocal relationship between character and action. While character is the motivating force behind action, the accumulation of actions helps to shape character. For example, the characterization of Medea begins with her depiction as a foreigner in a strange land, who is emotionally distraught after being abandoned by her husband, Jason. Medea's actions are driven by her inability to passively endure her maltreatment by Jason, but it is the course of action she chooses to take, that completes her characterization. This reciprocity fits Aristotle's view of characterization, as observed by Cameron (1968: 52) as including "complete identification of characters and action." Nevertheless, although Aristotle regards tragedy as a representation of life whose center is people's actions, not their characters, he maintains that characterization is needed to assure that the actions are consistent with the portrayal of the personae who carry them out. This is why he insists that playwrights fashion their characters only after fully considering how they would behave in the dramatized situations (cf. Mossman 1995: 94–102, 138–41).

Following Aristotle's emphasis on action, some consideration is given to how much the heroine's action(s) or inaction and their outcomes can be attributed to her personal character, and how much is imposed by societal and traditional mores. The characters' acceptance or rejection of the social norms within which they operate is thus of crucial importance. For example, while Antigone's actions may be ascribed to her personality, the results of those actions are imposed by societal mores, or, more precisely in this case, by Creon's edict. Her rejection of Creon's decisions seals her fate. In the case of both Deianeira and Phaedra, it would appear that their decision to take action led to their downfall, but their deaths also may be attributed to not being able to withstand the shame associated with their actions. Only Helen seemed to be able to withstand societal and traditional mores with complete impunity.

The Eleven Heroines

Eleven heroines who play dominant roles in the Greek tragedies were selected. Each one is the focus of the audience's attention for a large part of the tragedies within which they appear. Each has a well-developed, memorable character, having fascinated readers and audiences for over two millennia. The discussion of the heroines will start with the house of Atreus: Clytemnestra, Electra, and Iphigenia. Due to her similarity in character with the young, stubborn Electra, Antigone will come next. Helen and Hecuba complete the suite of heroines associated with the Trojan War (excepting Antigone). Due to their connection with the greatest of all Greek heroes Heracles, Euripides' Alcestis and Sophocles' Deianeira and will be discussed next. Finally, united in their use of love potions, poison, and murder or attempted murder, the final group are Medea, Creusa, and Phaedra. Many different orders could have been used, placing Antigone, Deianeira and Phaedra together, for example, as all three commit suicide. However the motives behind these suicides are so different that this was not considered a sufficiently good criteria for categorization.

Here is a brief summary of each character, as presented in this book:

Chapter 1: Clytemnestra

In the six plays in which Clytemnestra appears, her character changes from a powerful woman effectively combining both feminine and masculine traits when ruthlessly pursuing her goals in Aeschylus to a remorseful feminine mother in Euripides, via Sophocles' cruel and unremorseful wife. Lack of remorse is a masculine characteristic. Aeschylus hardly encourages us to sympathize with the murderous queen, although it is impossible not to respect her intelligence and determination. He also presents the men in her life in negative lights: a cowardly and ineffectual Aegisthus and an arrogant if obtuse Agamemnon. Clytemnestra's chapter considers the various accounts of Clytemnestra's culpability and explores whether the plays make us feel that she indeed deserved to die by the hands of her children. Furthermore, the chapter also looks at Clytemnestra's motivation. Was she functioning as a grieving, bereft mother or as a woman, frustrated by the limited realm of women, restricted to the domestic activities within the *oikos* (household), yet seeking to hold a public position of power in the *polis*?

Aeschylus' Clytemnestra displays magnificent rhetorical prowess, but also has no compunction about lying brazenly regarding her adultery and her intentions towards her husband. We see a gradual waning of Clytemnestra's power after the arrival of the enslaved prophetess Cassandra, eldest daughter of Hecuba. Cassandra rejects the subservience expected of her status, ignores Clytemnestra's directives to enter the palace, and while remaining on stage enters into a wild frenzy, envisaging the violent past of the House of Atreus. While doing so, Cassandra foretells her own end, but also predicts the eventual demise of the Aeschylean Queen. Sophocles' Clytemnestra lacks the grandeur of Aeschylus' ruthless murderess, but displays a hard-hearted cruelty to her children. The chapter closes with Euripides' softer characterizations of a wife and mother, who nonetheless meets her death at her children's hands.

Chapter 2: Electra

The chapter focuses on the intransigence of Electra in her pursuit of revenge while comparing the four treatments and interpretations of Electra's figure focusing on the revenge and betrayal Electra is resolutely and unwaveringly set to accomplish. All the tragedians present a highly feminine young woman, whose defiance finds expression initially more through her words than her deeds. Sophocles and Euripides both present princesses who make deft use of deceit after Orestes' return, while Aeschylus does not develop the young Electra's character, beyond her grief at her father's death and joy at being reunited with her brother. Sophocles presents a highly principled young woman, defiant of Clytemnestra and Aegisthus, and prepared to risk her own life, and that of her sister in avenging her father's death. Euripides gives two presentations of Electra, one before and one after the matricide. While the former is shown as a somewhat spoilt young woman, prioritizing her own discomforts over any principles, in *Orestes* Electra is shown to genuinely care for her brother. At the end of his *Electra* the protagonist does express misgivings over the matricide and in *Orestes* she also demonstrates some of her mother's astute strategic thought, defiant spirit and cold-blooded determination. The chapter also offers an analysis of the changing mother–daughter relationships between Electra and Clytemnestra through the different dramatizations.

Chapter 3: Iphigenia

Iphigenia features in two of Euripides' extant plays, *Iphigenia among the Taurians* and *Iphigenia at Aulis*, whose performative chronological sequence is the reverse of the mythic order of the events they dramatize. *Iphigenia among the Taurians* (414–412) initially presents a young woman numbed by trauma, but sufficiently clearsighted to understand that the human sacrifices demanded by the Taurians accord with the will of man and not that of the gods. Despite this unusual perspicacity, Iphigenia initially tows the line, submissively behaving exactly as is expected of her. Following an ominous dream that she interprets to mean that her brother has died, instead of defiantly refusing to cooperate with the cruel temple rites, Iphigenia initially promises herself to be more ruthless than before in dealing with sacrificial victims. However, when she discovers that the next victims are none other than Orestes her brother and Pylades their cousin she turns into a passionate, intelligent and resourceful figure. Her plans to rescue the young men and sail with them back to Greece, include deceiving Thoas, King of the Taurians. Euripides continues his positive take on Iphigenia's character in the second play. Young and innocent, Iphigenia is tricked by her father into coming to Aulis for her marriage with Achilles, which turns out to be her sacrifice. While initially bewailing her fate, and pleading with her father to change his mind, Iphigenia adopts a stance befitting a Homeric hero, choosing to die courageously, to allow the ships to set sail for Troy. Thus, while remaining supremely feminine, she frames her actions in purely masculine thought, seeking honor as the first victim of the Trojan War.

Chapter 4: Antigone

This chapter discusses Antigone's tragic visualization as a character of integrity, remaining true to herself, yet stubborn and intransigent. As with other Sophoclean heroes, Antigone is not only a young woman of uncompromising determination with no regard for compromise, bargaining, concession, or middle ground, but also a sibling, with a love-hate relationship with her sister as well as loyalty to her brothers. However, she is not calculating: Antigone also explores whether what she sees as the transient laws of man should take precedence over the eternal laws of the gods. Ultimately, the tragic combination of Antigone choosing to favor what she interprets as the laws of the gods, together with Creon's intransigence in executing his new-found power, indirectly leads not only her own death but to the deaths of Creon's nearest and dearest, his wife and son.

Chapter 5: Helen

Only appearing in a positive light in her eponymous play, Helen is portrayed as a devoted and loyal wife to Menelaus. Her appearance is transferred through the device of an *eidolon*, or living image, crafted by Hera and sent to Troy with Paris, while the real Helen was taken by Hermes to Egypt, where she stayed safely throughout the Trojan War. By contrast, Euripides offers a devastating portrayal of her in *Trojan Women*. She is shown to argue sophistically with Hecuba, refusing to acknowledge any responsibility for the war over her and blaming Hecuba and Priam and the goddesses, specifically Aphrodite, for the carnage. In the other plays portraying post-Trojan War events, Helen is almost irrelevant. *Orestes* depicts her as vain and self-centered, but as a woman who is no longer dangerous, but rather tricked and deceived. The ending of Euripides' *Orestes* sees Helen saved from Orestes' attempt on her life and taken up by Apollo to heaven's recess immediately on Menelaus' return from Troy. The dualities abounding in the depictions of Helen are emphasized throughout this chapter.

Chapter 6: Hecuba

Hecuba is discussed in two chapters: in the chapter on Helen, and in the chapter carrying her name. In *Hecuba*, she is the personification of female suffering. She has lost her husband, sons and daughters in the war caused by one woman, Helen. Hecuba is also the only example of an actively avenging tragic heroine whose superb rhetorical acumen does not render success. She has been enslaved and in *Hecuba* at least "a successful speech cannot be made by a weaker party" (Luschnig 1988: 100). Following Hecuba's depiction in the *Iliad* as a caring mother and wife whose wishes are always thwarted (Roisman 2011), Euripides does not allow her powerful rhetoric to save Polyxena from being sacrificed on Achilles' tomb in *Hecuba*, or to have Helen executed in *Trojan Women*. She does, however, eventually manage to persuade Agamemnon to look the other way in *Hecuba*, while she exacts a brutal revenge on Polymestor, maintaining the traditional link between rhetorical prowess and deceit.

Chapter 7: Alcestis

Euripides' dramatization has often been interpreted as depicting one of the most feminine of all of the heroines, the "perfect wife" submissive to her husband's wishes to the extent that she agrees to die in her husband's stead, when no one else including his parents will volunteer. She is seen by the Chorus and Admetus as following Semonidean Bee woman (see Box, p. 54), whose thoughts center only on her husband, children, and her household. However, a closer look at the text raises some doubts. It is clear that had she refused, she would have incurred the bottomless hatred Admetus feels now for his mother and father. Alcestis demands a "favor" in return for offering her life, that Admetus shall not remarry. When Heracles brings Alcestis back from the dead, without revealing the identity of the mysterious woman he has with him, after brief rebuttals Admetus agrees to accept the "stranger" into his life. We are left wondering how the reunited couple will get past this "incident."

Chapter 8: Deianeira

Deianeira is Heracles' second wife and his unwitting murderer. She is singular among the tragedies' heroines in the great care and good intentions she shows for Heracles, which nevertheless lead to a tragic outcome. Winnington-Ingram refers to her as the "most appealing of Sophoclean women" (1980: 74). Helplessness and fear of losing Heracles to

Iole, a younger captive woman, lead Deianeira to use Nessus' poisoned clotted blood, having been told by the Centaur that it was a philtre. The use of magic and poison was thought to be a feminine art especially in affairs of erotic emotions (Just 1989: 268), and Deianeira's deceit combines the two. The chapter follows the tragic development of Deianeira's awareness of the consequences of her actions.

Chapter 9: Medea

Medea is a wronged wife who is a foreigner with no rights; the mother of two boys stranded in Corinth. Her rapidly changing persona, adapted to suit the need of the moment, and her stunning use of rhetoric to confuse and deceive all around her make Euripides' characterization of Medea an unforgettable *tour de force*. This characterization also challenges many perceptions of what is feminine. Medea negotiates with Creon, Aegeus, and Jason, each time succeeding in gaining what she has hoped for. She presents herself as a suppliant to Aegeus, yet it is clear that she sees herself as his equal, demanding he swears an oath, in addition to his promise to receive her in his house. While seeking empathy from the female Chorus, by emphasizing her experience as a woman, like them, she also admits that she would prefer to fight on the battle field, rather than to give birth. Her attitude to her sons is at best ambivalent and at worst detached, seeing them as means to an end, her revenge on Jason. It is speculated that the killing of her sons was an innovation on the part of Euripides (e.g. Mastronarde 2002: 52–55), and this act, committed first and foremost to hurt Jason, as he has pained her, has condemned her for eternity. Whether this is true or not, the chapter asks why Euripides wanted her to carry out this appalling deed.

Chapter 10: Creusa

Creusa is the daughter of Erechtheus king of Athens, the barren wife of Xuthus, a non-Athenian who won her by helping Athens in a war. In her youth Creusa was raped by Apollo and abandoned her son at birth with trinkets of recognition in a cave. In the play she is in Apollo's temple with Xuthus asking for help in her barrenness. Unbeknown to Creusa, her son was rescued and serves at the temple she is visiting. Not realizing that Ion is her son and believing he is a foreigner, Creusa attempts to murder the young man by employing deceit, not of her own initiative but having been convinced to do so by her loyal old slave. She fears that once Ion is brought into her home by Xuthus, who believes him to be his own son, Ion, in spite of being a foreigner, will inherit the throne of Athens. The themes of female helplessness, motherhood together with the importance of family and ancestry form central themes to this chapter, while it briefly considers how Euripides involves the gods in his plots and character development.

Chapter 11: Phaedra

While Theseus is away from home, Phaedra develops an overwhelming sexual desire for her stepson Hippolytus. Euripides infers that Phaedra may be an innocent victim of a jealousy between two goddesses. How much control she has over her own fate is never clear. It is generally believed that the heroine of the lost *Hippolytus Veiled* was an overtly lascivious woman and that Euripides wrote the second extant version as a literal corrective, following a hostile audience reaction to the first. Most scholarship views the second Phaedra as a virtuous woman who does her utmost to control her passion and remain faithful to her husband Theseus. But is Phaedra indeed the chaste wife struggling to overcome the sickness of unrequited love? Or, is she a manipulative lascivious woman who uses her ability to play-act and her powerful rhetorical skills to manipulate her Nurse? Or is she an innocent victim of fate? Once again, this chapter like those preceding it, shows how careful inspection of the text can yield fascinating insights into Euripides' use of text and dramatic effect to create a powerful impact on all those reading or watching his play.

Translations

The translations followed in this book are the following:
Oresteia—C. Collard. 2002. *Aeschylus. Oresteia*. Oxford: Oxford University Press
Euripides' *Medea, Alcestis*—D. Kovacs. 1994. *Euripides: Cyclops; Alcestis; Medea*. Cambridge, MA; London, England: Harvard University Press
Euripides' *Hecuba*—D. Kovacs. 1995. *Euripides: Children of Heracles; Hippolytus, Andromache, Hecuba*. Cambridge, MA; London, England: Harvard University Press
Euripides' *Hippolytus*—My own
Euripides' *Electra*—D. Kovacs. 1998. *Euripides: Suppliant Women; Electra; Heracles*. Cambridge, MA; London, England: Harvard University Press
Euripides' *Helen, Orestes*—D. Kovacs. 1999. *Euripides: Helen; Phoenician Women; Orestes*. Cambridge, MA, London, England: Harvard University Press
Euripides' *Iphigenia among the Taurians, Ion, Trojan Women*—D. Kovacs. 2014. *Euripides: Trojan Women; Iphigenia among the Taurians; Ion*. Cambridge, MA, London, England: Harvard University Press
Euripides' *Iphigenia at Aulis*—C. Collard and J. Morwood. 2017. *Euripides*. Iphigenia at Aulis. Liverpool: Liverpool University Press. 2 vols.
Sophocles' *Antigone, Women of Trachis*—H. Lloyd-Jones. 1998. *Sophocles. Antigone; The Women of Trachis; Philoctetes; Oedipus at Colonus*. Cambridge, MA: Harvard University Press.
Sophocles' *Electra*—H. M. Roisman. 2008. *Sophocles: Electra. Translation with notes, introduction, interpretative essay and afterlife*. Newburyport, MA: Focus Publishing, Hackett, 2nd printing 2017 (with updates)

CHAPTER 1
CLYTEMNESTRA

Mythic background

In ancient Greek myth, Clytemnestra is the daughter of Leda, a princess in her own right, and of Tyndareus, King of Sparta. Leda was seduced by Zeus, who had appeared in the guise of a swan, and eventually gave birth to two sets of twins: Helen and Pollux are usually said to be descendants of Zeus, while Clytemnestra and Castor were the mortal children of Tyndareus. (In one account Castor and Pollux are both "sons of Zeus," and thus termed Dioscuri.)

Tyndareus offers hospitality to Agamemnon and Menelaus, the two sons of the cursed house of Atreus, from nearby Mycenae. They were exiled when their father was murdered by his brother's son, Aegisthus. According to some versions, Clytemnestra was already married at this point, and had an infant son. Menelaus marries Helen and succeeds Tyndareus becoming King of Sparta. Agamemnon returns to Mycenae, and with the help of Tyndareus' army deposes King Thyestes, Aegisthus' father, and claims the throne (see also Box on *daimon*, pp. 29–30). Agamemnon also kills Clytemnestra's husband and new-born son, taking Clytemnestra to be his wife.

When Helen was carried off to Troy by Paris, the son of Priam, Menelaus and Agamemnon gathered a Greek force to sail to Troy in order to bring Helen back. The ancient myths give few if any details of Clytemnestra's life during the ten years while Agamemnon is away at war. In the Ninth Book of Homer's *Iliad* (9.145) Agamemnon speaks of his son Orestes and his three daughters: Chrysothemis, Laodice and Iphianassa (the last two possibly alternative names for Electra and Iphigenia) without mentioning their mother, Clytemnestra. In the Third Book of the *Odyssey* (3.263–75) the old counsellor Nestor tells Odysseus' son, Telemachus, about the events leading up to the death of Agamemnon. Nestor attributes Agamemnon's murder to Aegisthus, Agamemnon's cousin *(Od.* 3.234–35). Nestor comments that Clytemnestra was naturally of good character, but that Aegisthus had tricked her with flattery and seduced her. Nestor adds that Aegisthus ruled for seven years after killing Agamemnon until Orestes returned home and killed Aegisthus in revenge, but nothing is said of Clytemnestra. In the Eleventh Book of the *Odyssey*, (11.409–10) during Odysseus' visit to the Netherworld, Agamemnon tells Odysseus that Aegisthus with the help of his 'accursed wife Clytemnestra' caused his death. He adds that the "guileful Clytemnestra" killed Priam's daughter Cassandra, whom Agamemnon had brought back from Troy as a prize (11.421–23). Agamemnon warns Odysseus that all women lack faithfulness/loyalty, even though he admits that Odysseus' wife Penelope is a very admirable woman (*Od.* 11.441–56).

THE HOUSE OF ATREUS

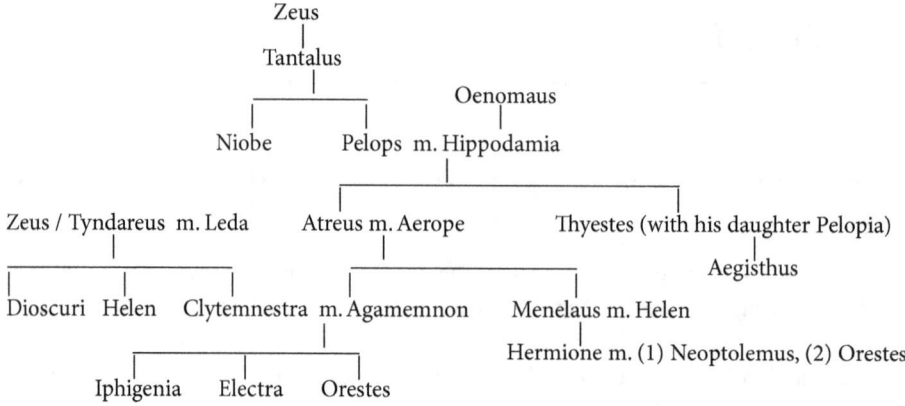

Introduction

Clytemnestra appears in six Greek tragedies: Aeschylus' *Oresteia* (*Agamemnon, Libation Bearers, Eumenides,* 458 BCE), Sophocles' *Electra* (418–410), Euripides' *Electra* (422–417 or 415–413), and *Iphigenia at Aulis* (405?). Aeschylus, whose trilogy was written first, presents Clytemnestra as cruel and ruthless, but also as intelligent and decisive. Sophocles' and Euripides' *Electra* plays are dramatic reactions to the Aeschylean treatment of Clytemnestra, although the queen's role in them is more comparable to that in *Libation Bearers* than in *Agamemnon*. This is not surprising since both of the *Electra* plays and the *Libation Bearers* are set after the regicide and focus upon planning the matricide resulting from Agamemnon's murder. However, the depictions of the queen in the plays by Sophocles and Euripides differ markedly from one another, reflecting to some extent the portrayal of her daughter Electra. The Sophoclean Clytemnestra is just as cruel and savage as the Aeschylean one, expressing neither regret nor remorse. She is even less motherly than the woman portrayed in *Libation Bearers*. Euripides, however, presents a more sympathetic Clytemnestra. She is, however, a formidable figure throughout: a highly intelligent woman, capable of strategic planning and fully committed to any task she sets for herself.

While the plays were not written in mythic chronological sequence, the timeframe of their plots spans from the start of the Trojan War to shortly after Clytemnestra's death. When Helen leaves Sparta for Troy with the young prince Paris, Clytemnestra has had several children with Agamemnon, the eldest of whom, Iphigenia, is already of a marriageable age. Agamemnon and Menelaus have mustered a fleet of a thousand ships to bring back the errant Helen, but the fleet is becalmed at Aulis. Clytemnestra brings two of her children, Iphigenia and the baby Orestes, to Aulis, only to discover that Agamemnon wishes to sacrifice Iphigenia to ensure fair winds for the fleet. The only play to depict these early events, *Iphigenia at Aulis*, was actually the latest composed—it was Euripides' last piece of work and was performed posthumously. This episode in Clytemnestra's life serves as a trigger for future events.

Clytemnestra returns to Argos without her daughter, and awaits Agamemnon's return from Troy for ten long years. Left alone, this defiant, resolute queen not only runs her home and hearth—the *oikos*—but also takes on the public duties of ruling the *polis*, and plots her revenge. She chooses as a lover, and possibly a collaborator, none other than Aegisthus, Agamemnon's cousin, who had murdered Atreus, Agamemnon's father, in order to restore his own father, Thyestes, to power. When Agamemnon returns, Clytemnestra employs every weapon at her disposal to ensure her plan is carried out without delay, and murders not only Agamemnon, but also the tragic prophetess Cassandra, whom Agamemnon has brought from Troy as his concubine. In the fullness of time, Clytemnestra meets her death at the hand of her son Orestes, who had, as an infant, many years earlier traveled with her to Aulis. By committing the horrifying act of matricide, Orestes avenges the murder of his father, Agamemnon, but risks losing his own sanity and life. The final glimpse of Clytemnestra is in *Eumenides,* after her death, when she is urging the Furies to avenge her murder.

The tragic portrayal of Clytemnestra is particularly interesting as the *Odyssey* is ambivalent about her role in Agamemnon's murder. While in Book Three only Aegisthus is named as the perpetrator of the plot, Agamemnon's ghost in Book Eleven indicates that Clytemnestra bore some blame in his murder, though her guilt may have partly been through adultery, and aiding and abetting Aegisthus. The *Odyssey* does, however, sow the seed in the readers' minds for imagining Clytemnestra as a cruel murderess.

* * *

Each tragedian constructs a complex character for Clytemnestra including a series of internal contradictions:

- traits considered masculine by the Greeks such as clarity of thought and strength of purpose intertwined with those considered feminine such as irrational hope, overwhelmingly strong passions, and the use of deceit;
- defiance of accepted conventions when she trusts her own judgment to rule the *polis,* yet later on submitting to a patriarchal order and willingly restricting herself to domestic pursuits;
- a loving mother who pleads for one daughter's life, who later abuses and casts out another;
- a wife and mother who stops at nothing to avenge her daughter's sacrifice, becoming herself a cold-blooded murderess;
- a mother who is prepared to defend herself even beyond her own death, demanding vengeance—against her own son.

This chapter will accompany the reader through an analysis of the texts of six plays as they each in turn cast light on the character so skillfully crafted by the tragedians. The sections of this chapter examine each depiction, starting with the complex character created by Aeschylus.

CLYTEMNESTRA IN AESCHYLUS' *AGAMEMNON*

Aeschylus' *Agamemnon*

The play starts with a Watchman lying awake scanning the horizon for a glimpse of beacons that will announce the long-awaited fall of Troy. His joyful outcry on finally seeing the beacons summons the Chorus of the city's elders and eventually Clytemnestra. Clytemnestra and the Chorus are arguing over the reliability of the beacons when a Herald arrives, announcing not only the fall of Troy but also Agamemnon's imminent return. Agamemnon arrives, accompanied by his concubine Cassandra. Clytemnestra lures him into an act of hubris when he demonstrates excessive self-pride, offensive to the gods, by walking into the palace on crimson tapestries. Cassandra ignores Clytemnestra's order to follow Agamemnon inside the palace, eventually entering of her own accord. Clytemnestra returns, exulting over the corpses of Agamemnon and Cassandra and tries to justify her actions to the Chorus. When Aegisthus joins her, accompanied by an armed bodyguard, the Chorus attack his cowardice. He belittles Clytemnestra and boasts of his own role in the murder.

In Greek tragedy the first reference to a character is usually revealing. At the start of *Agamemnon*, the first play of the *Oresteia*, Aeschylus' trilogy, a Watchman introduces Clytemnestra not by her name, but as an anomaly: "a woman with a hopeful heart which plans like a man" (*gynaikos androboulon elpizon kear*, 11). In the Greek text you can see that the word *gynaikos* (a form of the word for a "woman," *gynē*), appears directly before the word *androboulon* (which is composed of *anēr*, meaning "man" and *boulē*, meaning "mind and counsel"). Clytemnestra is thus immediately presented as a complex character who comprises one of the fundamental polarities on which Greek tragedy is based. She possesses traits that the Greeks associated mostly with men: eloquence, strategic intelligence, the ability to use her resources while guarding her secrets, and the cold determination to pursue her goals relentlessly. She is also linked to traits traditionally considered female: deceitfulness and willingness to alter facts to suit her purposes, as well as an uncanny insight into other people, which may be called "feminine intuition." The two antitheses she encompasses, that between the genders (male, *anēr* versus *gynē*, female) and that between "hope" (*elpis*), signifying the irrational, and "mind and counsel" (*boulē*), along with the reversal of their traditional assignations, feature as the main motifs in *Agamemnon* and the trilogy as a whole.[1]

When the male/female components of Clytemnestra's personality are synchronized, she is unstoppable. Choosing from her impressive armoury of rhetorical skills whichever "weapon" best enables her to overcome her opponents, Clytemnestra pits her wits against all around her. She constantly engages her opponents in sophisticated and devious rhetoric, so that those hearing her words can never be quite certain what her true meaning is. She outsmarts all who engage with her until a tipping point is reached during her encounter with Cassandra, the eldest daughter of King Priam and Queen Hecuba of Troy. Cassandra was gifted the power of prophecy by Apollo, but later cursed by him, never to be believed by those who hear her. Essentially Clytemnestra's power begins to wane when Cassandra simply refuses to engage with her. Cassandra, knowing her own fate, refuses to enter the palace when ordered by Clytemnestra. Remaining on stage after Clytemnestra leaves, Cassandra dances frantically and sings of terrors past and those yet to come. She appears to be possessed as those who prophesize sometime do. In keeping with Cassandra's curse, the Chorus think Cassandra is insane and do not respond to her warnings. Eventually Cassandra enters the palace on her own terms, without anyone's bidding, knowing full well that she is going to be killed. Clytemnestra murders Agamemnon, as she has planned for ten long years, but she murders Cassandra too. After this, it appears that the control she has over her own destiny slowly seeps away.

Aeschylus is interested not only in characters but in society as a whole. Significantly, he is writing at a time when a more radical form of democracy has been introduced in Athens, when in 462 BCE Ephialtes' reforms reduced the power of the traditional governing body, the conservative, aristocratic *Areopagus*, in favor of the democratically chosen elements of the council (*boulē*) and the assembly (*ekklesia*), to which all male citizens could be elected to by lot. The *Areopagus* retained jurisdiction over homicides and some other serious crimes.

Clytemnestra is a queen who plays many roles due to the ten-year absence of Agamemnon. She defies societal norms out of necessity and her actions flout some of her city's basic customs and moral codes. The Elders of the city, in spite of their polite declaration of their allegiance to her, carefully observe that the throne can be filled only by a male (258–60). That being said, the *Oresteia* highlights the importance of maintaining the wellbeing of the narrower frame of society, the "household" (*oikos*) variously meaning the family, the family's property and the house. Clytemnestra plays a complex role in the "household" and calls herself the "watchdog" of the house, yet her actions prove her to be nothing of the kind: she destroys it through her actions which lead to a cycle of murders and revenge.

Within the private domain, Clytemnestra is a wife and mother, although one of her children, Iphigenia, is dead and another, Orestes, has been sent away for his own safekeeping during his father's absence. Clytemnestra's claim of loyalty to Agamemnon is one of the first indications of her deceptiveness. Her powerful rhetoric, manipulative skills, and deceit make her a prototype of the so-called "unreliable female narrator." Her boast and the Chorus' concession that she speaks sensibly "like a man" emphasize her ability to use language to outmaneuver her male associates. In the public domain, Clytemnestra, having taken on roles normally filled by men, displays attributes associated with them. While pursuing her goals in a manlike fashion, she nevertheless displays the irrational hope that Aegisthus will protect her.

It may also be considered that Aeschylus' Clytemnestra not only plays a male role, but also subverts the social order by emasculating or "feminizing" the men she encounters: the Elders of the Chorus, the men of the city, Agamemnon, and Aegisthus. In Clytemnestra's interactions with all of these, it is the men who end up displaying a certain degree of irrational behavior—a trait the Greeks associated with women.

However, despite her various masculine attributes, Clytemnestra is very conscious of her female gender, to the extent of glorifying it. Clytemnestra is not attempting to be a man at all, but rather an empowered "super-female" who ruthlessly uses behaviors attributed to the male sex, correctly or otherwise. She successfully outwits the men around her, subjecting them to her will, outdoing them in "their" domain of rhetorical exchanges. In the ferocity which he attributes to Clytemnestra directly after the murder, Aeschylus is in effect preempting later authors such as William Congreve who wrote in his 1697 tragedy *The Mourning Bride*: *Heav'n has no Rage, like Love to Hatred turn'd, Nor Hell a Fury, like a Woman scorn'd*[2] or, even more aptly, Rudyard Kipling's famous line: *the female of the species is more deadly than the male.*[3] It is therefore fitting that, while Clytemnestra successfully outwits the men around her, she stumbles when she faces the female agents who oppose her, the first of these being Cassandra, Agamemnon's captive concubine. In the *Eumenides*, the last play of the trilogy, Clytemnestra suffers outright defeat at the hands of Athena, another female, albeit a special case.

Towards the end of *Agamemnon,* long before her final defeat, Clytemnestra, a manly woman, encounters a man displaying behavior more often attributed to women. Her lover Aegisthus has stayed at home while all other Greek men of fighting age have gone to battle. He deviously allows Clytemnestra to carry out the dangerous act of murdering Agamemnon alone. Ironically, it is in part Aegisthus' weakness and lack of insight that will eventually contribute to Clytemnestra's downfall as well as his own, as we shall soon see.

Clytemnestra's motives for murdering her husband have been much debated. Is avenging the sacrifice of her daughter her primary motivation? Is she a jealous wife punishing her husband for bringing home his spear-prize? Is she a wanton adulteress who needs to eliminate her husband? Or is she a woman whose abilities suit her for a life beyond the limitations society has placed on her? There is another question relevant to the contrast between Clytemnestra's unique strengths and her piteous end: what causes Clytemnestra's decline? The introductory description of Clytemnestra as "a woman with a hopeful heart which plans like a man" perhaps hints at the problematic contradictions in her personality. Although her combination of disparate qualities endows her with the power to plan and execute Agamemnon's murder with a chilling *sangfroid,* the internal tension is ultimately untenable.

The discussions about Clytemnestra below are divided into two parts: before and after her meeting with Cassandra. Throughout this section, an inspection of Aeschylus' use of language in the characterization of this tragic heroine sheds light on her motivations and the cause of her downfall.

The Ascendancy of Clytemnestra: Before Meeting Cassandra

Clytemnestra: "A Woman with a Hopeful Heart Which Plans Like a Man"

As we have seen, Clytemnestra is introduced by the watchman at the start of *Agamemnon* as incorporating both male and female traits, in that she is "a woman with a hopeful heart which plans like a man" (11). The watchman has been tasked by Clytemnestra to look out each night for the flames of a beacon, carrying the message of Troy's defeat, a signal agreed between Agamemnon and Clytemnestra. During the ten long years waiting for the sight of the flames, the watchman seems to have observed much of the behavior of the mistress of the house, but holds his tongue from saying more. When he finally sees the blazing flames, he joyfully alerts Clytemnestra who rapidly initiates citywide celebrations of the victory. Clytemnestra's clear mind and rapid decisive actions are brilliantly highlighted by Aeschylus through their contrast with the almost doddering pace of the Chorus of elderly men who were too frail to go and fight in Troy.

As the Elders enter, they sound an ominous tone by introducing the background to the Trojan War, reminding the audience both of the motive of vengeance and of the involvement of the gods from the very beginning. They also question what they regard as Clytemnestra's hasty actions in setting all the city's altars alight with burnt sacrifices celebrating the victory. While it is not clear whether Clytemnestra is on stage with them, if she is, they do not pause to give her the opportunity to answer. Instead, after settling on the *orchestra* (see Glossary) they sing of the ominous portents from the start of the war, recalling the terrible sacrifice that was required which resulted in "a fearsome, and unforgetting Wrath which avenges children" (154–55). They add a graphic description of Iphigenia's sacrifice, without referring to her or to her mother by name (205–47). If the queen was standing within hearing range, their words must have been deeply disturbing.

At the start of the first episode (258, see Glossary) Clytemnestra loses no time in telling the Chorus the good news that Troy has fallen: "The Argives have captured the city of Priam" (267). In the following confrontation, Clytemnestra first displays how a powerful woman may effectively use her feminine artfulness to enhance 'masculine' traits. The Chorus accuse Clytemnestra of irresponsibly claiming that Troy has been sacked without any proof. They insult her judgment by saying this is typical of her 'womanly disposition'. Later on, when Agamemnon makes the opposite accusation, blaming her of *not* behaving like a woman (940) she also outwits him. In both cases

Clytemnestra employs the rhetorical strategy recommended later by Aristotle: "what is persuasive is what persuades someone" (*pithanon tini pithanon*, *Rhetoric* 1356b) and pretends to give in to her accusers. In both cases she succeeds in eliciting irrational or "feminine" behavior from her opponents, while carefully feigning modesty and downplaying her abilities.

The Elders are slow to grasp what she has relayed to them (268) to which Clytemnestra sharply replies that "Troy is in Achaean hands: *am I expressing myself clearly?*" (269). When the Chorus ask Clytemnestra to repeat her explanation and, despite her precise presentation of a military-style signalling system, the Elders demand to hear the information again "from beginning to end" (317–19). Clytemnestra deftly turns the tables on the Elders who are incapable of understanding this factual report, by giving them an imaginary account which they accept. The dramatist essentially mocks the Chorus' "male" suspicion by having the Elders believe an imaginary story "as a woman would."[4] There is no other extant tragedy where both the schism between male and female, as well as the contrast between "normative" and portrayed behaviors of both genders, is so pronounced. To allay their suspicions of her, she gives the Chorus a graphic and vivid picture of the turmoil in Troy, the deaths and the misery of the conquered (320–50). As she proceeds with her tale, Clytemnestra focuses mostly on the conquerors of the city not the conquered, about whose misery one would expect to hear more. She suggests that there is still danger lurking for the successful victors. All depends on how they will behave in the fallen city.[5] Clytemnestra's ploy of drawing the Elders into her imaginary scene, and giving the impression that her sole interest lies with the wellbeing of the army, shows how she can divert their attention with a tale richly embroidered with imagined details. It is this description that convinces the Chorus, who are now the ones to behave "like a woman does," that is to say, they are relying on gossip and imagination rather than on the hard evidence which she had originally offered.

In manipulating the Chorus into accepting the product of her own imagination as fact, she not only shows them to be gullible, a trait deemed as being feminine in a traditional understanding of gendered behavior, but also gains for herself their ultimate compliment: she "speaks like a sensible man" (351). However, the Elders once again repeat their former criticism in spite of having just praised her "manly" speech: "It is just like a woman to command thanksgivings before the situation is clear … quickly a rumour proclaimed by a woman vanishes" (483–87).[6] This redundant criticism is immediately proven wrong-headed when the Herald arrives to make the official proclamation of the fall of Troy.

As soon as the Herald's official news validates Clytemnestra's order for thanksgiving, she taunts the Elders for accusing her of being naive and credulous *as women are* (591–92). She talks *at them* rather than addressing them, and describes how the thanksgivings she ordered were carried out: "throughout the city *one man here, another there* began loudly rising the auspicious cry of triumph *according to women's custom*" (594–96). Clytemnestra's masculine power is demonstrated by her ability to "womanize" men: the men of the city who express their thanks according to "women's customs", then the Chorus, Agamemnon, and eventually her paramour, Aegisthus.

Clytemnestra's Speech to the Herald

Between the "feminization" of the Chorus and her battle of wits with Agamemnon, Clytemnestra delivers an ironic speech to the Herald. The message she sends via the Herald to Agamemnon abounds with ominous *double entendres* cloaked in a "womanlike" guise. Clytemnestra refers to her wifely excellence while using overtly masculine speech and behavior. She emphasizes her happiness in greeting her husband: there is nothing sweeter for a wife than "to open the gates" for a husband returning from a war; she has never broken the seal or had pleasure from another man (610–12); she will make haste to give her "honorable husband" the best possible welcome. She expresses her famous wish: "may he find the wife in the palace just as *loyal* as when he left her" (606–07, my translation).[7] Since Agamemnon's departure for Troy necessitated the sacrifice of Iphigenia, these lines may refer to the very time when the queen abandoned any loyalty to Agamemnon. Finding her just as loyal as the time "when he left her" would thus indicate finding her not only disloyal, but also plotting her revenge.[8]

There is a particular significance to many of the words in Clytemnestra's speech. She describes herself as a loyal wife, watchdog of his household who knew no delight or scandalous report from another man any more than of tempering bronze (611–12). Her self-description to the Herald as *gynē pistē*, "loyal/faithful wife" (606), is a rhetorical *tour de force*. She uses the military concepts of "fidelity" or "loyalty," familiar to Agamemnon from the last ten years spent with his army. The use of language from his comfort zone creates a false sense of security. The phrase itself is triply odd. *Pistos* "loyal" is a rare personal epithet found previously only in Homer and limited to a military context, but Clytemnestra transports it into a domestic environment, where being a "loyal wife" becomes the heart of her wifely identity. Secondly, it is used formulaically and only for Homeric heroes who have proven their loyalty in death.[9] That Clytemnestra is attuned to this original meaning of the epithet becomes clear in her reference later to the slaughtered Cassandra, whom she calls Agamemnon's "loyal (*pistē*) bedfellow," meaning that she was so loyal to her master that she died for him (1442).[10] Is Clytemnestra insinuating that she is ready to die for Agamemnon if necessary? Or that her life without him was as a "living death"? Clytemnestra is speaking Agamemnon's language, lulling his senses before she strikes. Thirdly, her use of the epithet for herself is unique: there is no other extant case in epic or the tragedies where a person uses this epithet to describe himself/herself.[11] This usage reveals her as both self-masculinizing and brazen. There is also the possibility of a semantic ambiguity in the phrase as it appears in the text. When the two words *gynaika pistēn* are pronounced fluidly and emphatically together, they can be heard and understood as *gynaik'apistēn* meaning the exact opposite: "unfaithful/disloyal wife."[12] In terms of performance the text gives latitude to an actor to pronounce Clytemnestra's phrase as he pleases.

Clytemnestra continues to try to allay Agamemnon's possible suspicions by appealing to another set of values important in a military context. In order to present herself as a reliable partner and wife, she describes herself as a "watchdog" of his house (607), which implies that she represents his interests. The relationship calling for identification of interests, a requisite for marriage, was known to the Athenians as *philia*, "friendship," which covered a complex web of personal, family, political, and business relationships.[13] Emphasizing *philia* is another ploy to gain Agamemnon's trust. Although Clytemnestra imports this set of masculine values into her wifely role, she describes herself as a dog rather than "a friend." Her comparison of herself to a "dog" has long perplexed scholars. Hogan sees her reference in context with usage in ancient Greece as "brazen in light of the common meaning of dog as 'bitch' or 'slut'" (1984: on 614 ff). This comparison follows her claim to be "loyal" (*pistē*), which likewise implies subordination. By calling herself "a dog" or "a bitch" she debases herself further, granting Agamemnon more power.

Clytemnestra's self-depiction as a dog must have raised a smile in the audience, whose familiarity with the Homeric epics could be expected. In both *Iliad* and *Odyssey* "dog" is associated with a woman of loose morals.[14] It was Agamemnon himself who in the *Odyssey* famously called Clytemnestra a "bitch-faced" (*kynopis*, 11.424) murderess, who did not bother even to close his eyelids after piercing him with the sword. Clytemnestra's sister, the notorious Helen, refers to herself in the *Iliad* as both "dog" (*kyon*) and "dog-face" (*kynopis*, 6.344, 3.180), when expressing her sense of guilt.[15]

The puzzling allusion at the end of Clytemnestra's speech to "tempering bronze" (612) might be another use of language from the world of men to indicate Clytemnestra's alleged ineptness in this male sphere. In claiming that she knew no delight or scandalous report from another man any more than of tempering bronze (611–12), she claims that she knows nothing of masculine matters. All "real" men know that steel is tempered, not bronze. Clytemnestra could be saying that she is a helpless woman who doesn't understand the world of men. On the other hand, this *double entendre* might suggest that fidelity is as foreign to her as tempering bronze would be.[16] Is this yet another attempt at downplaying her ability, an intentional "slip of the tongue" as may befit a woman displaying her femininity, or is she making a mistake any man would spot to eliminate suspicion that she could handle a weapon?[17]

Clytemnestra and Agamemnon

"I will not be Ashamed to Speak to you of my Feelings of Love for my Husband"

The arrival of Agamemnon heralds the lengthy encounter between husband and wife. The rhetorical duel between the newly reunited King and Queen is the only scene in *Agamemnon* in which the two exchange words (855–974), and it forms the dramatic turning point of the play, the outcome of which seals Agamemnon's fate.

Agamemnon is overbearing, callous, and arrogant. Clytemnestra, by contrast, assumes the pose of an adoring wife. As the returning master of his house and the King of Argos, it is fitting for Agamemnon to project authority; however, his words still reveal a man with an exaggerated sense of his own importance. He finds deep satisfaction in having acted as an agent of justice, punishing the unlawful abduction of Helen, and takes pride in having sacked Troy. His entire address, although mentioning the gods as actors, dwells on vivid details of how *he* sacked the city, embellishing upon *his* own victorious achievement. Agamemnon's reaction to the Chorus' warnings about genuine versus false sincerity indicates that he is still thinking in terms of his sojourn in Troy when he claims that Odysseus seemed the most sincere of all of his comrades (793–98, 841–42). Clytemnestra was therefore correct in assuming that Agamemnon's associations would be within the realm of the Trojan War. Her address capitalizes on the weaknesses of a man full of his own vainglory.

Because Clytemnestra is unsure whether Agamemnon has heard any rumors about her infidelity, she must remain outside the palace to prevent the Chorus from saying anything to him.[18] She stands at the palace's gate listening to Agamemnon's lengthy address to the city, during which he ignores her. Furthermore, she can see the Trojan woman he has in tow. After his speech, Agamemnon intends to dismount and enter the palace to give thanks to the gods (851–54) thereby immediately resuming his position as lord of the house, but his wife thwarts him, blocking his way. Her position clearly demonstrates that she controls the entry into the house. He gives a positive interpretation of her dominant stance, calling her the "guardian" of the house (914), when he finally addresses her. However, a feeling of foreboding has already begun to mount in the audience: it becomes clear that Agamemnon can only enter his palace on Clytemnestra's terms.

Agamemnon's refusal to acknowledge Clytemnestra during his address to the Chorus might explain why she only turns to her husband about halfway into her own speech. As Agamemnon stands in front of her on his chariot, she addresses not him but the "Men of the city, you assembled Elders" (855). Furthermore, seeing Cassandra with him on the chariot,[19] Clytemnestra launches into an avowal of her love for her husband: "I will not be ashamed to speak to you of my feelings of love for my husband" (856–57). Her intimate words are astonishing, proclaimed as they are to the city Elders within Agamemnon's hearing. There is no similar expression of love for a spouse in extant Greek tragedy. Aeschylus presents us with an unparalleled scene of the greatest husband-murderess ever, professing her love for the husband she is about to kill. She is also a mother confronting for the first time the husband who has sacrificed their daughter ten years earlier. This husband shows no remorse, even daring to bring a concubine into their home. In her public proclamation Clytemnestra embarrasses a husband, a king, and a boasting general. The Watchman was right to emphasize her "heart which plans like a man."

Cassandra's presence may have been the catalyst for Clytemnestra's prolonged speech describing her suffering during her husband's absence. She casts herself in the Penelope mould. Like Penelope, who sought news about her husband from passers-by (*Od.* 14. 121–30), so it was with Clytemnestra "sitting alone in her home without her man" (861–62). She listened to one frightening report after another about her husband. In her description of Agamemnon's possible death, she equates his wounds to the number of holes in a fishing net. Having embarked on the description of Agamemnon wounded in battle, she then pictures him as triple-bodied, killed once for every shape, and describes the triple cloak of earth needed for his burial. As if suddenly aware of revealing too much of what she desires, she describes her own attempts at suicide.

When she finally addresses Agamemnon directly, twenty lines into her speech (877), she explains Orestes' absence. In a *most feminine* way, she credits her brother-in-law Strophius with the idea of removing Orestes from the dangerous city. Clytemnestra then resumes her tale of woe, which culminates with the claim that she dreamt of Agamemnon suffering even more wounds while she slept (893–94). However, as Hogan points out, this claim contains a slight ambiguity, since the "wounds" (or suffering) she dreamed of might have been those she is planning for Agamemnon (1984: on line). She takes advantage of the "frailty" attributed to women, pretending to be swayed by dreams, visions, and gossip, despite earlier on denying any such feminine weakness to the Chorus.[20]

Clytemnestra then turns her back on Agamemnon and addresses the Chorus anew, speaking of Agamemnon in the third person. Unlike her portrayal of personal feelings, she now delivers a strangely distancing panegyric (eulogistic oration) apparently filled with praise yet comparing him to a dog or something inanimate (896–901). The only human reference to him is that he is "only son of his father," a glaringly false statement. The spectators know well that he has a brother, on whose behalf he went to Troy. Is Clytemnestra suggesting that all the other comparisons are also false? In one breath she manages both to praise and insult him. For example, referring to him as a watchdog of the house recalls *Iliadic* insults. The original spectators, who were usually well-versed in the Homeric epics, probably recalled Achilles' angry address to Agamemnon following his extramarital escapades, calling him *kynopis* "dog-face" (*Il.* 1.159), and saying: "You heavy with wine, with a *dog's* eyes and with a deer's heart" (*Il.* 1.225) after Agamemnon refused to give up Achilles' concubine. By association Aeschylus allows Clytemnestra to condemn him for taking yet another concubine.

Whether praising or criticizing, Clytemnestra emphasizes her subordinate status, in contrast with images of Agamemnon's manly guardianship, strength and stability. However, Clytemnestra takes her duplicity to a new level when she invites Agamemnon to walk into the house on the "fine crimson fabrics". Clytemnestra has just expressed her wish that her husband should not "court jealousy" (*phtonos*, 903–04) in his victorious return. Having said that, she tempts him to act in a way likely to arouse this divine jealousy. She bids her slaves to spread fine crimson fabrics "so that Justice" may lead Agamemnon into the palace (911), a statement which contains another *double entendre*. While Agamemnon would probably understand "Justice" as alluding to his war of revenge on Paris and Troy, Clytemnestra most certainly is thinking of the revenge *she* is about to take.

Crimson Tapestries   The scene in which Clytemnestra urges Agamemnon to walk on fine fabrics on his way into the palace, and he finally agrees to do so, has attracted a great deal of scholarly attention.[21] The spectators are treated to a dramatic presentation that is perhaps reminiscent of Agamemnon's bloody sacrifice of his daughter, since these tapestries, the fruit of women's labor, are a deep crimson, the color of blood.[22] Additionally, as Agamemnon points out, the crimson color is designated for the gods. Clytemnestra thus entices Agamemnon into doing exactly what he feared to do: overstepping the realm of mortals and trampling on tapestries that only gods deserve to tread on, thereby arousing divine jealousy.

Spreading the sumptuous fabrics was a tremendous spectacle. Once the fabrics are laid, Agamemnon addresses his wife. His first words are terse and offensive: "Daughter of Leda, guardian of my house, you have made a speech that was like my absence—you stretched it out to a great length" (915–16).²³ He then lectures her on what is improper. His directive "Do not in a woman's fashion pamper me" (918–19, my trans.), or by extension as Sommerstein (with Fraenkel 1950: on line) translates: "Do not pamper me as if I were a woman," is of major importance, because he ends up doing exactly what he claims should not be done: "act like a woman."²⁴ His prohibition against *proskynesis* (known as foreign bowing or prostrating oneself before a person of higher social rank) reveals exactly what Clytemnestra has already figured out: that he has become accustomed to the norms of the east, and will ultimately succumb to a non-Greek custom: walking into his house on rich crimson tapestries. This scene highlights Clytemnestra's shrewd calculation.

Despite Agamemnon's many well-reasoned reservations, Clytemnestra's determination is unshakeable. Creating a series of hypothetical circumstances,²⁵ she first asks him whether he might have vowed to the gods to walk on the fabrics if he were in danger. The question makes little sense, because as far as Agamemnon knows he is not in such a position, although ironically he actually is.²⁶ However, instead of telling Clytemnestra "I am not in any dangerous situation," he answers her question, although in a qualified manner: if a seer had told him, he would have walked on tapestries. This positive answer from Agamemnon is, as Easterling (1973: 13) points out, crucial because Clytemnestra now has an opening to offer other circumstances in which it would not be improper to act as she is asking him to do. He fails to see that his wife is "pulling the wool over his eyes" and leading him down the slippery path to his fatal mistake.

Clytemnestra continues "Then do not fear shame at the criticisms of mortals" (937) although in fact he fears the anger of the gods. However, he falls for her argument, and allows her to allay his fear of public opinion by saying that the person who incurs no human jealousy is not "enviable" (939), capitalizing on Agamemnon's desire be envied.²⁷ Having no match for Clytemnestra's rhetorical prowess, Agamemnon strikes at her most obvious "weakness": *being a woman who does not behave like one*. In response she "plays the woman": "But for the fortunate, even a defeat can be honorable," she flatters him (941). Delivering her *coup de grâce*, she appeals to his masculine superiority: "You are still the master, you know, *if you yield to me out of your own free will*" (943). He acquiesces. By agreeing to her request, Agamemnon becomes submissive and acts "as if he were a woman." Clytemnestra succeeds in "feminizing" him.²⁸ She sees his ostensibly "unwilling surrender" as a victory for herself. Furthermore, by proclaiming that she would have vowed to trample many garments to contrive the return "*of this life here*" (pointing to Agamemnon, 965), she continues her depersonalization of Agamemnon. Those who know of or suspect her sinister plan would understand that Clytemnestra would have done anything to ensure the return of Agamemnon, so that she could kill him herself. Meanwhile, she ignores Agamemnon's order to bring Cassandra into the house.

Once he is inside, Clytemnestra utters a prayer to "Zeus the fulfiller" (973). The spectators know what the prayer is. Her victory is almost complete.²⁹ Only after her short address to Zeus does she enter into the palace, leaving Cassandra in the carriage without uttering a single word to her. As Taplin points out, "if two important characters go together, then the dramatically dominant tends to speak last" (1977: 310). Agamemnon's silence during his exit must have been noticed by the spectators, as was Clytemnestra's dominance. Clytemnestra's address to Zeus indicates that she is certain that Zeus desires the death of Agamemnon. She believes avenging her daughter is her religious and moral right.

The Decline of Clytemnestra's Power: After Meeting Cassandra

Clytemnestra and Cassandra   The only character to challenge and indeed cripple Clytemnestra's dramatic dominance is Cassandra. Clytemnestra follows Agamemnon into the palace and reemerges in line 1035. Clytemnestra's appearances on the threshold are always imperious, so the audience is not surprised when in a dismissive but commanding way she tells the captive princess: "You, get yourself inside too—I mean you, Cassandra" (1035). The verb she uses for "get yourself inside" is the simple form of Agamemnon's compound verb "bring in" (*komize,* 951). This rare verb, used only twice in Aeschylus, is apparently a marker for Cassandra.[30] Clytemnestra points out that Cassandra should be grateful to have come to such a wealthy household. The domineering queen is ignored by Cassandra, who remains silent and motionless.

Cassandra's inertia and silence in the face of Clytemnestra's imperious commands give her a potent grandeur. After all, how can one win an argument when faced with silence? Cassandra's motionlessness in the chariot parallels the usually static appearances of Clytemnestra. For now, there is a kind of "draw" in physical dramatic effect between the queen and the Trojan princess. This performative indecision between the two characters shifts when Cassandra refuses to answer the queen's quick succession of injunctions to descend from the chariot.[31] Clytemnestra understands that she is being insulted by the captive's silence and withdraws abruptly into the palace. Cassandra has taken control of the stage. The scene changes dramatically after Clytemnestra's exit: Cassandra bursts into words, and probably into song and dance.[32] She is as vital as only a young person can be, both frantic and surprising, dominating the stage.

Why did Aeschylus devise such an animated scene for the captive Trojan prophetess? The reason could have been the significance of Cassandra's arrival in Argos for Clytemnestra. While it was societally permissible for a husband to have extra-marital liaisons, bringing a concubine to cohabit with a wife was not acceptable.[33] Such an act threatened the wife. Here Cassandra is the character with the longest continuous presence on stage apart from the Chorus. After she starts speaking in 1072, she has the stage free of Clytemnestra's presence for 258 lines. In those lines she converses with the Chorus, sings, and dances. This distraught activity follows the silence and stillness which stripped the power from Clytemnestra's rhetoric. Her youthful energy, free expression, and almost voluntary entrance to the house not only nullify Clytemnestra's imposing dominance, but also show how nimble and mobile Cassandra is, in contrast with Clytemnestra's lack of motion.

In everything she does, Cassandra draws attention to the contrast between Clytemnestra's control over Agamemnon and the queen's lack of control over her, Cassandra, who maintains her free will. Agamemnon, the victorious hero, walks into the palace deceived, ensnared, and defeated by Clytemnestra. Cassandra, a female captive, goes inside of her own accord, in her own time. She is fully aware of her upcoming fate, which Apollo has unveiled to her. Symbolically, by depriving Clytemnestra of the rhetorical power in which her superiority resides, Cassandra undermines her status as the mistress of the house, embodying the threat any concubine poses to a wife.

The scene with Clytemnestra and Cassandra, second in dramatic effect only to Agamemnon's trampling the crimson cloths, does irrevocably damage Clytemnestra's stature, but in the following exchanges between Cassandra and the Chorus, Aeschylus uses an interesting dramatic device to pit the two women up against each other. Instead of directly showing Clytemnestra's preparation for the murder and the regicide itself, Aeschylus allows Cassandra to narrate the events, which she "sees" with the gift of her prophecy (1107–11; 1115–18; 1126–29; 1261–63). Cassandra also "sees" her own forthcoming death clearly. After Clytemnestra cedes dominance of the stage to Cassandra, she never recovers the calm, confident control she has exhibited up to this point. Could Clytemnestra have some inkling of the last part of Cassandra's prophecy that a man will come to avenge the murders, and slay his mother (1280–81)? Could this new uncertainty contribute to the loss of Clytemnestra's power? Although she retains the wherewithal to follow through with her plans, something has changed.

The *Daimon*—the "Evil Spirit" When Clytemnestra reappears on stage, she reveals the bodies of Agamemnon and Cassandra, which have been rolled out from the door of the skene on the ekkyklema (see Glossary). She immediately confesses that she had previously spoken deceitfully to achieve her purpose (1372–76). She had not previously attempted to justify her deeds, as she had not revealed her true intentions. Clytemnestra now enters into a bitter confrontation with the Chorus, and it soon becomes evident that the queen's confidence and rhetorical prowess are diminished. While she starts strongly, "You are testing me as if I were a witless woman" (1401), she quickly seems overwhelmed at the realization that she has committed the grave crime of regicide.

---

daimon

The origin of the idea of the evil or avenging evil spirit and avenging spirit of the House of Atreus stems back to Tantalus son of Zeus, who was the first of successive generations to perpetrate a series of outrageously bloodthirsty deeds against other family members. Tantalus invited the gods to a banquet and then insulted them by serving the boiled flesh of his own son, Pelops. The gods recognized the vile act and only Demeter, who was distracted, ate from the flesh. Tantalus suffered a never-ending punishment in the Netherworld and Pelops was restored to life. It was, however, Pelops who first provoked the curse on the family. He wished to obtain the hand of Hippodamia, but to do so had to beat her father, King Oenomaus, in a chariot race. All previous suitors had lost this challenge and been put to death. Pelops came up with a plan to bribe Oenomaus' charioteer Myrtilus to remove the linchpin from a wheel of his master's chariot. In exchange, Pelops promised to allow Myrtilus to lie with Hippodamia. Myrtilus kept his end of the bargain and Oenomaus was killed when the wheel fell off the carriage as he raced. However, Pelops refused to give Myrtilus his reward and threw him into the sea instead. Before he died, Myrtilus cursed Pelops and his descendants. Aeschylus focuses on the crimes of the next generation, Pelops' sons Atreus and Thyestes, who continued the family tradition of betrayals and violence. The two brothers were banished from Olympia after murdering their half-brother, Chrysippus. Having taken refuge in Mycenae they competed for the throne while the king Eurystheus was away at war. Having decided that the possessor of the finest ram would be king, Pan agreed to help Atreus by giving him a golden-fleeced ram. But Atreus' wife, Aerope, being in love with Thyestes, stole the ram and gave it to him. Atreus then convinced Thyestes to give up the throne if the sun went backwards in the sky. Zeus helped Atreus accomplish this feat and Thyestes was banished. Later on Atreus feigned a reconciliation, invited Thyestes to a banquet and served him his two murdered sons as food. When Thyestes discovered the truth, he went into exile after cursing Atreus. This seems to be the curse that haunts the house of Atreus. The acts of violence continued in the next generation. Thyestes fathered another son, Aegisthus, who was brought up by Atreus. Atreus planned for Aegisthus to murder Thyestes, but when the young man discovered the truth about his parentage, he killed Atreus instead. The curse is referred to in the play *Agamemnon* by both the Chorus and Clytemnestra.

Her decline goes hand in hand with the changes in her claims of responsibility for the murder of Agamemnon. She starts by declaring that she alone killed him: "*I stand where I struck...I did it this way—I won't deny it—...I struck him twice...and when he had fallen I added a third stroke*" (1379–86). The gruesome imagery describes her joy at Agamemnon's death, comparing her delight at being covered in the spurt of his blood to an ear of corn glad in Zeus' gift of rain. "No other speech in Greek tragedy contains so many (ten in all) and such insistent references to the speaker's responsibility for a deed," says Conacher (1987: 49). After the Chorus' outburst criticizing the way she dares to speak about her husband, Clytemnestra is even more defiant in her claim of murdering him: "this is Agamemnon, *my husband,* a corpse, the work of this right hand of mine" (1404–06), a vaunt reminiscent of heroic narrative and casting Clytemnestra as an even more masculine woman.[34]

However, as if she suddenly were weakened, and in need of some kind of moral support, she claims for the first time that her motive for the murder was Agamemnon's sacrifice of Iphigenia, saying that she has carried out the act for Justice (*Dikē*), Ruin (*Atē*), and Fury (*Erinys*). A new theme is also introduced: her fear. She will never *feel fear* as long as "the fire upon my hearth is kindled by Aegisthus and he remains loyal to me as hitherto; for he is an ample shield of confidence for me" (1435–37). This is the first mention of Aegisthus in the play. Her disparagement of Agamemnon and glorying in his death now seem grating. Calling Agamemnon an "abuser" in Greek (*lumanterios* 1438, a word which is usually used for a rapist) bringing up Cassandra, and heaping lurid insults upon the woman she has just murdered in cold blood (1440–43), whom the audience have just seen as intelligent, vital, and courageous, all further erode Clytemnestra's authority and further show the widening cracks in her confidence. The mention of Iphigenia should have sufficed.

In the lyrical exchange between the Chorus and Clytemnestra starting at 1448, Clytemnestra does not sing as the Chorus do, but uses the rhythmic units known as anapests, based on a repeated metrical foot composed of two short unstressed syllables, followed by a long-stressed syllable (˘ ˘ -). Anapests are suited to a chanted or recited vocal delivery which according to Hall "could be recited in a grand and declamatory manner more suitable than lyric song for indomitable masculinized females."[35] The vocal transition signifies both intensity and a certain emotional upheaval on her part when responding to the Chorus' comments.

Progressive movement in the arguments follows with both sides gaining some insights, although no truce or compromise is reached.[36] The Chorus blame Helen for the blood shed at Troy, but still liken Clytemnestra to "a hateful raven," perched over Agamemnon's body. Some common ground is found when the Chorus admit the intervention of a *daimon* (evil spirit), Zeus, and the avenging spirit (*alastor*).[37] Clytemnestra first accepts the intervention of the *daimon* as the source of her deed, and then claims to be the manifestation of the *alastor*, the avenging spirit itself (1497–504), "undercutting herself as fully autonomous agent."[38] Finally, she realizes she might become the *daimon*'s next victim and seeks a pact with the *daimon* demonstrating how far she has fallen from her lofty perch: she will accept all that has happened and give up her share of the royal wealth if only the *daimon* will go elsewhere and persecute some other house (1567–76).

Clytemnestra is standing with the Chorus, rattled by the murder's potential consequences, and trying to avert the "evil spirit," when suddenly Aegisthus and his guards arrive. For Aegisthus, the issue is clear: the conflict is over: the slain Agamemnon lies wrapped in the woven robes of the Furies (1580–81). This is not so for Clytemnestra. There is a clear possibility that the cycle of violence will continue now that the responsibility for the murder has been transferred to the *daimon*. Clytemnestra is no longer the representation of the evil spirit, as she was before, but is *the potential victim* of it. The scene started with her glorying in her responsibility for the murder, and it ends with her claim that she was overcome by the *daimon*. The only thing she still boasts about is that she is a woman and what she says is important.

Clytemnestra and Aegisthus In his first speech, Aegisthus, the man whom she has proclaimed her shield and protector, has not one word for her. Mirroring Clytemnestra's references to nature when she described Agamemnon, Aegisthus now praises the light of the day that brought justice. For Aegisthus, Agamemnon's death is all about him and the wrongs done to his side of the family. To make matters worse, Clytemnestra hears the Chorus castigating Aegisthus by calling him "You woman!!" for not fighting at Troy but sharing her bed instead (1625). In response to the Chorus' condemnation of his cowardice in not carrying out the murder himself, Aegisthus finally mentions Clytemnestra, dismissively at that: "Well, the entrapment was obviously a job for a *woman*" (1636). Clytemnestra hears that she has been relegated to the role of a generic agent of punishment for *his* family's sake, nothing more. She is stripped of her strategic role.

Hogan states: "it seems strange to use *woman* abusively when a woman has actually murdered the *lord of war*" (1984: on line). Hearing that Aegisthus has no regard for women, and is himself taunted by being called a woman, is a harsh blow for Clytemnestra. In effect, she has exchanged an applauded military hero for a nobody. After pacifying the Chorus, Clytemnestra takes one last shot at the Elders regarding her gender: "Such are the words of *a woman*, if anyone sees fit to learn from them" (1661). Her words are intelligent as always. She calms the Elders and prevents an unnecessary physical confrontation between them and Aegisthus. When the brawl is about to get out of hand again, she intervenes for the second time. As a mother would calm a child, she tells Aegisthus not to pay attention to the "empty howlings" of the Chorus (1672). Having pacified Aegisthus, she admits him into the palace, hinting at joint authority.

Clytemnestra's last two contributions seem to be the only positive ones which don't have overt dissimulations (but see below). However, they also point to her deteriorating stature from a self-confessed, avenging murderess glorying in her deed, to a representative of the avenging spirit, to the victim of this spirit. Aegisthus in turn emerges as a coward who not only did not fight at Troy, but claims victory over Agamemnon without having lifted a finger against the commander. Ignoring Clytemnestra, he considers her nothing but a convenient tool defined by her gender. He claims to be the architect, she only the executor, of the deed.

What might Clytemnestra's plans be for the man who has referred to her only as a tool for accomplishing his interests? Clytemnestra was present during his altercation with the Chorus, who call him "a stay-home woman" (1625–26). Unlike her former biting retaliations against the Chorus' insults, however, she does not interfere until weapons are drawn. Furthermore, she says nothing to Aegisthus of her bargain with the *daimon*. This omission becomes significant when we hear her including herself in the future rule of Argos: "*I and you*, ruling over the house, will make things well" (1672–73),[39] a claim made in spite of her having heard Aegisthus say that *he* alone will rule over the Argives.

It would seem that Clytemnestra plans to have Aegisthus in *her* palace on her own terms: he is needed at least for the sake of appearances. Clytemnestra cannot be a sole ruler: a male is needed on the throne. Aegisthus is a weak man and so a good choice for what she wants to do: to be the power behind the throne. Having managed to manipulate the great Agamemnon, she should be able to control Aegisthus, a much weaker man. The audience have no reason to think he would be successful in keeping his independence from Clytemnestra.

Some of the spectators might have entertained the possibility of a rerun of what has just happened to Agamemnon, especially since in many ways this is a "mirror scene" of Agamemnon's arrival. The dramatic portrayal of Clytemnestra as the one who engineered and committed the murder of the commander of the Greeks was, as far as we know,

Aeschylus' innovation and a surprise to the spectators.[40] Some in the audience might have wondered if Aeschylus planned to present this "manly woman" killing Aegisthus as well. At this point the spectators don't know what her scheme is.

If Aegisthus is to live, the play has to come a full circle. Despite the formidable courage and planning needed to commit Clytemnestra's horrific and "manlike" act of revenge, in the eyes of the men she is just "a woman," only useful as a tool for deception. Never mind her wits, intelligence, and rhetorical skill. Although the play started with a gender reversal, at its denouement the play retracts this reversal. The Elders almost act as "men" in standing up to Aegisthus, and Aegisthus, the most ineffectual male in the drama, manages to belittle the powerful, masculine Clytemnestra, turning her into the "subdued wife." In a way, the first part of the trilogy anticipates the trilogy's arc. It starts with the dominant Clytemnestra, a woman who successfully overcomes the commander of the Greeks symbolizing not only female control over a man, but also the principle of the blood tie between a daughter and mother. As we will see, the trilogy ends on a different note altogether. Not only is there no punishment for matricide, but the blood tie between mother and child is invalidated. It seems that there is a complete rehabilitation of the male as well as of child sacrifice and matricide.

CLYTEMNESTRA IN *LIBATION BEARERS* AND *EUMENIDES*

Aeschylus' *Libation Bearers*

About eight years after the murder of Agamemnon, his son Orestes returns from Phocis, where he was sent by Clytemnestra before the murder. He is accompanied by his cousin and friend Pylades. After leaving an offering of his hair on his father's tomb, Orestes notices the women of the Chorus and Electra approaching, and withdraws into hiding along with Pylades. Clytemnestra has sent these women to pour libations on Agamemnon's grave because she has been frightened by a nightmare. The nature of Clytemnestra's dream appears to auger things to come: she has given birth to a snake who sucks her blood. After Orestes comes out of hiding and reunites with his sister, the siblings pray for their revenge on Clytemnestra and Aegisthus. Disguised as travelers, Orestes and Pylades gain entrance to the palace. The disguised Orestes tells Clytemnestra that her son is dead. After Clytemnestra dispatches Orestes' old Nurse Cilissa to report the news to Aegisthus, Aegisthus enters and is killed by Orestes. Clytemnestra is then confronted by Orestes and Pylades. Her appeal to Orestes to spare her as a mother freezes him, until Pylades reminds him of the instructions he had received from Apollo's oracle at Delphi before returning to Argos, commanding him to kill Clytemnestra and her lover. Orestes kills them and is subsequently pursued by the Furies sent by his mother and seeks the help of Apollo at Delphi.

Aeschylus' *Eumenides*

The *Eumenides* concludes Aeschylus' *Oresteia*. The sleeping Furies surround Orestes at the Temple of Apollo, with the god now ordering the tortured man to travel to Athens and seek Athena's protection. The ghost of Clytemnestra awakens the Furies and sends them in pursuit of Orestes. In Athens, Athena questions the Furies and Orestes about their claims. Orestes maintains his innocence; the Furies demand his life for shedding the kindred blood of his mother. Athena decides to hand the adjudication to a group of chosen Athenians who will form the first homicide tribunal, the *Areopagus*. This significant development takes revenge out of the hand of the immediate family and gives the *polis* and the appointed court the task of seeing justice done. Apollo argues in defense of Orestes that the murder of a mother does not consist of kindred bloodshed, because the female is only a receptacle for the male's seed; it is the father who is the biological parent. Athena concurs, casting the deciding vote, apparently deciding that Orestes' matricide is to be judged not to be kindred killing, so therefore not punishable by the Furies. Athena convinces the Furies to become Benevolent Spirits (Eumenides), who will be beneficial to Athens.

While the first part of the trilogy is dominated by Clytemnestra, the next two parts both expand on and counter her prior portrayal. *Libation Bearers* demonstrates Clytemnestra's decline from a dominant 'manly' woman to a more submissive 'womanly' one, relegating her to wifely tasks, as well as having her succumb to masculine ideology. Although Clytemnestra is murdered at the end of *Libation Bearers* she appears once more after her death in the *Eumenides*. While initially Clytemnestra seems to have regained her defiant rage beyond the grave, as the plot unfolds it portrays her utter downfall. When Athena votes for the acquittal of Orestes, accepting Apollo's contention that a mother is no more than a receptacle for the father's seed, and that there is no blood relationship between mother and child, Clytemnestra is robbed of her gender's role in giving life to a child. Motherhood, which led her to the murder of Agamemnon, has been taken away from her.

In *Agamemnon* Clytemnestra had the stage for most of the tragedy; in *Libation Bearers* she appears only in two brief scenes. In the first one of 50 lines (668–718), obeying the tenets of hospitality usually offered by the wife, she invites her future killers into the palace, and in the second one of 45 lines (885–930), she is murdered. The introductory picture of the queen is grim. Before she herself appears, the Chorus of elderly slave women, Electra, and Orestes all have much to say about her, none of it good. She is odious to all of them, as a murderess and as a mother. Her children do not love her. In fact, Orestes sees her as a viper and vows to avenge his father.[41] Electra claims that Clytemnestra's godless spirit against her children belies the name of a mother.

Clytemnestra not only murdered Agamemnon but also mutilated his body and gave him an impious funeral, without lamentation or mourning.[42]

Unlike *Agamemnon*, however, this play does not consistently assign Agamemnon's murder solely to Clytemnestra, but usually includes Aegisthus. This version of events accords rather surprisingly with Aegisthus' own account at the end of *Agamemnon* which contrasted so strongly with what the audience had witnessed. This variability enforces the idea that the past can be rewritten or reinterpreted according to the present purposes. Orestes' Nurse Cilissa sees Aegisthus, not Clytemnestra, as the person who brought the house down (764–65, cf. e.g. 492), although she does not make it clear how he has done this.

Furthermore, the balance of power between Aegisthus and Clytemnestra seems to have shifted in favor of Aegisthus. He is now perceived as the person who calls the shots in the palace. Although Orestes assumes Aegisthus might refuse his access to the palace (569–70), he tells the Doorkeeper that he prefers to speak to *the man* of the house rather than to its mistress, because conversing with a woman involves blurring one's words, while "a man speaks to another man with confidence and reveals his meaning with clarity" (667–68, cf. 672–73, 716). This claim that men should speak to men is simply stated as part of the masculine ideology accepted even by women. The idea is reiterated by Clytemnestra, who orders the Nurse to summon Aegisthus as quickly as possible "so that he can come and learn about the newly-reported information more clearly, *from man to man*" (735–37). The women of the Chorus uphold this idea again when they lure Aegisthus into the palace under the pretext that no transmission of information is better than "inquiring directly *from man to man*" (850). They know that this argument, which accords with a male preferential ideology, would sway him best. Clytemnestra uses the same anonymity-producing strategy when she learns about her son's (supposed) death: "we (referring to herself) will communicate this to the *rulers* of the house," she says, referring to Aegisthus. Using "we" when referring to herself, as in the modern-day "royal 'we,'" is especially noteworthy in view of her previous emphasis on her own accomplishments (e.g. *Ag.* 1404–06). Her identity has been compromised. She seems to be intentionally disassociating herself from her former masculine role and willingly exiting the male world.[43]

It becomes increasingly evident throughout the play that Clytemnestra's power and confidence have been eroded. She blames the misfortune of the family on abstract forces. Clytemnestra's previous version of her own role has disappeared, as has Iphigenia.

In Aeschylus' work (unlike in Sophocles' and Euripides' plays), Clytemnestra is not shown to have children with Aegisthus. He himself has none, leaving no possibility for future revenge by descendants. Much is made of Cilissa's claim that Clytemnestra only pretends to be sad in front of the servants, concealing her laughter when she hears the news of Orestes' death, which is followed by a touching account of how she, Cilissa, served as his wet nurse and nanny (737–41, 749–65). In direct contrast to *Agamemnon*, which presented Clytemnestra's views and narrative, *Libation Bearers* shows the opposition to Clytemnestra on all fronts, even by Aegisthus, who not only mocks her womanish emotionality and excitement, but also strangely seems to reverse the attitude he expressed in *Agamemnon* and make her the culprit for the murder of Agamemnon, as if he had nothing to do with it (841–45).

Now that she is left with this far from perfect partner in the palace, the cowardly "womanly" man who had been taunted by the Chorus at the end of *Agamemnon* (*Ag.* 1625), Clytemnestra has somehow become attached to him emotionally (*LB* 893). Putting aside for the most part her own "manly" courage and persistence, she tries to live as "a woman" does, i.e. caring for her husband and trying to forget everything that connected her to Agamemnon. This may be another reason for her "seeming" disregard of Electra ("seeming" because when Clytemnestra is haunted by nightmares, she chooses to send Electra with drink-offerings to Agamemnon's tomb; she could have sent anyone, but she chooses her daughter). Clytemnestra's prophetic dream in which she gave birth to a snake that bit her as she suckled it (514–39 cf. 928–29) shows that the fear of revenge has started to consume her.

Although the status of the queen appears diminished, she is not essentially changed.[44] Clytemnestra retains her competence and successfully fulfills the role she has chosen in her new circumstances. Just as she resolutely followed her "heart which plans like a man" in *Agamemnon,* where she steeled herself to commit the murder of her husband, so upon taking Aegisthus to her house, she plays the consummate subordinate wife. She is the perfect hostess (cf. 707–15), but everything significant beyond physical care and comfort of the guests is relegated to the master of the house, as she tells Orestes and Pylades: "If there's need to do anything requiring more deliberation *it's work for men, and we'll communicate it to them*" (672–73). Clytemnestra, who had been introduced as having the deliberative capacity of a man, is now relinquishing this mental activity in favor of generic "men."

Furthermore, being the perfect wife to Aegisthus would demand that she ignore Agamemnon's children as much as possible. Iphigenia is not mentioned. Electra is utilized when necessary. Orestes is abroad, but she thinks she knows where he is, as her comment that he was smart not to return to Argos shows (696–97). Euripides followed this thought by making Aegisthus offer a reward for whoever should kill the exiled Orestes, and having Orestes return *incognito* and stay close to the border rather than enter the city (Eur. *El.* 32–33, 90–97). It is indeed clear to Clytemnestra that her current husband would not tolerate a competitor to the throne. Her motherhood is thus relegated to second place, while she is first and foremost Aegisthus' wife.

Even as Clytemnestra sheds her dominancy, the charge of emotionality clings to her. Both Aegisthus and the Chorus accuse Clytemnestra of reacting emotionally rather than thinking coolly and rationally. The Chorus oppose the "crafty plotting of a woman" (626) who is prone to passion and wishes to assume command (629–30). It is interesting that the charge of being motivated by passion is combined with the accusation of coveting the power to rule. This would have been an additional possible motive for Clytemnestra's actions in the first play of the trilogy. She needed to remove the strong male figure, Agamemnon, from the palace and replace him with a token male, Aegisthus, who would supposedly allow her to maintain her position of power.[45] However, in *Libation Bearers* things do not appear to have worked out in this way as she is never shown wearing the mantle of leadership.

Aegisthus' scornful attitude to Clytemnestra is evident in his response to the news brought by Cilissa from Clytemnestra. He suspects that it is overly dramatized and asks the women of the Chorus for corroboration: "What is it all about? Should I regard it as the living truth, or are these just the frightened words of women that leap high in the air?" (844–46). Aegisthus' contempt for women has already been seen in *Agamemnon* (1636). Here, however, Aegisthus proves himself more worthy of his own scorn. Clytemnestra's directive to him to come with his bodyguards shows perspicacity, whereas Aegisthus, unquestioningly following Cilissa's altered message, shows how easily he can be duped even though he is "a man."

We see glimpses of Clytemnestra's old self when she realizes that the guest she had invited to the house is none other than Orestes, and that he has just killed Aegisthus. Her reaction is courageous and instantaneous: "Someone give me … an axe that can kill a man!" (889). It takes a lot for a mother, however distant from her children she has become, to be willing to kill her son. Finding herself with no other choice, Clytemnestra is, as usual, quick to grasp the implications. However, her rebuttal of Orestes' accusations is far from the brilliant rhetoric she used in the crimson tapestries scene in *Agamemnon*.[46] Her quick wit and ability to improvise are absent, although she does try to soften Orestes by calling him "my son" or "my child" (896, 912, 920). She fails, however, to bring up issues that might have helped her. Instead of the sacrifice of Iphigenia, she decries Agamemnon's infidelities (918) and bemoans the pain of women kept apart from their men (920). She does not remind Orestes that he was sent to his uncle for his protection, in answer to his charge that she has cast him out of the house.

Aeschylus must have purposefully portrayed a more subdued Clytemnestra than we have seen before. After all, she is fighting for her life. She might have fought harder, but she did not. The best she could do was threaten Orestes with a mother's vengeful Furies (see Box on Furies, p. 38). There may be many reasons behind Aeschylus' dramatic choices. It is important to remember that he is writing a trilogy and the acts in the second play, the *Libation Bearers,* prepare for the drama still to come in the *Eumenides.* The point here is that Orestes is about to commit what has been considered throughout history a most heinous crime, that of matricide. This horrific act will lead to his temporary insanity mediated by the Furies. To understand fully the dramatic tension of this moment the audience need to identify with Clytemnestra, at least to some extent. Having depicted an invincible heroine in *Agamemnon*, and a woman who has distanced herself from her children so far in the *Libation Bearers*, perhaps Aeschylus saw the need to show that Clytemnestra is vulnerable too. He may have wanted to indicate that a mother confronted by her son may not have the wherewithal to defend herself, or he may have wished to frame Clytemnestra as a woman affected by her conscience following the murders she had committed. As the text does not give a decisive answer to these points, readers and the audience have to make up their own minds.

Clytemnestra's diminished stature is felt throughout the play until she finally enters the house followed by Orestes. She is forced to cross the threshold on Orestes' terms, not

> **Furies, or Erinyes**
>
> These chthonic (Netherworld) female spirits are described by Aeschylus as being frighteningly hideous. Their principal function is to punish kindred bloodshed. Furthermore, if a person failed to avenge the murder of a member of his family, the Furies avenged the death on him. This left Orestes in an insoluble position. Were he not to avenge the murder of his father by his mother, he would be punished by the Furies, and if he shed his mother's he would be punished for that. Thus, he would be hounded by the Furies whether he killed his mother or not. Athena in Aeschylus' *Eumenides* forces the Furies to stop prosecuting Orestes and convinces them to give up their primitive function as bringer of retributive justice in favor of becoming the gracious Eumenides (Benevolent Spirits).

her own. This contrasts strongly with the way in which Cassandra was able to choose to enter the palace on her own terms. However, the consequences are the same; staying outside means she lives, walking in means she dies.

The final part of the trilogy, *Eumenides*, allows one last glimpse of the domineering queen. The play starts with the sleeping Furies, whom Clytemnestra's ghost rouses from their slumber to track Orestes. Sleep and awakening connect the beginnings of the first and last parts of the trilogy. In *Agamemnon*, Clytemnestra's vitality energizes those around her into action. In *Eumenides*, the queen, no longer among the living, still demands action although she is only a vision in the minds of the Furies. Her persistent upbraiding of the sleepy Furies is reminiscent of her old decisiveness and determination. Sending the Furies after Orestes perhaps symbolizes another victory over the male. For a short while the audience is allowed to think that Clytemnestra's death might be avenged.

This impression continues through most of Orestes' trial which forms the heart of the play, with the Furies as Orestes' prosecutors and Apollo as his defense. Crucially Athena is adjudicating and she also holds the casting vote. The suspense is maintained throughout Orestes' confession to the murder of his mother, and Apollo's defense detailing the abhorrent trickery involved in the murder of a general by his wife. Both are forceful, but do not resolve the issue of spilled kindred blood which motivates the Furies. No insults cast by Apollo against the ancient goddesses can bring about Orestes' acquittal.

The situation only changes when Apollo introduces the ingenious theory of reproduction in which the fetus is merely gestated in the mother's womb and therefore not related by blood to the mother. However, this claim would not have carried any weight had Athena as the judge presiding over the court objected to the idea. Athena's own birth, mythically described as having been directly from the head of Zeus (Hesiod, *Theogony* 924; cf. Aesch., *Eumenides* 736) put her in a unique position not to contest

Apollo's claim. Clytemnestra is thus eventually defeated by a female goddess, as she was defeated in the first part of the trilogy by the quintessentially feminine Cassandra (see Box on The Vote of Athena, p. 40).

There is a difference, however. While Cassandra was Clytemnestra's competitor for Agamemnon's affection, Athena has no animosity towards Clytemnestra. Athena makes her decision to side with Apollo logically and impersonally, with a view to one thing: the best interests of Athens, the city whose protector she is. By ensuring that Orestes, who is indebted to her, succeeds to the throne of Argos, Athena secures Argos as a faithful ally to Athens. She also uses the occasion to found a homicide court in Athens and thus ends kindred bloodshed. The dramatic tempo is so swift that there is no time to realize that Athena's position does not actually address the idea that a woman is only a vessel for the male seed, but is based on Athena's own peculiar birth. Athena intervenes in the trial to support Apollo's position at the last minute, just after the jurors cast their votes. The Furies have no opportunity to ask questions due to the tempo of the scene. Athena allows no further argument.

It is not immediately clear why Aeschylus portrays Clytemnestra as being defeated by a goddess also having attributes considered as being traditionally masculine. Clytemnestra had two significant female opponents, one human, and the other divine. A very feminine Cassandra has diminished Clytemnestra's dominance; then the most masculine of the goddesses inflicts the final blow. Winnington-Ingram has already claimed that there is a sense in which Athena is the counterpart of Clytemnestra. The goddess serves as the poet's final comment upon Clytemnestra's character and motive. Athena is the "god-goddess to Clytemnestra's man-woman" (1983:125–26). He claims that everything that Clytemnestra's nature wanted to do but her gender prevented her from doing, Athena by virtue of her godhood was free to accomplish: she could fight like a man and roam the world as she wanted, while Clytemnestra was confined to running the house of a man who was abroad and had concubines elsewhere. Indeed, while Athena's masculinity brings her praise (she is famously praised for her wise counsel (*boulē*, *Theogony* 319, 896), Clytemnestra is chastised for her "counsel" (*boulē*), her womanly mind, which eventually leads to her own death as well as the death of those around her.

A powerful woman like Clytemnestra combining male and female attributes could not be brought down by a "feminine" woman alone, nor by a male god alone. The combined forces of both female and male were needed to overcome her. By giving the last blow against the formidable queen to a goddess, Aeschylus partially returns to Clytemnestra the dominant status that she has lost as the trilogy evolved. Yes, she is dead and unavenged, but it took a unique immortal to render her powerless.

As already noted by Betensky, Clytemnestra tends to think of events in terms of human fertility.[47] To have Athena sever the sacred bond between a mother and a child is the cruellest punishment of all. The formidable queen is finally not only stripped of her life and every positive attribute she ever had: she is ultimately made as barren as Athena.

The Vote of Athena

Mythically within the trial of Orestes, Athena put an end to the primitive divine mechanism of retributive justice executed by the Furies/Erinyes by founding the homicide court of the *Areopagus* (court sitting on the hill of Ares in Athens) in which homicide trials were adjudicated. There are various views on the number of the jurors, which may have been eleven or twelve. The acquittal of a defendant of murder was a result of majority votes in his favor or tied votes. The vote of Athena is thus either a vote that would make the votes equal if the number of jurors is uneven but lacking one, or a vote that would create majority in case the number of jurors was even and their votes created a tie. "The Vote of Athena" was always on the side of mercy.

CLYTEMNESTRA IN SOPHOCLES' *ELECTRA*

In Sophocles' *Electra*, Clytemnestra makes her entrance in the second episode (516–51). A key purpose of this scene is to enable the audience to decide whether Clytemnestra deserves to die at her children's hands after killing their father. Up to this point, the spectators have heard both Electra and the Chorus describe Clytemnestra's treachery, lasciviousness, and abuse of her children.[48] They repeatedly mention the axe with which she killed Agamemnon (99, 195–96, 484–85), the deceitful treachery involved in the murder (125–26, 197), and Clytemnestra's passion for Aegisthus (97, 197, 273–74). Her savage mutilation of Agamemnon's corpse, wiping the bloodstains from his head is a new twist, as is her designation of the day of the murder as a monthly festival (278–81, 445–46). Electra also complains that Clytemnestra does not behave like a mother (287–98). The cards have thus already been stacked against Clytemnestra by the time she enters. However, Electra is inevitably not impartial, and the utterances of the Chorus are not necessarily reliable. Therefore, before deciding on the justice of the matricide, the audience must see Clytemnestra in action. They witness her confrontation with Electra and then her response to the Tutor's false report of Orestes' death.

The formal debate (*agon*, see Box on Formal Debate, p. 45) between Electra and Clytemnestra (516–633) contains the play's only direct discussion of revenge. Clytemnestra, claiming that "Justice took him [Agamemnon], not I alone" (528), propounds the classical notion that homicide might be justifiable under certain circumstances, and that only an unjust murder is properly punishable.[49] Clytemnestra speaks first, which is significant because the first speaker in a Sophoclean formal debate usually has the weaker position.[50] She makes three related points. First, Agamemnon was exceptionally hard-hearted in sacrificing Iphigenia. Second, he performed the act for the benefit of people who had no right to profit from the death of her daughter (the Argives,

Sophocles' *Electra*

Sophocles' *Electra*, like Aeschylus' *Libation Bearers*, focuses on Orestes' revenge killings. Orestes, accompanied by his Tutor and Pylades, has returned from his exile in Phocis and reveals that Apollo's oracle told him to avenge his father by using deception. There are however several innovations in Sophocles' version. Sophocles introduces Orestes' and Electra's sister Chrysothemis into his plot, with the confrontations between the two sisters emphasizing Sophocles' recurring theme of conflict between pragmatic decisions and those based purely on high-minded principles. Sophocles' Electra is cast in the role of an extremist, zealously lamenting her father's murder, with no consideration of the practical implications of her behavior. Clytemnestra and Electra engage in a heated debate about culpability in the killings of Iphigenia and Agamemnon. The Tutor, disguised as a Messenger, announces Orestes' death in a chariot race. Clytemnestra is relieved of the fear produced by her night-time terrors, and Electra plunges into deep despair. Orestes and Pylades enter, carrying an urn supposedly containing Orestes' ashes. When Electra eventually recognizes Orestes the celebrations of the two threaten to reveal the deception. Orestes and Pylades kill Clytemnestra while Electra stands guard outside the palace. Aegisthus soon arrives and is shown Clytemnestra's veiled corpse which he takes to be Orestes. Aegisthus finally is ushered into the palace to be killed.

534–36), and for whose benefit it would have been more appropriate to sacrifice one of Menelaus' two children (537–41). Third, Agamemnon sacrificed Iphigenia because he no longer loved her (544–46).

However, her argument is undermined in two ways. In the first place all three points are based on an egocentric and proprietary view of Iphigenia, as "my daughter" (536). As Clytemnestra draws him, Agamemnon had merely sired Iphigenia and not endured the pains of childbirth; he had no right to take the girl from her (532–33), a charge similar to that made by the Aeschylean queen (*Ag*.1417–18). In accordance with this claim, Clytemnestra's murder of Agamemnon becomes retaliation for the loss of valuable property more than retribution for the loss of a beloved daughter. Indeed, any expression of love for Iphigenia or grief over her loss is conspicuously absent from her argument.

In her rebuttal, Electra presents the sacrifice (563–76) as the "price" that the goddess Artemis exacted as "redress" for the stag that Agamemnon had killed in her sacred grove. As she presents it, Agamemnon did not make the sacrifice lightly, but only under the most "severe constraint" (575). Electra does not mention Iphigenia by name, and expresses no sadness. However, Electra's emphasis on Agamemnon's difficulty in sacrificing his daughter weakens Clytemnestra's charge. Until he performed the sacrifice, the entire Greek army was stranded at Aulis, unable either to proceed to Troy or to return home (573–74). Electra's account is a fuller rendition of the familiar myth than

Clytemnestra's and brings out the terrible choice Agamemnon had to make between the life of his daughter and the lives of the entire Greek army, although it is marred by the same coldness that Clytemnestra had shown.

Clytemnestra's relatively weak performance in the formal debate contrasts strongly with the queen's rhetorical confrontations presented by Aeschylus in *Agamemnon*. There her timing is exquisite, and her dominance supreme. Sophocles' Clytemnestra is an older woman, more similar to the figure in Aeschylus' *Libation Bearers*; however, Sophocles has given her a different life. Here she is a mother not only to Orestes and Electra, but also to Agamemnon's daughters Chrysothemis and Iphianassa, as well as to other nameless children fathered by Aegisthus.

With the debate on the justice of Clytemnestra's revenge ending in a draw, Sophocles shifts to a furious personal clash between a mother and her eldest surviving daughter, in which both sides are undermined by the speaker's own behavior. From the substantive discussion in the first part of her speech, in which Electra explains the reason for her sister's sacrifice, Electra moves in the second part (585–609) to an all-out attack on Clytemnestra's character and conduct. Electra berates her mother for consorting with the man with whom she had conspired to murder her father and, moreover, for having cast off and mistreated Electra herself and her brother, the legitimate children, in favor of her illegitimate children. The implications of these accusations, consistent with previous treatments of the myth, are that Clytemnestra killed Agamemnon out of lust for Aegisthus. The murder is an irredeemably reprehensible act which warrants the severe punishment that will be meted out. Yet these accusations are not an objective condemnation of Clytemnestra, but the railing of an affronted daughter. Electra sounds like a furious teenager blaming her mother for flaws and misconduct that have affected mainly herself.

The Chorus condemn both protagonists for failing to consider that there might be justice on the other's side:

> I see she's breathing fury. But whether *she* might have justice on her side. I don't see *her* giving any thought to this. (610–11)

The pronoun references in this statement are confusing. Since the observation directly follows Electra's angry lambasting, Electra would seem to be the fury-breathing "she." However, it is Clytemnestra who rebuffs the Chorus' statement with the words, "What thought should I give her / when she's so insolent toward the one who bore her" (612–13), suggesting that Clytemnestra is the "she" in question, or sees herself as such. The audience is left to decide on the pronoun reference or to conclude that it refers to mother and daughter both. Whichever one may choose; one should note Clytemnestra's chilling reaction: in no way is she prepared to accept Electra's responses with any motherly compassion. Neither Electra nor Clytemnestra behaves well. Clytemnestra shows herself lacking as a mother. Electra shows herself misbehaving as a daughter. The altercation ends inconclusively.[51]

From here, the discussion focuses on the question of what kind of mother Clytemnestra is—and indeed on whether or not she is a true mother. Sophocles introduces this question into the play as an important antecedent to the revenge. If Clytemnestra can be cast as a "false" mother, then her murder is not quite matricide (which is the pivotal question in *Eumenides*, but biologically rather than morally based). Earlier in the play, the Chorus had urged Electra to accept their advice as that of a "loyal mother" (234), implying that they, not Clytemnestra, had a mother's love and concern for her. Electra, telling of her rancorous relationship with Clytemnestra, questioned whether "one can / call her a mother" (273–74). The audience learn from Chrysothemis that Clytemnestra is willing to see her daughter Electra entombed in a dungeon outside the country if she does not cease her lamentations (378–82). In the formal debate Electra continues to paint Clytemnestra as an unworthy mother.

In the second part of the episode Sophocles allows the audience to decide for themselves. The first intimation of things to come is in Clytemnestra's prayer to Apollo, which follows her dream presaging the upcoming vengeance. In the dream, Agamemnon has come back to life and planted his sceptre next to the hearth where he had been murdered, and the "leafy shoot" that sprouted from it overshadowed all the land (420–23). Terrified, Clytemnestra now prays to Apollo to alleviate her fears, asking him to make any ill tidings in the dream rebound on her enemies and to allow her to continue living the comfortable life she has enjoyed till now in the company of her friends and of "those of my children who / harbor no ill will toward me or a bitter grudge" (653–54). She couches her prayer in what she terms "veiled" language, since Electra is in hearing range, and ends it with a silent entreaty: "As for the rest, about which I'm silent, / I trust that you, being a god, know it full well" (657–58). Since the ancient Greeks made their requests to the gods aloud, and viewed requests made in silence as indicative of sinister intent, Sophocles allows the spectators to think the worst: that Clytemnestra is praying for harm to come to Orestes, the "leafy shoot" of Agamemnon's sceptre, who threatened to take over the land.

These intimations are made more explicit with the arrival of the Tutor. Clytemnestra accepts the Tutor's description of Orestes' death as "glad news" (666–67) and shows herself callous to Electra's distress. After the Tutor describes Orestes' death, Clytemnestra experiences a moment of mixed feelings, in which her sense of good fortune is tainted by maternal sorrow for the death of her son:

CLYTEMNESTRA:

Oh Zeus! What am I to say about this? That it's a piece of good luck?

That it's terrible but welcome? It's a sad thing

to save my life through my own misfortunes.

TUTOR:

Oh lady, why are you disheartened by what I've told you?

CLYTEMNESTRA:

It is a wondrous thing to give birth. For even

when you're treated badly, you can't hate your own children. (766–71)

The moment, however, is very brief: Clytemnestra soon reverts to her characteristic egotism. Assuring the Tutor that his visit has not been in vain if he has brought proofs of Orestes' death, she goes on to malign her son. Presenting herself as the injured party, she complains that Orestes "abandoned my suckling and my nurture and took himself off / and became an exile and a foreigner" (775–76)—misdeeds that, as a small boy, he could not possibly have committed. She blames him for never having returned to see her and for charging her with his father's murder, even though she knows full well that returning for a visit would have endangered his life, and that she did murder his father. A bit later, she tells Electra that Orestes is well off "as he is" (791)—that is, dead. The act ends with her once again demonstrating callousness toward Electra, as she invites the Tutor into the palace for "a proper welcome" (800–01) and urges him to leave Electra outside to "clamor" (802) about her sorrows. Whether the hostility of Electra and Orestes and the threat they pose justify Clytemnestra's behavior toward them is another matter. The episode raises the question of what sacrifices a mother should make for all of her children, not only those who do her bidding. Should she be expected to sacrifice her happiness, her pleasure, and her fecundity? Should she be expected to sacrifice her life? Is a woman who will not make these sacrifices not a "true" mother?[52] Whatever the answer to these questions, Clytemnestra is no longer depicted as a woman with a "heart that plans like a man," who functions beyond the realm of the home. Neither does she retain the male trait of courage. She does not take any action in self-defense as did her Aeschylean prototype. The Sophoclean Clytemnestra is depicted as a deeply flawed, cruel and vindictive woman who mutilated Agamemnon after killing him and designated the day of his murder as a monthly festival.

It is Sophocles' choice of casting Electra as the main figure that effects his "different" Clytemnestra. As we will see in the chapter on Electra, the mother and daughter are alike in many ways, but neither of them is portrayed as a woman who is a realistic independent actor. In Sophocles' play, Clytemnestra is past her glory as a woman who can plan and carry out major revenge. Her current "achievement" is scheduling a feast on the day she murdered her former husband. Electra has been lamenting for around eight years, but does not think of planning the matricide and the murder of Aegisthus until she hears that Orestes is dead. But even then, she makes no realistic plans. Sophocles' exquisite mastery of dialogue allowed him to develop his tragic characters to heroic stature, even if they did not have the most sympathetic personalities. The reader must decide whether Sophocles' portrayal of Clytemnestra is indicative of his opinion of women and their place in society in general, or merely effected by dramatic considerations.

There is no firm evidence as to which of Sophocles' and Euripides' *Electra* plays was written first, so it is not possible to conclude whether one is a reaction to the other.[53] However, as will be seen, one of the many significant differences between Sophocles' *Electra* and Euripides' play is that in Sophocles' version Clytemnestra's intransigent daughter still lives in the palace. The proximity of the mother and daughter, at continual loggerheads with each other, must have produced a powder-keg like atmosphere waiting to be ignited. What does it mean for a person like Clytemnestra to live with a daughter who day and night reminds her not only of the murder she committed but of her illicit relationship with Aegisthus? What does it do to a person knowing that at any moment her son could come to kill her? Sophocles raises questions that are not found in Aeschylus' plays, including what it means to be a good mother under the most trying circumstances.

Electra's preeminence in Sophocles' play is felt up until the last time Clytemnestra's words are heard. Although Orestes murders Clytemnestra in the palace out of the audience's sight, Electra is on stage, making callous comments in response to each cry heard from the woman inside being murdered. In Sophocles' play neither Orestes nor Electra display any remorse. There is no hesitation on Orestes' part before the murder and Electra has completely disowned her mother, leaving Clytemnestra once more bereft of the role of motherhood.

Formal debate (*agon*)

The full Greek phrase is *agōn logōn* "contest of words" which is translated into "formal debate". The *agon* "contest" is one of the structural elements of Greek tragedy, which is antagonistic by nature. The main characteristic feature of an *agon* is the formal and highly organized debate of two, or at the most three, characters who present antithetical views of a major conflict. Its origins are ascribed in varying degrees to influences from institutionalized and often combative debate in deliberative political bodies, from sophistic argumentation, from rhetorical techniques, and from law-court practice. The *agon* was not necessarily designed to depict one party swaying the opposing one(s) through its argument, but rather to show that the speakers lack the basis for mutual understanding, and therefore will remain at odds. However, there is a tendency in Euripides for the offended or hostile party to speak first and for the seeming "winner" or the one of more sympathetic view to speak second. At the end one side is considered to have prevailed. The formal debate is a symmetrically structured verbal duel, which may be an entire tragic episode or part of one, often followed by stichomythic (rapid exchange in single lines) exchange. Two opposing speeches of roughly equal length are its core; one speech sets out a case and may also anticipate that of the opponent; the other speech rebuts and tries to overcome the first. Its calculated progression is distinguishable from more naturally styled confrontations.

CLYTEMNESTRA IN EURIPIDES' *ELECTRA*

Like Sophocles, Euripides prefaces Clytemnestra's appearance by having others comment on her. Although she is portrayed as a murderess living with Aegisthus (8–10, 160–66, 211–12), she is also aware of her guilt and concerned for her children. This dual perspective on Clytemnestra permeates the play: while the Chorus and Electra complain

Euripides' *Electra*

One of Euripides' main innovations in his version of *Electra* is in moving the action away from the palace in the heart of the *polis* and giving his play a rural setting instead. Married off to a poor farmer by Aegisthus, Electra lives in a rustic hovel. Her considerate husband, a farmer, leaves their marriage unconsummated out of respect for her royal status, and tells her she need not perform menial tasks, but she insists on performing them anyway to demonstrate how miserable her life is. Crossing the border from Phocis, Orestes and Pylades arrive near Electra's home. Remaining *incognito*, Orestes pretends to bring her news of her brother. Electra sends her husband to Agamemnon's old slave to bring refreshments for the noble guests. The Old Man eventually recognizes Orestes, and helps Electra to do the same, after which the siblings plot to murder Aegisthus, who is holding a sacrifice to the Nymphs on his nearby estates, and Clytemnestra, who is expected to join him. Electra tricks Clytemnestra into coming to her hut by sending a message that she has given birth to a baby son and needs her mother's help with the proper ritual. After the matricide, both Electra and Orestes lament their deed. The Dioscuri, Clytemnestra's brothers, arrive through the sky to settle the fates of the murderers. Sending Orestes into permanent exile, they order Pylades to marry Electra and take her old husband with them to Phocis. Sister and brother tearfully part.

of her cruelty, the queen presents herself as a wronged woman whose husband murdered her daughter to retrieve his brother's unfaithful wife, and then on his return from war, brought a concubine into their home.

The Farmer, who has less animosity towards Clytemnestra than the other characters, gives the audience the first picture of the queen. Aegisthus, fearing revenge, wanted to kill Electra to prevent the birth of a noble heir obliged to avenge the murder. However, "her mother—cruel minded as she was—saved her," fearing criticism of the people (27–30).[54] The Farmer suggests that Clytemnestra believed she could get away with killing her husband but not her children. The opinions of humble and nameless figures (farmers, slaves, the Chorus) often serve in Greek tragedies as pointers for the views and assessments that the playwright aims to elicit in the audience.[55] It is noticeable, however, that unlike the Sophoclean queen, the Euripidean one has exhibited shame and self-awareness in the saving of Electra's life, although otherwise she has left the fates of her children to Aegisthus, who has married Electra off to a lowly farmer and put a price on Orestes' head. Electra's complaint that Clytemnestra treats her and Orestes "as the house's illegitimate offspring" (60–63, Kovacs 1998) compared to the children she begot with Aegisthus, is neither entirely true nor false. The spectators were not likely to be totally sympathetic to the cruel and bloody-minded Electra (281, 647). Orestes is actually more positively inclined toward his mother than Electra is. His use of language referring to the murderers of Agamemnon with a plural noun without specifying the names deflects attention from his mother implying that he sees his mother and Aegisthus as equally guilty (86–89, 93).[56] Unlike Electra, who hates Clytemnestra unreservedly, Orestes never forgets that she is his mother; he is tormented by the thought of having to kill her.[57] In a way, the bond between mother and child, which is severed legally in Aeschylus' *Eumenides* and repressed in Sophocles' play, is reinstated in Euripides.

Euripides reverses the sequence of the revenge murders: Aegisthus is killed before Clytemnestra. Her entrance is much later than in Sophocles: she comes onto the stage two-thirds into the play (988). Her arrival is orchestrated by Electra in a particularly noxious manner. Luring her mother to her hovel under the pretence of needing ritual purification due to the birth of a baby boy, she plans to kill her when she arrives (650–60, 1124–27). Detailing her plan to the Old Man, Electra claims that Clytemnestra will come to gloat over the unworthiness of a child fathered by the poor Farmer (658), whose marriage to Electra Clytemnestra had sanctioned. However, when Clytemnestra arrives, she shows none of this hypocrisy or false sentiment. Clytemnestra's maternal instincts make her come immediately when summoned, although we have heard earlier from the Old Man that she prefers to travel when it is dark out of concern for public opinion against her (641–43).

Clearly Clytemnestra does not come to debate with Electra. However, Electra is looking for a fight and immediately starts complaining about her mistreatment. Clytemnestra's reply is revealing. Instead of addressing Electra's charges directly, she delivers a lengthy justification for the murder that goes far beyond Electra's complaint. Her awareness of her guilt is clear from the fact that she avoids being seen in public. Although the spectators would not have condoned her crime, they would have appreciated her sensitivity to the importance of public opinion, which was a significant consideration for the society in which the play was written. Unlike the Sophoclean Clytemnestra, the Euripidean one does not ignore the values of the audience. This concern for good repute makes her insist that she be judged on the basis of facts rather than hearsay that serves as basis for prejudice.[58]

She proceeds as though a defendant in a trial, presenting her case meticulously and factually. Her father did not give her in marriage to Agamemnon in order to have her child killed by her husband. Clytemnestra employs adroit rhetoric when she compares Tyndareus, a father who cares for his daughter, with Agamemnon, who lures his daughter to Aulis under the pretence of marriage to Achilles when he is actually planning to kill her. While the circumstances of Iphigenia's arrival at Aulis are unclear, it is certain that Clytemnestra did not accompany her (according to this play). This shows not only how much she originally trusted her husband, but also the horrendous shock of realizing what Agamemnon had done.

Clytemnestra conjures up two imaginary situations in which she might have been able to pardon the sacrifice of her daughter: firstly, if it were in the public's interest, and secondly if Agamemnon had not brought his concubine Cassandra, an illegitimate interloper, into the private domain of her home. The purpose of Clytemnestra's comment that she would have accepted the sacrifice if it were done for the benefit of the many, rather than because of her sister's whore-like behavior, is not entirely clear. The remark certainly does not enhance the portrait of her motherliness. She seems to be examining what pushed her over the edge. She seeks to justify herself in spite of her crime, whereas Agamemnon had crossed a line from which there was no return. Even if she demeans women in general, saying that she recognizes their weaknesses (1035), the Euripidean Clytemnestra, who is the most feminine and least politically active version of the character, is nonetheless thinking beyond the roles traditionally assigned to women.[59] Ahead of her times, she demands equality between the sexes. If men can have new lovers, women should be allowed to as well. She resents that women are loudly blamed for such behavior while "men, the authors of this conduct, are free of criticism" (1036-40). In short, having just demonstrated that she, like a man, is concerned about the good of the community as a whole, she should also be treated like a man in the more intimate areas of life.

Clytemnestra returns to considering the murder of her daughter. She contrives a hypothetical situation in which she would be asked to kill Orestes in order to preserve Menelaus, her sister's husband. She asks Electra how her father would have put up with that (1043-45). The imaginary scenario shows two things: first that Clytemnestra's thinking was still gender-orientated: Iphigenia was sacrificed for Helen, so Orestes' sacrifice would fit Menelaus. Secondly this rather simplistic, inverse analogy indicates her endless quest for justification. When she finally summarizes her case: "So can you claim it would have been wrong for him to be killed for killing my child, yet right for me to suffer at his hands?" (1044-45, Kovacs 1998), she is clear and succinct: the suffering or killing of her child equals her suffering. This summation reveals her motherly feelings. Euripides left this argument to the end to emphasize Clytemnestra's motherhood, just before her children kill her.

The point she adds defending her collaboration with Agamemnon's enemy, Aegisthus, is of interest, mainly because of her self-centered reasoning: which of Agamemnon's friends would have conspired with her against him? (1047-48), she asks. Raising the issue, however, shows the extent to which Clytemnestra has been torturing herself and trying to find a justification for every decision she has made.

At the end of her speech, Clytemnestra grants Electra *parrhesia*, the freedom to speak without repercussions.[60] This invitation to Electra to speak her mind is the reverse of the situation in Sophocles' *Electra*, in which Electra asks her mother's permission to "speak truthfully about both the dead one and my sister" (Soph. *El.* 554-55). This dissimilarity emphasizes the difference between the two Clytemnestras. The Euripidean queen is open to listening to opposing views while the Sophoclean one is aggressively defensive, tyrannical and menacing. Nothing in Electra's reply counters Clytemnestra's main charge against Agamemnon: the sacrifice of Iphigenia. Electra does not say one word in reference to her sister's sacrifice; Clytemnestra's charges against Agamemnon remain as presented.

In spite of Electra's hateful tirade against her, Clytemnestra tries to be conciliatory and understanding. Some children, she says, love their fathers more than their mothers, and Electra clearly falls into this category (1102-04). Vellacott comments: "Her answer to thirty-seven lines of concentrated hate is to speak of love."[61] She never denies killing Agamemnon, but unlike any other Clytemnestra she does not gloat. On the contrary, she expresses remorse for what she has done (1105–10). Pressed about the way Electra and Orestes are treated, she says that Electra brings it upon herself. As for Orestes, Clytemnestra is afraid of him, which is why she does no bring him home (1114–15). Little does the poor woman know that she should fear her daughter more than her son.

Clytemnestra eventually goes to perform the ritual for which she was summoned. She enters the hovel where Orestes lies in ambush for her and is murdered by him while Electra helps.

Overall, Euripides describes Clytemnestra more positively than the other playwrights have done.[62] She is neither the majestically overbearing, calculating woman, of "a heart that plans like a man", nor the unmotherly, ruthless ruler who celebrates the day of Agamemnon's murder. She is a more maternal woman who regrets her deed. In spite of her unfavorable depiction by the various characters who describe her as a treacherous wife and cold mother, she strikes us differently in the last part of the play. When Electra utters a hateful tirade against her, Clytemnestra is conciliatory. She never denies killing Agamemnon, but does not describe the murder with glee. On the contrary, she is concerned about what others think of her and openly frightened of Orestes, in other words a person for whom the spectators can have some compassion.

In his portrayal of both Clytemnestra and Electra, Euripides responds not only to Aeschylus but probably also to Sophocles. If indeed the Sophoclean version was presented before that of Euripides the dates would have been fairly close, but Euripides presents a different take on the revenge and the characters. The rustic setting of the play allows the characters to act in a less grand fashion. He even allowed himself the latitude to lightly mock some of the scenes Aeschylus had presented. Euripides displays a wider breadth of human emotions and allows his characters to admit to being confused. Nothing is black and white as it had seemed with Sophocles' characters. There is a far stronger element of remorse with consequent appeals for compassion. The question he asks is: for how long should we deem someone guilty with no forgiveness? Wasn't Clytemnestra's self-torture and her constant fear of Orestes enough?

CLYTEMNESTRA IN EURIPIDES' *IPHIGENIA AT AULIS*

Decades after the original portrayal of *Agamemnon's* masterful queen was first performed, depicting a woman with a heart of hope and the deliberative capacities of a man (Aesch. *Ag.* 11, see p. 18–33), Euripides presents the nascence of her character. Euripides' Clytemnestra possesses the same traits depicted by Aeschylus, but to a lesser degree. In *Iphigenia at Aulis* Euripides dramatizes the cause of Clytemnestra's wish for revenge and eventual murder of Agamemnon, Iphigenia's sacrifice, and thus provides a mythic prequel to the other treatments.[63] As will be discussed in the chapter on Iphigenia, earlier mentions of the sacrifice do exist. Chronologically, *Iphigenia in Aulis* was Euripides' last play, performed many years later than Aeschylus' *Oresteia*. Euripides has been regarded as having been a free thinker, more interested in the relationships between people than in formal religion or the running of the *polis*. He may have felt disillusioned by the militaristic Athenian society of the day. It therefore seems fitting that he chose to highlight the horrors of war by depicting the act of child sacrifice associated with the very start of the Trojan War, emphasizing how violence bred violence in all directions. It is, however, doubtful whether the play is entirely by Euripides.

From the start of the play Agamemnon appears to be aware that his wife is not a person to be trifled with: he asks for Iphigenia to be sent to Aulis alone, without her mother, a request which must have seemed highly unusual in the circumstances. The mother of the bride was central to the preparations for a wedding ceremony. He may have wanted to avoid Clytemnestra's tears, as he indicates to Menelaus (539–41) or he may have been aware that his queen, coming from "a proud lineage" (594) would not allow him to continue with his plans without offering a powerful opposition. Indeed,

---

Euripides' *Iphigenia at Aulis*

The horrifying act of child sacrifice lies at the center of this, Euripides' last play, with the events described here preceding—and triggering the murder of Agamemnon and the revenge killings of Clytemnestra and Aegisthus. Agamemnon has learned that he must sacrifice his daughter Iphigenia to Artemis in order to ensure that the fleet at Aulis will have a favorable wind to set sail to Troy. He is caught between what he perceives as the good of the entire Greek army and his own personal interest. Agamemnon is not impervious to the horror of what is demanded of him. While he had ordered Clytemnestra to send Iphigenia to Aulis under the pretext of marriage to Achilles, he has since relented and tries to prevent Iphigenia's arrival, but it is too late. When Menelaus realizes that that the price demanded from Agamemnon is too high, he is prepared to call off the war. Agamemnon, however, has reached a point of no return. His own army will not let him back down he thinks, so he goes off to arrange the sacrifice. Achilles, who is unaware that he plays a role in Agamemnon's deceptive plan in summoning Iphigenia to Aulis, has an embarrassing encounter with Clytemnestra, during which the Old Man, who was privy to Agamemnon's secret, reveals Agamemnon's treacherous intentions to both Achilles and Clytemnestra. Achilles vows to save Iphigenia, but like Agamemnon, soon discovers that his own men are threatening to run riot, and will kill him rather than disband the army and return home. Iphigenia declares that she is glad to die for Greece and is led off to be sacrificed. In the epilogue, which is usually rejected by editors, a Messenger arrives and announces that at the moment of sacrifice, a hind already in its bloody death-throes was miraculously substituted for the girl, and that Iphigenia has flown to live among the gods. Calchas declares the miracle to be the work of Artemis. Agamemnon goes off to war, but Clytemnestra doubts the miracle.

from the moment that Clytemnestra arrives in Aulis she demonstrates her control over those around her, giving detailed instructions to her entourage, in preparation for her daughter's wedding. The audience, who already know that Clytemnestra has been cruelly deceived, must feel some pity for the happy woman joyfully anticipating her daughter's marriage to Achilles. Knowing that Agamemnon has brought Iphigenia to Aulis under false pretences and is intending to sacrifice his daughter on the altar of Artemis in order to acquire the proper winds for sailing to Troy must immediately frame Clytemnestra in a positive light in the eyes of the audience.

Throughout the play Clytemnestra emphasizes how good a wife she is, a telling reminder that Aeschylus' queen described herself as a "faithful/loyal wife" in her speech to the Herald in the *Agamemnon* (606–08) when that couldn't have been further from the truth. However, at this point Clytemnestra has no reason to suspect any duplicity on her husband's part, so her emphasis on tradition would appear to be sincere. Her very first words to Agamemnon when she arrives at Aulis focus on her obedience, a quality most appreciated in a wife: "we have come; we have *not disobeyed* your commands" (634). Her prudent omission of the fact that she has partly disobeyed Agamemnon's command in that she has accompanied Iphigenia, may hint at Clytemnestra's capability for rhetoric and for manipulating facts in her favor. She values the traditional aspects of being a dutiful wife, being strict about the division of responsibilities between husband and wife. She wants to fulfill the roles expected of her, including the proper religious observance of the wedding rituals for her daughter, such as the sacrifice to the goddess and holding high the wedding-torch (718, 732, 736, 739–41).

From this point on, Euripides endows Clytemnestra with some characteristics which the audience, having probably had the opportunity to watch re-performances of the *Oresteia*, could connect to her earlier characterizations by Aeschylus, Sophocles, or Euripides himself in his *Electra*. When Agamemnon gives in to his emotions, lamenting the fate of Iphigenia under the guise of a father who is about to lose his daughter to another family when she marries, Clytemnestra's answer is: "I am not so *devoid of understanding*—be sure that I shall suffer this myself as well" (691–92). Euripides pits Agamemnon's "emotions" against Clytemnestra's "understanding," exactly as Aeschylus pitted her intelligence against the Elders' emotional reaction to her imagined scene of the Sack of Troy (see p. 22).[64] Clytemnestra's response to Agamemnon's tears is soothing and natural, but some of the spectators could have discerned another layer of meaning in her response. Clytemnestra indeed should not be suspected of being "devoid of understanding."

Clytemnestra is indeed a quick-thinking woman who knows her own mind. She immediately discerns Agamemnon's attempt to capitalize on her obedience. When in his haste to avoid a likely confrontation with his wife and send her back to Argos, Agamemnon peremptorily tells her to obey him without actually telling her in what way she needs to show her obedience (725), her suspicion is immediately aroused: "What? Why, I am accustomed to obey you" (726). She is very explicit in her displeasure with Agamemnon when he orders her again (739) to leave Aulis. However, despite her inclination to be obedient, even if unhappy about it, when Agamemnon seems to be dismissive of the wedding rituals involving the mother of the bride, as Collard and Morwood (2017) state, Clytemnestra "speaks ... in a superb declaration of independence": "No, by the sovereign goddess of Argos! Go and arrange the things outside, and I will those indoors ..." (on lines 739–40). The defiance and tenacity that will resurface in the mythic future are revealed in her words and actions when she goes to the tent to prepare what is needed for a maiden in her upcoming nuptials. She holds firm to the norm that gives women control of the "inside" matters and is happy to do her part as a wife and a mother, but objects to Agamemnon's overstepping the bounds of a man's role as she sees it, and rebuffs his attempt to usurp her maternal duties.

Clytemnestra's self-depiction as a "blameless and sexually chaste" wife, who increased Agamemnon's estate (1157–64), is reminiscent of Aeschylus' queen's bidding the Herald to report to her husband that she knew no pleasure of another man nor was she a subject of scandalous rumor (*Ag.* 611–12). Her claim that she increased Agamemnon's estate establishes her as the Semonidean "Bee Woman" who by increasing her husband's possessions makes herself the best wife one could possibly have (see Box on Semonidean Bee Woman, p. 54). This Clytemnestra prides herself on being an excellent wife, and knows that a good wife is a rare "catch" (1162–63), as she puts it. This function of a wife echoes the older queen's claim in *Agamemnon* that she not only was a watchdog of Agamemnon's house while he was away, but also kept the seals of the storage room, where coffers and possessions were kept, intact (*Ag.* 607–10).

However, Clytemnestra's outstanding feature in *Iphigenia at Aulis,* unattested in other treatments, is what a loving mother she is. The closest might be Euripides' *Electra* where she shows herself as a very dutiful, understanding, and patient mother, but not necessarily a loving one. She does not send Iphigenia alone to Aulis, although this was Agamemnon's initial request, but accompanies her as a caring mother would. Nor does she leave baby Orestes behind with her other daughters, but brings him with her. When Iphigenia first catches sight of her adored father, she asks her mother's permission to run to embrace him (635–36). Being a good mother, Clytemnestra shows how perceptive she is of her children's wants and needs, observing that Iphigenia had always been the child who loved her father the most (638–39, cf. Euripides, *El.* 1102). While Clytemnestra counts her motherhood as one of the features of a good wife, we see in the end that, here at least, motherhood overrides her wifely duties. As soon as she learns the truth about Agamemnon's ruse, she takes the only action that she can she supplicates Achilles to come to her aid (900–14). In her attempts at intervention Clytemnestra demonstrates her clarity of vision and independence, quickly putting thought into action. She does not seem to be deluded as to the weaknesses of her husband, even daring to call the king and general "a coward" who is afraid of his own army (1012). In her exchange with Achilles, Clytemnestra displays some of the dualities discussed earlier. While she is adept at using masculine rhetoric, she also emphasizes her feminine characteristic of being willing to follow the male lead, managing to flatter Achilles, while asking him to risk his life, defending her daughter "How sensibly you speak! I must act as seems best to you" (1024).

When Clytemnestra tries to change Agamemnon's mind about Iphigenia on the grounds of how good a wife she was to him she mentions that she bore him three daughters and a son (1164). She does everything in her power to protect Iphigenia, as the Chorus point out (917–18), although there is a hint of the Sophoclean Clytemnestra, who saw Iphigenia as a possession, as "hers" (p. 41), when she says: "I have learned what you are about to do to *me*" (1141). Clytemnestra is reminding her husband that any pain inflicted on her daughter, is also directly inflicted on her.[65]

Eventually, Euripides plants a clear threat that materializes in the Aeschylean play. Clytemnestra tells Agamemnon: "Come now!—if you go off and fight, leaving me in the house and staying at Troy in a long absence from me, what do you imagine will be my feelings at home whenever I see every chair of hers empty, and the maidens' chambers empty?—while I sit alone weeping, forever singing my lament for her" (1171–76). Moreover: "For it needs only a slight pretext, and I and the girls who were left behind will receive you with the reception you should receive" (1180–82). If she nurses her bitter feelings for the duration of the war, he should hardly expect a warm welcome on his return, she tells him. Furthermore, even if the report that Artemis has spared Iphigenia at the last minute is authentic (1540–612), Clytemnestra's comment on this report is instructive: "Oh my child, which of the gods has stolen you? How am I to address you, how am I to say that this story is not false consolation, to make me cease from hideous grief for you?" (1615–18).[66] It is clear that Clytemnestra sees the report as an invented tale. If she did accept this version of her daughter's fate, it did not comfort her. The bottom line for her is that Agamemnon's actions have caused her to lose her child forever.

Iphigenia's sudden resolve to be sacrificed willingly is an innovation. The Chorus in *Agamemnon* describe quite a different scene with Agamemnon hardening his heart and callously slaying his daughter, with no indication that Iphigenia willingly goes to the altar. The Aeschylean Clytemnestra would therefore have either directly witnessed or have heard described a scene even more brutal than that which Euripides describes. Euripides' Iphigenia also goes some way to try to reconcile her parents to each other, with no mention of any such words in Aeschylus. Euripides' *Electra* and his *Iphigenia at Aulis* were written around forty years after Aeschylus' *Oresteia*, though as pointed out earlier there had been more recent revivals of Aeschylus' masterpiece. Euripides' "softer" versions of the queen may to some extent be related to a different version of the initial events in the playwrights' minds.

In conclusion, Clytemnestra is the only character in the play who is shown as a victim without recourse. Unlike Iphigenia she neither accepts the sacrifice nor forgives Agamemnon.[67] Whether her daughter has been sacrificed by human hands or taken away to the gods, she will live the rest of her life without this child. To make matters worse, the sacrifice of Iphigenia reminds Clytemnestra that years earlier she lost another child by Agamemnon's hand, when he murdered her baby from her first marriage, after he had killed her husband (1148–52).[68] Clytemnestra, who does not accept Iphigenia's sacrifice as a necessity, is the only character in this play who never has a change of heart. Agamemnon, Menelaus, Achilles, and Iphigenia all change their minds at some point; indeed, Agamemnon does so twice, but not Clytemnestra. As the story is narrated in *Agamemnon*, we see that Clytemnestra ultimately lives up to her warning in *Iphigenia at Aulis*: she will not welcome her husband upon his return. Clytemnestra enters the play as a strong and tenacious woman aware of her wifely duties. She exits as an even stronger woman, who clearly will soon become obsessed with the idea of taking revenge on her murderous husband.

Semonidean Bee Woman

Semonides of Amorgos (fl. 7th century BCE) was a Greek iambic and elegiac poet, who in his famous satire (Poem 7) depicts women as sprung from different species. The perfect woman is the one sprung from the bee. The Bee Woman has two main attractions: she increases her husband's possessions, since she is a formidable worker, and she is not prone to sexual engagement except for procreation. Clytemnestra depicts herself as filling all these requirements and hence as being the 'perfect bee woman' in both *Agamemnon*, and in *Iphigenia at Aulis*. However in *Agamemnon* she is speaking falsely while in *Iphigenia at Aulis* she considers that she is telling the truth.

Conclusion

Throughout this chapter we have discussed the character of Clytemnestra as it was presented by the three tragedians. If we allow ourselves to look at her treatment in chronological order in line with the myth, rather than as related to the date the plays were written, we witness the dramatic portrayal of the rise and fall of this supremely tragic heroine.

In *Iphigenia at Aulis* Euripides presents his audience with the youngest version of the queen. The relations between the king and queen throughout the play indicate that Clytemnestra is not quite as subservient to Agamemnon as she at first makes out. While the balance of their power is not entirely clear, Clytemnestra comes across as having the stronger personality of the two. By the end of the play the bond of trust between husband and wife has been irrevocably broken and the scene has been perfectly set (albeit retrospectively in terms of the dates of writing the plays) for the events that follow. It is interesting to note that Euripides completely ignores or contradicts the argument that Aeschylus gives Apollo in the *Eumenides*, i.e. that the child belongs only to the father. Could he be going so far as to ridicule the idea of complete patriarchal authority arising from the belief the woman is only the bearer of the father's child? In his *Electra* (524–39) Euripides pokes fun at Aeschylus' recognition scene in the *Libation Bearers* (168–210) so it is possible that here too his text is challenging the interpretation offered by Aeschylus.

The portrayal of the myth is continued in Aeschylus' *Oresteia*, treated in this chapter through its three separate plays: *Agamemnon*, *Libation Bearers* and the *Eumenides*. Clytemnestra's strength of character and determination are expressed to the fullest in *Agamemnon*. Not only does she meticulously plan her husband's murder, but she also carries it out herself. While planning the murder she is careful to cast any suspicions aside by portraying herself as a woman who cannot act independently, but only on the advice of *a man*. She shows herself to be highly intelligent, possessing sophisticated rhetorical skills and an impressive capacity for strategic planning. While taking on some aspects of a typical male persona, Clytemnestra also succeeds in feminizing all of the males around her. The one person who outmaneuvers Clytemnestra is Cassandra. From this point on, Clytemnestra's power appears to wane.

The *Libation Bearers* portrays the response to Agamemnon's murder. Clytemnestra is haunted by terrible nightmares, not about her own deeds, but of the revenge still to come. Clytemnestra also seems to subordinate herself to Aegisthus, as she never chose to do with Agamemnon. When faced with Orestes as her murderer, Clytemnestra does not hesitate in calling for an axe, intending to do battle with her own son in self-defense, but she fails to come up with her former powerful rhetoric while trying to argue for her own life and dies by her son's hand.

Sophocles gives Clytemnestra the opportunity to tell her side of the story, when she battles wits with her daughter in his *Electra*. However, Electra has no patience for her mother, and it would seem that the queen has more than met her match in her daughter. Sophocles, like Euripides in *Iphigenia at Aulis,* places a strong emphasis on Clytemnestra's role as a mother, even though the two tragedians show different aspects of parent-child relationships. Motherhood has not been easy for Clytemnestra. Her first son was killed by Agamemnon (according to Euripides), her eldest daughter sacrificed at Aulis, and both Electra and Orestes reject her to the extent of seeking her death. When Sophocles introduces a further daughter to the family, the relatively mild tempered Chrysothemis, she too turns against her mother. Clytemnestra is murdered by Orestes, with Electra urging him to stab once more after the queen is wounded.

In his *Electra,* Euripides, like Sophocles, allows Electra to paint a grim picture of her mother, while making sure to undermine the credibility of Electra as a narrator. She exaggerates the suffering in her life, and thus may also be exaggerating the cruelty of Clytemnestra towards her. Indeed, Electra has no doubt that her mother will come to her assistance immediately when summoned, and so she does. Clytemnestra allows Electra to berate her, and listens to all of her complaints, expressing remorse for the events that have come to pass. Clytemnestra is not seen to make any attempt to save her own life beyond piteously calling out "My children, in the gods' name, do not kill your mother" (1165).

Aeschylus provides one last glimpse of Clytemnestra after her death. She is urging the Furies to pursue Orestes, and avenge her death. However, when the case is moved to the court set up in Athens, designed to move the people forwards from an era of a never-ending cycle of revenge killing to a "modern" time, when justice is handled by the courts, the verdict deals Clytemnestra the cruellest blow of all. Athena, having the casting vote, does not refute Apollo's contention that a woman is a mere vessel for the father's seed. By this logic the father is the only parent with any rights to their child. Thus Clytemnestra, the woman who rose to a position of unparalleled power, challenging her husband Agamemnon in every way possible; his right to determine the fate of their children, his right to rule the *polis* and ultimately, his right to live, is herself finally defeated. She conceded to Aegisthus the right to rule the *polis*. She had little or no control over her surviving children, who eventually take her life. After her death, she even lost the right to be considered a true parent at all.

Given the varied presentations of Clytemnestra by the tragedians it is perhaps fitting that both scholarship and performance media have provided many different interpretations of Clytemnestra. Whether she is reviled, revered, or pitied may depend more upon current interpretative trends than on the original intentions of the tragedians. Nevertheless, the larger than life presence of Clytemnestra, her dramatic rise and fall, her complex character and controversial acts have fascinated those who have encountered her for generations, and it is probably safe to say that this fascination will continue for many generations more.

DISCUSSION TOPICS

1. Remembering that the tragedians were primarily interested in entertaining their audiences and winning the competitions within which the tragedies were presented it would seem feasible that Aeschylus' larger than life portrayal of Clytemnestra was intended to heighten the audience's reaction and indeed Aeschylus won first prize in the Dionysia festival in 458 BCE when his trilogy was first shown. Can you suggest other factors, both dramatic and political, which may have influenced the various different treatments of Clytemnestra's character?

2. In *Agamemnon* it appears that Clytemnestra took over some roles in running the *polis*. This would have been unthinkable to the Athenian audiences living in a strictly patriarchal society. Do you think that Aeschylus intended to shock his audience with a portrayal of what a woman may do once allowed to have a position of power? Thinking of the era when the plays were written, when women had far fewer freedoms than today, do you think that the entire *Oresteia* trilogy may be considered a warning about the possible consequences of changing societal structures and norms, in particular allowing women more freedom of activity beyond their roles within the family?

3. Do you feel that all three tragedians were misogynistic in their depictions of Clytemnestra or did any of them seek a broader understanding of the frustrations intelligent women must have felt when limited to mundane duties in the home? Do you feel that the three tragedians differ in this respect? Can you find examples to support your answers?

4. Another issue which readers may have found puzzling revolves around Clytemnestra's role as a mother. Can you outline her attitudes to each of her children throughout the tragedies? Do you think that these varying attitudes are realistic? Could you imagine them as holding true to mother-daughter or mother-son relationships in the present day?

5. The role of Clytemnestra, like all other female parts, would have been played by a man. Clytemnestra displays many character traits which were considered more masculine than feminine, especially in Aeschylus. How do you think the actor may have consistently ensured the audience were aware of Clytemnestra's feminine traits as well as her more masculine tendencies?

6. Clytemnestra committed regicide after her daughter was sacrificed. The regicide was punished by Clytemnestra's murder by her son. In the final reckoning, the matricide remains unpunished. Many societies throughout history have carried out blood feuds and revenge killings, usually between men, and honor killings where women are often the victims. Many recent portrayals of Clytemnestra either in modern revivals of the tragedies or in original adaptations in a variety of media from modern ballet to rock opera take a far more sympathetic approach to Clytemnestra, often adopting a feminist interpretation of her character. In a modern western context, what do you think should be the outcome of a trial of Clytemnestra?

CHAPTER 2
ELECTRA

Mythic background (see also Chapter 1, pp. 15–16)

The *Electra* plays present a chapter in the gruesome story of Orestes' return to Argos to avenge the murder of his father, Agamemnon, but place Electra at center stage in the planning if not the execution of the plot. The Athenian audience would have been familiar with the mythic background beginning with Tantalus, Agamemnon's earliest ancestor, who earned punishment in Hades for his attempts to deceive the gods. Tantalus' son Pelops carried out his own pair of treacheries. When he had to compete with Oenomaus, King of the Peloponnesian town of Pisa, in the chariot race, so he might win the hand of Oenomaus' daughter Hippodamia, he bribed Myrtilus Oenomaus' charioteer to remove the lynch pin from a wheel of Oenomaus' chariot. The promised bribe had been the reward of lying with Hippodamia. Myrtilus delivered, Oenomaus died, but Pelops rewarded the charioteer by throwing him into the sea. Before dying Myrtilus cursed Pelops' descendants. Electra's story is the last manifestation of this curse. Electra is a relative latecomer to the myth. In the *Iliad* (9.145, 287) Agamemnon is said to have three daughters, but Electra is not named among them. Proclus' fifth-century CE summary of the *Cypria,* a post-Homeric epic (of c. late seventh century BCE), names four daughters: Chrysothemis, Laodice, Iphigenia, and Iphianassa. Aelian, a Roman author (*c*.175–*c*.235 CE), reports the first known reference to Electra in the now-lost *Oresteia* by Xanthus (seventh century BCE) who claimed she was the daughter whom Homer calls Laodice, nicknamed 'Electra' because she remained so long "unmarried," *a-lektros* in Greek. The pseudo-Hesiodic *Catalogue of Women* (frag. 23a.13-15 M-W) identifies Electra as the daughter of Clytemnestra and Agamemnon, and Orestes as their son. It is also very likely that the *Oresteia* by Stesichorus (*c.* 630–555 BCE*)* mentioned Electra's recognition of Orestes by the lock of hair he left on his father's grave, thereby placing Electra firmly in the story of revenge and suggesting she played a role in it. The audiences of Sophocles' and Euripides' *Electra* plays would also probably have been familiar with the Aeschylean treatment of the myth.

Introduction

Electra, like Clytemnestra, is featured in extant works by each of the three tragedians, appearing in Aeschylus' *Libation Bearers*, Sophocles' *Electra*, and Euripides' *Electra* and

Orestes. The question of which *Electra* was first has not been resolved; the view maintained in this book is that both were performed in the 410s, with Sophocles' *Electra* being first (see Chapter 1, note 53). Euripides' *Orestes* is dated with more certainty to 408 BCE, the year Euripides left Athens. After Aeschylus' sparse depiction of Electra's character, Sophocles and Euripides present more developed, yet very different, portrayals, varying in their personal circumstances, the settings of the plays and on what motivates the women. Both are older than the Aeschylean Electra, yet the Sophoclean protagonist lives a single life in the palace, yearning for a husband and children, while the Euripidean princess is a married virgin, banished to the rural hut of a poor farmer.

Electra's early life remains constant in all of her characterizations. The eldest surviving daughter of Agamemnon and Clytemnestra, she was separated at an early age from her father, when he set off for the Trojan War. On his return, Agamemnon was murdered by her mother and her mother's lover, before Electra could be reunited with him. Mythically, in her early youth, Electra had been left at home when her older sister Iphigenia was taken to her father when the fleet was becalmed at Aulis. As Iphigenia never returned, the young Electra was never reunited with her sister either. The absence of Agamemnon for ten years and his subsequent murder also result in Electra's separation from her brother, Orestes. However, perhaps most importantly, after the murder of Agamemnon, Electra also loses her relationship with Clytemnestra. Left with her idealized impressions of her father, Electra devotes her life to his memory, and to seeking revenge for his murder. She is a princess by birth, but without any of the privileges one normally associates with that status. In each portrayal Electra is seeking justice, or what she perceives as justice, through avenging her father's murder.

When contemplating Electra's life, it may be concluded that, like her sister Iphigenia and her brother Orestes, Electra has been a victim of the Trojan War. Interestingly, her older sister Iphigenia never mentions Electra by name in *Iphigenia among the Taurians*, with Electra likewise never referring to her sister by name, even though both young women long to be reunited with their brother, Orestes. Is this simply an omission by the all three playwrights? Or is this a representation of the male-orientated society when a lost brother is a major tragedy, but a lost sister is a mere trifle? Similarly, all Electras mourn the death of their father, despite his implication in the sacrifice of her sister Iphigenia. They also all long for and connive towards the murder of Clytemnestra, or in the case of Euripides' *Orestes*, which takes place after this event, the deaths of other female family members: Clytemnestra's sister Helen and Helen's daughter Hermione.

Electra's highly subjective perceptions of justice become a pivotal part of her characterization and of the plot in each of the plays in which she is depicted. In Aeschylus' version of the myth, Electra is still young and impressionable, but already decisive about the pressing need for her father's murder to be avenged, even if she has not developed any clear ideas about how this should take place. Sophocles' Electra advocates for justice, which must be carried out at the expense of all else. She has no concern for her own human comforts, or for the wellbeing of any family members, as long as the dead is avenged. Euripides' very human Electra claims to want justice, but bewails the loss of her palatial comforts more loudly. Sophocles explores the mother–daughter relationship, while also introducing another sister—Chrysothemis—into his play. While serving as a foil to Electra, the relationship between the two girls highlights Electra's many weaknesses, the foremost one being her complete lack of consideration for her sister's feelings or wellbeing. Euripides' presentation of the mother–daughter relationship is more nuanced. His Clytemnestra is far more vulnerable, making Electra's harsh judgment and the matricide seem even more troubling.

While there may be an apparently simple gender divide between the way Electra treats the male and female members of her family, the treatment of gender in her various characterizations is more complex. In Aeschylus' *Libation Bearers*, the young Electra shows great respect for the motherly women of the Chorus but abhors her mother. In Sophocles' *Electra,* the protagonist respects the older women of the Chorus, but dismisses her sister, hates her mother, loathes Aegisthus, but shows love and devotion to her father and brother; while in Euripides' *Electra* she refuses to listen to both the female Chorus, who are women of her own age, and the male peasant who is technically her husband. Indeed, her treatment of people would seem to depend more on their class than their gender. Both of Euripides' depictions show a hard-hearted, selfish woman, capable of displaying affection to her brother, but apparently to no one else.

There is also some variability in the femininity of the character's depictions. All Electras despise Clytemnestra, adulate Agamemnon, and prioritize their relationships with the male members of the family, all of which could be considered typical feminine behavior. While Euripides' Electra rather comically goes through the motions of adopting the feminine roles of keeping the home for her peasant husband, Sophocles' Electra, who does not have her own home, is a far more political, and therefore in some ways masculine figure. She does however focus almost exclusively on the one major function that free Athenian women had: mourning the dead (see Box on Women's mourning and laments, p. 63). Sophocles' Electra performs all of the most extreme customs of mourning as she grieves for her father, claiming to have been beating her breast until it was bloodied (Soph. *El.* 88–90). Her actions, however, greatly exceeded ritual female duty, continuing the funeral's ritual lament in public view, or so loudly from within the palace that she could be heard outside, for years, transforming these laments into a form of public speaking, a political, and therefore masculine act. Sophocles may have been implicitly questioning the relative freedom women held in religious rituals, asking whether it could be exploited at times to the detriment of both the community and the family. Electra's extreme behavior may serve as an example as to why legislation was introduced in the sixth century to limit the time and place of the mourning. He may have been indicating that, by their behavior, women had forfeited this freedom.

Sophocles' feminine portrayal of Electra however, remains poles apart from the masculine Clytemnestra of Aeschylus. His Electra wants revenge, but it must be carried out by someone else. When this Electra thinks that Orestes is not coming, she proposes to Chrysothemis that they collaborate together in the murder. The lack of any detailed content in Electra's plan further emphasizes her femininity (*pace* Wheeler 2003). The act is to be accomplished simply by the power of having imagined it would be done. Relying on imagination rather than proof, as we know from Aeschylus' *Agamemnon*, was a marker of the unreliable female (e.g. *Ag.* 270–80, 590–92). Chrysothemis' caution to Electra that she is a woman and not as strong as a man, (Soph. *El.* 996–97) is irrelevant for Electra because using physical strength is simply not her role in life. Sophocles' Electra uses words to bitterly criticize the rulers of the *polis* (Soph. *El.* 266–81), and then again to lull Aegisthus into the trap where he will meet his death (Soph. *El.* 1451; 1464–65). Even during the revenge, Electra's only deeds are her words.

Like Sophocles' Electra, the Euripidean Electra initially prefers words to actions. Only towards the end of Euripides' *Electra*, and in his *Orestes*, does Electra finally show that she is indeed her mother's daughter, as far as strategic thought and taking action are concerned: ultimately she follows in her mother's footsteps planning cold blooded murder. Although Euripides' Electra acknowledges that it was her hatred for Clytemnestra that mostly brought about her mother's death, and that she actually held the sword (Eur. *El.* 1182–84, 1224–25), she goes on to voice gender-related concerns about what will happen to her. She fears that no man will have her as a wife and that she will not be able to participate in those civic activities permitted to women. Electra's fears do not materialize. Pylades will marry her (Eur. *El.* 1249, 1284–87), making her the lawful wife of someone of her status, a prince who will inherit the throne in Phocis.

In the extant tragedies, Aeschylus only deals superficially with the character of Electra. Sophocles presents a full-blooded characterization of a highly principled and trenchant young woman and Euripides deals with Electra in two plays: before and after the matricide.

* * *

The character of Electra includes the following traits:

- she displays the feminine trait of preferring words over acts defying both her mother and Aegisthus, but only verbally, until the return of Orestes;
- she easily resorts to using deceit;
- she is also given the more masculine attribute of strategic thought;
- all Electras are highly temperamental; with her volatility and lack of consistency being particularly emphasized in Euripides' *Electra*;
- her lack of consistency continues throughout her portrayals, as she disregards any culpability Agamemnon may bear regarding the sacrifice of Iphigenia, while refusing to expunge Clytemnestra's guilt over the murder of Agamemnon;
- while remaining highly inconsistent, she shows no remorse when planning the deaths of Clytemnestra, Helen, and Hermione, yet shows real pity for her brother when he is tormented by the furies after the matricide;
- after committing the matricide in Euripides' *Electra*, she does finally admit that what she did was wrong.

Women's mourning and laments

Women not only washed, anointed, and dressed the corpse but, as pictorial evidence shows, they were the formal mourners both during the *prothesis*, the lying-in-state or wake phase of the funeral, and during the funeral procession to the burial place.[1] In their laments, women generally focused on the common experiences the mourner shared with the deceased and on the bitterness of the loss, but they could raise complaints related to the death of the deceased. Women's laments and mourning included wild gestures: beating the head and chest, lacerating and clawing the neck, and as some pictorial evidence shows, pulling the hair. As Alexiou points out, the wake was a grand public occasion in the early period, but after the sixth century it was held indoors, or at least in the courtyard within the household, away from public view. This law, attributed to Solon (Plutarch, *Solon* 21.4; Ps.-Demosthenes, 43.62), only allowed women over sixty years of age to participate in the procession to the burial place. This curtailed the number of the participants, and lessened the emotional intensity. As Just (1989: 198–99) points out, this law evidences the social and political disruption that could be caused by women's lamentations.

ELECTRA IN AESCHYLUS' *LIBATION BEARERS*

Aeschylus' *Libation Bearers*

About eight years after the murder of Agamemnon, his son Orestes returns from Phocis, where he was sent by Clytemnestra before the murder. He is accompanied by his cousin and friend Pylades. After leaving an offering of his hair on his father's tomb, Orestes notices the women of the Chorus and Electra approaching, and withdraws into hiding along with Pylades. Clytemnestra has sent Electra to pour libations on Agamemnon's grave because she has been frightened by a nightmare. Electra is too inexperienced to figure out what prayer she should utter on her father's grave and asks the accompanying women of the Chorus for help. Orestes comes out of hiding and reunites with his sister. After, the siblings pray for their revenge on Clytemnestra and Aegisthus, Electra exists the scene without reappearing. Orestes and Pylades gain entrance to the palace, and eventually kill both Aegisthus and Clytemnestra. Electra plays no role in the murder. Orestes is subsequently pursued by the Furies sent by his mother and seeks the help of Apollo at Delphi.

Aeschylus appears to have drawn his material for the *Oresteia* from two divergent traditions, Homer's *Odyssey* and Stesichorus' *Oresteia*. Although Homer made no mention of Electra, Stesichorus gives her a leading role. The Aeschylean Electra only has a small part in *Libation Bearers*. Aeschylus does not develop the character: her function is to recognize Orestes, in a scene that has attracted considerable scholarly attention due to Euripides' parody of it in his *Electra* (508–46). Clytemnestra, worried by nightmares, sends Electra to pour libations on Agamemnon's tomb. This young Electra lacks confidence. Although she hates her mother, she is willing to ask advice from the Chorus of women accompanying her about how to properly honor her father's memory. They suggest praying for Orestes' return and vengeance. Electra prays to the gods and asks her father to make her more self-controlled and more worthy than her mother.

After pouring the libations at the tomb, she notices a lock of hair which matches her own. She and the Chorus quickly (perhaps too quickly) guess that the hair must have come from Orestes' head. Electra then notices footprints which also match her own. The similarity of their hair and footprints suggest the close bond between brother and sister, but when Orestes reveals his presence, Electra does not accept his true identity until he shows her a piece of cloth that she wove for him. Once the two are reunited, he says they are "not yet mature enough to bring our father's quarry to the net" (Aesch. *LB* 249–50). He prays to Zeus, and they both pray to Agamemnon to aid them. Once Electra exits during lines 510–22, she is never to appear again: she has no role in the ensuing murders.

This depiction of Electra towards the beginning of the second play in Aeschylus' trilogy raises some questions. The audience would have just seen the tragedian's powerful queen commit regicide after arguing that Agamemnon deserved to die because he killed her daughter Iphigenia. Now the queen's second daughter is reviling her mother's deed, and describing herself as a slave in her mother's home. It is generally agreed that Aeschylus' primary theme in his *Oresteia* is the pursuit of justice, including the problematic cycles of revenge. He is less interested in the family relationships. There is no condemnation of her father's deeds—they are not discussed. Electra prompts the women in the Chorus to call out for revenge. She then prays for an avenger to arrive, and when he does, she provides positive identification that he is Orestes. Having given Clytemnestra such a powerful role in his first play of the trilogy, Aeschylus chose not to develop the character of the surviving daughter. Electra states that the queen's behavior "profanes the very name of mother" (Aesch. *LB* 190–91), but little more is said about Electra's side of the relationship. Perhaps this vacuum was perceived as a great opportunity by both Sophocles and Euripides who went on to breathe life into Electra in their own unique ways.

ELECTRA IN SOPHOCLES' *ELECTRA*

Sophocles' *Electra*

Sophocles' *Electra*, like Aeschylus' *Libation Bearers*, focuses on Orestes' revenge killings. Orestes, accompanied by his Tutor and Pylades, has returned from his exile in Phocis and reveals that Apollo's oracle told him to avenge his father by using deception. There are however several innovations in Sophocles' version. Sophocles introduces Orestes' and Electra's sister Chrysothemis into his plot, with the confrontations between the two sisters emphasizing Sophocles' recurring theme of conflict between pragmatic decisions and those based purely on high-minded principles. Sophocles' Electra is cast in the role of an extremist, zealously lamenting her father's murder, with no consideration of the practical implications of her behavior. Clytemnestra and Electra engage in a heated debate about culpability in the killings of Iphigenia and Agamemnon. The Tutor, disguised as a Messenger, announces Orestes' death in a chariot race. Clytemnestra is relieved of the fear produced by her night-time terrors, and Electra plunges into deep despair. Orestes and Pylades enter, carrying an urn supposedly containing Orestes' ashes. When Electra eventually recognizes Orestes the celebrations of the two threaten to reveal the deception. Orestes kills Clytemnestra while Electra stands guard outside the palace. Aegisthus soon arrives and is shown Clytemnestra's veiled corpse which he takes to be Orestes. Aegisthus finally is ushered into the palace to be killed.

Sophoclean Electra is the focus of the play: she is on stage for nine-tenths of it and has one of the longest speaking parts in extant Greek tragedy. With the addition of the Tutor and Chrysothemis, Sophocles develops more complex sub-plots than Aeschylus. Sophocles' fanatical young woman contrasts greatly with the relatively mild girl willing to receive guidance from the Chorus in the *Libation Bearers*. Here she is a vengeful zealot with no interest in anyone else's opinions. The details of her earlier life are similar to those portrayed by Aeschylus: she has remained in the palace after Agamemnon's murder, but, continually lamenting her father's murder, she is not treated as one of the new royal family. She is on bad terms with both Clytemnestra and Aegisthus, Agamemnon's successor. There is nothing in either Aeschylus' or Sophocles' texts to indicate what the mother–daughter relationship was like before the murder. Although the sacrifice of Iphigenia was presented as sufficient motive for murder, the wellbeing of Electra apparently had no significance either at the time of Agamemnon's murder, or now, years later. Electra is, for all intents and purposes, an exile in her own home, cut adrift from parental guidance and support, left to create her own worldview. We left Aeschylus' Electra after she asked advice from the Chorus and let Orestes take any action needed. Sophocles' Electra may be older than the girl depicted by Aeschylus, but she retains many hallmarks of adolescence. Everything is black or white to this immature woman who has been forced to remain unwedded. She is similar to many young modern rebels and revolutionaries, outcasts from society whose worldview allows no compromise. Her rigid interpretation of correct religious practice and personal morality has not been tempered by the wisdom of older relatives. Electra's father's memory is sacrosanct: he could have done no wrong. Her mother, on the other hand, is the epitome of evil.

Another adolescent characteristic is Electra's overly dramatic presentation of her own situation, accompanied by her almost incessant grieving, which is reflected in her extensive, highly emotional lyrics. Indeed, she has more lyrics than any other Sophoclean character. Electra's mourning is not silent or discreet. Her cries from inside the palace are the first thing the spectators, as well as Orestes and the Tutor, hear (77–85), demonstrating to the audience that even when Electra is not outside the gates of the palace, her laments can be heard in public. Day in, day out, people both inside and outside the palace are subjected to Electra's constant lamentation. Their intensity may have been appropriate for a recent bereavement, but not for the loss of a parent some years previously. While proving Electra's zeal and resoluteness, her public display of grief also explains Clytemnestra's and Aegisthus' hostility toward her. For eight long years, Electra's dramatic descriptions of the murder have undermined their authority, as she reminded the citizens of the ruling couple's culpability for Agamemnon's death. However, this relatively passive act of resistance is only the beginning. Throughout the play, Electra is at first waiting and then actively seeking ways to rectify the situation by avenging her father's death.

Sophocles shows Electra engaging with all the characters of the drama: the Chorus, Chrysothemis, Clytemnestra, Orestes, Tutor, and Aegisthus. These encounters serve as vehicles for her characterization. Electra's conversations with the Chorus and with Chrysothemis in particular are highly significant, revealing her motivations and her moral stand. They serve as context when considering what is the appropriate response to the corruption and injustice in the world, here represented by the rule of Agamemnon's adulterous murderers. (This question posed by Sophocles' play is as pertinent today as ever.) Initially Electra's determination to adhere to her principles, no matter what, seems commendable, derived as it is from her strong sense of justice. She will not compromise her duty for the sake of her own comfort. However, the question soon arises as to whether revenge is equivalent to justice. Aegisthus and Clytemnestra have indeed committed murder, but does this give Electra and Orestes the right to be judge, jury, and executioners?

Electra's exchanges with the Chorus and Chrysothemis do not initially focus on these weighty questions, but on the more pragmatic matter of the way she is damaging her own health and wellbeing. The Chorus and Chrysothemis represent the non-heroic stance of ordinary people. They urge moderation and compromise—the Chorus for the sake of Electra's psychological wellbeing, and Chrysothemis for the sake of her physical survival. Their commonsense positions are affirmations of life against the pull towards death that characterizes Electra's position, as she "melts" (123, 283), "wastes away" (304, 819, 835–36, 1181), and exhausts herself in her unrelenting anger, grief and endless waiting for Orestes. Electra has so little sense of self-preservation that she responds to Chrysothemis' warning that Aegisthus plans to bury her alive if she does not hold her tongue with the defiant reply, "So let him come as soon as he can, if this is what he wants to do" (387).

From the opening monody (an ode sung by a single actor) and throughout the first episode (the act, performed between choral songs), Electra reveals the ideal that guides her. Her implicit message is that vengeance must compensate for the lost life of Agamemnon. Stopping her lamentation would be equivalent to not avenging Agamemnon, which would be a moral transgression (236–50): it is the end of reverence and of piety of all mortals (249–50). She has determined to lament her father forever of her own free will. All that matters to her besides the memory of her father is that justice take place.

Confrontation with the Chorus

The interactions of Sophocles' Electra with the Chorus differ dramatically from those of her Aeschylean counterpart. Sophocles' more mature character is no longer willing to be led by others, unlike Aeschylus' young girl who was seeking guidance. Electra's confrontation with the Chorus revolves around the unremitting intensity of her grief and rage, which are upsetting the *polis* and endangering Electra herself. The Chorus are depicted as women of unquestionable good will, whose counsel is clearly intended to benefit the young woman.[2] They point out the destructiveness (140–42) of Electra's insatiable and intractable grief: Electra herself, through her extreme behavior is the source her own troubles (215–19). The women kindly suggest that she "neither be overly vexed with those you hate / nor entirely forget them" (177–78) and that she let time assuage her sorrow (179). While the women's arguments make perfect sense to the rational listener, Electra is not inclined to be rational. She acknowledges the good intentions of the Chorus "Ah, noble-hearted maidens, you have come to relieve me in my troubles" (129–30), yet implores them to leave her to her grief (135). Her own argument shows a young woman not interested in any compromise. She understandably remarks that her situation is untenable, but makes her own unique response without regard to its consequences. She claims that her persistent, obdurate lamentation is unavoidable: "[H]ow can any well-born woman / not act this way when she sees the sufferings of her / father's house ...?" (257–59). In her following exchanges with the Chorus, Electra offers cogent and emotionally powerful supports for this claim. Describing her current circumstances, she paints a moving picture of her loneliness, frustration, and vulnerability after they prevented her from marrying. She describes her deprivation and abuse by her father's murderers, saying she has been turned into an ill-treated, badly dressed servant, who cleans her father's rooms and "stand[s] at empty tables" (189–92) in what had been her father's home. Her mother, she says, vilifies her (289), wishes her dead (291), and reproaches her for having sent Orestes out of harm's way (295–97).

Sophocles' Electra, who would have been older than her Aeschylean counterpart at the start of the Trojan War as well as when Orestes finally returns, is attributed with the decision to have sent Orestes away from home for safekeeping. As mentioned in Chapter 1, Clytemnestra framed that decision as having been taken to protect the young

Orestes from the citizens of Argos, who were unhappy at having lost so many of their loved one in the Trojan War. She also emphasized that Strophius, Agamemnon's brother-in-law, had initiated the move. With his changed version of events, Sophocles not only emphasizes the dominant personality of Electra who had been capable of taking such an initiative at a fairly young age, but also adds the sinister innuendo that Electra had sought to protect the young child from his own mother.

Electra also provides a number of moral arguments for her persistent lamentation. One is the imperative to continue her lamentations so as to honor her father. "Only a simpleton forgets parents who died piteously" (145–46), Electra declares. "How can it be good to neglect the dead? To what human being is this natural?" (237–38), she challenges. Another powerful reason for protest is the ongoing affront of the royal couple's conduct to public decency. Her mother, she says, celebrates her father's death in a monthly festival (277–81) and sleeps with his murderer Aegisthus (271–73) who sits on her father's throne, wears his clothes, and pours libations at the hearth where he killed him. Electra ends by stating that if the murderers go unpunished, the entire fabric of public order will collapse, as "shame and respect for law will forsake all mortals" (245–50).

These claims are unassailable. Electra would almost certainly have led a different life had she had been permitted to marry and have children. The moral obligation to remember and honor a parent is axiomatic, so fundamental to Greek society, that it cannot be denied. The outrageous conduct of the royal couple surely should not be allowed to continue, and the idea that if murder goes unpunished, there will be nothing to inhibit crime still has validity today.

In three gnomic pronouncements she reiterates that no other response was open to her. She first asserts that "Dreadful deeds forced me to dreadful deeds" (221). She then states that "unlawful force compels" (256) her to her grief and lamentations, and adds "in evil straits / one's conduct must be evil too" (308–09). These forceful assertions convey Electra's sense of personal compulsion and raise the "dreadful," extreme, and "evil" acts she will commit to a moral imperative.

Yet Electra's statements also contain discordant notes. In the exchange with the Chorus, the most grating is perhaps Electra's assertion of emotional affinity with Procne, "that mournful bird," and Niobe, two mythic women who grieved incessantly for their deceased children (147–52), references which might cause some discomfort. Mythic comparisons can impart grandeur to Electra's intense grief and perpetual mourning; however, both these figures were responsible for their children's deaths. Procne killed her son Itys and served his flesh to her husband, Tereus, in revenge for his rape and mutilation of her sister Philomela. Niobe's children were killed by the children of Leto, Artemis and Apollo, after Niobe bragged that she had more children than the goddess. Niobe herself was turned to stone to end her sorrows. Electra's references to these women thus highlight the murderous and destructive aspects of her grief, as well as its self-perpetuation and futility, since these figures never cease to mourn. These stories also underscore the horror of revenge.

Electra's repetition that she continues to grieve out of necessity does not stand up to closer inspection. Made in conjunction with her many assertions that she *will not* cease her lamentations (103–06, 132–33, 147–52, 223–25, 231–32), they illuminate characteristics shared by many idealistic, principled individuals who sacrifice themselves to a cause: they believe that they must act in accordance with their beliefs while confusing *will not* with *cannot*, denying the element of choice in response to life's ills.

Before bidding the Chorus to leave her to her grief, Electra asks them whether persons "whose wisdom is attuned to the moment", as theirs is, "can give me useful advice?" (226–28). The question is a powerful expression of Electra's, and the play's skepticism regarding the utility of conventional wisdom in the face of life's troubles. The Chorus cease to dispute Electra and admit that they would give her more support had they the courage to do so (314–15). Nevertheless, Electra's position remains problematic. The arguments on both sides are too flawed to either fully accept or fully reject.

Libations

Libations consisted of some kind of liquid, usually wine, milk, oil or honey poured from a vessel dedicated to this function onto an altar or straight into the earth. For fifth-century Athenians, visiting the graves of relatives was as important as attending the internment and included pouring libations. By pouring drink offerings, they would summon the spirit of the deceased to attend the rite being enacted in their honor. The libations were generally followed by a prayer to the deceased asking for a blessing or a favor. From Sophocles' *Electra* 894–95 we learn that Orestes poured milk. Offering a lock of hair on a tomb was also customary. Orestes does the same in Aeschylus' *Libation Bearers* 6–7, and Euripides' *Electra* 91. Chrysothemis will discover these offerings and the flowers and infer that Orestes has returned (893–904).

Confrontation with Chrysothemis

Sophocles uses his unique exchanges between Chrysothemis and Electra to reveal their character differences. Chrysothemis is the more conventional, pragmatic sister who, like Ismene in *Antigone* (see pp. 123–129), serves as a foil to the play's rebellious, headstrong heroine.[3] There are clear differences in the status of the two girls: Chrysothemis is on her way to Agamemnon's tomb bearing Clytemnestra's libations, Electra is not supposed to leave the palace. Chrysothemis' first address clarifies her pragmatism. Although scholars have typically praised Electra's highly principled stand and dismissed Chrysothemis as being meek and submissive, her clear-sighted, moderate realism could be considered admirable. Chrysothemis' advice shows concern for Electra's wellbeing, without a hint of spite or one-upmanship. She admonishes her sister quite sharply, saying that she should not be outside the palace, needs to curb her "foolish anger" (331) and to "sail with lowered sail" (335)—that is, to emulate her own restrained behavior, and recognize that for the time being at least, others have power over their lives. In effect Chrysothemis is the material demonstration of how Electra's life could have been, had she decided to relinquish her acts of mourning and at least outwardly accept the legitimacy of the royal couple. Chrysothemis enjoys good food and clothes and is treated as a member of the royal household rather than as a serving girl or slave.

Electra declares that if the price for the good things of life is ceasing her lamentations, she willingly foregoes the good things (352–54). Electra pours scorn on her sister's comfortable lifestyle (361–65). However, if this is how she feels, why does she complain so bitterly about her deprivations and mistreatment? Her admission to Chrysothemis that the purpose of her public lamentations is to "nettle them [the royal couple] so as to confer honor on the dead" (355–56) reveals a political agenda.

The sisters' interactions give the audience time to decide whether they think that Chrysothemis is a hypocrite, a coward or a pragmatist; and whether Electra's stand is based on principles and morality or on the wish to get her own way at any cost. Electra's arguments are powerful. She berates Chrysothemis for disloyalty to their father, hypocrisy (for hating the royal couple only in "words" and not in "deeds"), and cowardice (351). Chrysothemis is kinder, more caring, and more accommodating, and therefore unable to withstand Electra's assaults (cf. Ismene's genuine concern for Antigone, Soph. *Antigone* 39–99).

It soon becomes apparent that Chrysothemis' motivation is to warn Electra of Aegisthus' and Clytemnestra's plans to entomb her alive if she persists in openly reviling them. She cautions her sister to hold her tongue, even though her only reward is Electra's scorn. Despite being accused of being timid, Chrysothemis does have the courage to oppose her mother surreptitiously, by agreeing to Electra's demand that she exchange the libation offerings Clytemnestra had given her to place on Agamemnon's grave with offerings of their own (431–71).

At first Electra seems to hold the moral high ground. She does not pause to question her own judgment in condemning her mother's behavior, and having passed judgment on her mother she can hardly wait for punishment to be meted out. While waiting for "justice," Electra is prepared to pay the full price for openly sharing her beliefs with all around her. Whilst bemoaning her deprivations, she claims that they are insignificant compared with the price of being untrue to herself. Her words, compared to those of Chrysothemis, show the overbearing and simplistic nature of Electra's boasts. Her expression of contempt for the good life that Chrysothemis enjoys is unnecessarily sarcastic. Her assertion that she would like nothing better than "[t]o escape as far as possible from you people" (391) shows her utter lack of appreciation for Chrysothemis' attempts to warn her of danger.

In the second meeting between the two sisters, which takes place after Electra has heard the Tutor's false report of Orestes' death, a slightly different picture of Electra emerges. Chrysothemis is filled with excitement because she believes she has seen evidence that Orestes has returned. At first Electra treats Chrysothemis with much the same disdain that characterized the sisters' previous interactions. She does not really pay any attention to what her sister has to say. Even though Electra has heard evidence to the contrary, Chrysothemis has good reasons for what she announces. Electra now seems an almost delusional young girl. She is unable to listen to anything contradicting her own perceptions. Furthermore, she is now desperate to bring about her mother's murder, whatever means she must use. Her first idea is to enlist Chrysothemis' help, asking her sister to join her in avenging their father's murder on their own. There are two major problems with her proposals. First, she lies to Chrysothemis; and second, she has no practical plan of action. She is thus both manipulative and out of touch with reality. Her opening words play on the emotional bond and obligations that sisters are supposed to have for one another:

> But now that he's gone, I count on you
> not to shrink from killing, along with me, your sister, the man
> who by his own hand murdered our father:
> Aegisthus. I mustn't keep secrets from you anymore. (954–57)

This is the first time in the play that Electra, who had not previously expressed any warmth toward Chrysothemis, calls her "sister." Moreover, even though it is clear that Electra regards her mother as a full partner in Agamemnon's murder (97-99, 205–06, 585–88), she names Aegisthus as the sole target of their revenge. Electra's hatred has been principally directed against her mother, so it seems disingenuous for Electra to hide her true intentions from Chrysothemis.[4] This omission casts doubt on the candor of Electra's declaration that she must keep no more secrets from her (957).

Unlike her mother, who planned her revenge meticulously, Electra is completely detached from reality, as is evident in her fanciful vision of the outcome of the scheme (978–85): all the denizens of the place, citizens and foreigners alike, will greet them with praise as sisters who saved their father's house without concern for their own lives, Electra declares. At every public gathering, people will tell one another that they should love, honor, and revere the sisters for their bravery. Her dead father and supposedly dead brother may indeed praise Chrysothemis' piety; and it is not impossible that people will consider her a "free woman" (970). Electra may believe her own words, but they sound like delusional ravings. A woman who had killed someone was hardly likely to be viewed as a desirable wife and find a "worthy marriage." She is more likely to gain notoriety than fame by participating in a murder. Even if Electra is correct that people admire quality (972), fame for heroic acts was deemed a masculine virtue in ancient Greece.[5] Furthermore, Electra fails to contemplate the possibility that the attempt may fail. Dismissing Chrysothemis' warnings that they may be caught and die by slow torture (997–1008), she is determined to proceed with the scheme on her own (1017–20). This decision shows courage, but when Electra replies "I don't want to live by such laws" (1043) to Chrysothemis' observation that there are times when being right brings harm, she is displaying an ideologue's refusal to accept any reality that does not accord with her ideology.

Nevertheless, Sophocles does not present Chrysothemis as unflawed. Not only do Electra's criticisms stick, but Chrysothemis herself admits her weaknesses: she is afraid of power, does not defend her father's name, and hides her dislike of the ruling couple. Chrysothemis admits that "justice isn't in the course I recommend, / but in the course you've chosen" (338–39).

At the end of the second encounter, the Chorus come out in favor of Electra. They depict Electra as fighting a lonely and noble battle for her honor, suggesting that she is the better daughter and praising her piety in following nature's laws (1058–97). However, the sisters' exchanges show the problems with the choices that both have made. Choosing to follow a principle without considering any of the consequences might indicate courage, heroism and a devotion to justice and duty, but the choice comes with the risk of suffering or even death. On the other hand, opting for caution and moderation might involve abandoning the principles one holds dear. As often is the case in real life, there is no simple right or wrong.

Confrontation with Clytemnestra

We have already seen Electra's confrontations with her mother in the chapter on Clytemnestra (pp. 40–45). Focusing here on Electra, it becomes apparent that her behavior becomes less bold in her mother's presence. Clytemnestra appears after Electra refers to her mother and her "bed-fellow" splitting Agamemnon's skull with an axe as woodcutters cleave an oak (97–99), a violent and dramatic image clearly designed to shock. She goes on to paint a bitter portrait of the queen as a heartless and cruel woman who celebrates the day when she killed her husband; a mother who oppresses her daughter; and an adulteress who shares her bed with her accomplice to murder.[6] Clytemnestra's behavior is consistently depicted by Electra as that of an almost demonic woman who continually berates her daughter. On seeing her daughter crying, Electra reports Clytemnestra as saying:

> You godless, hateful creature! Are you the only one
> who's lost a father? Do not other people grieve?
> May you perish miserably! And may
> the gods below never free you from your wailing! (289–92)

Electra claims that when Clytemnestra hears that Orestes is on his way, she comes to Electra and shouts insanely:

> Aren't you the cause
> of this? Isn't this your doing? You, who stole Orestes from
> my very arms and smuggled him away!
> Know that you'll certainly pay for this as you deserve! (295–98)

When Sophocles' Clytemnestra finally appears, her actual behavior appears relatively mild in comparison with this hateful description. This queen does not have the power or presence of Aeschylus' Clytemnestra. She complains that Electra is defying her by going outside the gates, and that she dares to do this only because Aegisthus is away. This suggests that Aegisthus holds more power than Clytemnestra, and that he is Electra's main abuser.

The play has one formal debate (*agon*) between mother and daughter (516–609). Far from being the all-powerful, unfeeling ruler depicted by her daughter, Clytemnestra is a very human mother complaining that her daughter doesn't listen to her, or respect her. Furthermore, from Clytemnestra's perspective, she is only reacting to the daughter's behavior: "I speak vilely to you because you so often speak vilely to me" (523–24). Later, in her confrontations with Clytemnestra, drawing on notions of heredity, Electra blames her mother for her own character flaws and misconduct (608–09).[7] She admits that she is behaving "unreasonably and contrary to my nature" (618), but continues to blame her mother: "But your enmity and your actions force me to behave like this against my will. For ugly deeds are taught by ugly deeds" (619–21). By attacking her mother in this way and using this justification for her behavior, Electra weakens the power of her argument of necessity: her argument now seems personal.

Electra's claim that her mother just pretends to grieve and mourn for Orestes but that "she's gone off gloating" (807), does not receive any support from the text. Similarly, she exaggerates her sufferings to Orestes when she tells him that Clytemnestra hits her (1196), to which there is no attestation, and that she is a slave to Clytemnestra and Aegisthus against her will (1192), which is untrue. She herself has told Chrysothemis that it is her choice to live as she does, although her willingness to bend the truth was also a feature of her earlier speech to her sister. Electra's hatred for her mother has intensified over the years to the point that all her descriptions are tainted by exaggeration. The real Clytemnestra does not match up to the vileness of Electra's descriptions, and it is Electra herself, with her unrestrained outpourings, who appears extreme.

The main plot function of the mother–daughter encounters is to give the audience the opportunity to judge whether Clytemnestra is such an evil woman that she deserves to die. The verdict on the mother will reflect upon the daughter set on matricide. Electra's ugliest moment is certainly when, in response to her mother's death cries, she calls to Orestes: "Strike her a second time, if you have the strength!" (1415).

Reunion with Orestes

As in all versions of the myth, Electra's one positive relationship is with Orestes, from whom she has been separated since he was a small child. Her obsession with her brother fits with Electra's black-and-white relationships with her other family members. Electra has lavished all of her potential for love and affection on her memories of her absent brother, while also investing in him all of her hopes for the future. The audience have known that Orestes has returned from the start of the play, but Electra has no idea of this. When Orestes finally appears alongside Electra, he does not identify himself to her or the Chorus, but gives Electra the urn that allegedly contains his ashes. Electra sings a heart-wrenching lament over the urn. This intensely moving dirge is one of the most memorable expressions of sorrow in Greek literature. Aulus Gellius (*Attic Nights* 6.5) tells a story about the actor Polus (fourth century BCE) who, returning to the Athenian stage after the loss of his son, recited Electra's lament while holding the ashes of his own son. Everything in her lament conveys the intensity of her pain: from her recollections of the "resplendent" child that Orestes had been when she smuggled him out of Argos and the pleasure she had taken in nurturing him, to her sense of having died and her wish to join Orestes in death, "for the dead ... no longer suffer pain" (1130, 1170). The lines illuminate the intensity of Electra's relationship to Orestes: both as his favorite sister, "the one you always called 'sister'" (1148) and his true mother: the urn she cradles would have been about the size of an infant. Her account of having nurtured Orestes and of having rescued him from murder when he was a small child makes *her*, not Clytemnestra, the person who gave him life and care. "You were never / more loved by your mother than by me" (1145–46), she declares. The distress she feels from Orestes not having received a proper burial at home is so intense that she wishes he had died before she had sent him away so he could have been buried with their father. Now their enemies are laughing. Their "mother, who is no mother, is delirious with joy" (1153–54). Electra's grief compels Orestes to reveal himself to her (1098–231); their interactions reveal how important each is to the other, despite their long separation.

Following the recognition, the brother and sister sing a unique, joyful duet that has been recognized as Electra's most powerful dramatic scene in all her 1435 lines on stage (Scott 1996: 159–60). Electra's song is arranged by strophe and antistrophe, that is to say by two metrically corresponding stanzas followed by an epode, a stanza with no correspondence. Sophocles uses meter as a tool intensifying the projection of the character's emotions. Electra's initial excitement is reflected in her use of a variety of lyric meters while the cool, rational Orestes responds in iambic trimeters, which, according to Aristotle, was the meter most suitable for normal spoken language and the one that dramatic dialogue was composed in. The difference in their meters highlights the difference between Orestes' calculating logic and Electra's unbridled passion.[8]

Sophocles' Electra is so emotional that despite her great love for him, she initially fails to heed her brother's warnings when he uses a moderate tone. At first when trying to calm her down, he tells her to "hush" (1236, 1238) and reminds her that the women in the palace, whom Electra does not deem worth fearing, may be dangerous. Orestes then cautions her not to speak of their past sorrows until "the situation calls for it" (1251–52) and, more sharply, warns her to "safeguard your freedom ... by not wanting to talk at length when the time isn't right" (1257, 1259). However, even in cautioning her, Orestes shows understanding for his sister's feelings ("I'm loath to curb your jubilation, but I fear / you're overcome by too much joy", 1271–72). It is only when he becomes exasperated with her failure to appreciate the mortal danger they are in that he cuts her off rudely ("Spare me the verbiage" 1288) and commands her to tell him only what he needs to know so that they can carry out the vengeance (1288–95).

Despite her jubilation at being reunited with Orestes, Electra does finally listen to him and agrees to do as he says: "Well, my brother, whatever suits you / will suit me too, because it's / from you I've taken all my joy" (1301–303); she further assures him that her mother will never "see my face radiant with smiles" (1310). Coming from a woman who, until this point in the play, has not agreed to do anything that anyone asked of her and who has shown neither the willingness nor ability to control her emotions, these concessions are significant.

Electra and the Act of Revenge

After the reunion with Orestes, Electra again seems somewhat out of touch with reality. To Electra, Orestes' return means revenge, even though the act has not happened yet. Despite all of her talk about revenge, she is not herself an active character. She is absorbed in reliving her memories, but is disengaged from the present. All the years of waiting; all the years of lamenting; all the years of being unmarried and childless, of dressing in rags, and surviving on leftovers, have culminated in the single moment of her brother's arrival, which means the revenge can take place. Orestes does not only signify "revenge" to her, but this is fairly close to being the case.[9] Electra sees herself and Orestes almost as one entity, united by their wish for revenge. When complaining about Clytemnestra's mistreatment of her children from Agamemnon (589-90), Electra disregards Chrysothemis and Iphianassa who live comfortably in the palace. This resembles Antigone's song when being led to her death, claiming she is the last offspring of Oedipus, completely dismissing Ismene (see pp. 131–134).

When the tutor finally silences Electra (1364–66), he advises Orestes and Pylades to make haste, while no man is inside the palace (1369). Electra supplicates Apollo to be their champion. While there is almost no time to consider the gravity of the matricide they will commit, the tension is heightened by the dark imagery of the choral ode. The Chorus describe the avengers, including Electra herself, as "inescapable hounds / hunting down evil" (1387–88). This image identifies the avengers with the Furies, who are frequently likened in Greek literature to hounds that track drops of blood (cf. Aesch. *Libation Bearers* 924; *Eumenides* 246–47).[10]

Outside the palace, Electra acts as a narrator of the events taking place inside, and as a watchman looking out for the arrival of Aegisthus. There is no dialogue between Orestes and Clytemnestra. The audience only hear Electra's reactions to Clytemnestra's words in her final moments. When Clytemnestra cries out that the house is filled with murderers (1405), Electra coldly remarks to the Chorus "Someone shouts inside. Do you not hear, friends" (1406). While the Chorus show some emotion, Electra continues with her cold responses, again referring to her mother as "someone" crying out (1410). When Clytemnestra begs for mercy, for her son to take pity on his mother, Electra's heartless retort is "But he [Orestes] was never pitied by you, nor the father who begot him" (1411–12). When her mother cries that she has been stabbed, Electra brutally cheers Orestes on to strike her again (1415). Her only question to Orestes is the callous retort, "Did the wretched woman die?" (1426). The impatience with which she anticipates Aegisthus' arrival (1416), the cool calculation with which she gets Orestes out of the way when

Aegisthus approaches (1430, 1435), the deftness and aplomb with which she sweet-talks Aegisthus into believing that she has turned over a new leaf, her gratuitous rejection of his request to be allowed to say some last words, and her urging Orestes to "kill him as quickly as possible" (1483–87) are designed to appall.

ELECTRA IN EURIPIDES' *ELECTRA*

> ### Euripides' *Electra*
>
> One of Euripides' main innovations in his version of *Electra* is in moving the action away from the palace in the heart of the *polis* and giving his play a rural setting instead. Married off to a poor farmer by Aegisthus, Electra lives in a rustic hovel. Her considerate husband, a farmer, leaves their marriage unconsummated out of respect for her royal status, and tells her she need not perform menial tasks, but she insists on performing them anyway to demonstrate how miserable her life is. Crossing the border from Phocis, Orestes and Pylades arrive near Electra's home. Remaining *incognito,* Orestes pretends to bring her news of her brother. Electra sends her husband to Agamemnon's old slave to bring refreshments for the noble guests. The Old Man eventually recognizes Orestes, and helps Electra to do the same, after which the siblings plot to murder Aegisthus, who is holding a sacrifice to the Nymphs on his nearby estates, and Clytemnestra, who is expected to join him. Electra tricks Clytemnestra into coming to her hut by sending a message that she has given birth to a son and needs her mother's help with the proper ritual. After the murders, both Electra and Orestes lament their deeds. The Dioscuri, Clytemnestra's brothers, arrive through the sky to settle the fates of the murderers. Sending Orestes into permanent exile, they order Pylades to marry Electra and take her old husband with them to Phocis. Sister and brother tearfully part.

The following discussion assumes that Euripides' *Electra* was written partially in response to Sophocles' version. Euripidean Electra is roughly the same age as her Sophoclean counterpart, but she has been married off to a poor peasant farmer (descended from true-born Mycenaeans) with whom she lives in the countryside, far away from the city of Argos. Although this humble marriage was intended to prevent her from giving birth to noble offspring who might challenge Aegisthus, it was also supposed to be a demeaning insult. However, the farmer treats her with great respect: the marriage remains unconsummated because the simple peasant believes that he is beneath his aristocratic wife. At times Electra is the one who seems unworthy of her spouse.

The rustic setting by the peasant's simple home shifts the focus away from city politics to family drama. The characters, particularly the Chorus, discuss at length both the justice and questionable morality of revenge, but Electra does not show the political drive or revolutionary zeal of her Sophoclean namesake. She concentrates instead on her deprivations while living in poverty and her expulsion from her family home (cf. 300–13).[11] This Electra has none of the grandeur of the Sophoclean figure who stands by the palace doors reminding the citizens of the regicide committed years ago.

Electra's State of Mind and Motives

Electra is presented to the audience just before the break of dawn, dressed in rags and carrying a water pitcher on her shorn head. She makes it clear that while her marriage, her exile from her home, and her humble circumstances were all imposed upon her by Aegisthus and her mother, it is her choice to play the role of the peasant's wife to the fullest extent, at least as far as taking part in household chores. Her main objective in fetching the water from the nearby spring is not, however, to be a helpful wife, but to show her misery to the heavens, thereby directing the attention of the gods to Aegisthus' callous behavior (58). She complains not only to the gods but also to her father in the heavens (59). The fact that Electra first mentions her father not to lament his death, but to bewail her own miserable circumstances is telling. Although she is a married woman, Electra is still focusing on her parents. Her first mention of her mother is similarly revealing. In a single sentence she both defines her mother as being "all-destructive" or deadly, and complains about being sent away from her, cast out from her home while Clytemnestra continues bearing children with her new husband (60–63). Although she hates her mother, Electra's main complaints consist of having been sent away from her family, from the palace and from the luxuries she had known there.

Electra is so absorbed in bemoaning her fate that she fails to notice her husband's appearance at her side. The peasant has seemingly already told Electra that she need not take part in household duties that are beneath her. When talking to him, Electra suggests that she is going to fetch the water to keep the house in order (74–75) since he has work to do outside. However, her words do not ring true. As soon as she is alone, her true nature is revealed. Euripides uses an extraordinary device to achieve this portrayal. He makes Electra recite a highly unusual monody (112–67) filled with instructions to herself about the role she is playing. The lines start with imperatives repeated in the corresponding stanzas and throughout her solo:

Hasten the tread of your steps with song,
O *march on, march on* in tears! (112–13, 127–28)

Come, raise the same lament once more,
stir up the delight that comes of much weeping! (125–26)

Ah, ah strike the head! (150)

These repeated commands to herself emphasize her reluctance to actually bring the water from the spring. She knows that she could easily avoid this task. Her aim, however, is not to avoid hard work, but to return to the luxuries of life in the palace. Thinking that she needs divine assistance to achieve her goals, the first audience for her play-acting is the gods. She is not very convincing: it is quite obvious that even her grief is feigned since she is instructing herself to cry out. This Electra stands in bleak contrast to her Sophoclean counterpart who was prepared to suffer deprivation in order to continue lamenting her father. The Euripidean Electra requests her own freedom first in her appeal to Zeus, "Come to free me the unfortunate from trouble O Zeus, Zeus!" (135–37), and only after this does she ask for Orestes' return, so that he can avenge his father's murder (137–39). Although she might believe that she is seeking a just vengeance rather than simply the alleviation of her discomfort, she is never very convincing.

The most bizarre section of her monody occurs when Electra reaches the peasant's hovel with the full water pitcher. She gives herself instructions for all of her actions:

Take the vessel from my head and set it down
so that I may raise my night cry
before dawn to my father! (140–42)

Electra is essentially talking to her own hands in these lines. Some scholars have suggested she is addressing a handmaid, but if she were accompanied by a serving girl or slave, surely this helper would be carrying the water.[12] Throughout her monody, and later in her interactions with Orestes, Electra always gives second place to the idea of seeking justice and revenge for her father's murder, with her wish to return to the palace and live in comfort taking precedence. Later on, when talking to Orestes before his true identity is revealed, Electra once again places her own troubles ahead of her father's murder: "I shall tell . . . the heavy woes that are mine and my father's" (300–01).

Electra's monody is interrupted by the arrival of the Chorus, young women from the area, who have come to inform Electra that all the Argive maidens are invited to go to festivities at Hera's temple (167–74). Electra is determined not to take any part in these festivities, even though it is what is expected of her. She has no concept of duty, but finds an excuse in her filthy hair and rags unbefitting a princess (185–89). These excuses don't have much validity since they can easily be remedied, as the Chorus point out (191–93). Only when the Chorus remind Electra that they have a duty to revere the gods, does Electra bring up the murder of her father (195–97, 200). Having mentioned her father and brother briefly, Electra quickly returns to the description of her own sorrows, saying that she, herself, lives in a poor man's home, wasting her life away as an exile, a term usually reserved for Orestes (208–10). The final lines of Electra's exchange with the Chorus give the greatest insight into Electra's motivation: while Electra is living "in exile," her mother is still living in luxury in the palace with her new husband (211–12). Typically for this Electra, the allusion to her father's murder comes almost as an afterthought (211).

Orestes' Return, the Recognition Scene—and Planning a Matricide

Electra's exchange with the Chorus ends abruptly when she sees Orestes and Pylades, whose identities are unknown to her, coming out of their hiding place near her hut. Immediately assuming that they are bandits, she shouts to the Chorus that they must flee for their lives (215–19). However, when hearing that the "stranger" has news of her brother, Electra goes almost instantaneously from one extreme to another. After screaming at the unrecognized Orestes to go away and that he must not touch her (223), a few moments later she calls him "the best of friends" or "dearest of men" (*philtate*, 229). This is just the first of several examples of Electra's excitability and mood swings.

Euripides extends the dramatic tension in the scenes before Electra recognizes her brother for over 300 lines of text. Electra's volatility is perhaps a way to hold the audience's attention over this long period of time. The unrecognized Orestes goads Electra by asking her to imagine a scenario that could occur on Orestes' return, more specifically asking whether she would dare kill her own mother (274–79). Electra's immediate and excited affirmation of her willingness to commit matricide without hesitation is emphasized by her spontaneous response: "May I die once I've shed my mother's blood as well" (281). Orestes retorts "If only Orestes were nearby to hear this" (282), raising the audience's tension, while they wait to see if Orestes will reveal himself. The scene's momentum is broken when Electra confesses, "But, stranger, I would not know him if I saw him" (283).

Electra is depicted as out of touch both with reality and with the niceties of acceptable behavior. When Electra's husband arrives while she is talking to the two young men, he comments that it is not proper for her to be seen in their company. The peasant's comment would have been in line with the traditional morality of the times. He then exhibits the noble behavior of offering hospitality (*xenia*), to the men, who are to him complete strangers, inviting them into his home even though he is aware that his house must be far simpler than the places they are used to. Electra's sullen behavior displays no such decorum. When Orestes, impressed by the farmer, asks whether this man is indeed her husband, Electra replies "This is the one who is called my husband" but finishes the sentence with a phrase drawing attention to her misery "unhappy as I am." Electra is behaving disgracefully. Even after Orestes' long speech on how virtue may be hidden, Electra continues to belittle and insult her husband in front of their guests, berating him for having invited such noble guests into their meager home. The peasant's invitation ultimately serves as a plot device, as Electra sends him off to find her father's old slave, who will supply suitable provisions to feed their guests. It is this Old Man who subsequently recognizes Orestes. Electra's responses reveal another aspect of her character. She is incapable of bridging the gap between the two periods of her life: as a young princess growing up in a palace and as a peasant's wife. When she realizes that the messengers are in some way connected to Orestes, the contrast between the two becomes unbearable, and Electra becomes incapable of behaving in a way befitting either role.

In line 431 Electra's husband departs to fetch the Old Man. The peasant has now fulfilled his role in the play. Electra had been exquisitely ill at ease, torn between her present role as wife of a poor farmer and her other identity as princess, sister of Orestes. From this point onwards, she is free of that schism. When the Old Man, whom Electra's husband has been sent to fetch, arrives, he reports that he passed by Agamemnon's grave on his journey, and that he saw there a lock of yellow hair together with a sacrificed ram. The next lines (520–44) parody Aeschylus' recognition scene. When the Old Man suggests that the similarity between the shade of hair he saw and that on Electra's head must indicate that the hair was left by Orestes, Euripides' Electra mocks the Old Man saying that female and male hair could not be similar due to the different treatments they had received, and correctly points out that siblings may not necessarily have hair of a similar shade. When the Old Man notes he saw a footprint, similar in size to Electra's foot, she scoffs that there could not have been prints in the stony ground. The last element of potential proof, taken directly from Aeschylus' version of the myth, is dismissed even more rudely, when the Old Man suggests that Orestes may have clothes with him that Electra wove. She replies that she was only a young girl when Orestes was sent away, and would not have woven clothes at that age, and even if she had, clothes do not grow with the body.

While there has been much debate on why Euripides would treat Aeschylus with such disrespect, it is possible that Euripides is adding layers to Electra's character and emphasizing her own great disrespect. It is also remarkable that Electra did not recognize Orestes before the Old Man's arrival, especially considering that a scar on Orestes' forehead is what prompts the recognition. Could Euripides be insinuating that Electra only observes what she wants to see, hear, and think, without much connection to reality? Furthermore, having sent for the Old Man, who describes at length how hard it has been for him to climb up to her home, although he nobly expresses how happy he is to do so, Electra upbraids him on his arrival for being illogical and unwise (525). The irony is that while Electra is technically correct in saying that there is no reason for siblings' hair or footprints to be identical, they do both in fact come from Orestes. Electra's discourteous treatment of the Old Man reinforces the negative impression she has already made. When the Old Man recognizes Orestes, Electra continues with her rude comments, suggesting that he has lost his mind, until she is finally convinced by the scar on Orestes' forehead.

Volatile and Unrealistic or a Strategic Planner?

After the recognition scene, during which Electra shows none of the exuberance of her Sophoclean counterpart, the plot moves swiftly to the planning of the matricide. Electra does not speak after the Choral ode until she volunteers to make the preparations for killing her mother (647), while Orestes seeks out and kills Aegisthus. This has been Electra's longest silence in the play, except for when she is twice briefly off stage. Nobody asks Electra to take an active role in killing her mother, but her interjection reinforces her earlier statement that she is prepared to do so (281). From this point onward Euripidean Electra displays a new side to her personality, a masculine propensity for strategic thinking reminiscent of her mother's formidable abilities, different from anything seen in Aeschylus or Sophocles. She dispatches the Old Man first to show Orestes the horse fields where Aegisthus will be making the sacrifice to the Nymphs. When Orestes wonders how he will kill both Aegisthus and Clytemnestra, Electra offers to take care of their mother's death (647, 660). Electra even tells Orestes that if he fails to kill Aegisthus and dies, then she will commit suicide with a two-edged sword, but if he is victorious, she will celebrate his victory (685–92). Electra plans the matricide by herself, instructing the Old Man to go and summon Clytemnestra to her hut, by falsely reporting that Electra needs her mother's help with the ritual purification required ten days after childbirth. This scheme, unique to Euripides, is particularly shocking, because Clytemnestra will die at the hands of the daughter she has willingly come to help while welcoming her first grandson into the world. Despite Electra's negative opinion of her mother, she never doubts that Clytemnestra will immediately come to help her daughter once she hears that Electra has given birth. The lie with which she lures her mother to her death shows how easily she is prepared to make negative use of feminine sensitivities and is particularly despicable in its exploitation of her mother's concern for her.

After Orestes departs to hunt down and kill Aegisthus, Electra stays in her home waiting for news. The Choral ode that follows recounts the ominous history of the house of Atreus (699–746). This builds an atmosphere appropriate for the dark events still to come. When the Chorus say they have heard shouts (747–49), they call for Electra and report that they have heard a cry of death that means there has been bloodshed. Electra then loses the cool calculating demeanor with which she had planned to kill her mother. With no one knowing which side has had the upper hand, the tension mounts until Electra reaches such a state of frenzy that she fails to recognize the Messenger accompanying Orestes only a short while earlier. Of all the twenty-six messengers in surviving Greek tragedy, this is the only one who is not immediately recognized and believed as a matter of course. Electra's near hysteria abates when the Messenger announces that Aegisthus is dead. She admits that her acute anxiety had effectively blinded her. Moving from the rude suspicion she had expressed, Electra then showers the Messenger with emotional superlatives, much as she had done earlier with Orestes. Calling the Messenger "Dearest of men" *(O philtate* 767) she uses the same term of affection that she uses for her husband and brother, which is an inappropriate way of addressing a slave.[13] When Orestes returns to the hovel with Aegisthus' corpse, Electra offers Orestes and Pylades crowns for their victory. It is only after the matricide that both Orestes and Electra realize the enormity of their actions.

The Mother–Daughter Relationship and Confrontation with Clytemnestra

Throughout the play Electra is obsessed by the difference in station between her mother and herself. As the daughter of Agamemnon, Electra feels it is she who ought to be living in the palace, while the murderess Clytemnestra should, at the very least, be suffering in exile. She is shown as more eager than Orestes for her mother's death.

When the two women finally encounter each other, their speeches emphasize the difference in their social positions. Clytemnestra is markedly insensitive, boasting of the Trojan slaves who ornament her house, in compensation for her lost daughter Iphigenia—while standing in front of her living daughter forced to live in exile. By offering to take the place of a slave girl and help her mother with her own hand, Electra emphasizes that she herself is living like a slave. In the formal debate (*agon*), between the two, Clytemnestra briefly tries to defend her own behavior, but Electra is more than a match for her, rebuffing each of her mother's points (see also Chapter 1, p. 46–49). The tone of the two women is quite different. Clytemnestra seems to be showing some remorse, even admitting, "woman, to be sure, is a thing of folly" (1035). At every possible juncture Clytemnestra tries to soften her approach to Electra, freely offering to listen to Electra's arguments without rebuke: "it is a pleasure to accommodate myself to your mind" (1059), she says. The lines ending the formal debate show Clytemnestra treating Electra in a conciliatory and caring manner (1102–1146). She acknowledges that Electra was always particularly fond of her father, and that she, as a mother, may forgive everything Electra has said. On the other hand, Electra is relentless in her criticisms. She never once acknowledges that Clytemnestra saved her life by distancing her from Aegisthus. Even at the end of the formal debate Electra seems unwilling to let the argument go, but must proceed with her plan to invite Clytemnestra into her hovel, where Orestes is hiding. Clytemnestra enters, intending to make a sacrifice on her daughter's behalf, but immediately discovers that she is the intended victim.

The Ending

After urging Orestes, almost against his will, to kill their mother, moments after the murder Electra cries out: "Pitiable, indeed, my brother, is this sight, yet I am the one to blame. For I burned with hatred against the mother who bore me as her daughter" (1182–85). Electra has been unrealistic all along, not only in protesting her condition, but also in understanding what she herself most desires. Perhaps this young woman did not really want to kill her mother, but like many other daughters, her true desire was to receive the love, recognition and affirmation she yearned for from her mother. Any understanding of this inevitably arrived too late. Orestes also realizes the gravity of the matricide, regretting their actions, commenting on the obscure justice of Apollo's commands along with the clear pain they have brought him:

> Ah Phoebus, the justice your song spoke of
> is all too obscure, but all too plain to see
> are the woes you have wrought, and the lot you gave me
> was that of murderer banished from Greece!
> What other city shall I go to?
> What friend, what godly man
> shall look upon me
> now that I have killed my mother? (1190–97)

Orestes' words are heart-wrenching. The only relief the brother and sister have from their torment is provided by the intervention of Castor and Polydeuces, Clytemnestra's divine brothers, who appear as *dei ex machina* (gods making a sudden appearance to save the day, making use of a special crane holding them aloft above the stage) and announce that although Clytemnestra met a just fate (1244), Apollo did not give Orestes wise advice (1246). These authoritative assertions of the Dioscuri are never refuted and thus eliminate the moral justification for the matricide. Indeed, they cast a pall over the avengers, especially Electra. Orestes' agony derives from the realization that, urged on by his sister, he has done something he knew was evil.

Electra, the prime mover of the matricide, is to marry Pylades (1249, 1284–87), making her the lawful wife of someone of her status, a prince who will inherit the throne in Phocis. Electra had wondered what man on earth would be willing to marry a matricide. Pylades, who was privy to the machinations of his cousins and stood by them, was the only man for this task. Indeed, he was ordered by Castor to do this. Electra will now have an almost ordinary life, other than for the fact that the new couple has to take with them to Phocis her previous husband as a constant reminder of life in the dry hills outside Argos. It seems that Euripides, having composed a play rejecting the morality of the matricide, as well as the blood vengeance at the core of the myth, is highlighting once again the injustice resulting from the gods' interventions in human affairs, who allow Electra to achieve her greatest desires: a noble husband and life in a palace.

Deus ex machina

"God from the machine" in Latin. This machine is a stage crane that could lift a character, most often a god's statue, from behind the stage-building to appear suddenly on high above the stage and the mortal characters. This technique was closely associated with Euripidean drama and was usually used to resolve a seemingly unsolvable conflict.

ELECTRA IN EURIPIDES' *ORESTES*

Euripides' *Orestes*

Electra is tending her brother Orestes, who has become ill through being haunted by hallucinations sent by the Furies (Erinyes) after the murder of Clytemnestra. Meanwhile, the Argive assembly is about to decide whether to impose the death penalty on the siblings, who are hoping that Menelaus, who is rumored to have arrived at the port of Nauplia, will sway the assembly in their favor. Helen arrives and angers Electra by suggesting that the young woman make an offering at

Clytemnestra's tomb. Electra retorts that Helen should send her daughter, Hermione, instead. Clytemnestra's father Tyndareus, who arrives soon after Menelaus, argues that Orestes should have exiled his mother rather than killing her. Accordingly, he urges the assembly to pass a death sentence, while Menelaus merely offers moral support. The assembly, having heard from Orestes himself, at the suggestion of Pylades, sentences Orestes and Electra to death but grants them the option of taking their own lives. While they lament their fate, Pylades encourages them to avenge themselves on Menelaus by killing Helen. Using her new-found strategic skills, Electra forms an additional plot to take Hermione, conveniently returning from her mission to Clytemnestra's tomb, as a hostage in order to force Menelaus to rescue them from death. Helen disappears in the midst of the attempts to seize her. Meanwhile, Menelaus, believing Helen has been killed, is trying to at least save his daughter, whom Orestes is about to kill. Suddenly Apollo and Helen appear on high. Apollo reveals that Helen was brought to heaven according to Zeus' will. Orestes will eventually become the king of Argos, and marry Hermione, while Pylades will marry Electra.

Euripides' *Orestes*, produced at the City Dionysia of 408 BC, was performed just before he left Athens for Macedon the same year. The play offers an innovative plot revisiting the myth of the *Oresteia* with echoes from, and responses to, not only the Aeschylean and Sophoclean treatments, but his own as well.[14] He confirms his previous view of the matricide as a vile and inexcusable act by portraying the revenge in *Orestes* as unpardonable, and depicting the participating characters accordingly.

The play focuses on how close family and the citizens of Argos view the matricide and on whether they are willing to forgive Orestes and Electra. Unlike the previous treatments, in which Orestes leaves Argos, in this play he and Electra are at the palace in Argos. Now the focus is no longer solely on the family relationships. All of the political and moral aspects related to the royal palace, the house of Atreus, and the horrendous consequences of revenge return. The questions of divine intervention and mortals' responsibility for their own actions are also considered. That Apollo has authorized the murder is undoubted, but he has abandoned Orestes, who is suffering a desperate sickness brought about by the Furies (Erinyes) of his mother. Pylades, who returned to Phocis after the murder, is cast out by his father, Strophius, and joins the siblings back in Argos, helping Electra tend to Orestes. The citizens of Argos are not interested in the divine authorization of the matricide and are repelled by the pollution brought upon the city by the children of Agamemnon. They convene an Assembly to decide their fate. Tyndareus, Clytemnestra's (and Helen's) father, demands the death penalty for his grandchildren; Menelaus suggests exile. The debilitated Orestes appears with the help of Pylades in the assembly and pleads his case, but a death sentence is passed. He and Electra have to take their own lives this very day.

Love, Hatred, and Bloodthirst

Electra displays a full gamut of emotions during *Orestes*. At the beginning of the play, she appears as the loving sister of Orestes, who attends to him in his agony (1–315). Toward the end she concocts a brutal plan to kill Hermione unless Menelaus saves Orestes and her from their impending suicide (844–1352). In between she encounters Helen, for whom she displays deep hatred.

Electra first appears as a devoted sister. Her unconditional love for her sick brother is reminiscent of her heart-wrenching lament in Sophocles, when she holds the urn that allegedly contains Orestes' ashes and bemoans his and her lot (Soph. *El.* 1126–70), one of the saddest passages in extant Greek literature. Her love for her brother is now shown by the way she tends to all Orestes' needs.[15] She takes physical care of him until Pylades arrives. Orestes is incapacitated. He sleeps and wakes up, seized by madness. When he is asleep, Electra covers him with a cloak, and asks the Chorus to hush, fearing that he will die if he is disturbed (132–72). She wipes the foam from his face (217–22). He asks her to support his body and brush the hair from his face (223–26), to position and reposition him in his bed (227–32). Electra tends to him with love and compassion, as in Sophocles where she took care of him as a child (Soph. *El.* 1143–48). In Sophocles her sisterly love was implicit while her most salient emotion was hatred toward her mother. We have seen her lamenting and grieving, desperate and hopeful, abusing a corpse in Euripides' *Electra*, cruel and bloodthirsty during the murders. However, we have not seen her taking care of anyone out of sheer love. This is a new Electra.

But alongside her apparent capacity for love, Electra continues to display her signature hatred, this time for Helen, whom she loathes with an intensity replicating her former hatred toward her mother. From the moment Helen appears, Electra exhibits animosity. Helen asks her niece to take her hair and libations to Clytemnestra's tomb. Electra's answers reveal her feelings towards her aunt:

EL. But are you not allowed to visit your sister's tomb?
HEL. No: shame prevents me from showing myself to the Argives.
EL. Your good sense comes late: previously you left your home disgracefully.
HEL. Your words are true but unkindly spoken.
EL. But what inhibitions do you feel toward the Mycenaeans?
HEL. I am afraid of the fathers of those who died at Troy.
EL. Yes: in Argos your name is fearsomely shouted out. (97–103).

The motif of avoiding crowds out of shame has been already noted in Euripides' *Electra*, when Clytemnestra waits till dusk to join Aegisthus' sacrifice to the Nymphs to avoid being seen by the Argives. To be fair to Electra, Helen's request that Electra take the libations to Clytemnestra's grave is insensitive at best, if not macabre. Even when Electra says that she could not bear looking at her mother's tomb, Helen tries to shame her for refusing by saying it would be improper for slaves to take these offerings (105–06). When Electra suggests that Helen ask Hermione, Helen's answer is "It is not good for unmarried girls to appear in public" (108), although she had stated earlier, quite offensively, that Electra too is still a virgin (72). The fact that Electra does not restate this fact here suggests that the mention of her virginity was not lost on her. Electra's exclamation after Helen reenters the palace shows the magnitude of her disdain toward her aunt:

> O inborn nature, what a curse you are to mankind
> ...
> See how she cut off just the ends of her hair,
> trying to keep her beauty unchanged! She is the old Helen still.
> May the gods' hatred fall upon you for ruining me
> and him [Orestes] and all of Greece! (126–31)

This Electra is as observant of women's beautification attempts as her earlier Euripidean counterpart, who claimed that as soon as Agamemnon left for Troy and even before Iphigenia was sacrificed, "you [Clytemnestra] began to primp your golden tresses before a mirror" (Eur. *El.* 1071). Electra is deeply cynical about bonds between women, and does not appear prepared to admit that any ties of sisterly affection may exist. Indeed, throughout all of her depictions Electra only displays love and affection to her male relatives. When Electra realizes that there will be no reprieve for her or her brother, her truly vindictive side reappears. Before the verdict of the assembly is given as to whether Electra and Orestes will be stoned to death, they believe that their one hope may lie with Menelaus, who has finally returned from Troy. Orestes approaches his uncle as a suppliant. Menelaus is shocked at the sight of his nephew, who looks like a living corpse (385). However, while Orestes is still addressing Menelaus, Tyndareus arrives, and Orestes immediately realizes that all is lost (459–60). Tyndareus instructs Menelaus not to help Orestes, and to leave him to his fate of death by stoning. Meanwhile, Pylades arrives with the news that he has been banished by his father. Orestes and Pylades then go to the assembly to plead for Orestes' and Electra's lives. A Messenger brings to Electra and the Chorus an account of the assembly and the verdict that the siblings are to take their own lives that very day. Pylades has sworn to die with them.

Electra cries out in despair, lamenting not her brother's imagined death, as in Sophocles, but her own (960–70), the end of all the race of Pelops (971–75) and the descendants of Tantalus (982–1012). However, when all seems lost, the former Electra of Euripides reappears, proving herself to be of independent thought and capable of cold-blooded murder. She, not one of the men, comes up with a plan to save the three of them. As in the murder of her mother, morality plays no part in her actions. She is past remorse. When Pylades makes the chilling suggestion that they kill Helen, simply to punish Menelaus for abandoning his nephew and niece, Electra tops his plan by suggesting that after the murder they take Hermione as hostage and threaten to kill her in order to force Menelaus to rescue them from death (1105–154, 1177–245). The fact that Hermione, daughter of Menelaus and Helen, is also a descendant of Tantalus and Pelops is conveniently ignored.

Her overall plan is more creative and practical than that of Pylades, while the details reveal the old bloodthirsty and heartless Electra. She is specific in her instructions to Orestes: "You must hold your drawn sword right up against the girl's neck" (1193–94), and if Menelaus refuses the conditions, "You must proceed to the cutting of the girl's throat" (1199). Once she has snared Hermione, she hands her over to Orestes and tells him: "Place the sword against her neck and bide your time, so that Menelaus sees that he has met with real men" (1349–52).

This ruthless, cold blooded, strategic ability is also reminiscent of the Sophoclean character, who watches at the gates of the palace for Aegisthus' arrival. In *Orestes* after Orestes and Pylades enter the palace to kill Helen, Electra resumes her watching role, this time not alone but with the Chorus. So that no one learns what Orestes and Pylades are doing in the palace, she divides the Chorus into two groups. She sends one group to the east side of the palace, the other to the west. Next, she lures Hermione, who is returning from pouring libations at Clytemnestra's tomb (1323–35), to the palace to be held hostage in order to blackmail Menelaus. Electra's deceit of Hermione is reminiscent of her cold and calculated deception of her own mother. In both cases Electra capitalizes on the trust of the two women unaware of her deadly duplicity.

Revenge and Gender

Electra says that Apollo persuaded Orestes to kill their mother, and that she also "had such a part as a woman may have in this murder" (28–32). The question of what it means to be a female participant in a murder is problematic. The play offers several explanations, one from Electra herself and the others from Tyndareus and Orestes. Electra claims she has "put my hand on the sword" (1235), which Willink (1986) defines as "a *figurative* insistence upon full complicity" (on 1235–36), a statement that seems to hint at the kind of active participation in the murder engaged in by Euripides *Electra*, who similarly claims in the remorse scene after the matricide

> And I, *I urged* you on
> and, as I did so, *put my hand to the sword*! (Eur. *El.* 1224–25)

as if she were actually guiding the sword (Roisman and Luschnig 2011: on 1224–25). In *Orestes* however, the verb indicating the action of "putting the hand on" is different than the one in *Electra*. While in *Electra* she uses a compound verb that means that she actually put her hand "on" the sword, or rather "grasped" it (*eph-hēpsamān* 1225), in *Orestes*, she is only "touching" the sword (*hēpsamēn*) without any insinuation of pushing or guiding it. Orestes is clear that he was the one who killed their mother and that Electra only "agreed" to it; Electra herself attributes the act solely to him (89). In *Electra*, on the other hand, her active participation in the act of murder is confirmed by Orestes' comment to his slaughtered mother: "It was your own murderers, then, that you gave birth to" (1229), indicating that his sister also played an integral part in the murder.

Euripides further modifies Electra's complicity in *Orestes* by giving the description of her part a different context. In *Electra*, the claim is uttered during the intense remorse and regret scene in which Orestes and Electra finally realize the magnitude of their crime.

Furthermore, Electra's active complicity is believable. She was behind the murder of her mother all along, inciting Orestes to kill her, as well as planning the matricide. Not so in *Orestes*. Electra claims to have touched the sword when she, Orestes, and Pylades pray to Agamemnon asking for his help with their plot to force Menelaus to save their lives. Electra needs to impress upon her father that she too had a part in avenging him in the hope that he will react out of gratitude. Accordingly, when Orestes proclaims: "I killed my mother..." (1235), Electra immediately adds her part in the act "I put my hand on the sword" (1235), but the active nature of Electra's complicity is doubtful in *Orestes*. In *Electra*, the protagonist claims to have been "urging" Orestes to commit matricide; in *Orestes* she is merely "agreeing" to it. The initiative belongs to Orestes; she is complicit morally but not actively.

Since in *Orestes* Electra has not taken an active part in the murder proper, in what way did she participate "as a woman would"? The men's narrative reveals the nature of womanly participation. It is not simply tacit participation: it involves words. The play presents the gender roles in the matricide in the traditional antithetical mode of "word" versus "action" (*logos* versus *ergon*). In his tirade against Orestes, Tyndareus exclaims: "She [Electra] deserves to die more than you do [Orestes] ... She put you in a mad rage against your mother by always whispering stories in your ear to make you hate her, telling you reproachfully of Agamemnon's fate and Clytemnestra's affair with Aegisthus ... until she set the whole house alight with a fire not of Hephaestus' making" (615–21). Tyndareus refers to Electra's inflammatory missives urging Orestes to return from exile and kill their mother. In this accusatory account, although Electra is not involved in the act proper, she is the instigator. Women can effect murder with their words. However, this interpretation of the events seems to refer to another treatment of the revenge story, and to contradict Orestes' account that Electra merely agreed to the act. Euripides seems to be conflating another treatment of the myth with his own, and does not offer any resolution of the variant versions.

For Orestes, too, womanly participation takes the form of words. Unlike Tyndareus' accusation of inflammatory rhetoric, Orestes fears that Electra's words could make him weak. When Electra starts lamenting after she hears the verdict of the assembly, Orestes scolds her: "Stop these *womanish laments* and endure in silence what has been ordained! To be sure, these things call for tears, but nevertheless! [You must endure the present misfortunes.]" (1022–24). Euripides brilliantly recasts the scolding given by Sophoclean Orestes to Electra to stop *rejoicing* once she has realized he is not dead: here his rebuke centers on *lamenting*, how unhelpful it is and how cowardly it might make him (1027–28, 1031–32). The playwright also makes a possibly humorous reference to the notorious "lamenting Electra," when he has Orestes and Pylades keep her in the dark about their plan to face the assembly, because they fear that if they divulge their plan to her, she will immediately start shedding tears for Orestes, even though the outcome is still unknown:

> OR. Shall we tell my sister?
> PYL. In heaven's name, no!
> OR. Well, she would shed tears for me.
> PYL. Would this not be a powerful omen of woe?
> OR. Clearly better to say nothing. (787–89)

Ironically the more critical of the two is Pylades, destined to be married to the princess. Although this exchange might be a commentary on Electra's penchant for lamenting in previous dramatic treatments, in this play it also indicates the men's reluctance to listen to annoying female outpourings.

Orestes' inclination to criticize Electra's utterances is also shown in his reply to her disparaging remarks about Clytemnestra and Helen "Marked for censure were the daughters Tyndareus bore, ill-famed throughout Greece" (249–50). Orestes responds: "Take care then to be different from the wicked, since you can: do not merely mouth these sentiments but have them in your heart" (251–52). The reason for this sour reply is unclear. Is it Euripides' reminder of the previous Electra, who goads Orestes into killing his mother? Is it a general rebuke of a woman who talks too much? Does Orestes find his sister's comment irrelevant in the current circumstances? While all the possibilities have some validity, the last one seems the most probable because Orestes reverses his judgment of her comments when she devises the scheme to force Menelaus to help them. He exclaims: "Oh you have *a masculine mind*, yet an outstanding body among women, how well you deserve to live rather than to die!" (my translation, 1204–206). Electra's "masculine mind" is of course reminiscent of her mother's "heart that plans like a man" (Aesch. *Ag.* 11). By words alone Electra becomes her mother Clytemnestra. One can only pray that Pylades will be more fortunate than Agamemnon (1207–10, 1658–59).

We can conclude, therefore, that the male view of female participation is not in their giving an active hand, but in the words they utter regarding the act, and this must be what Electra means when she says that she took part in the matricide as a woman would. According to Orestes, she simply "agreed" to what he was doing, but did not actually give a hand. By stating this at the very onset of the plot, Electra shows herself as a different creature from the earlier Electra, who actually took part in the slaughter itself. This claim is significant for another reason as well. It frames the entire *Orestes*, in which Electra's idea of kidnapping Hermione saves the lives of the siblings and Pylades. It is Electra who plans and verbalizes a way to bring Menelaus to his knees. Orestes gives her the highest possible praise for this idea: she has a "masculine mind." When she directs Orestes to hold the sword to Hermione's neck, she reveals her cruelty, her willingness to shed the blood of an innocent girl, and her moral depravity. How do these traits accord with her love for Orestes? Electra in *Orestes* is a composite of previous portrayals, with different characteristics taking the stage at different moments. Electra's criticism of Helen contains a significant message: "O inborn nature, what a curse you are to mankind" (126): one's nature does not change. Electra can love, but her underlying nature consists of hate and bloodthirstiness. She is the old Electra, no matter how or why she attends to Orestes.

Conclusion

The portrayals of Electra in extant Greek tragedy cover a broad spectrum, from Aeschylus' young girl who does not participate in the planning, let alone the execution, of the vengeance on her mother, to the Electra in Euripides' *Electra* who not only strategizes the revenge but also takes an active part in it. The monumental Sophoclean Electra, who cannot strategize a revenge even when she is determined to carry it out by herself, is selfless and idealistic to the point of being unable to face reality. She shows absolute devotion to her father and belief in the justice of the revenge and loves her brother deeply, but is callow and cruel during her mother's murder, when she pitilessly demands that Aegisthus be murdered as well. As Euripides' Electra developed, she changed from a miserable, ineffective young woman into a woman capable of planning a matricide. While her bitterness towards her mother is a common theme throughout the play, Electra experiences extreme mood swings and a lack of connection to external realities and her own feelings. Electra's dissociation from her own emotions appears most poignantly immediately after the matricide.

These multiple characterizations are at the root of the ambivalence inherent in Electra's part in the revenge in *Orestes*. Her namesake in Euripides' *Electra* is a self-centered young woman for whom the revenge serves as means to obtain her own comforts. She is melodramatic, overbearing, and domineering; abuses a corpse; incites her brother to kill their mother by shaming him with cowardice; and does not shun bloodshed. She actively participates in her mother's murder. *Orestes'* Electra borrows the Sophoclean character's capacity for love and the "woman's" participation in the revenge: by words only. Given this modified Electra, *Orestes* can be regarded as giving testimony to Euripides' views of revenge as a source of great evil.

DISCUSSION TOPICS

1. Aeschylus gives his Electra a relatively small role in the *Libation Bearers*, especially when compared with Sophocles' treatment of his eponymous heroine. This contrasts strongly with the major role he gave to Clytemnestra in the first play of the *Oresteia* trilogy. Suggest reasons for this.

2. Sophocles' *Electra*, like Aeschylus' *Oresteia* deals with the topic of justice and revenge. Do you think that Sophocles' Electra is primarily motivated through a wish for justice? Explain your answer.

3. Euripides ended his *Electra* using the *dei ex machina* device, with Castor and Polydeuces passing judgment on both Orestes and Electra, yet in his *Orestes* a slightly different fate awaits the brother and sister. In both plays Euripides presents a bloodthirsty young woman. Do you think that the plot of *Orestes* may be correcting the treatment of Electra as a murderess? Which treatment do you find more justified? Explain your answer.

4. Euripides chose to give his Clytemnestra a more motherly character than that presented by Aeschylus and Sophocles. How do you think that twist impacts on his dramatization of Electra?

5. Mother–daughter relationships have been studied intensely in the modern era. Do you think the mother–daughter relationship is the key to the characterization of any of the Electras by the three tragedians? From the evidence in each of the plays discussed in this chapter, do you think that any conclusions can be made as to the importance of mother–daughter relationships in ancient Greece?

CHAPTER 3
IPHIGENIA

Mythic background

One of the challenging aspects of writing about Iphigenia is that her mythic background is patchy and full of conflicting details on every aspect of her life, including her name, her parentage, whether or not she was a human sacrifice at Aulis and thus one of the first victims of the Trojan War and if she did indeed survive an attempted sacrifice what happened to her after leaving Aulis.

The epic *Cypria* (a poem dating from the seventh or sixth centuries BCE) appears to have given the earliest written account of myths relating directly to Iphigenia. However, this source is compromised as no original versions exists and it is now only known through a summary written by Proclus during the fifth century CE. The *Cypria* offers a prequel to Homer's epic cycle, explaining the origins of the Trojan War, including Aphrodite awarding Helen, wife of the Greek King Menelaus, to Paris, son of the King Priam of Troy. Helen's elopement with Paris was the trigger to the ten-year campaign waged by the alliance of Greek kings and their armies together with an entourage of heroes and their followers who eventually destroyed Troy. However, before the ships set sail, the assembled leaders made a sacrifice at Aulis, during which a serpent ate eight young sparrows in a nest and the mother bird before turning into stone. The prophet Calchas warned the Greeks that Zeus was angry and that the war would last ten years. The fleet set sail making navigational errors and the Greek army plundered the wrong city. The fleet was scattered by a storm and returned to Aulis where the prophet Calchas now persuades King Agamemnon that he must sacrifice his daughter Iphigenia to appease Artemis. Iphigenia is brought to Aulis under the ruse fabricated by Odysseus that she is to be married to Achilles. When Agamemnon attempts to sacrifice her, Artemis snatches her, transports her to the Taurians (people living on the southern coast of the Crimea peninsula) substituting a deer for her on the altar, while making Iphigenia immortal.

Unlike the *Cypria*, Homer's *Iliad* does not mention Iphigenia by name at all. Instead in Book Nine (145) Agamemnon tells Achilles that he has three daughters: Chrysothemis, Laodice, and Iphianassa. This may have been the origin of supposed nuptials between Iphigenia and Achilles as Agamemnon offers Achilles any of the three girls he chooses for his wife. It is not certain whether the latter two daughters later become known as Electra and Iphigenia, or whether they are different girls.

The pseudo-Hesiodic Catalogue of Women (23a.12-18 M-W) describes a beautiful daughter of Clytemnestra called Iphimede ("strong in counsel") and claims that she was sacrificed by the Achaeans but saved by Artemis.

The name Iphigenia means "strong-born" or "mighty in childbirth." In his *Hellados Periegesis,* an ancient travel guide to Greece citing mythic traditions of the areas he visited, Pausanias (c. 115–80 CE) mentions many different temples and local traditions associating Artemis with Iphigenia (see Box on Pausanias, p. 109).

The historian Herodotus, a contemporary of Euripides, tells about the Taurians' sacrifice of shipwrecked sailors to the maiden whom they identify as Iphigenia, daughter of Agamemnon, not Artemis. Her immortality was later associated with that of Achilles, and she became the divine spouse of the hero. This is reiterated in the *Metamorphoses* by Antonius Liberalis (c. 200 CE) in which Iphigenia was spirited off to the island of Leuke, just west of the Black Sea where, under the new name of Orsilochia, she was wedded to Achilles after all.

Iphigenia features in two of Euripides' extant plays, *Iphigenia among the Taurians* and *Iphigenia at Aulis,* whose performative chronological sequence is the reverse of the mythic order of the events they dramatize. The order of discussion below follows the methodology employed in Chapter 1 where the figure of Clytemnestra in *Iphigenia at Aulis* was discussed last, in spite of portraying her in an earlier chapter of mythic chronology. It is important to note that there is nothing to indicate that Euripides thought of writing a prequel to *Iphigenia among the Taurians*, and that the two depictions of Iphigenia do not fully correspond with each other. Each play and its characters need to be analyzed on their own merit.

Nevertheless, there is a certain similarity between the heroine's situations in that they are both facing constraints of their circumstances beyond their control. They also have two basic character traits in common: being free and independent thinkers and each one convincing herself to do what she knows a priori is not right. However, there are no further commonalities between them. Thus, Euripides' two different presentations of the same heroine allows us a glimpse into the creative process of a playwright in his adaptation of myth in service of characterization. For example, in *Iphigenia among the Taurians,* written about nine to seven years before *Iphigenia at Aulis,* Euripides tells a version of the myth whereby Clytemnestra remained in Argos, sending Iphigenia alone to what she assumed would be her daughter's wedding. Clytemnestra's absence from this significant event may have broken the bond between mother and daughter, which could have been the reason for Iphigenia's unemotional reaction in *Iphigenia among the Taurians* to the murder of Clytemnestra by Orestes. A few years later when Euripides wanted to emphasize Clytemnestra's love for her daughter, he created a situation in which Clytemnestra not only accompanies her daughter to Aulis, ready to take an active role in preparation for the wedding, but also has her bring baby Orestes too. These plot differences have ramifications for Iphigenia's relationship with Orestes too. In *Iphigenia at Aulis*, baby Orestes' presence is tearfully employed in Iphigenia's plea to her father to spare her young life. By contrast, in *Iphigenia among the Taurians,* with Orestes not having been present in Aulis, Iphigenia expresses feelings of guilt that she did not take him in her arms before hurrying to her wedding with Achilles.

* * *

As presented in Euripides' *Iphigenia at Aulis* and *Iphigenia amongst the Taurians*, Iphigenia's portrayal is rife with contradictions in that she is seen to be a highly feminine character who defers to the males around her, yet casts herself in male roles where necessary, showing the capacity for intelligent strategic thought. Some of her traits and internal contradictions include:

- in *Iphigenia at Aulis* she portrays herself as a Homeric hero when, after initially being shocked on discovering the fate planned for her, she chooses to willingly sacrifice herself for the greater good of Greece;
- in *Iphigenia among the Taurians* after submissively going through the motions of leading her life amongst the Taurians, including preparing human victims for sacrifice, once she has met with Orestes this formerly passive woman takes it upon herself to devise a daring escape plan;
- as part of her escape plan, Iphigenia uses a complex subterfuge to deceive King Thoas;
- in each play, Iphigenia is seen to change her mind and alter her path of action, yet in moments of extreme hardship she proves resolute, and carries through with her plan of action until the end.

IPHIGENIA IN *IPHIGENIA AMONG THE TAURIANS*

Euripides' *Iphigenia among the Taurians*

Deviating from the story in Aeschylus' *Eumenides*, where the Furies, persuaded by the judgment of Athena, accept the offer of sanctuary in Athens, here a faction of the Furies remain unpersuaded by the trial's verdict and continue to hound Orestes. He goes back to Apollo, who sends him on a quest to retrieve the statue of Artemis from the land of the Taurians, where Iphigenia serves as the priestess of Artemis, and every Greek stranger is sacrificed by her to the goddess. Iphigenia was brought to this remote outpost through the intervention of Artemis who has not allowed her to be sacrificed. Iphigenia has had a dream which she interprets to mean that her only brother, Orestes, is dead. In the meantime, Orestes and Pylades, who were awaiting nightfall to steal the goddess' wooden statue, are captured by a herdsman and brought before King Thoas. They are supposed to be sacrificed by Iphigenia to Artemis. In spite of Iphigenia's resolve to show no mercy, she feels immediate kinship with them. Through interrogation she learns that they are from Argos and finds out about the fates of various Greeks including her own parents. Though one prisoner informs her that Orestes is alive, he adamantly refuses to give his own name and she remains vague about her identity. It comes into her mind to offer to spare one of the prisoners if he will take back to Argos a letter written for her by an earlier victim that she has preserved in the temple. Orestes insists that Pylades be spared, rather than himself. Iphigenia retrieves the letter, recites it and gives it to Pylades. Recognition is achieved and the three make plans for their escape and the theft of the image of Artemis. The ruse makes use of the truth in the service of deception. Iphigenia will use Orestes' pollution as a matricide as an excuse for cleansing him in seawater and for removing the statue from the temple for purification alleging that Artemis herself had turned away and rejected the sacrifice as unclean. Once at the seashore they will make for Orestes' ship and achieve their escape with the prized image of Artemis. The deception of Thoas is carried out. Iphigenia, Orestes, and Pylades leave for the seashore carrying the statue and accompanied by an escort. A Messenger arrives with urgent news of the escape of the captives. In a surprising turn of events, the ship has been driven back to shore, making pursuit by Thoas and his army possible and thus putting the escape in danger. Athena arrives in time to stop Thoas from deploying his troops. She instructs Orestes to build a temple at Halae and deposit the wooden statue there, and tells Iphigenia that she will be Artemis' priestess at Brauron, ordaining cults of Artemis at both sites.

Introduction

Euripides' *Iphigenia among the Taurians,* produced between 414 and 412 BCE, revisits the myth of the "House of Atreus," as previously dramatized in Aeschylus' *Oresteia* and both Sophocles' and Euripides' *Electra* plays, presenting a dramatic epilogue to the previously described events, while focusing upon the life of Agamemnon's elusive eldest daughter, Iphigenia. Unlike her mother Clytemnestra or her sister Electra, Iphigenia did not have previous dramatic treatments. The audience might have vaguely remembered the account of the victimized helpless Iphigenia portrayed as if in a painting being raised above the altar to be slaughtered as an animal from the re-performed *Agamemnon* of Aeschylus (*Ag.* 231–43). If the audience did indeed have this image of the young victim in mind, they may well have wondered whether, given that she is now shown to have survived such a terrible experience, she might be tainted by it for rest of her life. It would appear that the event lived on in the victim's mind, as Iphigenia opens the play by referring to it (4–9). This experience may well have fundamentally changed her reactions and behaviors. Modern discourse on young victims often includes the notion of a survivor growing up to victimize others, thus perpetuating a cycle of abuse. Euripides seems to hint subtly at this possibility as well, while capitalizing on the opportunities that such an expectation allows for dramatically.

Mythically Euripides presents Iphigenia as the first victim of the Trojan War, albeit a victim of terror who was not actually killed. With the Greek fleet becalmed at Aulis, the seer Calchas claimed that their plight could only be remedied through the death of Iphigenia, as Artemis demanded her sacrifice.[1] When the notoriously deceitful Odysseus devised a plan calling for the girl to be brought to Aulis under the false pretences of being wed to Achilles, Agamemnon acceded. The terrified Iphigenia had been bound and held above the altar, with Agamemnon holding the knife to her throat. However, one split second before her death Artemis had snatched Iphigenia from the altar, replacing her with a deer.[2] Iphigenia gives no indication here of having reconciled herself to being sacrificed, as presented in Euripides' later play *Iphigenia at Aulis*. The young girl in this play's description is taken forcefully to the altar, with no choice in the matter. One can only imagine her terror.

From this point onwards, Euripides presents the audience with his own original version of Iphigenia, the loving daughter of a king and queen, who not only was traumatized by her early life experience, but whose survival led her to face continuing horrors. Iphigenia's harrowing experience at Aulis, would, in itself, be enough to leave the young girl in a prolonged state of shock. Indeed, as we will see in considering Iphigenia's behavior she may be characterized as suffering from what would be called in today's terminology Post-Traumatic Stress Disorder (PTSD). A person in this state typically avoids distressing thoughts and emotions, and may seem in some way disassociated from their life. While avoiding the trauma in wakeful hours, the person may be plagued by distressing dreams as the events resurface in different ways during sleep. While the term PTSD was obviously not coined in Euripides' time, we will see that his characterization of Iphigenia gives a remarkable presentation of someone damaged by a stressful experience. Iphigenia seems a cryptic character, certainly far more self-effacing than any of the other female characters of her family presented by Euripides or the other two tragedians. When she describes the events at Aulis she speaks without emotion, as if she were repeating a story about things that happened to someone else.

However, the audience soon learn that Iphigenia's trials did not end in Aulis. She was whisked away by Artemis to the land of the Taurians, often thought to be located on the coast of the Black Sea in the southern part of the peninsula now known as the Crimea, where she was made priestess serving at the temple of Artemis. The Taurians are depicted as savages who kill all strangers who happen to come to their land. If ever a Greek should land in in this wild place it is Iphigenia's miserable task to prepare him for sacrifice. This is how the playwright starts his extraordinary dramatic tale of the victim who is supposed to take part in victimizing others.

But Iphigenia does not necessarily follow the schema of PTSD. On the one hand, as would be expected of a character who narrowly escaped with her life after her father had held a knife to her throat, Iphigenia displays many signs of someone dissociated from her emotions. On the other hand, she does not appear to be cast in the mould of a victim mindlessly continuing the cycle of violence. As will be discussed further below, she does unwillingly fulfill the role of the priestess, thus perpetuating what to us seem to be needlessly brutal acts of sacrifice which she herself was once caught up in. However, she questions whether this is really the will of the goddess, and is astute enough to suggest that the sacrifices are actually wicked deeds of mankind, rather than a religious duty.

At first glance, the characterization of Iphigenia is somewhat opaque, with her behavior being full of contradictions and inconsistencies. It is not easy to follow her motives or understand the thought processes behind her decision making. She is clearly conflicted over whether she bears a bitter grudge to those who sacrificed her at Aulis or should fall back on her natural loving disposition. While she is generally rather "closed down," not displaying strong emotions, she probably expressed enough hatred of Greece at the beginning for the Taurians to be confident that she would carry out the important role they had entrusted her with, of preparing Greeks for sacrifice.

However, nothing is completely transparent about Iphigenia. For one moment the audience might think that her better nature may triumph and she will refuse to participate in human sacrifice, only to be disappointed when she agrees to go along with it, although circumstances lead her to change her mind again. Her attitudes to her family members are similarly baffling. We hear nothing of her relationship with her mother, although Euripides' later work *Iphigenia at Aulis*, a chronologically mythic prequel, indicates a close bond between mother and daughter, with Clytemnestra desperately attempting to thwart Agamemnon's plans to sacrifice his daughter. That earlier mythic chapter also indicates that father and daughter had been extremely fond of each other before the events at Aulis. Despite the fact that it was her father who had almost taken her life with his own hand, and her mother who had tried to protect her, Iphigenia (when she learns what happened in the aftermath of the war) follows Orestes' antipathy for their mother seamlessly without a single protest at Orestes' actions, and with total sympathy for their father.

In addition to her puzzling attitudes and relationships, Iphigenia also exhibits an almost bizarre ability to jump to the wrong conclusions while remaining blind to obvious truths in front of her. She is so completely convinced by her own convictions, that she is capable of persuading others that her rather improbable tales are solid truths. This trait works to her advantage when she concocts a story to help with her escape plan and manages to convince all around her of the veracity of her words. The audience realize that Iphigenia's strong convictions are based only on thin air when she recounts her dream of her house's physical ruin. Iphigenia is so sure that Orestes has died that she performs for him the ritual libation due to the dead. Only after performing the libations does she stop to wonder whether Orestes may actually be still be alive.

These shifts and turns, together with her suppressed emotions, prevent any clear conceptualization of Iphigenia's persona. It is hard to fathom her cold account of her near death at her father's hand. While she clearly battles her anger and grudge, at the same time she seeks to be able to pardon.[3] Unlike her mother and her sister Electra, Iphigenia is unable to hold on to a grudge and act upon it. Her natural kindness intervenes. While her musings about human sacrifice indicate she knows the right thing to do, she almost never follows her heart. The only constant in her behavior is her looking after her own interest in leaving the Taurian land. For that purpose, she seeks Orestes in the hope that he would come and rescue her. But Euripides puts even this plan on its head when ultimately she is the one who rescues her brother and Pylades.

As the play starts and she delivers a formal dialogue that sets the background for the drama, the audience might have expected a detailed description of what she has undergone. But one gets to know very little about her own musings; she seems cryptic and self-effacing. Only in her opening soliloquy (her spoken monologue, expressing her thoughts to herself) do we meet a young woman who has not forgotten her past and begrudges her suffering. She is depicted as a person who can intelligently figure out that no divinity wants human sacrifice and that the fearful ordeal is something humans dictate, yet when called to do her duty she does not refuse. Her inclination to obey an order that is obviously wrong, in spite of knowing what is right, is also emphasized by Euripides in the later prequel *Iphigenia at Aulis*, where she knows she should refuse to be sacrificed and yet complies with it because she is told to.

Iphigenia's Entrance

Iphigenia delivers the prologue standing outside the doors of a temple of Artemis situated above a cliff next to the shore of the Black Sea. Her robes identify her as a priestess. She delivers a monologue that begins in a strictly conventional manner. But while it describes at some length her supposed sacrifice at Aulis, there is an apparent lack of emotion on her part, which might indicate either that she is not vengeful or bitter about it, or that she is still in a delayed state of shock, detached from her true emotions. She puts the blame for her sacrifice strictly upon Calchas, the seer, who interpreted Agamemnon's vow and ordered her sacrifice, she says. And it was Odysseus who formulated the ruse about her marriage to Achilles, so she would voluntarily come to Aulis. She dryly states the facts with no indication of her feelings toward these two men. She fails to mention her father, who, as we learn later, was the one to put the knife to her throat. She doesn't even say whether he objected to her sacrifice or not. In fact, nowhere in the play are we told what Agamemnon's reaction to Calchas' demand was. It is only in the later *Iphigenia at Aulis* that Euripides describes Agamemnon's dilemma and the way he copes with it.

Iphigenia's lack of emotionality dissipates when the subject of her brother comes up bound with her function in the temple. She dreamt last night that she was in Argos, she tells the audience, asleep in the women's quarters; the house is shaken by an earthquake; she runs out; she sees the whole building fall in ruins; one pillar remains standing and from its top shoot locks of auburn hair; it has a human voice, and she finds herself performing upon it the sacrificial ritual her position compels her to perform upon stranded Greeks. In spite of its unworldly atmosphere, the symbolism of the dream betrays the feelings and fears of Iphigenia: her longing for home, her anxiety about her family of whom she had no news since Aulis and which she suspects has been annihilated except for one survivor: Orestes, whom she loves deeply. But her repulsive present duties compel her to consecrate him for death. The dream thus foretells the future as dreams seem to do, and as prologues often forecast.

On the basis of this dream alone, she assumes her family has been destroyed and is confident that Orestes is dead too. With the Greek women whom king Thoas has placed at her disposal, she decides to perform for him (but not for the rest of her family!) the ritual libation to the dead. She accompanies the ritual with a song of lament for his soul in Hades, continued by the Chorus who deplore the ills of the house of Atreus. The double dirge, in the course of which Iphigenia pours libations of wine and honey, forms the main part of this lyric scene (123–202). Iphigenia then mourns her own fate, pointing out the difference between the bloody sacrifices she must help perform in the land of the Taurians and the joyful rituals of Greece (221–28). As a princess she would have had a leading part in festivals in honor of goddesses, and would have been busy with intricate colorful weaving (cf. 816–17). Instead she prepares foreign men for death and has to listen to their piteous cries in their final agonies instead of the gentle music of the lyre. But even during this reminiscence of her ordeal of watching men die, there is not one mention of her own horrific experience as a sacrificial victim, of helplessly awaiting the knife.

Address to her Heart

In the soliloquy to her heart (344–91) Iphigenia starts out by explaining how her dream had affected her. Before the dream, despite the Taurians assumption that she sought to avenge herself on the Greeks, she had actually felt great pity for the victims about to be sacrificed and cried for their fate. She goes on to suggest that since her dream, which persuaded her that Orestes is dead, she has become savage and goes on to enumerate the reasons for her change of heart. But as she tries to force herself to be savage her thinking becomes befuddled, and her reasons are so illogical that they actually point to her inability to be cruel. In a similar way Euripides will make her younger persona in *Iphigenia at Aulis* convince herself to accept death: by illogical self-persuasion. But in this earlier play her self-persuasion will eventually fail. Her reasons are as follows: she has to become savage because of her dream about the alleged death of Orestes. How and why the dream should cause her savagery is not addressed. We could surmise that since she thinks that her brother is dead, she no longer anticipates being rescued and brought back to Argos. But why this new circumstance should turn her savage is left unclear. After all, no Greek was implicated in Orestes' supposed death. And why would the death of Orestes weigh more in her expected grudge against the Greeks than her own experience? Instead of explaining her statement, she bears out her case by citing the old adage that misery cannot pity greater misery, which still does not explain her change of mind toward the new captives.[4] Iphigenia's inclination to base her reasoning on accepted wisdoms will resurface in *Iphigenia at Aulis* in relation to what is thought about women.[5]

Iphigenia next focuses on Helen and Menelaus whom she would apparently be only too happy to sacrifice. The way she goes about mentioning them does show, however, that Aulis remains firmly in her memory. She does not mention them immediately but complains that there is no breeze from Zeus (354) reminding the audience immediately of the lack of winds at Aulis that caused her sacrifice (according to one version—the other is of adverse winds). But it is not *any* indiscriminate lack of breeze she complains about, but a specific wind that would have sent adrift the ship of Helen and Menelaus and brought it to the shores of the treacherous and murderous Taurians. The lack of specificity about the winds as well as the logic of the dissatisfaction are nebulous, but the complaint implicitly demonstrates the extent that her experience is on her mind. Why she should hate the two victims because of Helen and Menelaus is as entirely unclear as it was in the case of believing Orestes was dead. The notorious couple has done nothing harmful to Orestes himself. Platnauer seems to be right in pointing out the illogicality of her last complaint about Helen and Menelaus. He paraphrases Iphigenia's logic as follows: "I shall deal harshly with these strangers undeserving of harshness, though they are, for I cannot avenge myself on the real culprits."[6] In sum, the two young Greeks become in Iphigenia's mind a replacement for Helen and Menelaus on whom she cannot avenge herself.

But it seems that these reasons are not satisfactory even to her; she needs a more salient reason to bring herself to be merciless toward the innocent Greek victims. For that purpose, she finally turns to her own experience in the hope that she will be able to make herself savage and cruel. Her description is curt but poignant: "There [at Aulis] the Greeks manhandling me as a calf *tried to slaughter me* (*esphazon*), and the priest was the father who begot me" (359–60, my translation).[7] The choice of the verb *sphazō* "to slaughter" is significant. It is a brutal word. As Parker (2016: on lines 8–9) points out, in Homer it is used only for "to cut the throat" of an animal whether for sacrifice or food. Tragedy uses it for brutal killing in any form. Iphigenia clearly wants to rouse the worst emotional response in herself and capitalize on her latent grudge and anger. For that purpose, she brings up her father as the willing executor, which she shunned doing in the prologue where only Calchas and Odysseus were mentioned. To intensify her rage, she qualifies her father by the phrase "he who begot me." This is not a fleeting attribute but semantically significant. When Clytemnestra bewails her daughter in *Iphigenia at Aulis*, she uses the same phrase to show the utter treachery and perfidy of Agamemnon toward their daughter: "the father who begot you, my child, has slain you" (*IA* 1177). Euripides is very careful to make a back-reference to these words in *Iphigenia at Aulis* intimating that the Taurian Iphigenia has not forgotten her mother's words. It is the first time she brings up her father as participating in the ruse of the sacrifice and turning a deaf ear to her helpless pleas. The mention of her father to incite herself is significant because he was the one who plunged the sword into what he thought was her neck (784–85).

She brings up her pleading with her father before being manhandled. On the face of it, this recollection should bring up the highest possible grudge and indignation and thus harden her resolve and serve as a prop for her hatred of the Greek young men. But the mention of her father causes her mind to betray her and instead of making her strong and unfeeling, it brings up the mellowing memories of her family, those of the warmth of the women's home life. Her supplication of her unrepentant father centers on the most important event in a girl's life: her marriage. Although she realizes that he was marrying her to death, the mention of marriage releases latent memories of her mother, brother, and sister as well as recollections of sounds opposite to those of her begging for her life and crying: the wedding song. She fantasizes about hearing the voice of her mother's singing her wedding song, the last gift a mother gives her daughter upon departing the family house. She imagines herself as already dressed for the wedding ceremony when leaving Argos, and her resolve to be cruel and unfeeling melts as she recalls the quick look she gave her baby brother Orestes through her veil. Various details of her departure come to haunt her: she didn't take the baby Orestes into her arms to say goodbye, nor did she kiss her sister. Being sure that she would return to Argos after her wedding, she shunned many other embraces, for which she now longs. Similar thoughts of missed opportunities often haunt people who have lost a dear one as they recall the very last time they saw the person, but Euripides reverses the situation: it is the supposedly sacrificed victim who recalls the last moments before her death. Iphigenia is "haunted" by the warmth and love she experienced before reaching her destination at Aulis, where she faced the vast unruly army mob that demanded her death. These uncontrollable thoughts, instead of unleashing cruelty, soften her heart against her will and prepare her and the audience for the next scene in which she will be willing to spare one of the Greeks even though she would not yet know their identity.

Her thinking, however, is shaky and nebulous and her thoughts of Orestes are confused. After her dream she was sure he was dead, but now her confidence is eroded. And as she is reliving her last moments at Argos, she says: "O poor Orestes, *if you are dead,* what a fine and enviable heritage from your father you have lost!" (378–79). Is she sarcastic in reference to her father as she is next in reference to Artemis and her wisdom (380)? It is difficult to know, since she both criticizes her father and yet sometimes talks affectionately of him.

The last segment of her address to her heart reveals a horrifying and stupefying realization on her part: it is not the gods who demand the human sacrifice, it is murderous men who demand it, assigning the blame for it to the gods. What becomes clear is that she has given up on trying to be cruel and merciless to the victims. Her uninvited recollections of her mother, brother, sister and other dear women whom she left behind have made her gentle rather than fierce. Her attempt to be savage toward the two Greek victims as substitutes for Helen and Menelaus has failed. The Taurians may want the death of Greek wanderers for their own reasons, but she has no part in that. They were unwise to count on her to wish to participate in such a sacrilege. Her realization that men attribute their own wishes to divinities, could have also led her to the realization that it was Calchas rather than Artemis who wanted her death. There is no evidence that she thinks *all the Greeks* were murderers who demanded her death. This is underscored by the Chorus when the leader states that such human sacrifice "by the law of our (i.e. Greek) land it is unholy to offer" (465–66, Cropp). The audience should therefore expect her to be forgiving to Orestes and Pylades and refuse to consecrate them, but she continues with the ritual. Once they are brought in, however, and she is left alone with them in the temple, her compassion for them is clear, and there is no vestige of the savagery she claimed to have after assuming that Orestes is dead (348–50).

Iphigenia with Orestes and Pylades

The realization of the injustice of human sacrifice and the appearance of the two young Greek men further evoke Iphigenia's latent longing for her country and for her family, especially once Orestes reveals to her that he is from Argos, her city. Will her mellowing disincline her from participating in the cruel ritual?

Initially it does not seem that she will stray from what is expected from her—that she will consecrate them. However, when she meets the two strangers, it is as if her former musings about her family reawaken, and instead of proceeding immediately with the consecration, she starts questioning them. Her conversation with the two young Greeks is peculiar in that she does not identify herself to them as a Greek or as Iphigenia, and she uses circumlocution, using many more words than she needed, while keeping her questions vague. As a result, the dialogue is awkward and obtuse. When she hears that Orestes is from Argos, she comments that his "coming here from Argos is much longed for" (515). Orestes of course is baffled and must find the comment sarcastic, because why would his arrival to a place where he is about to be killed be termed "much longed for." Especially since the Greek phrase Iphigenia uses to convey the idea of "much longed for" indicates a special favorite reaction for Orestes himself, although she does not reveal to him that she too comes from Argos.[8] Iphigenia's following questions to Orestes are clearer but still periphrastic, not getting straight to the point. While Iphigenia's affectionate response to the news that Orestes is from Argos, and therefore might bring her direct news of her family would be easily understood by the spectators, the reason for the following verbal evasions is not immediately clear. One could obviously explain it by Euripides' intent to create dramatic suspense before the upcoming recognition scene (which is one of the longest in the extant Greek tragedies), but it also needs to be plausible in terms of character building.

Her questions reveal a clear interrogation strategy which aims to find out whether Orestes is still alive, while trying to mask her identity the best way she can. She starts in the most general way, asking about Troy while apologizing that she even knows about the war (or, the city) by saying that it is "talked of everywhere" (517). When Orestes is not too informative about Troy, she baits him further by saying "They say it has perished, destroyed by war" (519). Since Orestes' answer is still unsatisfyingly vague, Iphigenia brings up Helen, saying that Helen owes her a debt for grief, but immediately melds her personal hurt with that of all Greece saying that Helen is hateful "in Greece's eyes, not only in mine!" (523–25). She follows with further questions, first about the agents directly responsible for her sacrifice: Calchas and Odysseus (curiously leaving out her father yet again). Then she moves to those most beloved by her: Achilles and her family. Her periphrastic references to the "son of Laertes" or "son of the Nereid Thetis" (533, 537), which possibly were meant to make her questions more formal and distant, actually have the opposite effect on Orestes, because they indicate knowledge about these heroes. "Who are you?" he asks, expressing amazement at how keenly she searches for news from Greece (540).

This is the second opportunity for Iphigenia to reveal herself, but she remains evasive. She admits now that she is from Greece, although she still does not mention Argos, and follows with a wonderfully ambiguous statement "I was still a child when I was lost/ruined/died." The Greek verb she uses (*apōlomēn*, 541) allows for all these meanings. Iphigenia could easily identify herself now, but she chooses not to. On the face of it, there is no compelling reason for camouflaging her identity. There is no reason for her to think that the Greek youth would decline giving her news about her family once she has identified herself. Has her traumatic experience made her suspicious of any Greek, even an Argive one?

The circumlocution continues. Although her father is no other than "the general they say is prosperous" (543), about whom she questions Orestes, she does not state her relationship to the man she is enquiring after. She does not even mention him by name. Only when Orestes replies that he does not know whom she means, does she identify him as "son of Atreus" and then "*one* King Agamemnon" (545). When Orestes says Agamemnon is dead after having ruined someone else (548), Iphigenia could see in this a reference to herself and yet another opportunity for revealing herself but yet again she foregoes it. Instead she focuses only on how he died, and bursts into "Ah poor me!" (549). Her outburst must have surprised both her in-play and spectator audience. To Orestes it would be unclear why such a personal outcry comes from a woman who seemingly has no connection to the "prosperous general" ("Why lament at that? He surely had nothing to do with you?" 550, Cropp) and to the play's audience, her heartfelt sorrow for a father whose knife-armed hand was on her throat and who as far as he knows killed her (565), would be unclear as well. Instead of naming her family, she circumvents Orestes' direct question for the fourth time by saying that she laments for the good fortune Agamemnon once had. After hearing that it was her mother that killed her father, she expresses pity for both of them (553). It is peculiar that Iphigenia fails to ask why her mother killed him. Was she distraught by the news, thinking that her mother had killed her father to avenge her sacrifice? Unlikely, because in line 926 she explicitly asks what her mother's reason was for killing her husband. Perhaps she simply did not wish to digress while seeking information about Orestes? Her consternation is evident in the ambiguous phrasing she chooses when she reacts to Orestes' statement that the son killed his mother as revenge for the murder of his father. As Kyriakou (2006) points out, Iphigenia's sentence can mean in Greek two opposite things at the same time: "How well he performed a righteous wrong" or "How well he exacted wrong justice" (559). The syntactical structure allows for both meanings although Orestes obviously understands it to mean the former, i.e. that he has performed a "righteous wrong." Actor's delivery would be crucial here in making clear which is the noun and which is the attribute, but for a reader there is no way to decide. Clarity is obviously not Iphigenia's concern. She wants to know if Orestes is alive and progresses methodically to get this information following her former periphrastic method of inquiry when she asks about whether Agamemnon has left any "child" in his household, without specifying gender. Her interest is obviously in Orestes only, but when Orestes mentions her sister Electra and not her brother, she follows with a question about herself: "Does anyone still speak of the daughter who was sacrificed?" (563).

Told that everyone assumes she is dead, her reaction is as breath-taking as it is revealing: "Poor daughter, poor too the father who killed her!" (565), she says. She both abhors her murdering father and yet feels sympathy for him. There is a deep streak of hate and love in her for her father which was revealed already in her opening monologue when she refused to tie him with Calchas and Odysseus, as if he had no choice but to kill her. This is the excuse Euripides will mount later in *Iphigenia at Aulis*, where Iphigenia has convinced herself that her father had no alternative but to sacrifice her. The root of this later justification lies in this passage, in which Iphigenia intimates her utmost desire to be able to forgive her father. Indeed, the order of the people Iphigenia asks about is peculiar. She makes a clear distinction between the two who harmed her, Calchas and Odysseus, and those who tried to help her, Achilles and Clytemnestra. Agamemnon has his own place, being not linked to neither of these two categories.

"The murdered man's son, is he still alive in Argos?" (567) is her last question, and the one she meant to ask from start. Iphigenia seems so set on finding out whether Orestes is alive and is no longer concerned that this question could reveal her identity, which she was previously so careful to hide. It is also clear that she is now far less confident about her interpretation of her dream. This more explicit question should have made Orestes aware that the priestess knows far more about his family at Argos than she reveals. As Iphigenia had four opportunities to divulge her name to the Greek youths, so does Orestes have three chances to figure out that the priestess is not as clueless as she pretends to be. She knew about Agamemnon, about the daughter who was sacrificed, and she knows about Agamemnon's son. Interestingly, the following comment of the Chorus, who, having understood that Iphigenia had received information about *her* parents and family, wish now to know about theirs (575–76), should have led Orestes to the conclusion that Iphigenia is at least a relative of his.

In order to disguise the weakness and implausibility of the plot, Euripides packs the scene with fast paced developments (for a modern parallel, see Box on George Lucas, p. 106). Iphigenia is taken so suddenly by realizing that she converses with someone who knows about her family that she does not seem to care about disguising her identity. Orestes, on the other hand, does not have much time for contemplation. The play now moves rapidly and methodically from subject to subject without giving either Orestes or Iphigenia time to speculate about each other's identity. Only later does Orestes comment to Pylades: "Pylades, in heaven's name do you feel the same as I do? ... Who is this young woman? How Greek were her questions" (657–68). Orestes knows at this point that he is going to die, so it may be considered strange that he is contemplating the identity of the priestess who is going to consecrate him and promising him to afford him full burial. But Euripides does not want his audience to think about this implausibility. Instead, he shows Iphigenia so concerned about losing the momentum that when the Chorus try to inquire further of Orestes about their own families, she ignores their concern and delves into a completely new subject: the letter and her promise to keep one of the young Greeks alive.

George Lucas' strategy

Euripides adopts here similar although not identical tactics applied by George Lucas 2500 years later in his filming of The *Empire Strikes Back*, the second part of the *Star Wars* second trilogy. According to his editing assistant Duwayne Dunham, George Lucas' philosophy was: "Don't dwell on a shot that becomes boring. Keep things defined and interesting, with the emphasis on action and dialogue. Keep it moving, keep the pace going." This part of *Star Wars* was 105 pages long and contained three main acts scheduled for about thirty-five minutes each. Lucas wanted the script to be "short and tight." Everyone else involved agreed that *Empire* had to grapple with the philosophical issues raised by the first part of this trilogy and argued for longer scenes. But Lucas wanted the philosophical issues disposed of quickly. *Empire* had to be fast-moving, not complex. "The trick is to know what you can leave to the audience's imagination," Lucas maintained. Kasdan, his co-director, thought the ending of the *Empire* failed to resolve the characters' conflicts and that Lucas was relying too much on the revelations contained in part three of *Star Wars*. Lucas' response was: "Well, if we have enough action, nobody will notice."[9]

Iphigenia's Initiatives

Iphigenia shows an initiative geared toward her rescue on three occasions. The first one happened in the past, when a prisoner wrote a letter for her, in which she asks Orestes to come and take her back to Argos. We do not know what prompted this action. According to Iphigenia the prisoner took pity on her because he understood that her participation in human sacrifice had been imposed on her. Had she complained about it? Had she first revealed to him her origin? The playwright leaves the details to the audience's imagination, as George Lucas does in his masterpiece. The second initiative is her plan to let one of the Greeks go free carrying this letter to her dear ones, specifically to her brother whom she has found alive contrary to her former thinking. Iphigenia's third initiative takes place after the recognition between the two siblings. Her meticulous plan to deceive Thoas is as impressive as it is implausible. It is only her exquisite performance that allows her to almost succeed in executing the plan.

The Recognition

Although Iphigenia's incredulity that the young man standing in front of her is Orestes himself seems to be just another occasion where she believes the implausible but does not readily see what is in front of her eye, it matches well with other dramatic recognitions in which Orestes is involved. In Aeschylus' *Libation Bearers* as well as Sophocles' and Euripides' *Electra* plays, another sister of Orestes, Electra, is slow to believe that Orestes has arrived to take revenge on their mother and rescue her from her miserable life. Here likewise, Iphigenia cannot believe that Orestes has arrived to rescue her. Orestes brings up three key events in the family's fall from grace—Pelops' chariot-race for the hand of Hippodamia, the quarrel of Atreus and Thyestes, and Iphigenia's sacrifice—that eventually convince Iphigenia about his identity. This is more evidence than in any case of recognition between Orestes and Electra.

The joyful reunion is ultimately followed by Iphigenia figuring out the rescue plan. Her initiative reminds us of the Euripidean Electra who likewise is the one to who comes up with a plan: to lure Clytemnestra to her death.

After Orestes tells Iphigenia about his life as a matricide, saying that only if he brings the wooden statue of Artemis that fell from the sky and sets it in the land of Athens will those Erinyes who still madden him loose their grip over him. He promises to take Iphigenia back to Mycenae, if she helps him to get the statue (976–86). Iphigenia asks Orestes and Pylades to come up with a plan. Orestes suggests they kill King Thoas, but fails to explain how this would help them escape. Iphigenia refrains from killing the king, who is her host, thus demonstrating her piety: "I cannot do it," she says (1023). Instead she comes up with the idea of using Orestes' and Pylades' pollution as a matricide and his accomplice to their advantage. She will tell Thoas that the statue needs to be purified in seawater because a matricide has touched it. The victims, too, have to be purified in sea water. And this she does. Her deception performance goes without a hitch. She has thought of every little detail, and every possible question Thoas might ask her. She acts with confidence and decisiveness, so Thoas does not suspect her. The king is a courteous and a kind man but simple-minded, who is convinced that Iphigenia hates all Greeks. She not only tells him so now (1187), but the Taurians must have heard this from her before, as we know from the cowherd that this was generally believed to be her attitude (336–39). Thoas is thus unsuspecting and quite willing to defer to the priestess as to what should be done to wash away the supposed pollution. He does not have the presence of mind to ask how it has happened that one of the Greeks got the chance to touch the statue and pollute it. This is one further of the implausibilities that this play abounds with.

And so it happens that after Pylades and Orestes are being led in shackles and with covered heads from the temple, Iphigenia orders the guards to keep away as she goes to perform the cleansing rites alone with the prisoners. Since they have been gone for a long time, the guards became suspicious, and when they go to investigate, they find the fugitives just on the point of embarking in Orestes' ship, hidden nearby. A fight ensues in the course of which the fugitives manage to get on board and make for the open sea. But an unexpected tempest has blown up and in spite of their prayers and the efforts of the rowers, it is carrying them back to shore. Unless the wind drops, they cannot get away. Eventually Athena intervenes and saves them from Thoas' troops. She addresses both Iphigenia and Orestes, providing final confirmation of the rightness of Apollo's plan, and tells them where in Attica they must establish a temple to Artemis, where Iphigenia must be the priestess and in the end be buried. Iphigenia's plan thus succeeds and is blessed by the divine. Although she herself is not going to see her native home at Argos, as she hoped, she has managed to save her brother from the madness imposed on him by some of the Erinyes.

It is therefore somewhat unclear why Orestes felt it necessary to make a comment, which in translation sounds possibly complimentary, but in the Greek, sounds more like a criticism. As soon as Iphigenia started to outline her escape plan, Orestes comments "Well, women are clever (*deinai*) at inventing subterfuges" (1032). The Greek adjective *deinai* that Orestes uses means both "clever" and "frightening" and is unlikely to suggest a positive sense. In view of the tradition of female notoriety for cunning and deception in Greek, and acknowledged by both male and female characters, the comment is more likely to be a barb directed by Orestes at his sister.

So why does Orestes put Iphigenia down in this instance? Iphigenia had immediately pointed out flaws in two escape plans that Orestes had suggested. Could this simply be a case of sibling rivalry, with Orestes finding it hard to accept that his sister, however much he loved her, could take the male role of devising their escape? On the one hand, while the sudden criticism may seem out of place with the euphoria of brother and sister being reunited after so many years, perhaps it also indicates that the relationship quickly settles back down to normal, with the male claiming his dominant role, even when the sister has better ideas. On the other hand, may Euripides simply be following a Greek tradition of criticizing woman as deceptive? The latter seems more apt and goes straight to the heart of the success of the ruse. Yes, it was a ruse, the playwright tells his spectators (1031), but it saved the lives of Iphigenia, Orestes, and Pylades and brought them back to Greece without the bloodshed that Orestes' plan entailed.

The attack on female trustworthiness does not end with Orestes' comment. Even though Orestes assents immediately to Iphigenia's plan (having no alternative to offer), he raises doubts about the trustworthiness of the women of the Chorus. Here again the women outdo his suspicion. They not only live up to their promise to Iphigenia to keep her secret, but by doing so they expose themselves to being punished by Thoas (1431–34). Still, the question of women's treachery does not end here. The Messenger, with no clear proof, accuses the women of the Chorus of treachery when they tell him that they do not know where Thoas is. "See how treacherous (*apiston*) the female sex is!" exclaims the Messenger (1298). Euripides might be capitalizing here on the famous warning of Agamemnon to Odysseus in Book Eleven of the *Odyssey*: "since there is no longer *trustworthiness* (*pista*) in women" (11. 456) which would be familiar to the spectators well versed in Homer. But Euripides also seems to be playing on the assumed duplicity of women. Indeed, the women of the Chorus knew that Thoas was in the temple but their aim was to postpone the news getting to him as long as they possibly could, so the trio could gain time in their escape. In other words, their treachery toward the Taurians was out of their loyalty to the Greeks, contrary to Orestes' suspicion. This kind of dramatic irony concerning trustworthiness or loyalty continues during Iphigenia's deception scene with Thoas in which she explains her request that the prisoners be bound because *one cannot trust* a Greek, she says (1205). She states this of course in order to further gain Thoas' trust, but in reality, she, a Greek, is actually betraying him, and thus proving that her statement is correct. If the Athenian audience enjoyed the implied compliment to their traditional cleverness, they should have also supported the claimed generic cleverness of women. But does this logic work? It is difficult to know, but it may be feasible to assume that Euripides has created these *double entendres* intentionally, and out of desire to clear women of the traditional criticism. There is no absolute value to loyalty or treachery, he says. It all depends on whose side one really is on when employing it. As usual Euripides undermines the values one is traditionally instructed to employ.

Pausanias' writings about Iphigenia

The ancient travel writer Pausanias (*c.* 115–180 CE) mentions many different temples and local traditions associating Artemis with Iphigenia, including a temple to Artemis at Aulis considered to be site where Artemis substituted a deer on the altar. While Homer doesn't relate anything of Iphigenia's sacrifice at Aulis, he did however mention sacrifices made there to Artemis by a plane tree and according to Pausanias, remains of that tree were preserved in the temple. Pausanias encountered other temples to Artemis around Greece adorned with ancient images of Iphigenia, including one at Aigeira, and one at Limnaeum, where a wooden image is claimed to be that which Orestes stole from the Taurians. The local population associated this wooden icon with various blood rituals. When describing his visit to the sanctuaries in ancient Argos, Pausanias presents various alternative myths on Iphigenia's ancestry and her fate. He notes that the lyric poet Stesichorus (*c.* 630–555 BCE) had given Iphigenia a different parentage: she had been born to Helen after she had been abducted by Theseus. Helen's brothers the Dioscuri rescued Helen and ended Theseus' rule over the city of Athens. When the Dioscuri took Helen back to Sparta, Iphigenia was given to Clytemnestra to raise, as she was already married to Agamemnon, and Helen was as yet unwed. Pausanias also reports a temple to Hecate beside a sanctuary dedicated by Helen in connection with the birth of Iphigenia. This is of interest as Stesichorus claimed that in Ps. Hesiod's *Catalogue of Women* (23b M-W) Iphigenia was transformed into Hecate.

IPHIGENIA IN *IPHIGENIA AT AULIS*

Euripides' *Iphigenia at Aulis*

Having been told by Calchas that the only way to achieve proper winds for the army to sail to Troy, was to sacrifice his daughter Iphigenia, Agamemnon wrote to Clytemnestra to send Iphigenia to Aulis under the guise of marrying Achilles. The play opens with Agamemnon regretting doing this. He is writing a letter countering his previous one, which he gives to his trusted servant, the Old Man, whom he urges to make haste to reach Clytemnestra before she departs. Clytemnestra, Iphigenia, and the baby Orestes, however, have already arrived at Aulis. In the meantime, Menelaus has intercepted Agamemnon's second letter, and angrily argues with his brother. This scene reveals Agamemnon's ambition for office and military leadership. Eventually the two brothers change their minds. Menelaus decides against the sacrifice, but Agamemnon does not see a way out of it and goes off to make preparations while continuing to deceive Clytemnestra and Iphigenia as to the true purpose of their presence in Aulis. Iphigenia is overjoyed to see her father, and asks him painful questions about the details of her forthcoming ceremony, which she still believes will be a wedding. Agamemnon tries to persuade Clytemnestra to leave Aulis, but the queen refuses, wishing to oversee her daughter's wedding preparations herself. Agamemnon is dismayed and takes his leave. Achilles enters to complain about the delay in setting sail and has an embarrassing meeting with Clytemnestra, in which she greets Achilles warmly, only to discover he knows nothing of any forthcoming wedding. The Old Man reveals Agamemnon's treacherous intentions to both of them. Achilles vows to help save Iphigenia. Agamemnon returns, ignores the pleas of his wife and daughter, and attempts to justify himself. Iphigenia piteously laments her fate. Achilles returns, announcing that his men will kill him if tries to prevent the sacrifice. After hearing Achilles speak, Iphigenia changes her mind and declares that she is glad to die for the glory of Greece. Achilles hails her as a true hero. Iphigenia believes she will be the first to die in the war that will eventually defeat Troy. She takes her leave of her mother and is led off to the sacrifice. In the epilogue, which is usually rejected by editors, a Messenger arrives and announces that at the moment of sacrifice, a hind already in its bloody death-throes was miraculously substituted for the girl, and that Iphigenia has flown to live among the gods. Calchas declares the miracle to be the work of Artemis. Agamemnon goes off to war, but Clytemnestra doubts the miracle.

Introduction

In both Aeschylus' *Agamemnon* and Sophocles' *Electra* Iphigenia has really been sacrificed at Aulis, without being saved by Artemis. Euripides also follows this narrative in his *Electra,* but in his two extant Iphigenia plays, he chose a milder and perhaps later version of the story. And if we have the conclusion of *Iphigenia at Aulis* as he wrote it, Artemis at the last moment rescues the girl, and substitutes a deer in her place on the altar (see Box on the ending of *Iphigenia at Aulis,* p. 116). Why did Euripides choose to save Iphigenia? It may be that his own humane disposition led him to change the fate of the young girl, or maybe he wanted in a roundabout way to point to the horrific sacrifice wars may demand of a father. In earlier plays, however, he did not shun immolating

Polyxena and Macaria, but no parent was involved. (See Box on Polyxena and Macaria, p. 116.) There is no clear answer. It might well be, that in the case of Iphigenia, consistency required him to save her, since in his chronologically earlier play *Iphigenia among the Taurians* the princess is alive some twenty years after her appearance at Aulis.

The way the playwright has structured the play may be significant. Although Iphigenia's sacrifice is the main subject of *Iphigenia at Aulis,* her appearance in the first four-fifths of the play of 1510 (or 1629) lines amounts only to 24 lines: when she steps off her carriage and is happily looking forward to reunite with her beloved father. Her actual verbal and other participation in the drama resurface only at line 1211 when she tries to supplicate and beg her father not to kill her. After her second entrance she speaks 179 lines altogether in three speeches and conversations with her mother and Achilles, more than half of the remaining 300 lines in the play (counting the final disputed Messenger scene). Euripides thus delays Iphigenia's appearance for four-fifths of the play, and then in the last fifth lets her speak the majority of the lines. What is gained by this structure? It obviously gives an emphasis to her persona. After seeing her as the subject of machinations and pleas for rescue, the spectators can finally meet her in person and what they see is a scared child pleading to her parent not to harm her and, when realizing she has no recourse, changing her mind. At least some of the spectators would leave the drama with a heavy heart about the loss of young life to an aggressive war. Iphigenia's absence for four fifths of the play might also symbolically indicate how she is deprived of any independent initiative regarding the course of her own life. She is talked about, fought about, quarrelled about, but when she finally gets to speak everything has been decided about her, as she realizes fairly soon.

Iphigenia

Realizing why she has been brought to Aulis, Iphigenia does not berate her father, as her mother does, but utters a heart-breaking appeal for pity and love. Again and again she professes her innocence and begs Agamemnon to save her and not to kill her. Her only leverage is their shared memories. She reminds him that she was the first to call him father and that he called her his daughter; she was the first to be dandled on his knees; that she used to promise him to take care of him at his old age. She echoes Menelaus' comment when he professed to have changed his mind about her sacrifice: what does she have to do with Helen's absconding with Paris. Her utter helplessness is compounded when she asks her *infant* brother, Orestes, to plead for her: "See, father, he supplicates you by his *silence*," says the poor girl in her despair (1245, Kovacs). Although young, she knows her fate has been decided.

Agamemnon declares that he is so compromised with the Greeks that he cannot renege. His own life, that of her mother, and his family in Argos, as well as that of Iphigenia will all be in danger from the infuriated army if he further delays making the sacrifice with the appointed victim. Iphigenia knows she has no recourse. She sings a plaintive monody about Paris' exposure as an infant, the judgment of Paris, and the consequence of Helen's elopement; she sees Helen as the cause of her upcoming death. Her sorrow is especially bitter because she sees herself as betrayed by her "impious" father (1317–18). However, her outline of the "history" that brought affairs to where they are now makes her see her upcoming fate and its effects as part of an overarching pattern. Her part is the result of a sequence of events originating from the judgment of Paris, as is the Trojan expedition itself, of which she will ultimately become not only an integral part, but a prime mover (1279–335). Her account of the "history" of what precedes the Trojan War serves to depersonalize and universalize her fate, which is about to become no more than an episode in the long sequence of events following the birth of Paris. It might well be that this realization of her role in this long yarn began or even decided her change of mind. Her comment that her death might bring "fame to Danaan girls" (1309–10) would also be an indicator of this. Her quest for fame is repeated later on as one of her own motivations to die. This must have been noticed by those spectators acquainted with the former play in which Iphigenia finds out that hardly anyone remembers her (*IT* 563–64). Fame, Euripides says, is not a value that should motivate people, thus casting a cloud over the epic tradition.

Achilles' rushing in with the news that his soldiers have sworn to kill him, if he detains them any longer at Aulis for the sake of a young maiden, might have cemented Iphigenia's initial change of mind (1345–68). She has already heard her father's claim about the menacing host and Achilles just repeats the threat.

Aristotle uses Iphigenia as a prime example of anomaly in a character, since she first supplicates her father for life, and afterwards consents to die (*Poet.* 1454a26–33). For him a character needs to be consistent, and she is not. But Iphigenia's change of mind is not that difficult to understand or so abrupt as he suggests; it is presented in a singularly natural way throughout.[10] Iphigenia is a young girl. She was excited about coming to meet Achilles and about her wedding. Suddenly not only are her wedding plans cancelled, but she is to be sacrificed. In modern terms we could say she is in shock. It would be quite understandable to go from one extreme state to another in the short time she is given to digest her new situation. As things present themselves to her, the only way to maintain the state of high excitement is to make a grand gesture—if she's not going to have a grand life, she can have a grand death. Of course, her first impulse is to live, but when she clearly perceives how much depends on her voluntary death, and how Achilles, her champion, is so compromised by his dangerous resolve to save her, and how the Greeks are bent on the expedition from motives of national honor, she yields herself up a willing victim. What else is there for her to do but welcome her death and be the victim the goddess demands? If her father and Achilles cannot withstand the host, how can she? It is not out of sheer heroism as many suppose. It is out of no choice.[11] Furthermore, with the exception of Clytemnestra, the only consistent character in the play, everyone changes his or her mind. It is thus unclear why Aristotle does not criticize Menelaus' change of heart from demanding the death of the girl to the refusing to consent to it; or Agamemnon's double shift from first agreeing to sacrifice his daughter, then wanting to spare his daughter, and then again agreeing to kill her; or Achilles who gives up on his resolve to save the girl.

As Lawrence puts it: "Obviously Iphigenia is not free to choose whether or not to be sacrificed, though she may appear to be free to choose what attitude to adopt to the inevitable" (1988: 100). Once Iphigenia realizes that her death is inevitable, she musters all the possible aphorisms she must have heard growing up to help her face her death. She comes up with a remarkable array of statements and claims that would serve well any commander trying to rally his troops, but here this young girl is attempting to cheer herself to welcome death. Her consternation rather than courage at the news and her artificial verve to die show up in the contradictions of some of her newly fashioned claims. Other statements are simply astonishing, but all of them show the extent of her desperate attempt to justify a decision that was forced upon her. She goes back on her claim to Agamemnon that living is a most welcome thing. When she begged for her life, she told him "you see the light is sweet" or "the light is the sweetest thing to look on" (1219–20, 1250), but now she undercuts the claim by saying "truly it is not right that I should be too in love with my life" (1385). Why it is not right to love what is "the sweetest thing" she leaves unsaid.

She also goes back on her rejection of the heroic code: "To live ignobly is better than to die nobly" (1252). Now she wants to die young and achieve fame (*kleos*), which is most famously articulated in the *Iliad* through Achilles' choice of glorious death over long inconspicuous life. Fame is what an epic hero like Achilles strives for: he wishes to become the subject of a bardic song in recompense for his deeds and early death in battle. This striving for fame contradicts the invisibility that is recommended for a traditional woman of fifth-century Athens. After praising the heroes who died in battle, Pericles recommends to the women of Athens the following "For you great reputation comes from not falling short of your assigned nature. A woman achieves fame (*kleos*) who is least talked about among men, either with blame or praise" (Thuc. 2.45). Iphigenia's desire to attain fame does not match what she probably was taught. Her claim that Clytemnestra bore her "for all the Greeks in common, not for yourself (i.e. Clytemnestra)" (1386), was certainly not her mother's view, nor even that of her father who claims to be forced by the host to murder his daughter. For lack of recourse she subdues her death to the patriotic ideology of war.

Euripides next has Iphigenia utter an extraordinary *double entendre*, which seems haphazard and not entirely thought through but shows her inner disorientation. He has Iphigenia say: "This man (i.e. Achilles) should not do battle with all the Greeks and be killed *for a woman's sake*" (1392–93, Kovacs). The audience can understand one of two things or both: they might hear in the phrase a literary echo of the many references to Helen as the woman on account of whom the Greeks fought, suffered, or died (e.g. *Homer, Il.* 9.339; Aesch. *Ag.* 800); or a reference to Iphigenia. That is to say, if Achilles will try to save her life now, he will be killed. In either case the idea of the incontrovertible benefit of war as a concept is undermined. No matter what the cause, the zeal for war kills. The notion that no one should die for the sake of Helen, who eloped with a lover leaving behind her lawful husband, is fairly straightforward, but if Iphigenia refers to herself—as her following words suggest: "It is better that one man should see the light of the day than numberless women" (1394, Collard)—the meaning of the two sentences is more complex.

The ambiguity of *"for a woman's sake"* conflates into one meaning both saving and killing Achilles. The spectators know that while Iphigenia may save Achilles from the mobocratic spirit of the army, he will still die in the Trojan War, "because of a woman," i.e. Helen. This aggressive revenge-fraught war has only victims. But Iphigenia's saving of Achilles has two further ramifications that cast a shadow on her repeated disparaging comments about women and on the ethos of the Homeric archetype. First, although Achilles pledged to save Iphigenia's life, she, a woman and very young to boot, is the one who saves *his* life from the menacing army. Second, at the end of the play and contrary to Homeric lore, the Chorus call her, not Achilles, "the sacker of Troy" (1511–12).

Her claim that the life of one man equals that of numberless women is by itself rather stunning. It seems that she is somehow still unaware of the sacrifice she is about to undergo even though she will soon demand fame in return. Is she simply repeating the common misogynistic view of the worthlessness of women she must have heard growing up without giving it full examination because of the constraints of her situation? It might well be. But could it also be that Euripides undercuts here, however subtly, for the external audience the prevalent notion of the inconsequentiality of women's lives by showing how a young girl dares herself to die to satisfy the blood lust of the men in this play?[12]

Iphigenia's comments and reasons are not fully thought through but are an impulsive and instinctive response to what she hears from her father and Achilles. While in her appeal to Agamemnon she sees the sacrifice as entirely depending on her father, after listening to both Agamemnon and Achilles about the threat of the army, she understands that the decisive power is not her father's, but belongs to the mob-like army, and that her father's master is "Greece" (1271). She is not given any time to digest what her father tells her and fails to understand that even now he could save her life by giving up his position. The idea that what he does is for the good of Greece must have convinced her: this is what she gives her mother as her motivation to die. She buys into her father's and Achilles' preoccupation with the army and, following her former depersonalization of her fate, she seems to attempt *be part* of the war effort. As the soldiers are willing to sacrifice their lives for Greece's honor, she simply is doing the same. The only difference is that she precedes them in her sacrifice of her life. She tries the best she can to adopt their motivation: to honor Greece. It is a simplistic turn but a natural and adequate response to what she is facing. In other words, since she cannot fight them, she joins them, and for that purpose she tries to come up with all she can think of in order to justify her collective abuser.

Her fantasy that by allowing the army to sail she is about to become an integral part of the larger throng of the warriors borders on transgendering. At the end of her speech and contrary to her former denigration of women, she, although a woman, repeats her former hope for fame (1383), a known marker of a Homeric hero and above all of Achilles as the spectators know. After all, by sailing to Troy he chose fame over long life. When she declares that her sacrifice will be her "memorial that for me will be my children, my marriage, my good name!" (1398–99, Kovacs), she exchanges her female expectations of marriage and children with what a Homeric hero, that is to say, a hero participating in the Trojan War, is motivated by and aspires to.[13] She wants to see her death as the next chapter in the history she outlined in her monody, after which she is sure the sack of Troy will follow. She is so focused on achieving the fame that will accompany her death that she is sure that it will even bring a good name to her mother (1440). Somehow she thinks that her mother's tears can be replaced by the fame of her dead daughter. Fame for her now is the ultimate goal that will sustain her walking to the altar and offering her tender neck to the knife.

After expressing her belief that she is going to attain fame and be part of the Trojan War she asks for two things of her mother. First, she does not want her death to be considered a mournful event. She asks Clytemnestra not to grieve for her, not to shed tears, dress herself in black, or have her sisters dress in black, nor does she want sacrificial animals to be buried with her or a grave mound to be raised for her. Second, she asks Clytemnestra not to hate Agamemnon. In contrast to her former reference to her father as "impious" for planning to kill her, she now forgives him because "He killed me for Hellas's sake against his will." Iphigenia has now bought in completely into her father's nationalistic ideology and even speaks of her death as past event (1456). She does not allow her mother to come with her to the altar. She sings her departing lyrics and now speaks of herself as a triumphant savior of Greece, her feelings here reaching their highest pitch of exaltation, in the strongest contrast to her earlier lament monody. Now she sees herself not only as facilitating the voyage against Troy but as the actual "sacker of Ilium and the Phrygians" (1475-76). As she disappears on her way to the altar, the Chorus echo her words and they too refer to her as the "sacker of Ilium and the Phrygians" (1510-11). In her last moments, Iphigenia has finally achieved her goal in fame and in being seen equal to the Homeric hero *par excellence*, Achilles. Now she and Achilles share in the glory of Troy. They are not husband and wife, but two comrades in arms.

It is easy to conclude from Euripides' depiction of Iphigenia' in *Iphigenia at Aulis,* as well as from his *Hecuba* and *Trojan Women* (see Chapters 5 and 6) that he hated war. His presentation of a young innocent girl, who pathetically misconceives the blood-lust and aggression of the mob-like army for patriotic verve (with which she seemingly identifies because no other alternative is offered to her), can serve as an example for army's misguided by propaganda. Like Iphigenia, numberless young men were brainwashed into believing their deaths could help the cause of an abstract notion like Greece or any other impersonal entity deemed greater than their young life. At the same time the play unveils the greed for power and honor as invested in the army's leaders: in this case, in the ambitious Agamemnon, the cowardly and whiny Menelaus, and the conniving Odysseus and Calchas. If Iphigenia stands for the innocent who lose their lives in any war, it would not be the first time that Euripides' criticism of wars resurfaces in his plays, especially of aggressive war as the Trojan War was. In his play *Rhesus* (of an uncertain date[14]), Rhesus, a son of a Muse and an ally of the Trojans, comes with his army to help the Trojans fight against the Greeks, but is murdered in his sleep by Odysseus. In the final act of the play, the Muse appears carrying the dead body of her only son and singing a heart-wrenching dirge. Like Thetis, the mother of Achilles, the Muse knew that Rhesus would die if he went to Troy (*Rhesus,* 898-99, 934-35), and she also knows that soon enough Achilles, the enemy of Rhesus, will die at Troy too, and that she will mourn him as well, together with

Thetis his mother. The mother of the defender, Rhesus, and the mother of the aggressor, Achilles, will both have dead sons at the end of this war. The play as a whole thus subverts the entire notion of heroic war, and shows its futility, as much as the sacrifice of the young Iphigenia points to the atrocities a war brings about. War has victims only.

The ending of *Iphigenia at Aulis*

The play *Iphigenia at Aulis* was produced posthumously around 405 BCE by Euripides the Younger, identified in the sources as either son or nephew of the playwright. The text of the play, however, is not entirely sound throughout and various scholars bracket various passages as not authentic. Whether the play's "epilogue" (the section of the final act after Iphigenia exits to the altar, in which a Messenger appears announcing that Iphigenia was saved from the sacrifice) is by Euripides or the work of writers later than Euripides is unclear, but it is seen by most scholars as spurious. The style of the Messenger's speech, the language, and the prosody are said to disqualify this ending from being written by Euripides. Either the play was left unfinished, or what we have has displaced a genuine conclusion of which we may have a fragment quoted by Aelian in his work *On Animals* (7.39) and attributed indiscriminately to Euripides' *Iphigenia* (although not found in either one of the extant plays on Iphigenia). Aelian: "But I will place in the very hands of the Achaeans an antlered hind, which they will slay and boast that they have slain your daughter." The speaker must be Artemis who might be announcing to Clytemnestra that Iphigenia will not be sacrificed.

Polyxena and Macaria

In Euripides' *Hecuba* the Greeks sacrifice Polyxena, the daughter of Hecuba and Priam, on Achilles' tomb following Achilles' demand that they do this or he will stop the winds and prevent their sailing home. Polyxena decides to go willingly to her death and conducts herself with such heroic decorum before and during her sacrifice by the hand of Achilles' son Neoptolemus that she inspires the Greeks with admiration.

The maiden in Euripides' *Children of Heracles* is unnamed, but the *hypothesis* (the ancient summary of the plot of a Greek drama that usually precedes in the manuscripts the dramatic text) calls her Macaria. When the oracles state that Athens can win the battle with Argos on behalf of the children of Heracles only if a noble virgin is sacrificed, one of Heracles' daughters volunteers her life. She rejects the idea that lots be drawn among the female children of Heracles and insists that the glorious death must be hers alone. She wants to thank Athens for its protection of the children of Heracles with her own life.

Conclusion

The two portrayals of Iphigenia present the oldest daughter of Agamemnon and Clytemnestra at two different times of her life: in around her mid-thirties, after she has been transported off to a foreign barbaric land where she is forced to take part in ritual human sacrifices, and in a mythic prequel, written a few years after her first portrayal, as a younger woman who thinks she is about to marry Achilles, but then discovers that she herself is to be the victim of human sacrifice. The commonality of the horrors of human sacrifice between Euripides' two portrayals cannot be ignored. Having had his protagonist reject the idea that the gods require human sacrifice in *Iphigenia among the Taurians*, Euripides may be seen as exploring man's brutality to man (or woman) further in his *Iphigenia at Aulis*. The difference in age and circumstances between the Iphigenias portrayed in the two plays may be seen as explaining their differing characterizations. The naïveté and passion of the younger girl has given way to a certain degree of jaded cynicism and compliance in the older woman.

In both characterizations however, there is something endearing about Iphigenia. In *Iphigenia at Aulis*, she pleads for her life when she thinks there may be some hope, but quickly submits to fate when she understands the possible consequences to others of her actions. In *Iphigenia among the Taurians*, she refuses to countenance the murder of Thoas, however much she has suffered. As soon as there is a glimmer of hope, she is inventive enough to devise an escape plan, saving Orestes and Pylades as well as herself, without involving the murder of her host. Many ascribe certain misogynous views to Euripides. In his characterizations of Iphigenia and in Orestes' speeches in *Iphigenia among the Taurians*, it may be considered that rather than holding such views himself, he is allowing the expression of such views, which may be held by members of his audience, without allowing for an unequivocal interpretation.

DISCUSSION TOPICS

1. Considering Iphigenia's deception of Thoas, how would you judge the act of "lying"? Is it always negative?
2. What is the meaning of friendship? How would you view the relationship between Orestes and Pylades?
3. In *Iphigenia among the Taurians*, Euripides presents Iphigenia as being quite distant to start off with. He also lets the audience know that she is fully aware that she is complying with something that is morally wrong when she takes part in the human sacrifices practised in the temple. Do you think this is the reason for her portrayal as being fairly cold and emotionally "closed down"? The dilemma she is faced with sadly has many modern parallels. Can you think of any? Can you imagine how you would behave if you lived in a regime which

forced you to inflict violence on someone because they were a foreigner, or in any way "other" according to the rulers of the regime?

4. Throughout *Iphigenia among the Taurians,* Iphigenia seems to place far more emphasis on the importance of having a brother, Orestes, than on having a sister, Electra, although she would have been far closer in age to Electra. Can you give any reasons for this?

5. In presenting plays which touch upon the myths of the House of Atreus, Euripides was following on from Aeschylus' *Oresteia*. Do you think that his two portrayals of Iphigenia are influenced by Aeschylus' presentation of his female heroines, Clytemnestra and Electra? Do you think that his characterization is a response to Aeschylus' work, and if so, how?

6. Both of the plays in this chapter deal with heavy themes including human sacrifice. However, both plays could be interpreted as having "happy endings." Do you feel that they are actually tragedies? Give reasons for your answer.

7. If Euripides had not thought of dramatizing the events at Aulis when he wrote *Iphigenia among the Taurians,* can you think of any reasons for deciding to write *Iphigenia at Aulis* when he did? Can you think of anything he might have changed had he written the plays in a different order? In particular, do you think that the way in which Iphigenia relates (or does not relate) to her mother might have been different in *Iphigenia among the Taurians* had it been written after *Iphigenia at Aulis*?

8. In Greek tragedy, murders and extreme violence usually occur off-stage, with the events being narrated by a character, usually the Messenger. The final scenes of *Iphigenia at Aulis* are a good example of this. This contrasts strongly with the modern tendency to show focus upon every gory detail in both film and theater. Do you think that the Athenian playwrights managed to maintain the audience's interest without visible graphic depictions of violence? Is there anything to be learned from this for today's producers and directors, or have accepted norms moved too far to "turn the wheel back"?

9. In *Iphigenia at Aulis* Iphigenia is portrayed as doting upon her father. Do you find this believable in the light of Agamemnon's portrayal in the play? Do Agamemnon's various changes of mind of Agamemnon in *Iphigenia at Aulis* have an impact on his character as a father?

10. Both Agamemnon and Achilles present the army as an unruly mob that rules its generals to Iphigenia. Do you think that it is realistic that great "heroes" would express themselves in this way to a young girl? Try to explain what may have caused their behavior. Is it possible that Euripides may have been insinuating that they were taking advantage of a young girl's naïveté, or do you think that is too modern an explanation?

CHAPTER 4
ANTIGONE

Mythic background of Antigone and her father, Oedipus

The Theban saga of the Labdacids, Laius and Jocasta, their son Oedipus and his children is one of the best known and most frequently treated of Greek literary topics. While growing up in the court of Pelops, Laius was the tutor to Chrysippus, son of Pelops (son of Tantalus, forebear of the House of Atreus). He was supposed to accompany the lad to the chariot races, but instead abducted and raped him. In some versions of the story the humiliated young man then kills himself out of shame. Years later, Laius as the King of Thebes marries Jocasta, daughter of Menoeceus and sister of Creon. When the couple fail to conceive, Laius consults an oracle and learns that as punishment for his earlier misdeed he is doomed to perish at the hands of his own son, who will then marry Jocasta. Therefore, when Jocasta does give birth, Laius pierces and binds his son's ankles and commands a servant to expose the child on the slopes of Mount Cithaeron. Pitying the infant, the servant hands him over to a Corinthian shepherd, who takes the baby to Polybus and Merope, the childless king and queen of Corinth. When Oedipus grew up and was taunted by his friends as being adopted, he journeyed to Delphi and asked the oracle who his true parents were. Upon hearing that he would kill his father and marry his mother, he decided not to return to Corinth. Driving his chariot through Phocis, he encountered Laius at a crossroad. Each man refused to give way; as a result Oedipus killed Laius with his retinue, except for one slave, and drove on to Thebes. Upon his arrival at Thebes he solved the riddle of the Sphinx, who has been tyrannizing the city, causing her to fall to her death. Creon meanwhile has announced that the person defeating the Sphinx will be the next King of Thebes. Oedipus is given Jocasta, Laius' widow as his wife; two sons and two daughters are born to the couple. Years later, when Thebes is being ravaged by a plague, Oedipus sends Creon to the oracle to find how to rid the city of the plague, only to discover that he himself has unwittingly defiled the city. Upon discovery of the truth, Oedipus blinds himself, and Jocasta commits suicide. By most accounts, he continues to live at Thebes, while others say he goes into exile.

According to the version that he stays in Thebes, Oedipus claims to be disrespected by his sons, Polyneices and Eteocles, and curses them, condemning them to die at one another's hand. Polyneices and Eteocles quarrel over their inheritance. After gaining the support of the city, Eteocles exiles Polyneices, who returns to attack the city with an army he has raised with his father-in-law Adrastus, King of Argos. This army is led by seven champions, each of whom attacks one of the seven gates of Thebes. At the seventh gate, Eteocles and Polyneices meet and kill each other, fulfilling Oedipus' curse. All the other champions, with the exception of Adrastus, are also killed. Eteocles' forces are victorious, and Thebes is saved.

Introduction

Antigone appears in four surviving plays. The fullest depiction of Antigone is to be found in Sophocles' *Antigone*, the date of which is not certain, but if it is true that Sophocles

Aeschylus' *Seven against Thebes*

The play was produced in 467 BCE as the final play of a thematically connected trilogy. *Laius* and *Oedipus* are lost, as is the satyr play *Sphinx* which followed. The bulk of *Seven against Thebes* consists of a dialogue between Eteocles, now the ruler of Thebes, and the Chorus of Theban Maidens. The Chorus are fearful of the army marching against the city, but Eteocles scolds them for causing panic. He urges all to take their stand in defense of the city. In a lengthy description consisting of seven pairs of speeches, the Scout describes each of the seven champions who are leading the attack and the devices on their respective shields. Eteocles in turn announces which Theban commander he will send against each Argive attacker. After every pair of speeches, the Chorus give a brief response wishing success to the defender or death to the attacker. The champion before the seventh gate is revealed to be Polyneices. Eteocles refers to their father's curse when he posts himself against his brother. The Chorus try unsuccessfully to dissuade him from going. A Messenger reports that the attackers have been repelled, but that Eteocles and Polyneices have killed each other at the seventh gate. The Chorus split into two groups, which sing alternate stanzas lamenting the brothers' deaths. The part of the play with contested provenance starts with the Herald's announcement that the people's council of Thebes has decided that Eteocles, who died defending the city, will have a proper burial, but his brother Polyneices, who brought a foreign army to try to recapture the city, is to be left unburied, a prey for dogs. In what amounts to a reductive version of Sophocles' play, Antigone objects vehemently to the city's decision. She leaves with half of the Chorus to bury Polyneices. Ismene, who is not given any lines, leaves with the other part of the Chorus to bury Eteocles.

Euripides' *Phoenician Women*

Antigone appears also in Euripides' *Phoenician Women*, most probably produced in 411–409 BCE. There are many discrepancies between the plot of this play and Sophocles' *Antigone*. For example, both Oedipus and Jocasta are still alive when Polyneices and Eteocles kill each other. Appearing in the "viewing from the wall" (*teichoskopia*) in the prologue, Antigone asks questions about the attackers at the gates of Thebes, and the Tutor informs her of their identities. Later in the play, Jocasta summons Antigone from her maiden quarters to accompany her to the battlefield in an attempt to end her brothers' quarrel, but the two women find the brothers dead. Taking a sword, Jocasta plunges it into her body, sinking down upon her sons' corpses. Antigone sings a dirge for the dead and calls for her father to come out of the palace. Creon arrives as well, announcing the exile of Oedipus and adding the two requests of Eteocles before the duel: the future marriage of Antigone and Haemon and the prohibition of burial to Polyneices. Antigone refuses to leave Polyneices unburied. She also decides not to marry Haemon but to leave the city as a guide to her blind father. The burial does not take place in the play.

served as a general during the Samian expedition shortly after the production of the play, as suggested by the play's ancient preface (*hypothesis*), then the tragedy was performed around 440/41 BCE. The determination of a possible earlier appearance of Antigone, depends on whether the ending of Aeschylus' *Seven against Thebes* is part of the original play. If that ending is authentic, Antigone has already appeared as a dramatic character in 467 BCE, albeit very briefly. If the ending of *Seven against Thebes* is spurious and was inserted after the production of *Antigone* and/or that of Euripides' *Phoenician Women*, Antigone is not attested anywhere before Sophocles' play.

Both *Seven against Thebes* and *Phoenician Women* offer minimal characterization of Antigone beyond her defiance of the edict issued by Creon. Sophocles' later play *Oedipus at Colonus* presents a younger Antigone, before her father's death. Antigone receives some individuation here, being sympathetically characterized as the support and guide for her blind and aged father in his exile. Her part in various supplications is also meaningful in this "suppliant drama". Antigone supplicates the Chorus to hear her father, she supplicates Oedipus to hear Polyneices' entreaty, and unsuccessfully supplicates Polyneices to desist from attacking Thebes. Her resolute nature is shown at the end of the play when she asks Theseus to ensure her and Ismene's passage to Thebes, where she hopes to prevent the upcoming fratricide. Looking back to *Antigone*, this play makes reference to the burial of Polyneices. Faced with Oedipus' refusal to retract the curse he has laid upon his sons, and foreseeing his upcoming death, Polyneices asks both Antigone and Ismene to assure his proper burial.

Sophocles' *Oedipus at Colonus*

The now blind Oedipus has wandered ten long years after being exiled from Thebes, guided by his daughter Antigone, who has no independent life of her own. When Oedipus discovers that he has arrived at the grove of the Eumenides (Erinyes) at Colonus (close to Athens), he is convinced that this is his ordained final resting place, despite the refusals of a Peasant and a Chorus of Old Men of Colonus to grant his supplications to stay in this holy place. When Ismene arrives, Antigone and Oedipus are overjoyed to be reunited with her, but she brings worrying tidings. Eteocles, the younger of the girls' two brothers (in this version), has seized the throne and exiled the eldest, Polyneices, who is raising an Argive army against Thebes. Also, Creon is on his way to Colonus to force Oedipus to return to the vicinity of Thebes (without entering the country itself) because an oracle has foretold that whichever side Oedipus is attached to will be victorious. On the Chorus' advice Oedipus sends Ismene to the other side of the grove to carry out certain purification rituals on his behalf. Theseus, king of Athens, arrives and, after hearing of Oedipus' promised benefit to Athens, accepts Oedipus under his protection, entrusting him to the people of Colonus, before taking his leave. Creon arrives, revealing that he has already captured Ismene, and instructs his guards to seize Antigone. The Chorus call upon Theseus, who returns immediately, instructing his men to intercept the Theban kidnappers. Antigone and Ismene rejoin Oedipus. Finally, Polyneices arrives to ask for his father's help against Eteocles. Oedipus angrily refuses to help his son, stating that neither of his sons had done anything to help him when he was exiled. Furthermore, Oedipus foretells that his two sons will kill each other in the upcoming battle. Antigone unsuccessfully tries to persuade Polyneices not to attack Thebes and so avoid dying at his brother's hands, but Polyneices refuses, asking both of his sisters to honor him with proper funeral rites when he has met his preordained death. A violent thunderstorm is interpreted by Oedipus as a sign from Zeus of his own impending death. Theseus returns, and Oedipus tells him that it is time for him to give his gift to Athens. He allows Theseus alone to accompany him to his final resting place. A Messenger then reports Oedipus' death. After Antigone and Ismene lament the death of their father, Antigone asks for passage back to Thebes, where she hopes to stop the accursed fratricide.

Sophocles' *Antigone*

The play starts at dawn after the fratricide of Eteocles and Polyneices. Antigone tells her sister Ismene that Creon has issued an edict (from the battlefield) directing that Polyneices will remain unburied while Eteocles merits all the proper burial rites. Antigone asks Ismene to help her bury Polyneices in defiance of this edict.

After pointing out the risks involved, Ismene refuses to join her sister and tries to convince Antigone to rethink her plan. In response, Antigone rejects Ismene, vowing to act alone. After the Chorus of Theban Elders sing a hymn of thanksgiving to the gods for the victory, Creon enters and formally announces his edict to the city. One of the Guards of Polyneices' unburied body arrives with news that someone has sprinkled earth on the corpse. Creon accuses him of participating in the burial, threatening him with torture if he fails to find the culprit. The Guard returns bringing Antigone, explaining that the watchmen uncovered Polyneices' body and then caught Antigone as she tried to re-cover him and perform funeral rituals. Questioned by Creon, Antigone admits her deeds, proclaiming the immorality of the edict and the morality of her own actions. The incensed Creon assumes that Ismene must have been a partner in what he sees as a serious act of sedition. Ismene tries to confess falsely to the crime, wishing to die alongside her sister, but Antigone angrily denies that Ismene shares any responsibility; the honor should be hers alone. Ismene now tries to use Antigone's betrothal to Haemon, Creon's son, to make Creon reconsider, but he refuses to relent. Creon condemns the two women to death.

Haemon tries to intercede on behalf of Antigone but fails to change his father's mind. Following a suggestion from the Theban Elders, Creon decides to spare Ismene. Even though his edict said that the transgressor would be stoned to death by the people of the city, he changes the punishment, deciding to entomb Antigone alive in a deserted place to avoid pollution. Antigone laments her approaching death. The Chorus offer the consolation that she will be honored, but also recall her family history and scold her for flouting those in power. In front of Creon, Antigone deplores her unmarried state, but justifies her deed by stating that her obligation to her brother overrode that to a husband or child. She is led to her tomb.

Teiresias the blind prophet warns Creon that Polyneices should be buried at once. When Creon accuses Teiresias of being corrupt, Teiresias responds that due to Creon's transgressions, he will lose his son. Creon sends his men to free Antigone, but they are too late: Antigone has hung herself. They find Haemon in the tomb as well. He tries to smite his father with his sword, but misses and decides to use the sword on himself, dying while clasping Antigone's body. Upon hearing of her son's death, Eurydice, Creon's wife, kills herself as well. Creon declares that he is responsible for the deaths of Eurydice and Haemon, and asks to be led away.

ANTIGONE IN SOPHOCLES' *ANTIGONE*

In many ways Antigone is one of the most masculine of the tragedians' heroines. Her strongly characterized persona includes the following traits:

- she defies societal norms, going against the expressed wishes of Creon, adhering instead to what she perceives as the laws of the gods;
- she exhibits extreme bravery, showing no scruples about risking her life, or the lives of others in adhering to her principles;
- she lacks compassion when prioritizing the needs of her dead brother over those of her living sister.

Antigone's Intransigence

In contrast to more mature heroines like Clytemnestra or Medea, Antigone, like the Sophoclean Electra, is too young to be concerned with either loving or avenging a husband. Her passions are instead directed towards the fulfillment of abstract ideals, and her life is totally subsumed by her determination to attain her goals against all odds and in defiance of societal expectations. Tragedy's depiction of the dogged resolve of these two young women is not free from criticism. Both heroines exhibit stubbornness beyond that of any male character in tragedy or epic. As Knox has pointed out: "Ajax and Philoctetes at least discuss the possibility of surrender" (1966: 67), but not Antigone or Electra. However, they differ from each other considerably. Antigone acts alone, planning and acting quickly, paying with her life for her deeds. She is an impulsive heroine who buries her brother against Creon's edict, out of instinctual feeling that this is what one should do for a brother, without first formulating the principles theoretically justifying her action. Sophoclean Electra instead waits many long years for her brother to return and avenge her murdered father. The tasks the two young women set themselves differ fundamentally from each other, although the risks they carry are similar. Antigone wants her brother to receive proper burial, while Electra seeks revenge, entailing matricide and regicide. When Electra believes her brother is dead, she is prepared to take action herself. Both young women become famous for their fervent idealism and bravery. Along with their highly idealistic stances, both are prepared to adopt unprincipled means in attaining their goals. They have little concern for how their acts affect those around them. Both treat their sisters poorly, and both use some slight deception.

Antigone's Single-Mindedness

Sophocles is known for his antithetical style, which is attested in *Antigone* in the debates between the protagonist and her sister as well as in her quarrel with her uncle. The binary depiction of Antigone and Ismene is especially fruitful in revealing the intricacies of the animosity between Antigone and Creon.[1] Antigone is portrayed as a character of natural integrity, true to herself, yet stubborn and intransigent. In focusing on what she regards as the moral way to behave, she not only ignores the opinions of others, but is also, as in the case of Electra, willing to endanger them. Furthermore, on not receiving the cooperation she seeks, Antigone casts her sister off, prioritizing the needs of her dead brother over those of her living sister. A careful reading of her opening address to Ismene also reveals that in order to convince her sister to cooperate, Antigone misrepresents the facts by telling Ismene that she has heard that Creon had already "buried" Eteocles (*ekrypse*, 25).[2] For some reason scholarship has ignored this discrepancy between what Antigone claims has already happened to Eteocles' corpse, and Creon's proclamation to the Elders about what he wants to see happening to the brothers' corpses in the future. Does this slight deception align with Antigone's other attributes, or does it perhaps serve as a signpost of her gender?

As with other Sophoclean heroes, Antigone is characterized by her single-mindedness and steadfast determination. The ideas of compromise, bargaining, concession, or middle ground do not exist for her. She is also a sister capable of extreme, steadfast devotion to at least one of her brothers. Apart from her attempt to elicit Ismene's aid by the premature claim of Eteocles' burial, she is *never* calculating. Her usual integrity and instinctual reaction are also reflected in her lack of persuasive rhetoric. In keeping with her impressive independence of thought, her impetuous nature and unswerving devotion to her cause, Antigone is a woman who takes direct and immediate action. She does not beat about the bush. In her arguments with Ismene and Creon she also shows a straightforwardness that is not found in the speeches of Clytemnestra, Medea, or Phaedra, all masterful rhetoricians.

Antigone's Loyalties

Antigone cannot fathom a world in which she would not give a proper burial to her brother, claiming that this is a responsibility she owes her kin. The same obligation falls upon her sister, yet Ismene believes that Polyneices will forgive her for not participating in his burial, which the law of the city, as imposed by the ruler Creon, prohibits. Creon is also a blood relative of Polyneices, being his maternal uncle, but for him the safety of the city is paramount: Polyneices attacked the city and so will be denied burial. It thus seems that there is some latitude in fulfilling obligations to kin. On the face of it, blood relation trumps every other consideration for Antigone, yet she rejects both Creon and Ismene when they do not act in accordance with her wishes. Ismene and Creon prioritize external circumstances, whereas Antigone chooses some deep inner conviction over pragmatism and any other considerations. Antigone's duties and allegiances begin within herself. She insists on burying Polyneices not only out of loyalty to him but also out of loyalty to herself. Although she explicitly claims that she buries him because he is her kin (e.g. 73, 81, 503), there is more to this assertion. Polyneices is *hers*, and the refusal of burial for him is not only disrespectful to him, it is a personal matter for Antigone; it is her *self* that it wounded. "Creon has no right to keep me from *my [own]* family" (48), she tells Ismene when attempting to clarify to her sister the magnitude of Creon's transgression. The emphasis in this statement falls on "my own." Because Polyneices is not only a brother but indeed *belongs* to her, Creon cannot separate the two of them. Her religious duty to what is *hers* overrides any edict. In her first depiction of the edict, this emphasis on *her* is striking:

> This is the proclamation which they say the good Creon
> has made to *you and me*—yes to *me*. (31–32, after Lloyd-Jones[3])

On Antigone's double mention of herself, Brown (1987: on 32) notes: "It is not often in Greek tragedy that we are invited to assess a speaker's motivation and character from such implicit clues as this. There is a note of fierce pride here: Antigone takes the decree as a personal insult, assuming without hesitation that she, at least, could not possibly be expected to obey it." Similarly, O'Brien (1978: on 32) writes: "Antigone's repetition here conveys her incredulous indignation that Creon should think she would obey such an order."

The attachment of the sisters to their brother Polyneices is emphasized when Ismene asks if Antigone is going to bury Polyneices in spite of the prohibition; Antigone tries again to pressure her sister into her own way of thinking:

> Well *I* will bury *my* (*emon*) brother, and *yours* (*son*), if *you*
> will not; *I* will not be caught betraying him. (45–46)

Antigone's rebellion arises from somewhere within herself, from a deep inner spring where custom and propriety reside. There is no question that she feels responsibility for Polyneices as her brother, which she declares *viva voce*. However, this explicit declaration is also the way she formulates what she is experiencing inside herself, and the way she explains to herself and Ismene the motive for what she is about to do. This blend of allegiance to herself and to her family may be why, despite her ardent resolution to assure proper burial rights for Polyneices, she shows no sign of grief for his death, or for that matter for Eteocles' death either. One can compare Electra's heart-wrenching lament in Sophocles' *Electra* (1126–70, performed years later) when she holds the urn of ashes supposedly of Orestes, who she thinks has been killed in a chariot race. This is what a loving sister is expected to do. Antigone seems to replace grief with absolute adherence to custom, which for her nullifies any laws contradicting her will. In fact, we do not hear Antigone express affection for any of her siblings (*pace* O'Brien 1973: 7). Her determination is for her *self*, as much as for her brother's sake. Her loyalty to family, however, is by no means unconditional or automatic, as the case of Ismene reveals. Antigone repudiates her living sister, whom she cannot forgive for not agreeing with her. She appears to be infuriated by the thought that Ismene, an unworthy and cowardly sister, might share the glory which she thinks she alone deserves. This is why she refuses to let Ismene share her fate, which in fact would be the right thing to do, and also rebuffs her in hurtful terms. When Ismene begs to take her share of the blame, Antigone answers: "Why, justice will not allow you this, since you refused and I was not your associate" (538–39). To Ismene's question: "And what desire for life will be mine if you leave me?"

(548) Antigone answers cruelly: "Ask Creon! You are his champion!" (549). This must be why when Antigone walks to her death-chamber, she says: "And I, the *last* of them, and by far the worst off of all, shall go down [there] before the due portion of my life had come" (895–96, cf. 941 Griffith, 1999). Antigone considers herself the last scion of the house of Labdacus. Previously the Chorus spoke of the "last root" of the house of Labdacus, but their comment could include both Antigone and Ismene (599–600). For Antigone, however, Ismene does not exist any more.

Antigone's worldview is personal: whoever counters her wishes or disagrees with her principles is her enemy. From the very beginning, Antigone feels that it is she against everyone else. This might be why Sophocles gave her a high incidence of use of the first person. Even Creon, in spite of the ideologically formulated proclamations that he is imposing on the citizens of Thebes, has a lower incidence. In the 214 lines that Antigone speaks, she uses the first person every 4.5 lines on average (58 times), while Creon, who speaks 38% more lines than she does, (344) uses the first person only every 7.2 lines (48 times).[4] The first person singular is embedded in Greek in the verb itself and does not need to be mentioned separately, but Antigone fortifies the verb with the first person pronoun (in nominative *egō*) every 15 lines on average compared to Creon's every 26 lines.[5] The ratios are significant because Antigone is careful about her usage of personal pronouns. When she tries to coax Ismene into participating in Polyneices' burial, she refers to the two of them by the pronoun "we" or "us", which in Greek she puts into the 'dual' grammatical form. The 'dual' is a grammatical number in addition to singular and plural that the Greek grammatical system offers to the speaker so that two people considered as a unit can have their own grammatical form. Sophocles uses both systems, the plural and the dual, to indicate a pair (Morwood 1982: 2–3). The dual, however, is often used for emphasis, and in our case, the grammar contributes to Antigone's purpose of forming a tight union with Ismene (e.g. 3, 21). Further along, both sisters speak of themselves and their two dead brothers in the dual (13, 21–22, 50, 58, 558), since they think of themselves and their brothers as an inseparable unit. However, once Ismene refuses to aid in burying Polyneices, Antigone stops using the dual, in a grammatical reflection of the rupture between her and her sister, thus reinforcing her isolation for the rest of the play (O'Brien 1978: 2–3).

The use of the first-person signals motivation beyond grammatical needs. It reflects Antigone's insistence that she alone will do, or has done, what no one else is or was willing to do for her brother: bury him. This act of piety reflects a devotion resulting from her inner piety, from her inner *self*. This inner zeal for what is right regardless of what the outside world might think, expressed either by the emphasis on the first person, or by identifying herself with what is owed to her dead brother, might be why she serves as an example for all the "Antigones" to come. These idealistic, unbending, and uncompromising heroines and heroes who pursue what they believe in with complete disregard for the consequences of their actions often die for their ideals. Antigone, however, has the zeal of youth, rather than the seasoned ideologies of an older zealot. She knows the customs and norms that obligate kin, and reacts intuitively to what she hears both in words and deeds.

Antigone's Impulsiveness

None of Antigone's actions is premeditated nor are the ramifications considered. Antigone acts on the spur of the moment reacting to the situation in hand and acting quickly on her decision. Once she leaves Ismene, she goes at dawn, unobserved, to the battlefield and pours dust on Polyneices' corpse. She must have performed her deed in the short interval between the announcement of the edict to the people and the beginning of the watch over the corpse (Jebb 2004 [1900]: on 253–54), or else the guards were situated too far from the corpse to see her (Griffith 1999: on 253). She returns in full daylight to perform the necessary burial rites, that is, libations, possibly with a lament, or combination of the two. However, once she discovers that the dust has been removed, leaving Polyneices' malodorous remains uncovered, she screams and tries to reperform the partial burial. Her attempt to re-cover the corpse indicates that in her eyes the uncovering has nullified her former burial. Teiresias later concurs with this view when he tells Creon that leaving Polyneices' corpse unburied and bereft of funeral rites is against gods' wishes (1070–73).

It is significant that Antigone is not afraid to come again during the day to complete her task. Her screaming "with a sound like the piercing note of a bird when she sees her empty nest robbed of her young" (423–25) shows how absorbed she is in what she is doing, unmindful of the danger of being caught.[6] Did she want to be caught? Those who find the "double burial" (her former covering the corpse with dust and the attempt to re-cover it) problematic take this view. However, it is also possible that, as on other occasions, she is acting impulsively, responding to an immediate need rather than out of a wish to get caught in the act. She knew that sprinkling dust was only a symbolic burial. Since it was not in her power to dig a grave and lift and place Polyneices into it, the least she could do is provide such further obligatory burial rituals as libations, which she brought with her in a brazen urn (430–31). She might have also intended to raise a burial mound from the sand (80–81). Being caught by the guards, she fails to do this, and is brought before Creon.

Antigone and Ismene

Later adaptations of Sophocles' play see Antigone as the apogee of the rebel martyr, which intimates she is courageously following a conscious, idealistic doctrine,[7] while Ismene is usually regarded as a less courageous character without defined principles.[8] However, when one analyzes Antigone's utterances in response to Creon's edict, it is clear that she is reacting *ex tempore* without any motivation other than the fact that Polyneices is *her* brother, and therefore she has to bury him. Because Creon opposes her view, he is her enemy.

Her visceral disdain for Creon emerges in line 8, when instead of using his name she refers to him by the term *stratēgos*, "general," which, because it is a military title, has ramifications for what she is asking her sister to do. The plot assumption is that the victorious Creon has issued his edict when still on the battlefield functioning as a "general" after the death of Eteocles (7–8). He is on his way back to the city to make a public statement about his decision (33–34). By using this title, Antigone adds gravity to her demand that Ismene follow her lead in defying Creon, because an edict given by a *stratēgos* would require more absolute obedience than a similar edict from a *tyrannos,* a civil ruler. Antigone is thus characterized from the start as doubly rebellious, a woman who stands up not only to a civil leader but to a military commander. Her use of this military term also shows that she does not filter or consider her words, for she is using terminology that would reinforce Ismene's reluctance to help her.

Antigone approaches Ismene because she needs help lifting Polyneices' body and lowering it into a properly dug grave. As the guard will later tell Creon, the ground where Polyneices lies is hard and dry, not easy to dig (250–51). Antigone therefore relies on a close relationship with Ismene. In the first line, she emphasizes the family bond between them: *koinon autadelphon,* which literally translates as "my connected-by-common-origin / kindred, very sister." Every word suggests endearment and an atmosphere of unity and mutual support, which Antigone goes on to underscore in the next five lines when she speaks about their common past of suffering and endurance. However, once Ismene rejects her request, Antigone immediately severs all ties with her and focuses only on her unburied brother. Suddenly she claims that even if Ismene were to agree to cooperate with her in the future, she would not consent to have her as a collaborator (69–70). It seems that while Antigone thought of rhetorical ways of gaining Ismene's support, she did not expect a rejection, and her reaction is impromptu, spontaneous, and petulant. She spurns any possible future cooperation with Ismene by intensifying her own commitment to her brother. She now, for the first time, brings up her willingness to die if this is what it takes to bury her brother: "It is honorable for me to do this and die" (72), a claim that she will struggle with later when it is about to happen. The same is true of her outburst when Ismene suggests she tell no one about her plan. Antigone erupts: "Ah, tell them all! I shall hate you far more if you remain silent, and do not proclaim this to all" (86–87).

She justifies her resolve by an arresting and rather uncomplicated statement: she compares the relatively short time she will be with the living to the long time with the dead (73–76). This uncalled-for declaration smacks of an attempt to find a rational justification for her instinctual commitment to die, and will be repeated with greater detail when she marches toward her death in 904–20, explaining that she has buried Polyneices because she cannot have another brother now that her parents are dead. Her early, impromptu reasoning is a leitmotiv for the rest of her acts. Antigone is not a planner: she does not employ tactical gambits, but rather reacts *ex tempore.* As she digs herself into doing the "impossible," as Ismene defines it (92), she not only seems to be accepting certain death but also convinces herself that she will not suffer anything so terrible as to prevent her from dying honorably (96–97).

Antigone and Creon

Antigone admits to Creon that although she knew about his edict, she has not acted out of audacity but out of "consciousness of the penalty for disregarding gods' statues"

(Griffith 1999: on 458–60). Her self-defense involves the famous phrase "unwritten laws" that has been scrutinized incessantly by scholars. Was her belief in the unwritten laws what prompted her to bury her brother in the first place? If so, one would have expected her to mention it to Ismene when asking for help in burying Polyneices, especially since Ismene equated Creon's edict with the "law," *nomos* of the ruler, *tyrannos*, that is to say, Creon (59–60). One gets the impression that while Antigone "felt" she needed to bury Polyneices, saying that custom and propriety demand that she bury *her* kin (e.g. 71–77), she had not yet formulated the theoretical grounds for objecting to Creon's edict. She has busied herself with the burial and pouring libations, having no time for reflection on her stance and motivation. However, as she is escorted onstage by the guard and listens to both the Chorus rebuking her for transgressing Creon's "laws" (*nomoi*, 381–82), and as she hears Creon identifying his "proclamations" (*kēruchthenta*, 447) with "laws" (*nomoi*, 449), she rebels wholeheartedly against the assertion that Creon's broadcast "edict" (*kērygma*, 8) is a *nomos*, a "law" she should obey. The idea and phrase "unwritten laws" have not been formulated by her beforehand, but borrowed on the spot from what she hears as she is forcibly led in. What she hears sparks her emotions.

Creon's "law," *nomos*, defies the timeless and eternally valid, divinely sanctioned laws. These are distinct from the positivistic laws created by men (450–60). Divine laws do not need to be written or pronounced because they were always there and are taken for granted. Antigone is not positioning the laws of gods in opposition to those of men: for her, they are a continuum. By refusing to give proper burial to Polyneices, Creon has transgressed the human sphere of influence, and therefore his edict—or as he would like to call it, his "law"—is invalid in her eyes. On the other hand, by performing the duty dictated by kinship, she is obeying the laws of the gods. She has acted not from a set of preconceived principles, but from a semi-articulated idea of devotion to those of her own blood and from an assumed divine awareness. The scene is a forerunner of the one before the execution of her sentence, where Antigone makes a long speech in which she tries to reason out her own motives, as if to clarify to herself why her way was the right one. In phrasing her "unwritten laws," Antigone reacts on the spur of the moment to what she has just heard from Creon and the Chorus. Faced with Creon's legal terms, she answers in legal terms with carefully selected words. She has twice heard the word *nomoi* referring to the edict, and counters with *nomos'* derivative *nomimon*, which conveys better the original meaning of *nomos*, "what is customary," the neuter plural of which, *nomima* (455), usually meant "customs" (Knox 1966: 97). Her natural integrity and knowledge of right and wrong is intuitive.

Antigone's contentious reply to Creon's threats further demonstrates her impulsivity. Without any proof of inner audience sympathies, Antigone claims that "all these men [i.e. the Chorus] would approve this [i.e. her burial of Polyneices], if it were not that fear shuts their mouths" (504–05, cf. 508). How does she know this? She did not hear the conversation between the Chorus and Creon, in which the Elders refused to commit to Creon's demand that they not support his opponents (220), and only much later do they tell her that she has shown reverence by honoring her brother (872). Her claim about the Elders' fear arises from her own *fear* of a sure punishment that Creon has threatened in his last speech (473–96). She reacts to the idea of *fear* by transposing it from herself to the Elders.

When Creon questions her burial of Polyneices, who was the enemy of the city, and pits him against Eteocles, who was also her brother, Antigone utters her famous answer: "never was it in my nature to join in hating, but to join in loving" (Bayfield 1960). This statement, in which, as Griffith puts it, Antigone describes her own nature "and its inextricable involvement in 'family'" (1999: on 523), strongly contradicts the hatred she has expressed only a short time before for both Creon and Ismene, who also are her very close family (10, 86, 93). This spontaneous answer, however, is consistent with her former utterances, because she does not think things through in advance but reacts to what is in front of her.

It might well be that Antigone's silence about her betrothal to Haemon is not intentional or indicative of her disregard for him. All her utterances are reactive, mostly to what Creon has done or said, or to what Ismene says both when she rejects Antigone's request to help bury Polyneices, and when she later wants to share in Antigone's guilt. Since there is no context in which Antigone hears Haemon's name, she fails to mention him. She is not present when Ismene refers to Haemon begging Creon to save her sister's life (568–76).[9] However, the absence of Haemon in person in this scene and when she is on her way to her tomb enhances her growing feeling of complete abandonment.

Is Antigone Manly?

Some view Antigone as masculinized or as "androgynous" (e.g. O'Brien 1973: 6–7) because she has "masculine daring" and performs "chilling deeds."[10] However, the text containing Ismene's application of these "blemishes" to Antigone (92, 88) does not term them as masculine. There is nothing more chilling than Medea's killing of her children, but this act does not mark her as manly. It is true that Antigone hopes for fame (*kleos*, 502), which is the mark of a Homeric hero who strives for fame through battle, but a woman can also strive for fame (*Eur. Alc.* 150–51, 445–54) in her own sphere of accomplishments. She is an active heroine (unlike Ismene, whom scholars usually view as the average obedient female who does not defy authority), but this does not make her masculine. Sophocles' method of the binary presentation of the protagonist with a foil whose characterization often reveals the intricacies of the major figure, partly by allowing them to explain their motivations, is well known; he uses the same strategy with Electra and Chrysothemis (Kirkwood 1994: 100–01; Bowra 1952: 79–82). However, Antigone does not seem less feminine than Ismene. The plot gives her a fiancé, and by having Antigone mislead Ismene about the burial of Eteocles, as if it has already occurred, the playwright signposts her femaleness, as it was a common belief that women deceive. Antigone does not even bother to answer Ismene's caution that they are "women" who cannot battle against men (61–62), because this fact is not disputable. Antigone was aware, as every one of the spectators was, that women were subordinate to men. She is not fighting men, but following her conscience, and if this has ramifications beyond her control, she simply ignores them. In Aeschylus' *Seven against Thebes,* Antigone proclaims defiantly: "I shall myself, *woman though I am,* contrive to provide him [Polyneices] with funeral and burial" (1037–38). Antigone does not intend to strip away her womanhood when she decides to bury Polyneices. On the contrary, she does her duty as both kin and woman. The women of the family normally washed, dressed, and laid out the corpse in preparation for burial. They also undertook the subsequent libations over the tomb. Antigone also commits suicide in the traditional female way by hanging herself. Creon's emphasis on Antigone's femaleness, for instance, vowing that if Antigone is to enjoy impunity for her disobedience, "I am no man, but she is a man" (484, cf. 677–80, 746), reflects Creon's insecurity and personal anxiety over a woman's defying his authority rather than Antigone's masculinity.

Antigone's Punishment

Antigone laments her own death in a lyrical exchange with the Chorus without expressing any regret or surrender (806–82).[11] Such a lament is usually sung by the surviving members of a family after the death of a loved one. Since Antigone dis-acknowledges Ismene as her remaining kin and sees herself as the last of the house, she sings her own lament, one of the most lyrical dirges in extant Greek tragedy. The Theban Elders respond coldly, placing the full responsibility for her imminent death on Antigone's own head. She feels she is being mocked by them when she compares herself to Niobe, suspended between life and death, and they reprove her for her presumption in comparing herself to a goddess. Antigone's continuing rejection of the "laws" angers the Chorus, who despite their pity for her, still have no doubt that she has incurred her death by a willfully criminal act. They do, however, soften their harshness by addressing her as "child" (855) and by the suggestion at 856 that an inherited curse may be to blame.

Antigone again reacts to what she has heard last: that she belongs to an accursed house (1–6). She feels now that her fate can be explained in terms of her father's crimes. Ironically, her father's "crimes" were committed with no knowledge of what he was doing. Antigone by contrast, while she believed she was in the right, knew exactly what she was doing. She also bewails her brother's luckless marriage, which she now believes is cutting her life short, before she could be married. The Chorus for once show some sympathy for her in their final rather enigmatic comment: "The respect that you showed is a noble kind of respect" (872), but they immediately qualify their half-hearted commendation by claiming that one should not flout the power of the person to whom power belongs. They end by saying: "You were destroyed by your self-willed passion" (875). Antigone's final stanza shows how lonely, isolated, and abandoned she feels she is: "Unwept, friendless, unwedded, I am conducted, unhappy ... my fate unwept for, is lamented by no friend" (876–82). Antigone has no one at this hour of need. Why she is not calling upon Haemon, the play does not explain.

Creon intercedes, commenting that weeping and wailing before death will never end, and orders the guards to take Antigone to her tomb immediately (883–90). The guards, however, allow Antigone one last speech, which continues for thirty-eight lines (891–928). The speech is delivered in iambic trimeter, the spoken meter of reflection and analysis in tragic drama. Antigone tries to reason out her motives, which had remained unclear due to her spontaneity. She not only reiterates her sadness for not having a husband and children, but also gives an explanation for her insistence on burying Polyneices: since her parents are dead, she could not have another brother, while a husband or a child is replaceable (in spite of their oddity, no compelling scholarly grounds exist for athetizing 904–20). Her reasons might sound strange to our modern ears, but this explanation is also found in the *Histories* of Herodotus (3.119): when a wife is given the option to save one person from her condemned family, she chooses her brother instead of her husband or her children, giving the same reasoning.[12] It seems that it is the first time that Antigone explicates *to herself* what she has done on the basis of an impulse rooted in faith and piety beyond the realm of reason. Her act was caused by the inextricably intertwined personal love of what was hers, and by a supra-personal spiritual sense. She has no regrets.

Some critics are baffled when trying to reconcile the single-minded, intransigent heroine portrayed up to this point with the very human and sensitive Antigone of the lyrical exchange with the Chorus and her last speech. Has she changed her mind? Does she regret her decision to bury Polyneices now when she is faced with imminent death, as Creon predicted? There is absolutely no evidence for a change of mind. In fact, after hearing her speech, the Elders confirm her former passionate stubbornness and unbrokenness: "The same blasts of the same winds of the spirit still possess her" (929–30). She stands fast by what she has done, but she cannot truly understand why she is being punished: "What justice of the gods have I transgressed?" she asks (921). She also bemoans the horrid and cruel death chosen for her. As Brown has pointed out (1987: on 801–943), to the Greek thinking the transition of a person who died from the world of the living to the world of the dead is enacted by a "rite of passage," that is to say, the funeral procession from the person's home to the tomb (*ekphorā*). In Antigone's case the procession and the entombment, which formally part her from the living, take place while she is alive, and her forthcoming actual death will remain unmarked and unsolemnized, which for Antigone (with her keen sense of the importance of proper burial rites) is unbearable.

She reacts to this reversed sequence of events suddenly and, as always, without prior reflection. In the lyrical exchange she starts with what she feels is the most important to her and every young woman: her loss of marriage. When the Chorus mention that she is going to die with no illness, she dwells on the unusual living death that was decided for her, and hence compares herself to Niobe. When the Chorus mention the possibility that she pays for some crime of her father's, she again holds to what is important to her: the marriages that brought doom, while she dies still unmarried. When the Chorus rebuff her self-pity, she focuses on her loneliness. These kinds of impromptu reactions are in line with her former conversations with Ismene and Creon. She is not sorry for what she has done, but she laments the consequences, which she thinks are unjust: "For acting piously I have been convicted of impiety" (924 cf. 942–43). Antigone thinks that her death is a disgrace to Creon, but she also questions and reproaches the gods' lack of concern for her. Antigone expected to die (72–76, 460–64), but as she faces death, she cannot help feeling abandoned by the gods to whom she showed reverence.

Antigone is not mentioned by name once she exits with the guards to the place of her entombment. The Messenger will later report that Creon and his men, who came to release her, find her hanging with a noose around her neck and Haemon with his arms around her body lamenting his bride and the deeds of his father (1220–25).

The penalty laid down by Creon for disobeying his edict was stoning by the whole city (35–36). The spectators who remember this may suppose, after what Haemon said about the support that Antigone among the citizens, who were crying over the fate of the girl who they do not consider deserves to die (690–700), that Creon changes now his sentence because he is afraid that the people would refuse to carry it out. If so, he masks this fear by claiming that Antigone's slow starvation will prevent the pollution of the city since it will not have any violent contact with her death.[13] Teiresias, however, will disabuse him of the notion that he can avoid miasma by immuring Antigone alive. In his address to Creon, Teiresias underlines the symmetry between Creon's two crimes: refusing proper burial rites to Polyneices and entombing Antigone alive (Brown 1987: on 1068–71). Leaving the dead unburied is a form of pollution; burial of a living person would probably have been considered a form of homicide. Teiresias effectively shows that the crime against Antigone is a religious offence equivalent to Creon's crime against Polyneices. Creon's two offenses relate to the two fundamental categories of existence: life and death, each requiring its own form of respect. The dramatist's attitude to the practice of leaving a corpse unburied is not veiled. He reminds us repeatedly of the physical nastiness of the exposure (410–12, 697–98, 1016–22, 1039–44, 1080–83, 1198). The audience is made to feel that this is no way to treat the body of a human being. He is, however, less obvious about what he thinks of Antigone's entombment.

Conclusion

What is the play's verdict on Antigone? While the play is clear on Creon, it is not transparent in its view of Antigone. In spite of the fact that the play does applaud the principle she has died for, no one praises her except by implication. Although in their fourth song when already positioned on the *orchestra* (944–87) the Chorus try to reconcile Antigone to her fate by mythic exempla, nowhere do they justify her act, and we are pretty much left with their former cold chastisement of her. Creon is severely punished for his acts by the loss of Haemon and his wife. He is also clearly judged by the cold reproach from Teiresias. Antigone's act is not explicitly assessed by anyone. While the altars that refuse fire and the polluted sacrifices are blamed on the rotting corpse of Polyneices, no one says that Antigone's actual attempt to bury him was justified, even if symbolically it might have been the right thing to do.

Teiresias reproaches Creon for not burying Polyneices, but does not praise Antigone for trying to do so. She is not only abandoned to die in her dungeon, but, unlike the corpse of Eurydice that is displayed for the audience to pity, and the corpse of Haemon carried in Creon's arms, Antigone is disentangled from Haemon's embrace and left behind. Why is she commended in this scene only by implication? Is it because the scene was meant to focus on the fall of the house of Creon, and any mention of Antigone would have been a distraction?[14]

Is it possible that Sophocles is cautioning against Antigone's immature, self-centered view of the world with her particular first person speech patterns, her outright dismissal of all who disagree with her, and her own repeated emphasis on her youthful unwed status? Youthful zealots view the world as "black and white," disregarding the complex nuances that typically fill our lives. Antigone is so convinced that the ends justify the means that she does not spare a single thought for the consequences of her actions, until it is too late. She is then forced to face these consequences with such sudden brutality that she only has a few moments to reach some kind of maturity and start to consider the reasoning behind her actions and where they have led. These moments are too short, and she does not attain any understanding of why she is being punished. For her, if an action is in itself right, there can be no pertinent mitigating factors or reason to consider extenuating circumstances.

DISCUSSION TOPICS

1. In his dramatization of his two young heroines, Antigone and Electra, Sophocles chooses to use dialogues with their sisters, Ismene and Chrysothemis respectively, to add extra dimensions to his protagonist. Compare and contrast the relationships between the two sets of sisters.

2. Antigone's decision to bury her brother Polyneices is caused by Creon's decision to forbid his burial. Further in the play the two figures constantly oppose each other without any inclination to find a middle ground between them. Are the characters of the two main opposing protagonists, Antigone and Creon, very different from each other?

3. If Antigone had been the ruling monarch at the time of Polyneices' attack on the city, do you think she might have acted differently with regard to his corpse?

4. The appeal of Sophocles' Antigone has lasted until modern day, with many adaptations focussing on Antigone as a rebel defying Creon's authority. Interestingly, the play has also been popular with supporters of tyrannical regimes. So, for example, during the Second World War productions were presented by the Nazi regime in Germany and by those sympathizing with the resistance in France. During the last decade a film version was produced focusing on displaced immigrants in Canada, while an adaption focussing on women's rights has been shown in Teheran. Do you think that the play can be interpreted as supporting Creon as well as Antigone? How do you think that the characterization of Antigone may allow these varying characterizations?

5. Antigone's resistance to Creon is presented as being rooted in preferring the immortal laws of the gods, over transient manmade laws. Can you think of modern-day parallels where preferring ancient behavioral codes over modern ones may also be perceived as being rebellious or revolutionary?

6. The play punishes both Antigone and Creon. Antigone loses her life while Creon loses his son and wife. Do the punishments meted out in the play seem just? Why or why not?

7. Antigone bemoans the fact that she will die unwed, yet she is engaged to be married. Had she already been married, do you think she would have continued to prioritize her loyalty to her dead brother over that to her husband and family?

8. Various references are made by both Haemon and Antigone to their upcoming marriage. Do you think that Sophocles presents their differing attitudes in relation to gender or that his characterizations go beyond that? Do you think that either of them is committed to the idea of this marriage? Do their actions follow their words?

9. What does the play say about single-mindedness, whether Antigone's or Creon's? While Antigone is a young girl, Creon is a grown monarch. Do you think that either circumstance excuses or gives reason for their stubborn attitudes? Explain.

10. Ismene's characterization contrasts strongly with that of Antigone. It is reasonable to consider that sisters with such differing personalities would clash over many issues. Is Ismene portrayed as cowardly or loving, although she defies Antigone and refuses to participate in a proper burial?

CHAPTER 5
HELEN

Mythic background

In myth, Helen, the semi-divine offspring of Zeus (in the form of a swan) and the mortal Leda, was born from an egg. Helen's supreme beauty attests her divine parentage. Through her adoptive mortal father Tyndareus she has a twin half-sister, Clytemnestra. As a young girl Helen, was abducted by Theseus, with some versions claiming that this rape resulted in the birth of Iphigenia, who was then given to Clytemnestra to raise. When Helen reached marriageable age, Tyndareus chose Menelaus from among the many suitors competing for her hand, having previously required an oath from them that they would help the winner if Helen were to abscond. Tragedy inherited two competing mythic accounts of Helen. The first version comes from the Homeric epics, wherein Helen, the most beautiful of all woman, has eloped with Paris to Troy and a Greek armada has been launched to retrieve her. While the gods were supposedly partially responsible for Helen's actions, since Helen had been awarded to Paris by Aphrodite (who disregarded her marriage to Menelaus), it is often assumed that Helen was complicit in her abduction. Troy is burnt to ashes after years of carnage on both sides, and the Trojan women are enslaved. Helen is brought back to Sparta, where she lives a rather unhappy life with her lawful husband Menelaus. Both Homeric epics describe a woman who castigates herself for eloping with Paris, but despite blaming herself for the war, she does not necessarily condemn her own lack of morality. In fact, the *Iliad* portrays Helen as a complex and suffering figure with a good mind, who strives for autonomy, expression, and belonging, within and despite the many constraints to which she is subject: she is a captive and a possession; she is subjected to the whims of the gods; and she is an abhorred foreigner viewed as the cause of suffering and strife. The epic contains six encounters, which show her maneuvering within those constraints, while retaining and asserting her own personhood.[1] The *Odyssey* shows her back in Sparta living with her husband. No judgment is made of her except her own self-recriminations.[2] Lyric poetry (Alcaeus frags. 42, 283, Page 1970: 275–81, nos. 2–3; Campbell 1982: 256–59, 332–33) tends to condemn Helen for the adulterous behavior that provoked a devastating war. In the 420s, however, Gorgias of Leontini, a Sicilian Greek orator, wrote *Encomium of Helen,* a rhetorical attempt to exonerate Helen for her elopement.

The alternative version of events is presented by texts from as early as the Homeric version. Both Hesiod (frag. 358 M-W) and Stesichorus (in his *Palinode,* frag. 192–93, Page *PMG*: 104–06) attest that only a phantom (or *eidolon*) of Helen is in Troy, while the "real" Helen in Egypt is absolved of wrongdoing. Herodotus (2.115–120), preceding Stesichorus, makes no reference to this phantom story, but like Stesichorus claims to have learned in Egypt from priests at Pharaoh's shrine in Memphis that Paris had indeed abducted Helen from Sparta, but on his way back to Troy was blown off course and was forced to make landing in Egypt. Discovering Paris' crime, the Pharaoh detained Helen and sent Paris back to Troy despoiled of his prize. The Greeks, unaware that Helen was not at Troy, waged their war against Troy and discovered the truth only after they had sacked the city.

The treatments of the myth of Helen have had to grapple with these inherited dualities: her mortal and immortal origins; her depiction as a shameless beauty seduced by Paris versus the blameless heroine who never went to Troy; and her own conflicting attitudes of distress and self-disapproval contrasting with complete rejection of any responsibility.

Introduction

While tragedy is not flattering to Helen, it does not dwell on the woman whose face has launched a thousand ships (Christopher Marlowe, *Doctor Faustus,* Act V, scene 1). Although she is mentioned numerous times and always with ferociously negative implications, she appears less often in her own persona. She is reminiscent of the many beautiful women who are objectified: talked about, but seldom heard. The only dramatist who brings Helen on stage is Euripides, in three of his tragedies: *Trojan Women* (415), *Helen* (412), and *Orestes* (408). The *Trojan Women* and *Helen*, the two plays that deal with Helen's persona at length, present contrasting depictions of Helen since Euripides based the two characterizations on different versions of the myth.[3] Thus it is unclear whether Helen is to be considered a passive receiver of the will of the gods or as a woman to be held fully responsible for her deeds. While *Trojan Women* and *Orestes* depict a vain, self-centered Helen repeatedly blamed for all the carnage, *Helen* offers a complex portrayal of Helen's alternate tale and rebuts images of her culpability, being closer to Stesichorus' account of Helen in Egypt than to Gorgias' *Encomium of Helen* (D-K F B11). The latter work, however, may have influenced Helen's speeches in *Trojan Women*.[4]

The dualities inherent to the persona of Helen have been useful in analyzing the treatment of women in tragedy, and particularly in Euripidean tragedy.[5] While distinctions are made between male subjects and female objects, tragedy as a whole gives the objects a voice. As with the varying characterizations of Helen, this voice may participate actively in events or merely offer her subjective view, but by being articulated, the woman's position becomes active, practical, and political. The texts may be oppressive, but could also be subversive, containing an active negotiation between the hegemonic (dominant groups) and the counter-hegemonic (those opposing or criticizing those groups).[6] Helen, as the most beautiful of women, could be regarded as the most feminine of the heroines, with some claiming that beauty is definitive of female excellence in Athenian culture.[7] However, in at least some of the portrayals, as in *Trojan Women*, Helen is far more active in her own defense than would be expected from an "ideal" female. Furthermore, Helen's lack of loyalty to her husband and daughter would, at least for the Athenians, detract from any potential qualities of feminine excellence. However, while she may be considered a 'failed' woman for her transgressions, she can hardly be considered "masculine" like her half-sister Clytemnestra, who has killed a man. The very ambiguity in Helen's characterization invites discussion not only of gender and social relations, but also of divine intervention in human affairs, some of the main concerns of tragedy. However, the misdemeanors attributed to Helen might also have served to help convince the Athenians that social controls restricting women's visibility, movement and voice were well justified.

* * *

Perhaps the most feminine heroine of all, famed for her many suitors, Helen is described later by Christopher Marlowe, an English playwright of the Elizabethan era, as the woman whose "face launched a thousand ships." Euripides presents three different versions of Helen, with only one trait agreed upon in all three: her physical beauty. Other traits and contradictions in her characterization include:

- contrasting with her physical beauty, Helen receives a broadly negative characterization in tragedy, achieved in part through the deep hatred towards her expressed by many other characters;
- as the daughter of Zeus, Helen combines her femininity and beauty with an innate intelligence, a combination which she often uses to manipulate those around her;
- as opposed to the self-centered woman who has betrayed Menelaus portrayed in *Trojan Women*, in *Helen* she is portrayed as a loyal wife, capable of using deceit, strategic planning and logical thought in order to rescue herself and her husband; despite or perhaps because of her supreme femininity Helen is a rule unto herself, showing no regard for societal norms, and apparently fearing no man or no woman, perhaps a prerogative of those gifted with extreme physical beauty!

HELEN IN EURIPIDES' *TROJAN WOMEN*

Euripides' Trojan trilogy: *Alexander, Palamedes,* and *Trojan Women*

Trojan Women was the third play of a trilogy produced in the City Dionysia in the spring of 415 BCE, when Euripides was already 69 years old. *Trojan Women* is the only play extant; the others were the *Alexander* and the *Palamedes*. The fourth play was the *Sisyphus*, a satyr play. The trilogy won second prize (Aelian, *Varia Historia* ii. 8; *scholion* to Aristophanes, *Birds* 842), one of the five prizes (one posthumous) won by Euripides in the City Dionysia. All three tragedies concern events from the long story of the Trojan War. While each playwright competing in the Dionysia presented a series of three tragedies and one satyr play at the City Dionysia, this trilogy had several distinctive features (Barlow 1986: 26–27). First, the thematic connection between the three tragedies is unusual in Euripides' repertoire. At the date when the trilogy was presented, tragedians did not typically present a series of three plays following on from each other; over 40 years had passed since 458 BCE, when Aeschylus first presented his *Oresteia*, in which the plays told a connected, ongoing story. Second, although events on stage may be assumed to be metaphorical and not directly associated with the physical world of the audience, it is still reasonable to surmise that they may well have been reminded of the recent siege and total destruction of Melos by the Athenians in the winter of 416–415 BCE, whether intended to do so or not.[8] (See Box on the Peloponnesian War; the Destruction of Melos, pp. 141–142) The third distinctive feature of *Trojan Women* is the portrayal of the effects of war through the eyes of women as the war's main victims, something Euripides has done previously with the play *Hecuba* (see Chapter 6, pp. 167–177). In this respect the play rejects the epic tradition that presents war predominantly as a glorified male affair.

The first play, *Alexandros,* of which we have only some 193 lines (Kannicht, 2004: vol. 5.1 3 frags. 41a–63) focused on the recognition of Paris, who was abandoned in infancy by his parents, discovered in his adulthood, and reinstated as a prince of Troy.[9] The second tragedy, *Palamedes*, of which fewer than 40 lines survive (Kannicht 2004: vol. 5.2: frags. 578–90), dealt with the Greek mistreatment of their fellow Greek, Palamedes, probably casting blame on Odysseus. When Odysseus was feigning madness to avoid going to war against Troy, Palamedes exposed his trickery. Odysseus then forged a letter, framing Palamedes as a traitor. While Palamedes is not mentioned by Homer, Aeschylus, Sophocles, and Euripides all dealt with this episode. It seems that the theme of Palamedes, who is attributed with inventing writing, dying because of a written letter, was understandably popular with tragedians. The third play, *Trojan Women*, depicts the horrors faced by the women of Troy after the long war resulting from Paris' actions. Only one tiny fragment of *Sisyphos* survives (Kannicht 2004: vol. 5.2: 62 frag. 673).

Euripides' *Trojan Women*

Set shortly after the fall of Troy to the Greeks, the ruins of Troy serve as the background. Poseidon laments the fall of the city, placing the blame on Hera and Athena; naming Helen as being justly counted amongst the captives, and describing the fate of 'Hecuba the Queen of Misery'. Angered by Ajax the Lesser's dragging Cassandra out of her temple, Athena seeks to make peace with Poseidon and asks for Poseidon's help in destroying the Greeks' fleet on its way home. Poseidon is happy to oblige.

Lying in front of Troy's ruins, alongside the Chorus of Trojan women, Hecuba sings an emotional monody for herself and Troy. Talthybius, the Herald of the Greek army, announces that the Greeks are due to sail that day, and announces to whom the women have been allocated as slaves: Cassandra is to share Agamemnon's bed; Polyxena, another daughter of Hecuba and Priam, is to serve Achilles' grave; Andromache is to go with Achilles' son, Neoptolemus; and Hecuba with Odysseus. Before Cassandra is taken away she predicts Agamemnon's murder and Odysseus' future troubles. Hecuba's tale of woe seems to be more than she can physically bear, until Andromache enters and tells her that Polyxena was sacrificed on Achilles' grave. Then Talthybius returns and announces that Odysseus has convinced the Greek commanders that Astyanax, the toddler son of Hector and Andromache, must be thrown to his death from the ramparts of Troy. After two thirds of the play Menelaus enters, announcing that he will take his wife Helen back to Greece for execution to punish her for her elopement with Alexandros to Troy. Hecuba immediately intercedes, appealing to Menelaus to slay Helen immediately, without looking at her, lest she may bewitch him. Helen demands to speak in her own defense and Hecuba urges Menelaus to hear Helen out but to also give her, Hecuba, the right to counter Helen's claims. In the formal debate that ensues, Hecuba clearly defeats Helen's arguments. Menelaus agrees that Helen should be killed, but takes her away, against Hecuba's advice, to his own ship for the journey home. Talthybius returns with the corpse of Astyanax on Hector's shield, and the little boy is buried. The Greeks set fire to the city. Hecuba tries to throw herself into the flames but is held back by the soldiers. The play ends with Hecuba and the Trojan women lamenting the city as they are led away to their appointed Greek masters.

Peloponnesian War, the end of an era

After several defeats of their armies, the Persians' attacks against Athens abated from 478 BCE. By this time the Athenians had forged a broadly based alliance called the Delian League. Athens built up economic and military power rapidly at this time, with newly found precious metals financing the building of a large naval fleet. While Sparta maintained the advantage during onshore warfare, they felt threatened by Athens. The so-called First Peloponnesian War was fought mostly between Athens and Sparta's allies, from around 461–445 BCE. After attempting a series of truces from 449, a peace treaty was finally ratified in 445, but only lasted fourteen years. The balance of power between the warring factions was affected by the outbreak of plague in 430–427, when many Athenians died, including the Athenian general, Pericles (d. 429). The new leadership including Cleon and Demosthenes were more aggressive and led Athens into a series of offensive campaigns. Cleon, spreading an atmosphere of distrust in Athens, also prosecuted playwrights on the charge of impiety. This may well have affected the freedom of expression, with an appearance of neutrality necessary for survival. By 421 both Cleon and the Spartan general Brasidas had been killed in battle, and the Peace of Nicias was signed. Although the treaty lasted almost six years, the period was not devoid of political maneuvering as Argos, Mantinea and Elis, three states to the north of Sparta, formed a coalition with Athens against Sparta but were defeated in 418. Following a devastating defeat in 415 in an offensive campaign against Syracuse and ten more years of fighting, the Athenian fleet was finally destroyed in 405 and Athens was defeated. The 'Golden Age' of Athens had come to an end.

The destruction of Melos

Alcibiades, an Athenian leader, encouraged the Athenians to adopt an aggressive foreign policy. During the summer of 416 BCE, the Athenians sent 3,400 armed men to the tiny island of Melos which lies about 160 km to the southeast of Athens. Probably influenced by the rhetoric of Alcibiades, the Athenians demanded that the islanders pay tribute as subordinate allies. Having maintained neutrality throughout the Peloponnesian war, the islanders refused. The Athenians laid siege to the city, captured it, executed all of the men and sold the women and children into slavery. Both the Athenians and the Spartans had carried out similar atrocities after previous battles, but this felt particularly dishonorable to the historian Thucydides, who chose to immortalize the siege and the negotiations in his Melian Dialogue.

Helen's Vilification Before Her Entrance: Poseidon, Hecuba, Andromache, Cassandra and Menelaus

Although Helen herself only enters the stage in *Trojan Women* after 894 lines have been spoken (out of 1332 lines), the idea that Helen is culpable for the woes of both Trojans and Greeks is hinted at from the first moments of the Prologue, when Poseidon describes a city in smouldering ruins. Indeed, after he describes Troy's sudden downfall, famously brought about by the introduction of the wooden horse into the city, Poseidon names Helen before referring to any of the Trojan women waiting to hear their fate. Poseidon then mentions the long-suffering Queen of Troy, Hecuba; her daughter Polyxena, who has been put to death (although Hecuba is as yet unaware of this); and her surviving daughter Cassandra, who has lost her senses. Although Poseidon initially blames Hera and Athena for initiating the destruction, he is happy to oblige when Athena (his niece) enters, asking to make peace with him, and requesting his help in punishing the Greeks for desecrating her temple. It seems that no one is to return unharmed from this miserable war.

Euripides presents the spectators with increasingly devastating descriptions of what the Trojan women have endured, allowing these brutalized survivors of the horrors of war to blame Helen repeatedly for their suffering. Hecuba is lying on the ground, a defeated and broken woman, in sharp contrast to her previous position as Queen of Troy. In her song, Hecuba assigns the blame for the fall of Troy to "Menelaus' hateful wife," who disgraced Castor (see p. 15) and brought ill fame upon Sparta. The Chorus of captive Trojan women enter, asking Hecuba for news. When she tells them that the Greeks are sailing home that very day and that each woman will learn to whom she has been assigned as a slave, they beg not to be taken "to the hateful home of Helen" (211).

Talthybius, the Greeks' Herald, enters (235) announcing that Cassandra has been assigned to Agamemnon and Polyxena to Achilles' tomb: that is, she is to be sacrificed on his grave. Andromache will be given to Neoptolemus, and Hecuba to Odysseus. While Hecuba bewails her fate, it is only the frenzied Cassandra who finds something to rejoice at, as she has foreseen that her wedding to Agamemnon will bring about his death, thus avenging the fall of Troy. However, her celebrations are perverse to say the least, as she knows that she too will meet her death in Agamemnon's palace. Cassandra defines the devastating effect she will have on Agamemnon by calling herself "a wife more disastrous than Helen" (357). Helen seems to be the reference point against which all evil women can be measured. Her words serve as another reminder of how deadly Helen proved to Menelaus, Paris, and Deiphobus, all of her husbands. In terms of family relationships, Cassandra maintains that Troy, although vanquished, is more fortunate than Greece. The Trojans fought for their own city; those who did not perish were daily at home with their wives and children. The Greeks on the other hand were far away from their families, and those who died were buried in foreign soil, with no family members to attend them (372–99). Thus, Cassandra poisons further the future appearance of Helen by stating that countless lives were lost because of Helen, and that Helen "was abducted of her own free will, not forcibly" (373), a potent oxymoron, as the contradiction between being "abducted" and "free will" is blatant.

After Cassandra is led away, the audience's attention returns to Hecuba lying on the ground in hopeless misery. She describes her fall from being the royal mother of valiant sons and beautiful daughters to her present status as a captive, who has suffered the ordeal of seeing her husband slain at the altar, her sons die, and her virgin daughters torn away from her. She laments her future as a servant in the household of Odysseus. Hecuba sums up her unhappiness by saying: "what sufferings I have and shall continue to have because of a single marriage of *one woman*" (498–99), referring of course to her hated daughter-in-law.

The following scene with Andromache continues to undermine Helen's persona. Andromache blames Paris' hateful "couch," a reference to his marriage to Helen, as the reason for the smouldering Troy. Her self-portrayal as the "perfect" wife emphasizes the deficiencies of Helen. She claims that Helen is the offspring of the Avenging Spirit, Envy, Slaughter, Death "and all the miseries that the earth breeds" (767–69). While Andromache, widow of Hector, joins Hecuba in her laments, neither woman is yet aware of the full extent of their troubles. Talthybius arrives with bitter tidings: Astyanax, Andromache and Hector's baby son, is to be thrown from the city ramparts to his death. Talthybius blames this horrendous deed on Odysseus, who has convinced the army that it was necessary. This shocking news, delivered shortly before the arrival of Menelaus, serves as a backdrop of horror and anguish, and further emphasizes the pain Helen has caused.

When Menelaus finally enters at line 860, the spectators might have expected a fiery verbal castigation of his straying wife. Surprisingly, however, he claims that he did *not* come to Troy to retrieve his wife at all, but to avenge himself on Paris (864–68). This statement does not compliment Helen, though it implicitly supports her upcoming claim that she had no say in her departure. However, here again Euripides shows his mastery of saying and unsaying a fact. Menelaus' statement suggesting that retrieving Helen is secondary to his desire for revenge is undercut by his claim that he won't call his wife by name but only as the "Spartan woman" after having just called her by name a few lines earlier and continuing to do so few lines later after this bizarre announcement (862, 869–71, and 877).

To the spectators, Menelaus' claims about his motivation, as well as his intent to kill Helen, were unbelievable, not only because killing Helen would counter Athenian law, according to which a husband could not kill his adulterous wife but only banish her (see Box on Trial anomalies, p. 145),[10] but also because this would be an unlikely reversal of a very well-known myth. Furthermore, later sparring between the spouses indicates that Menelaus has not forgotten the pain of being abandoned.

Menelaus' entrance puts Helen in the spotlight again, even though she has still not been seen on stage. Menelaus' statement that he will put her to death as compensation to all those whose loved ones have been killed at Troy (873–79) is another reminder to the audience of the numerous deaths she is responsible for. Hecuba, however, is wary of the effect Helen might have on her husband. She is well aware of Helen's charms and the magic she can work on men (890–94). She fears that Helen will quickly persuade Menelaus to change his mind if they are ever alone together.

Helen has not yet appeared; her entrance is delayed as behoves the star of the drama. Moreover, here her late entrance gave Euripides the opportunity to prejudice the audience's judgment of her through the other characters' vilifications. Taking further advantage of her absence, Hecuba tries to convince Menelaus to kill Helen on the spot rather than take her back to Sparta.

Helen's Entrance

At long last Helen emerges from the tent where the captive women are being held by Menelaus' attendants. She is dressed splendidly, in contrast to the other Trojan women. Concerned only with herself, she asks Menelaus about her fate. On hearing that it is up to him whether to kill her or not, she asks to show him that killing her would be unjust (901-904). Menelaus vacillates, but Hecuba presses him to agree, promising to crush Helen's self-defense. The speeches of the two adversaries are cast as a formal debate (*agon*, see Box on Formal Debate, p. 45) with Menelaus as the judge, in the manner of a court trial, the proceedings of which were very familiar to the audience, who also liked such dramatic scenes.[11]

A few anomalies mark this formal debate, however, none of which favor Helen. While it is usual for the defendant to speak second, Helen speaks first, perhaps because Euripides wants to present her as over-confident, or because the outcome has been already decided—Menelaus wants to take her back to Sparta—and the customary sequence would not serve to create suspense.[12] On the face of it, by allowing Helen to speak first,

---

Trial anomalies

The evocation of legal oratory in a tragedy must have been popular with Athenian audiences, since Euripides includes "formal debates" in most of his tragedies.[13] A few anomalies mark the one presented in *Trojan Women*. While it is usual for the defendant to speak second, Helen, like Clytemnestra in Euripides' *Electra*, speaks first, perhaps because the outcome has been already decided and the customary sequence would not serve to create suspense. A further procedural twist marks Helen's speech. In cases of adultery, the wife had no place in the pleadings: the business at the court was conducted solely between the husband and the man with whom the wife had the affair. If she wished to assert her innocence, she could do it only through her *kyrios*, the man who was in charge of her, or another well-disposed person.[14] Euripides, however, allows Helen not only to plead her case but also to treat Menelaus as her opponent rather than as the judge, while ignoring Hecuba, her actual adversary (a strategy that ultimately backfires).[15] This formal debate has attracted frequent scholarly attention mainly because of its unusual court-like ambience and rhetoric. Under Athenian law, well-known to the spectators, Menelaus could banish Helen as his straying wife and was forbidden from continuing to live with her, but he could not legally kill her for adultery (Harrison 1998: vol. I, 35–36). He could execute her only if he viewed her as an enemy captive. After the formal debate, Menelaus at first decides to have her stoned, but changes his mind in favor of taking her back to Sparta, promising to kill her there, a decision he had already made before the two speeches. Thus, the trial has a foregone outcome.

contrary to the practice of the law courts, Euripides lets Helen control the narrative of the charges against her, and thus seemingly gives her the upper hand. However, such a strategy allows the accuser to produce additional accusations and redefine those already made, which the defendant cannot then counter. This is why such a sequence was not allowed in the courts. Indeed, Hecuba capitalizes on this anomaly by mounting accusations that Helen has no opportunity to answer and by redefining those Helen has admitted to.

Helen's Speech in Her Formal Debate With Hecuba

GORGIAS OF LEONTINI

Gorgias of Leontini in Sicily (c. 483–c. 385 BCE) was an ancient Greek sophist, pre-Socratic philosopher, and rhetorician. He was one of the most influential sophists who specialized in teaching rhetoric. With great ingenuity he could find arguments to support any case as is evidenced in his extant *Encomium of Helen*. His prose style is marked by word-play, verbal echoes, short symmetrical clauses, and rhythmically balanced antitheses. In the *Encomium of Helen* Gorgias uses these stylistic tools to overturn criticisms of Helen, presenting her instead as a worthy woman who deserves great praise.

Despite scholarly opinion that Euripides, as an Athenian playwright writing tragedies competing at the Dionysia festival, was not writing political commentary, and was unlikely to express any personal criticism of the incumbent regime,[16] it is hard to escape his focus on the suffering of people who did not hold political power in fifth-century Athens, particularly women and slaves. Euripides frequently demonstrates a remarkable creative drive, presenting his characters in new ways, and not shying away from unpopular topics, or from interpretations that differ from the consensus. Subversive as he is,[17] Euripides portrays Helen defending herself along the lines of Gorgias in his *Encomium of Helen* (see above Box on Gorgias of Leontini), which aimed to exculpate Helen from blame for the Trojan War by arguing that she was

- taken by force;
- compelled by the gods;
- persuaded by speeches; or
- blinded by love.

Thematically, Helen's speech is divided into four topics. They are logically connected together, but when viewed in isolation from each other, each actually vies with the others for their lack of plausibility:

1. Rather than Helen being in any way culpable it is Hecuba and Priam who are to blame for giving Paris life and not putting the infant to death after being warned that he would bring harm to his city (919–22).[18]
2. The three goddesses who awarded Helen as a prize to Paris were to blame for Helen arriving in Troy and the war that followed. Furthermore, Helen claims that she actually deserves gratitude from Greece (924–37). Had Paris chosen Hera or Athena as the most beautiful, Greece would then have been enslaved by Trojans.
3. She was victim with no agency of her own, with Aphrodite being to blame for her leaving Sparta. Thanks to Aphrodite's machinations, she was overpowered by love for Paris. If even Zeus was a slave of Aphrodite, what chance had she? (940–50).[19]
4. After Paris's death, Deiphobus took her as his wife *by force*. Again, she is not to blame. She had no hand in this and wanted in fact to escape to the Greek ships as the gatekeepers and the tower watchmen can testify. She finishes her points with a bold statement in which she equates her possible punishment at Menelaus' hands to an affront against the gods: "if you wish to overpower the gods, your desire is a foolish one" (964–65). Helen shows no fear.

The arguments are well developed in line with Gorgias's arguments, holding their own internal logic. Beyond that context they seem incredible. They are tainted by the Sophist rhetorical style connected with Gorgias, that favored style over factual content. The Athenians at this time were highly suspicious of the Sophists, who taught rhetoric designed to argue either or both sides of a case with no concern for the truth. This Sophist rhetoric has already been attacked before Helen's appearance when Talthybius announced that Odysseus' power of speech has brought about the decision to throw the young Astyanax from Troy's ramparts (721–24). Hecuba even earlier accused Odysseus of double talk and of twisting words (285–87). Helen's rhetorical attempt to nullify the reality of her guilt falls into the category of such a double speech: she is portrayed as another Odysseus, with the connotations of death and destruction that come with his name at this point of the story.

Helen's argument about the power of (sexual) love (*eros*) has also been thematically undermined before her entrance. Talthybius described Agamemnon's irresistible passion for Cassandra, which Cassandra herself prophesied as his death verdict, and the Chorus have just sung about the *eros* of Zeus and Aurora for the Trojans Ganymede and Tithonus, respectively, which did not save Troy (413–16, 840–59). Helen's self-defense, with its strategic reliance on Odyssean rhetorical acumen and the invocation of the power of *eros*, has been countered even before it begins.

Like Gorgias', Helen's speech shows intellectual acumen and linguistic skill, but its almost perfect logical flow and carefully constructed narrative-dividers in the form of chronological tricolon ("first," 919; "next," 923; "then," 931; cf. 938–39, 945, 951) make it sound rehearsed. It is clear from her three counter points (topics 2, 3, 4 above), in which she tries to show the lack of her own agency, that she not only has thought about the claims that can be brought against her, but also knows how she should have behaved. Her studied excuses are less emotive than Hecuba's more spontaneous-seeming claims which will be discussed soon, making Helen's speech less moving to the audience.

Although predating Aristotle by many decades, Euripides' contrast between the effects of the two speeches validates Aristotle's recommendations for the structure of a persuasive speech, written decades later. Aristotle recommended that first the orator should project a moral character (*ethos*) that will render him/her worthy of the hearer's confidence (*Rhetoric* 1355b–1356a = i.12-i.ii.7, esp. in i.ii.3) – a confidence due to the speech itself, not to any preconceived idea. Second, the speech ought to put the hearer into a favorable frame of mind by arousing emotion (*pathos*). Third, a logical argument (*logos*) is needed.[20] Euripides seems to foresee Aristotle's ideas. The speeches Euripides developed for Helen and Hecuba could almost be prototypes for successful and less successful speeches according to Aristotle. Whereas certain aspects of Helen's character and her unique circumstances prevent her from following every aspect of a persuasive speech, Hecuba is not hampered by these encumbrances.

The first Aristotelian requirement for projecting a moral character is obviously difficult for Helen. Her speech cannot be isolated from her dramatic persona. As we have seen, she has already been vilified by almost every other character, Greek, Trojan, or divine. The list of people Helen chooses to blame for her own actions, including Hecuba and Priam as well as the gods, destroys her credibility from the outset. Her refusal to take responsibility for any of her acts by claiming either divine or human coercion, which is Gorgias' first excuse, does not put her in a positive light. Aristotle was cautious about the second attribute of a persuasive speech, *pathos* – the emotion a speech should arouse in the audience; yet he deemed it necessary for convincing an audience. When the audience is predisposed to hate the speaker, any attempt at pathos may be doomed to failure. Finally, when forming the logical elements of Helen's argument, *logos*, Euripides favors implicit dialectic (within which type of discourse the connection between points is not always immediately evident) as the most successful strategy for persuasion, with Euripides being the master of it.[21]

However, Helen not only accuses Menelaus of being stupid enough to leave her alone with Paris by sailing away from home (940–44), she also explicitly expresses her grudge about not being appreciated as the savior of Greek freedom (932–37). More significantly, the audience hear her blaming Hecuba, an old woman in rags, a captive, a widow, and a mother who has lost her children and grandchild. Such coldness cannot arouse a favorable attitude from the external audience. She fails to convince even her most ardent listener, Menelaus, who does not believe she was divinely coerced but rather left of her own free will for the bed of a "stranger" (1037–38).[22] He thinks that the divine element was introduced by Helen as a boast about her beauty (1038–39), indicating that he has not bought into Helen's implied appeal for pity as victim of her own attractiveness (935–36). In sum, Euripides presents Helen as skillful in setting and formulating her argument, but unable to arouse the listeners' emotions in her favor. A logically designed argument without a morally convincing persona and the ability to arouse positive feeling in the audience, even when adorned by eloquence, cannot render a speech convincing. This becomes very clear with Hecuba's rebuttal.

Hecuba's Rebuttal

As she promised to Menelaus, Hecuba overturns and undermines Helen's points one by one (except the first one[23]), and adds additional damning blame which Helen, having spoken first, cannot counter. In the first part of her speech (969–86), in the spirit of the enlightened fifth-century myth-criticism, Hecuba demythologizes and dismantles Helen's claim of divine compulsion, and thus strips Helen of her main claim that she is not responsible for her acts. Hecuba mocks the claim about the three goddesses. Indeed Aristotle himself cites this speech, considering the weakest and most easily refuted of Helen's pleas, to be this one, and using the beginning of Hecuba's speech as an example of a second speaker successfully undoing the impression left by an opponent (*Rhetoric* 1418b17–22 = iii.xvii.15). Hecuba shows that it would be foolish for Hera, the main deity of Argos, to sell Argos to the barbarians, as it would have been for Athena to subjugate Athens to the Phrygians.[24] She paints Helen's excuse as an affront to the goddesses and thus denies Helen divine favor, while declaring herself the goddess's champion, thus countering Helen's threat to Menelaus that her punishment would be an affront to the gods. Her demythologizing also contradicts Helen's arrogant claim that she ought to have been publicly honored for assuring Greek freedom.

In the spirit of rationalization, Hecuba points to the improbability of either Hera or Athena vying in a contest about beauty, which for Hecuba is important only in the case of marriage. She wonders sarcastically whether Hera sought the judgment "so that she could get a better husband than Zeus", or whether Athena, who had begged for the gift of maidenhood, would be desirous at all of marriage (978–81).[25] Hecuba warns Helen not to attribute "foolishness" to the goddesses in an attempt to excuse her own misconduct. "I fear that you won't convince the sensible," she says (982).

After absolving Hera and Athena of any involvement in Helen's misconduct, Hecuba turns to the exculpation of Aphrodite. She derides Helen's claim that Paris arrived at Sparta "with no small goddess at his side" (940), under whose influence she eloped with him to Troy. By rationalizing Helen's words, she declares the claim "an utter absurdity" (983–84), wondering why the goddess couldn't transport Helen, and for that matter all of the city of Amyclae, to Troy without bothering to leave heaven at all (985–86).[26]

After combating and demolishing her opponent's main arguments about divine interference, Hecuba substantiates her own case against Helen, as Aristotle will later recommend (*Rhetoric* 1418b5–22). In the second part of her speech (987–97), she details the roots of Helen's malfeasance. It was not divine coercion but uncontrolled lust for the handsome Paris and a craving for Troy's wealth and life of luxury that motivated the adultery. Sparta was known for its stringent life bereft of luxury and comfort, as the audience knew well. As Lee puts it, Euripides attributes to Hecuba "a sound piece of psychology": Aphrodite, the external force Helen blames for her actions, was nothing but her own desires.[27]

In the third part of her speech (998–1028), Hecuba continues her assault by belittling Helen's claims that Paris dragged her away to Troy (962),[28] and that Deiphobus forced her to stay there (959–60). Why did no one hear Helen's cries for help while being abducted, asks Hecuba. Furthermore, Helen refused an offer from Hecuba herself to help her go back to the Greek ships, thereby ending the war. Hecuba emphasizes Helen's love of indulgence by portraying her unscrupulously basking in the Trojan custom of prostration before her. This would have been a major blow to Helen's character in the eyes of the external audience as the Greeks considered the custom degrading, believing that no human being should prostrate himself before another.[29] The implication is that Helen has in fact turned barbarian.

Furthermore, Hecuba continues, she intentionally aroused jealousy in Paris: any time that Menelaus was winning, she praised him to cause grief to Paris, "but when the Trojans were successful, Menelaus was nothing" (1007). This is calculated by Hecuba to arouse Menelaus' rage. After countering Helen's main points and demolishing her claims of being a victim of the divine and the mortals alike with no personal responsibility, Hecuba crowns her assault by pointing out Helen's sumptuous attire, which underscores for the viewers the difference between the cold-hearted Helen resplendent in her finery and Hecuba's degradation. No further words are needed to show who the victim is in this picture. Helen of course cannot counter the claims against her at this point in the *agon*. Having refuted Helen's self-defense, Hecuba turns to Menelaus, asking him to crown Greece with glory by killing Helen, and thereby establishing a law: "Death to her who betrays her husband" (1029–32).

Hecuba's speech towers over the sophistic, unemotional self-defense of Helen. Her speech fulfills all the demands later identified by Aristotle for convincing one's audience, which in this case is Menelaus. She has an immaculate moral character, which Helen does not. Her claims against Helen are powerful and logical. Her additional points that Helen left of her own volition, lured by Paris's handsomeness and Troy's wealth; that she basked in barbarian customs; that she rejected Hecuba's help when the older woman begged her to leave; that she is still adorned with beautiful clothes while the other captives wear rags, all arouse *pathos* in the audience. She proves point after point how deceitful and self-seeking Helen is, and how no divine agency was involved in her eloping. In sum, Hecuba's speech has what Helen's lacks: the emotive power to convince her audience, whether on-stage or off. In addition, Euripides presents Hecuba in rags and degradation, while Helen appears in all her finery. Hecuba wins all the sympathy, and does so according to Aristotle's (later) rules.

After this triumphant speech, Hecuba prompts Menelaus to order Helen to be stoned at once (1036–41).[30] He, however, changes his mind after Helen supplicates him, reverting to his former decision to take her home to be killed. We cannot know what the external audience thought would happen:[31] they certainly knew that Helen is living, however unhappily, with Menelaus in Book 4 of the *Odyssey*. However, experienced theater-goers understood that a playwright could alter Homer's story.[32] As Lloyd has pointed out, Euripides could have presented Menelaus as either forgiving Helen after being persuaded by her speech, or, although agreeing with Hecuba, still pardoning Helen "because justice meant nothing for him" (1984: 204). Instead, he chose to follow the Homeric template in which Hecuba never attains what she wants even if her argument is sound and right under the circumstances and her conduct irreproachable.[33] Should the spectators reach the conclusion that morality is no match for beauty?

Conclusion

Euripides gives voice to this beautiful woman who is often spoken of but rarely heard, but at the same time has her reveal herself as cold, insensitive, and deceptive. She is presented as a woman who does not accept any responsibility for her acts, always finding someone else to blame for her malfeasance: gods; Hecuba and Priam; Menelaus, or Deiphobus. If we extend her argument that parents are responsible for their offspring's wrongdoing, we could almost imagine her blaming Zeus, who was considered to be her father, for her own actions, but that was perhaps a step too far for any Athenian tragedian. Euripides' characterization of Helen is so negative that it almost cries out for some redress, which we will see was not long coming in his play *Helen*. In *Trojan Women*, at least, one can only wonder whether her imaginary mythic figure and persona might not have fared better if no dramatic voice had been given to her.

However, there is another point to be considered. While it is understandable that the Trojan women, seeking someone to blame for their suffering, direct their wrath at Helen, there is great irony in the fact that one of leaders of the Greek armies is standing in front of them. The men remain blameless, and the woman, who is perceived as the *causa belli*, whether or not she acted of her own free will, is found guilty. Even while shining the spotlight on women as the victims of war, Euripides participates in the convention that legitimizes trading women as property and castigates them when they fail to fulfill the roles of perfect womanhood demanded by their society. In the formal debate, Helen uses any argument that comes to mind. Even though Hecuba wins the audience's sympathy and their pity, it is important to remember that Helen is fighting for her life. She knows that her one chance of survival is to be alone with Menelaus so that she can resort to the feminine charms which have always been her strongest suit. While men may go to war with their honor unblemished, a woman taking an active stance, fighting for her life by using feminine wiles, receives harsh condemnation.

HELEN IN EURIPIDES' *HELEN*

Euripides' *Helen*

The play was produced in 412 BCE in the Greater Dionysia festival, a short time after Athens' defeat in Sicily in 413 BCE. The plot takes place near the tomb of Proteus, former king of Egypt, not far from the mouth of the Nile. Helen, who is standing alone in front of the tomb, introduces herself and tells how Hera, having lost the contest with Athena and Aphrodite, created an *eidolon*, an image of Helen, which she sent with Paris to Troy. In the meantime, Hermes, under order from Zeus, brought her, the real Helen, to Egypt. Hermes had warned her not to share her bed with anyone, if she wants to be reunited with Menelaus in Sparta. Proteus' son Theoclymenus is now king of Egypt, and seeks Helen's hand in marriage. Helen has taken refuge by his father's tomb, from where Theoclymenus cannot take her by force.

Teucer arrives and is stunned to find a woman with such a strong resemblance to Helen, whom he had seen in Troy. He comes to seek advice from Theonoe, Theoclymenus' sister, on how to reach Cyprus. He tells Helen that the Trojan War ended seven years earlier, and that a storm had scattered the Greek ships, with the rumor being that Menelaus is not alive. Helen does not identify herself to Teucer, who hates the Helen he had met in Troy because of the war she had caused. Helen advises Teucer to leave Egypt immediately because Theoclymenus murders all visiting Greeks. Helen and the sympathetic Chorus of enslaved Greek women lament the wrongful condemnation of Helen. Reflecting on her lot, Helen decides to commit suicide. The Chorus suggest she leave the tomb and consult the omniscient Theonoe about the veracity of Teucer's report.

After Helen and the Chorus enter the palace to seek Theonoe, the shipwrecked Menelaus arrives wearing rags. He boasts of sacking Troy, and says the winds prevented him from reaching Greece. After his ship was broken to pieces, he clung to the keel until he arrived at the coast of Egypt. He has left the *eidolon* he thinks is Helen in a cave guarded by survivors from his ship. He has come to the palace to ask for clothes and food. In a comic scene the Old Woman Gatekeeper prevents him from entering the palace and tells him that Helen, the daughter of Tyndareus, has lived in the palace for many years, from before the time when the Greeks set out on their voyage against Troy. The befuddled Menelaus contemplates the meaning of the duality, questioning whether there is one Zeus or two, etc., but eventually decides it must be a coincidence.

Helen and the Chorus return to the scene. Theonoe has prophesied Menelaus' arrival. Questioning illusion and reality, Menelaus rebuffs the actual Helen till his servant reveals that the cave's phantom Helen has exonerated the real Helen, then disappeared. Recognition follows. Menelaus wants to be sure Helen has not shared any man's bed. The two plan their flight and decide to commit suicide if they are caught. Their success depends on Theonoe, who comes out of the palace and reports that Hera will not prevent them from escaping to Sparta, but Aphrodite is now enraged because it might become known that her victory in the beauty contest was a result of her offering the best bribe to Paris (in that Paris preferred Helen over becoming a powerful king or gaining more wisdom).

Theonoe says she will have to disclose Menelaus' arrival in Egypt to her brother. The two beg her to keep silent and she agrees. Helen and Menelaus try to figure out an escape plan. After rejecting Menelaus' impractical schemes, Helen suggests Menelaus pretend to be a Messenger who saw Menelaus die. She will mourn and ask to perform the burial ritual in the open sea. Menelaus will join her as the man organizing the ritual. Once they are in open sea, they escape in the ship that Theoclymenus gave them for the ceremony. A Messenger arrives and tells Theoclymenus that the Greeks have escaped after killing the Egyptians on the ship. Theoclymenus wants to kill his sister for betraying him. Castor and Pollux (see p. 15) appear *ex machina* and tell Theoclymenus that it is the gods' will that Helen return to Sparta with her husband and that Theoclymenus should refrain from harming his sister. Helen will share in the Dioscuri's feasts of "Hospitality," and Menelaus will go to the Blessed Isles.

In *Helen,* Euripides follows the spirit of Stesichorus' (640–550 BCE) *Palinode,* according to which she is not to blame for eloping with Paris. Her phantom was taken to Troy, while the real Helen was stranded against her will in Egypt. The play is built on several antinomies: paradoxes or contradictions between being and appearances, illusion and reality. The credibility of the senses is questioned, asking whether our eyes tell us what is really around us, or not. Helen herself is a paradox, since she is allegedly the antithesis of what the world believes her to be. She is not the unfaithful wife who left Menelaus for Paris, but the most faithful of wives, contending only with Penelope for the title. However, Euripides seems to undermine both explicitly and implicitly the positive female character offered by Stesichorus (*pace* Allan 2008: 54–55). We find in her character the good, dedicated, faithful wife, but from time to time the mythic, traditional features of Helen trickle into the positive image of the faithful wife; although immediately erased, they give an impression of some sort of a struggle, either within the character herself—or perhaps within the playwright, who struggles with the Stesichorian version.

Euripides' undermining of Helen's persona starts at the very the beginning of the play, when Helen reports that Hermes cautioned her not to share anyone's bed during her sojourn in Egypt, if she wants to return one day to Sparta with Menelaus (56–59). Her usual mythic tendency toward promiscuity is therefore immediately brought to the spectators' minds. Secondly, Euripides' casting of Menelaus in this play as something of a *Miles Gloriosus* (as a Braggart Soldier, whose accounts of his accomplishments have little or no basis) undercuts her stature in general, by indicating that she has spent the long seventeen years waiting for a rather flawed man. Thirdly, her suggestion after the recognition that Menelaus leave immediately for Sparta without her, and that she will marry Theoclymenus, contrary to her steadfast shunning of this event beforehand, hints at the antithetical and dual presentation of Helen. Fourthly, the play's shift toward a tragicomedy or comedy of errors and mistaken identity, undermines our belief in Helen's "suffering" as a wife who has lost her good name for no valid reason. Does Euripides imply that viewing Helen as a rival to Penelope for the title of most faithful wife is somewhat laughable? He has already shown her to be far from blameless in *Trojan Women,* when he demolished her claims in the vein of Gorgias of Leontini. Is he doing the same to the imaginative creation of Stesichorus but in a more subtle and funny way?

The above four ways of diminishing Helen's persona create a duality in the character of Helen beyond the one that the play explicitly presents: appearance and reality. While

Stesichorus created duality by presenting an alternative plot, Euripides seems to play on this theme more implicitly, by creating a multi-layered character suggesting internal contradictions. Euripides indicates that while Helen is physically in Egypt, she nevertheless still seems to possess some inherent features that qualify her to be thought of as the cause of the war. Helen's character is not entirely positive or negative but a mixture of tendencies and actions that make her both a singularly devoted wife, and at the same time, at certain junctures, one who could revert to the mythic version the audience is more used to.

Euripides' skill as a dramatist allows his portrayal of Helen as a Penelope type to verge on seriousness while, at the same time, casting doubt that such a portrayal could ever be possible. His characterization does not simply cast her in simple in Penelope's mould, but he makes her appear to surpass the original. While like Penelope she awaits her husband for years, Helen outdoes Penelope's despondency when she is told that her husband might be dead: she contemplates suicide, which Penelope never did. However much other portrayals have brought this into question, here she is portrayed as a good mother, who cares about her daughter Hermione, just as Penelope cares about her son Telemachus. She and Menelaus also have secret tokens of recognition; and she is no less resourceful than her prototype. Eventually Helen makes use of deception, as Penelope does, not only in order to remain married to Menelaus, but also in order to save her husband's life. All this is a much taller order of accomplishment than Penelope's. Hermes' warning to Helen not to share any man's bed while in Egypt, however, makes the audience alert to any potential deviations on her part from her Penelopean persona. Penelope, after all, did not need such a warning in order to wait for her husband for twenty years. On the contrary, Odysseus had told her that when Telemachus started growing his beard, she should remarry (*Od.*18. 259–70). But she did not. Is Hermes' warning a dramatic parallel to Odysseus' words? At any rate, Hermes' advice has the effect of tainting Helen.

Menelaus

The Penelope model that creates the comparison between Helen and the renowned Odyssean queen calls for a comparison between the two husbands.[34] On the face of it, Helen's steadfastness in remaining faithful to Menelaus builds up Menelaus' persona, but his grandeur is diminished the moment he appears (386–436). First, his entrance as a tattered, shipwrecked survivor clad in bits and pieces of his sail contrasts with the heroic persona he intends to portray in his speech.[35] Euripides continues to chip away at his "greatness" by allowing him to claim sole responsibility for gathering the force against Troy and sacking the city. Such a pronouncement would immediately sound false to the external audience who knew that it was Agamemnon who amassed the army and commanded it on behalf of Menelaus. Furthermore, it was Odysseus who devised the Trojan horse stratagem which is usually given the credit for taking the city.

Euripides alludes to two further scenes in the *Odyssey* in which the comparison of Menelaus and Odysseus only further denigrates Menelaus' conduct. Menelaus recounts how he had wandered in misery for seven years over the waves of the sea, blown from the coast of Greece and never allowed to come home. Finally, his ship was smashed into countless pieces, leaving only the keel, on which he reached land safely. This description hints at Odysseus' arrival both at Ogygia, Calypso's island, and later at Scheria. After Odysseus' comrades devour Helios' herd, Zeus smites Odysseus' ship with his thunderbolt. The surge tears the sides of the ship from the keel. Odysseus holds on to the keel and, sitting on it, is borne by the strong winds to Calypso's island, where he is held by the goddess for seven years (*Od.* 12.403–25). Riding the keel, as Dale notes, was a classic shipwreck escape, however, "it is more effective for a solitary survivor than for a tandem" (1967: on 412). So how did Menelaus' crew and Helen arrive at the cave (424–27)? The resulting image is that unlike Odysseus, as Dale points out, the wreck was close to the shore. If so, while Menelaus' crew and Helen must have been struggling through the waves until they reached the shore, Menelaus was floating in relative comfort on the keel. Menelaus is revealed as not only unable to withstand real hardships but also extremely selfish.

Menelaus' lack of proper attire is reminiscent of Odysseus arriving naked at Scheria and supplicating Princess Nausicaa while holding a well-positioned olive branch—a humorous scene.[36] Like Menelaus, who claims that his luxurious garments were swallowed by the sea (423–24), Odysseus too had been nicely clothed by Calypso when he departed Ogygia (*Od.* 5.264), but the clothes weighed him down so that he almost drowned in the storm stirred up by Poseidon. In order to survive, he had to remove all of his beautiful clothing apart from the magic veil that Leucothea had given him (*Od.* 5.313–50). Odysseus arrives at Scheria naked (*Od.* 6.128–29) and has to cover himself with a branch before supplicating Nausicaa, the Phaeacian Princess, whom he meets on the seashore doing her laundry. She gives him princely attire and leads him to her parents' palace. Menelaus is not as lucky. He begs an Old Woman Gatekeeper for entrance to Theoclymenus' palace in hope of getting food. Menelaus' uncouth and gruff approach to the Old Woman paints him as arrogant, and she physically pushes him out. She even mocks Menelaus by saying that although he might be an important person somewhere else, in Egypt he *is not*. The "great" victorious hero Menelaus, is intimidated by the Old Woman.

Helen's image is inevitably damaged by the denigration of her husband. The Old Woman explains to Menelaus that Theoclymenus' ire against the Greeks stems from the presence of Zeus' daughter Helen in the palace. When asked to clarify her statement, she tells him that Helen had arrived before the Greeks sailed for Troy. Menelaus is confused. He alleges that he has brought his wife by force from Troy and stuck her in a cave; now he hears that there is another Helen, who is also the daughter of Zeus. In a proverbial prequel to Plautus' Sosia, who wonders whether there might be some other Sosia who is exactly like him, Menelaus asks: "Is there some man called Zeus by the banks of the Nile?" (490–91) (see Box on Plautus' *Amphitruo*, p. 159).[37] He decides that it must be a coincidence, that she must be an entirely different person. The world is a big place and many people and places share the same name, he states.

Intellectual ability or curiosity is not a strong suit of Menelaus; Dale notes, "incapacity for hard reasoning is not out of place in Menelaus, like his later failure to devise a plan of escape" (1967: on 497). His encounter with the Old Woman has not shattered his sense of self-importance; he decides valiantly to seek help from the king despite the Old Woman's warnings (500). He is confident that hearing his name alone will be enough to make anyone give him food, since he is "well known throughout the world" (502–04). This is another contrast with Odysseus. The latter prudently kept his identity secret, at least at first, and introduced himself to the Cyclops as *Outis* ("No One") out of precaution. This tactic proved to be auspicious, because the Cyclops had been warned that he would lose his sight by the hands of a man called Odysseus (*Od.* 9. 364–67, 507–12). Menelaus, who would actually be putting himself in grave danger if Theoclymenus heard his name, broadcasts his identity with little or no forethought. Despite his brave statements, he actually decides that he will hide and run away to the shipwreck if the king proves to be cruel (505–09).

These three humorous, unflattering comparisons lend levity and frivolity to the play.[38]

Recognition

After poking fun at Menelaus' appearance, boasts, and lack of courage, Euripides turns to the recognition between husband and wife, in which he again draws a comparison to the *Odyssey*. The ambiguity in the recognition of Odysseus by his wife is notorious. It may not be far-fetched to suppose that Penelope recognizes her husband, who is disguised as a beggar with a divinely altered physiognomy, but refuses to acknowledge him as such and tests him out of spite caused by his mistrust of her.[39] Helen, on the other hand, indisputably fails to recognize her husband. As the recognition scene progresses, the reunion of husband and wife is set as a romantic tragicomedy of errors. It is of interest that neither of them uses the "tokens of recognition" that Helen claimed they had (290–91). Were they mentioned in the beginning of the play only to cast Helen in the Penelope mould?

Helen initially suspects Menelaus of being Theoclymenus' emissary who is trying to ambush her in order to drag her from the tomb by force and make her marry the king. Scared, she cries for help from the Chorus in a similar fashion to Euripides' hysterical Electra, who thinks that Orestes is about to violate her (Eur. *El.* 215–27; *Hel.* 541–54). Helen eventually recognizes and acknowledges Menelaus first. Menelaus is still convinced that he has left his wife in a cave, and despite acknowledging the resemblance of the two women, he is certain that she is an apparition of some sort. Only the arrival of Menelaus' servant, who recounts the disappearance of the phantom from the cave, permits the recognition.

The couple's reunion is filled with emotion, reminiscent of the reunion of Electra and Orestes in Sophocles' *Electra* in both language and structure. It is therefore rather surprising that in the midst of their impassioned encounter, Helen clouds the moment by telling Menelaus that he has to leave Egypt *immediately*. If he does not flee, he will be killed because his unexpected arrival hinders her marriage to Theoclymenus (778–83). Helen's words are astonishing. She has just met Menelaus after waiting for him for seventeen long years, part of which she spent at the tomb of Proteus to avoid this marriage. If she thinks that Menelaus can escape Egypt unscathed, why doesn't she plan to join him? Because she does not include herself in Menelaus' suggested flight, it sounds as if she intends to marry Theoclymenus.

What happened? Was all her suffering in vain? Has the appearance of Menelaus discouraged her? Has she realized that this is not the man whom she left? Where is her former love and care for Hermione? Or maybe, Menelaus' arrival puts a stop to her "suffering chaste persona" which she has cultivated for the last seventeen years?[40] Indeed, line 780 ("Flee with all speed from this land") has bothered editors, some of whom delete it, but this is unnecessary on textual grounds and thematic ones (see Allan 2008 on line). As quickly as this fleeting suggestion of what could be interpreted as Helen's intention to marry Theoclymenus appeared, so it vanishes. Helen no longer mentions the need for Menelaus to leave, but is suddenly overly solicitous to him and concerned about his lack of food (791).

What are we to make of this brief scene? Is Euripides having fun with the audience, hinting that as much as one wants to believe that Helen can be faithful, her traditional promiscuity and predilection for good looks and comfort reappear every so often? After getting a glimpse of the tattered and ineffectual Menelaus, is she ready to go with Theoclymenus, as her traditional persona did with the glamorous Paris?

Helen's Ruse

Like his nephew Orestes in *Iphigenia among the Taurians,* Menelaus not only fails to come up with a feasible plan of escape, but thinks it is Helen's place to deal with Theonoe, the main obstacle to their escape, because there is "nothing like a woman to deal with a woman" (830). In other words, he rather begrudgingly admits that he needs to ask for help from a woman. They need to convince Theonoe not to divulge to Theoclymenus Menelaus' arrival on the shores of Egypt. Helen's emotional pleading with Theonoe succeeds in spite of Menelaus' arrogance when asking Theonoe for help.

Helen, who is mindful of Menelaus' disregard for women's power or ability, listens carefully to Menelaus' two unrealistic plans of escape: by a chariot or by ambushing Theoclymenus in the palace. When she notices that he has reached the end of his "planning ability," she carefully says: "Listen and see whether a woman too might say something clever" (1049). As Burian comments "the sentiment ... sounds an ironic, almost a mocking note here after the utter lack of cleverness in Menelaus' proposals" (2007: on line). Helen goes on to describe how Menelaus will come as a messenger announcing his own death, and she will ask Theoclymenus for a ship to give him a mock-burial at sea. After presenting her plan, she softens her suggestion by giving Menelaus a feeling of superiority and nullifying herself as the devisor of their escape saying "You must be in charge of everything" (1073).[41] Helen is shown to be not only a clever and resourceful woman, but also one who submits to the social hierarchy and subordinates her persona to her husband as expected, while knowing his deficiencies.

In giving Helen the wherewithal to concoct an escape plan that will work perfectly, Euripides characterizes Helen as the practical woman whom men suspect of being conniving and devious, and therefore dangerous. However, in this instance, Helen is deceiving others for the sake of her husband, and therefore she is not pernicious but helpful. The love and devotion that she exhibited in the seventeen years of waiting are linked to her willingness now to lessen her beauty by having her hair cropped and her cheeks scratched in her mock grief. This is no small sacrifice on Helen's part; after all, her beauty is her essential feature. In the end she not only succeeds in escaping an unwanted marriage, but thanks to her intelligent maneuvering she has returned his heroic, Homeric persona to her not-so-courageous and not-so-clever husband.

What the beginning of the play presented only as a hearsay by having Helen herself tell of her fidelity and devotion to her husband, is exemplified through her ruse. The play ends with an act that proves the extent to which Helen is committed to being the wife of Menelaus, in spite of his inefficacy in planning and poor grasp of reality. Helen's apotheosis, prophesied by Castor (1666–69), is suitable for a faithful wife.

Conclusion

Euripides fleshes out Stesichorus' idea of the phantom of Helen by portraying the "real" Helen living in Egypt while both Greeks and Trojans fought for her in a senseless war at Troy. He could have presented a serious dramatic portrayal of the Queen of Sparta, for which there was already a Homeric model in the faithful Penelope, a woman approached by suitors whose persistent advances she manages to cleverly frustrate. While this superficially is the chosen framework, throughout the play Euripides casts doubts on the ability of this Helen to behave like Penelope.

Helen's status is further compromised by the comic and unflattering depiction of Menelaus. The play seems to ask: "Has it been worthwhile to wait for seventeen years for this kind of a man?" Could painting Menelaus as a braggart and a pretentious hero somehow justify the alternative story of Helen's elopement with the handsome, wealthy Paris? Should we think that the message is: "Casting Helen as a faithful wife contradicts the very essence of this heroine: it just cannot be." Her persona is captivating in her irresistible, magnetic attraction for men and the antithesis between her outward beauty and inner immorality. Portraying her as a faithful wife detracts from her individuality and turns her persona into a somewhat boring, clichéd depiction of a subservient woman which she does not deserve. Furthermore, the mismatch between the beautiful, clever, and intelligent woman and her lawful but unworthy husband might have driven a less beautiful wife to seek an extra-marital relationship, let alone the "most beautiful woman known to men."

In sum, the comic depiction of Menelaus and some fleeting, darkly humorous moments, such as the abbreviation of Helen's suicidal musings by the realization of the difficulty of figuring out where she should strike herself with the sword (301–02), or the servant's sarcastic, ironic comment when he finds Helen with Menelaus after she has vanished from the cave, that "I did not know that you had wings" (618–19), are simply a way to indicate that the entire premise of the play is a comic one, not to be taken too seriously.

Plautus' *Amphitruo*

Amphitruo is the only comedy written by the Roman playwright Plautus on a mythic subject. The play is a comedy of disguised identities based around Amphitruo, the commander of the army of Creon, King of Thebes. While Amphitruo is away at war, accompanied by his slave Sosia, the god Jupiter (Zeus) falls in love with Amphitruo's wife Alcmena, who has been left at home expecting Amphitruo's child. Jupiter takes Amphitruo's form and seduces Alcmena. Jupiter's son Mercury (Hermes) changes his appearance to look like the slave Sosia, to confound any possible interventions. The real Amphitruo and Sosia return to Thebes, with the real Sosia going on ahead. On Sosia's arrival at the house the disguised Mercury beats him up and sends him away. Thoroughly confused by having been beaten up by himself, Sosia returns to the ship to relay what happened to his master. Amphitruo, annoyed by his slave's unbelievable story heads to his house. Jupiter leaves only moments before Amphitruo's arrival. Alcmena, seeing her husband, is confused as to why he is returning so soon after leaving. Amphitruo doesn't appreciate this strange welcome after being gone for so many months, and confusion turns to anger and jealousy after learning that she has slept with a man who was not himself. After a long argument, Alcmena is ready to leave her untrusting husband but is stopped by Jupiter. The god soon begins to set things right, and in a miraculous event, Alcmena gives birth to twin boys. One is the son of Amphitruo, the other is Hercules, the son of Jupiter, who shortly after birth kills two serpents, saving himself and his twin brother. Amphitruo has been overcome by his own anger and faints on hearing thunder following flashes of lightning. Jupiter finally reveals himself to Amphitruo explaining what has occurred. Amphitruo now accepts having shared his wife with a god and is reconciled with Alcmena.

HELEN IN EURIPIDES' *ORESTES*

Euripides' *Orestes*

Electra is tending her brother Orestes, who has become ill through being haunted by hallucinations sent by the Furies (Erinyes) after the murder of Clytemnestra. Meanwhile, the Argive assembly is about to decide whether to impose the death penalty on the siblings, who are hoping that Menelaus, who is rumored to have arrived at the port of Nauplia, will sway the assembly in their favor. Helen arrives and angers Electra by suggesting that the young woman make an offering at

Clytemnestra's tomb. Helen claims she cannot do this herself because shame prevents her from showing herself to the Argives. When Electra suggests that Helen ask Hermione, Helen's daughter, Helen answers that it is not good for unmarried girls to appear in public, ignoring the fact that she has stated earlier, quite offensively, that Electra too is still a virgin. Electra's firm refusal forces Helen to send her daughter to Clytemnestra' tomb. Clytemnestra's father Tyndareus, who arrives soon after Menelaus, argues that Orestes should have exiled his mother rather than killing her. Accordingly, he urges the assembly to pass a death sentence, while Menelaus merely offers moral support. The assembly, having heard from Orestes himself, at the suggestion of Pylades, sentences Orestes and Electra to death but grants them the option of taking their own lives. While they lament their fate, Pylades encourages them to avenge themselves on Menelaus by killing Helen. Using her new-found strategic skills, Electra forms an additional plot to take Hermione, conveniently returning from her mission to Clytemnestra's tomb, as a hostage in order to force Menelaus to rescue them from death. Helen disappears in the midst of the attempts to seize her. Meanwhile, Menelaus, believing Helen has been killed, is trying to at least save his daughter, whom Orestes is about to kill. Suddenly Apollo and Helen appear on high. Apollo reveals that Helen was brought to heaven according to Zeus' will. Orestes will eventually become the king of Argos, and marry Hermione, while Pylades will marry Electra.

Orestes was performed in 408 BCE and was the last of the extant plays putting Helen on the stage. The fluidity in the portrayal of Helen continues in this play. On the face of it, Helen seems sympathetic and generous; on the other hand, it is impossible to ignore her obtuseness, refusal to accept responsibility, and predilection for barbarian luxury (see also Chapter 2, pp. 83–89).

Euripides applies to this version of Helen characterization techniques similar to those he used in *Trojan Women* (415 BCE), except that in *Orestes,* Helen is vilified throughout the play by every character but Menelaus. In the prologue delivered by Electra we hear that: "Menelaus married that god-detested Helen" (19–20) or "as for Helen, *cause of so much woe,* he [Menelaus] waited for nightfall and sent her on ahead to our house so that those whose sons died at Troy might not see her walking by day and throw stones at her" (55–59). The audience therefore know from the start that the play is not going to be forgiving to Helen, despite the portrayal of Electra herself as obviously unhinged.

The duality in Helen's depiction is evident in Helen's single scene on stage (71–125), when she meets with Electra:

Daughter of Clytaemnestra and Agamemnon, Electra, unmarried now for so long, how are are you faring, poor woman, you and your brother, unhappy Orestes who murdered his mother? Speaking to you does not bring pollution upon me: I attribute any guilt to Phoebus. Yet I do lament the death of my sister Clytaemnestra.

After my unfortunate voyage to Ilium—a voyage caused by god-sent madness—I never saw her again, and in my bereavement I lament her sad fate. (71–80)

Is it a cordial and sympathetic address to her miserable and suffering niece, as Vellacott (1975: 61–62) believes? True, she does not scold or blame Electra for the murder, but let us consider what she does say.

Helen emphasizes Electra's spinsterhood, which is a major cause of misery to any young woman, as we hear later from Orestes's words to Menelaus when he decries Electra's status in order to elicit pity (663). Therefore, it is uncommon and rather insulting to talk about it so bluntly to someone's face. Helen augments her insensitive words a few lines later when she implies that Electra has no chance of marrying.

Helen's second improper remark is about Orestes. Does she have to mention the matricide, especially since she bemoans her sister's death in the next lines? How can she be so sympathetic to the duo if she misses her sister so much? It soon becomes clear that her sympathizing does not come without a price for Electra, but for a moment she strives to establish some common ground with the murderous siblings by comparing her god-sent madness, which she blames on the injunction of Apollo, to that of Orestes. The "price" comes next. She wants Electra to pour libations and put an offering of hair from herself on Clytemnestra's tomb. To Electra's suggestion that Helen send Hermione, Helen's daughter, to Clytemnestra's tomb, Helen says that "It is not proper for unmarried maidens to go out in public" (108, my translation), presumably because it would mar the maidens' chances of marrying. But why would it be appropriate for Electra to do so? Has she no chance to marry? One can only wonder whether Helen's emphasis on marriage does not bring to the audience's mind the fact that Helen has had an abundance of husbands: Menelaus, Paris, Deiphobus, and Menelaus again. We will never know whether the spectators suspected that this insensitive request was the reason for the apparent sympathizing. However, there is no dispute that asking a daughter who participated in her mother's murder to perform ritual offerings on this same mother's grave seems tactless, if not macabre.

Her obtuseness and shallowness might also be reminiscent of the scene in *Trojan Women* when Helen walks out of the tent of the captives adorned in her finest while the other women wear rags. Helen's claim that she would have gone by herself to the tomb but "shame" prevents her (98) holds out the possibility of rehabilitation for this beautiful but shameless woman, but her traditional portrayal reemerges immediately when, under pressure from Electra, she admits that it is rather "fear" of the fathers of those who died at Troy, not shame, that keeps her in the palace (102). After all, had she wanted to visit her sister's grave by herself, she could have waited for nightfall, in the same way that she was smuggled to the palace during the previous night.

The attacks on Helen's character escalate in accordance with the heightening plot tensions. When Orestes understands that his fate and that of his sister have been sealed and that they must die in punishment for the matricide, he and Pylades seek a way of exacting revenge on Menelaus, their kinsman, who did not stand by their side. Pylades decides that the best course of action is to kill Helen (1105). He justifies the planned murder saying "If we were to take the sword to a woman of greater virtue, the bloodletting would bring disgrace on us. As things are, she'll be paying for her crimes against all of Hellas, those whose fathers she slew and whose sons she destroyed while depriving brides of their husbands" (1132–36). The Chorus add insult to injury: "Tyndareus' daughter deserves the hatred of all women. She has disgraced her sex" (1153–54).

These attacks on Helen's character include an insinuation initially made by Hecuba in *Trojan Women*: Helen has a penchant for eastern luxury. As we shall see in *Orestes*, Euripides emphasizes this characteristic right up until Helen's last mortal moments. Not only do the audience hear that Helen brought mirrors and myrrh bottles back from Troy, but she was also pampered by her Phrygian slaves. In discussing their plan to kill Helen, Orestes refers to Helen's barbarian attendants (1110–15), and Helen's predilection for eastern comfort is well presented by her Phrygian slave who escapes the palace: he describes his role of fanning Helen's fair locks while she was weaving "with a disk of well-set plumes, wafting them past her cheek in barbaric fashion" (1427–30). Being fanned by plumes of peacock or ostrich, as described by the Phrygian slave, was an exotic luxury attributed usually only to Egyptian, Assyrian, and Persian kings. What is even odder here is that it is not a female but a male Phrygian slave, probably a eunuch.[42] While preferring a life of luxury to one of deprivation does not in itself condemn a person to death, it is difficult to imagine that this description would have won the hearts of the spectators. Later, Euripides has the Phrygian slave add one final detail of Helen's opulence in the midst of a horrific murder scene: after describing Orestes' and Pylades' threatening cries and Helen's screams and attempts to escape, he says that Helen "then with fleeting foot her gold-sandaled step she bore away" (1467–68).

However, it is not only Orestes and Pylades who attack Helen, verbally and then physically. Before they set off to carry out their plan, Electra adds her own twist to the proceedings. She suggests that she and the Chorus kidnap Hermione, who is due to come back from pouring libations on Clytemnestra's tomb. Hermione is to be held hostage to guarantee the siblings' safety once Menelaus discovers that his wife is dead. This side-plot allows Electra to be on stage with the Chorus, watching out for Hermione, when the audience first hear a scream indicating that Helen's murder is taking place. Helen's voice is heard crying out. She calls to Menelaus, who, perhaps predictably, fails to come to her rescue (1301). Even when Helen is apparently dying, the Chorus continue their bloodthirsty cries for Helen's death: "Slay, slay, smite, destroy her, plying at close range your twin double-edged swords" (1302–04).

Following the course of events in other tragedies, we might have expected to be presented with Helen's dead body, but Euripides continues to surprise the audience with new developments. Instead of being presented with a corpse, the Chorus encounter the Phrygian slave fleeing from the palace. He describes how Orestes and Pylades made their way to the throne chamber under the guise of wishing to supplicate Helen but after dispatching most of Helen's slaves, put the sword to her throat (1395–473). The scene is rather confusing. The spectators are told by the Phrygian slave, "From the realm of death I have escaped the Argive sword" in "Asian slippers" (1369–70). One of the many bizarre elements of this scene seems to be identifying everyone by their footwear. He bewails the loss of Phrygia, destroyed because of the beauty of a woman "born to a bird, Leda's cub, Hellish Helen" (1386-87, my translation). So even Helen's slave with his barbarian slippers condemns her. The audience then hear that Orestes was thwarted on the very point of cutting Helen's throat: "Orestes darted his fingers to her hair, putting his Mycenean boot ahead, and yanking her neck back to his left shoulder meant to thrust his dark sword into her throat" (1469-73). When Helen screamed, and turned her golden sandaled steps in flight (1468-69), her slaves battered down the doors.[43] A fight ensued between the slaves and the two murderers, but the following movements of Orestes and Pylades have been left vague. There is a suggestion that Helen is already lying dead or dying, bleeding on the ground (1491), as Hermione enters. But when Orestes and Pylades were returning to the slaughter of Helen (1493-94), she (or her bleeding corpse) amazingly vanished from their clutches as if by magic. The image of her bloody body sinking to the ground is consistent with what could have been understood as the already accomplished slaughter in 1491, but also consistent with what Apollo will reveal in 1633-34: the saving of Helen "from beneath Orestes' sword." The "vanishing" of Helen is reminiscent of the Phantom-Helen's disappearance from the cave in which she was hidden by Menelaus in *Helen* (486). Helen seems to be constantly escaping.

Dramatically, the confusing tale fits well with the descriptive song sung by a terrified Messenger, who is hard to understand, as he is a Phrygian. We are given no time for rational analysis before the narrator's concluding words and the following scene, both of which are designed to reinforce the impression that Helen has perished. Was Euripides playing with the audience when for a brief moment he gave the impression that Helen was murdered, then made her disappear? Did he do it because he assumed the audience would have liked to see the shameless woman dead? We will never know, but the description is gripping, if hard to follow.

Helen has only one speaking appearance at the very beginning of the play, but as the drama unfolds, she is repeatedly vilified and despised by Electra, Orestes, Tyndareus, Pylades, and the Chorus of married women. She is thus in the audience's mind all the time. She appears in person but as a mute character *ex machina* (see Box on *Deus ex machina,* p. 83) with Apollo at the end of the play. Apollo tells us that he spirited her away from under the sword of Orestes, "For she is Zeus' daughter and must live an imperishable life, and with Castor and Polydeuces in heaven's recesses she will be enthroned as a savior of seafarers" (1635-37), a role given to her solely by Euripides. What does this appearance with Apollo tell the audience? Perhaps Apollo is smitten by this beautiful "divine" woman in spite of her vilification of him to Electra. This view might gain some support from Electra's suspicion that Helen's beauty could have blunted Orestes' and Pylades' swords. The difference in age between Helen and the two young men does not seem to play a role in Electra's musings (1286-87). Helen's beauty bridges the chasm between mortal and divine, between young and old. We know from the *Iliad*, that the old Trojan men on the wall were smitten by the beautiful daughter-in-law of Priam.[44] Hecuba in *Trojan Women* is right when she begs Menelaus not to take Helen on his ship back to Argos lest Helen make him change his mind about killing her. In the end, beauty is imperishable, and morality does not necessarily go hand in hand with it.

Conclusion

As stated by Zeitlin: "when it comes to the figure of Helen, although she is singular in the entire mythic tradition as the emblem and indisputable exemplar of incomparable beauty... the quality of singleness is not among her attributes" (2010: 263). If there is one repeated motif for Helen, it is that of duality. Perhaps the most startling duality is the contrast between her outstanding physical or exterior beauty, and her internal persona reviled by almost every character who mentions her name. While the three extant plays placing Helen on the stage present differing and sometimes conflicting versions of her life story, *Helen* takes the dualities one step further with the plot revolving around the existence of two Helens, the real woman and her phantom, or *eidolon*. While Zeitlin gives a list of doublets connected with Helen (2010: 263–64), including having both a divine and a mortal father (Zeus and Tyndareus), Helen's life story hints perhaps at another motif behind Helen's characterization: the problematic nature of divine intervention in the affairs of mortals.

Helen herself is an embodiment of divine intervention: Zeus seduced her mother Leda, who was married to the Spartan King Tyndareus, and Helen started life most unnaturally in a swan's egg. Helen's divine origins seem to have expressed themselves in a kind of supernatural beauty, supernatural in that mortal men, and possibly some of the gods, seem unable to withstand it. However, this "gift" of beauty may have been seen as being more like a curse, when Helen attracts far too much attention for anyone's good.

In keeping with her birth, the rest of Helen's life seems to have been affected by the lack of clear boundaries between the affairs of gods and those of mortals. Helen, like her mother, was married to the King of Sparta, now Menelaus, whose right to the throne came through his marriage to Helen. As with her mother, the gods seem to have had little respect for her marriage, and Aphrodite thought nothing of offering Helen, the most beautiful mortal woman, as a prize to Paris if he judged the infamous beauty contest of the goddesses in her favor. Whether Paris, who was almost supernaturally good-looking himself, seduced Helen on his own "merits," or he abducted her with the help of Aphrodite, or Hera intervened and in order to punish Paris left him with an "airy-nothingness," a mere image of Helen, is immaterial to the miserable outcome: the Trojan War.

Euripides began *Trojan Women* with Poseidon's speech as he took leave of Troy, which had, in his own words, been destroyed by Hera and Athena. When Athena describes her plans to wreck the ships of the Greeks returning home, it seems that the gods intend to finish the destruction they had begun, and wipe the world clean of mortals who do not revere the gods. Euripides began *Helen* with the heroine describing her suffering, which she attributes to beauty: both her own and that of the goddesses, which was judged in the beauty contest. Finally, Euripides began *Orestes* with Electra recounting the suffering of her family, which began with Tantalus, reputed to be the son of Zeus.

The styles of the three plays are very different: *Trojan Women* is a tragedy in every sense of the word; *Helen* has at times been described as a romantic comedy, and there is little consensus as to whether *Orestes* is a tragedy, a tragicomedy, or a melodrama. However, they share the theme of the miseries resulting from the Trojan War, a war caused at least in part by the lack of a clear boundary between the domain of the gods and that of mankind. The three plays were written during the Peloponnesian War, which had caused great suffering to all those involved. A religious scandal had taken place in Athens before their expedition to Syracuse in Sicily, in which statues of the god Hermes had been mutilated. This was taken as a bad omen for the war. Although it is doubtful that Euripides, who was dependent on the authorities choosing him to present his plays at the Dionysia, would have made any public criticism of the gods or the traditional religious practices of Athens, he may have included criticism of man's interpretation of the will of the gods. There may also be a particular emphasis on mankind taking responsibility for their actions instead of blaming the gods for their misfortunes. The formal debate, the *agon*, between Helen and Hecuba in *Trojan Women* revolves around the question of who was responsible for Helen eloping with Paris, and subsequently remaining in Troy instead of returning to Menelaus, an act which apparently prolonged the war and led to the eventual destruction of Troy. Helen demonstrates sufficient resourcefulness in *Helen* once Menelaus has arrived, but is powerless against the will of gods and does not attempt to reveal her whereabouts, which might have prevented the destruction of Troy. In *Orestes,* despite the few moments of remorse expressed by the hero, no one takes any responsibility for anything that happens, least of all Helen. The trio, Pylades, Orestes, and Electra, gradually resort to increasingly violent tactics demonstrating a criminal lack of responsibility by blaming their troubles on the gods and everyone else. Yet in the midst of descent into complete chaos, Euripides resorts to a *deus ex machina* to resolve the crisis. However, the solution includes the return of a certain kind of order: Helen, whose origins were part-divine, is taken out of the realm of mortals and placed alongside her brothers in the heavens.

In Helen, Euripides has given audiences a character with little consistency except perhaps for the dualities she is identified with. She is, however, a prime example of the misadventures resulting from the gods' interference with the affairs of mortals. Her divine father made her too beautiful. Her beauty meant that mortals could not resist her, and without laws and boundaries chaos ensued.

DISCUSSION TOPICS

1. Helen is widely considered the most feminine of all the tragic heroines. She seems to hold an almost irresistible allure for various male characters while at the same time is almost universally loathed by female characters including Hecuba in *Trojan Women* and Electra in *Orestes*. Do you think the hatred is related to jealousy over Helen's beauty or to Helen's behavior? Explain.

2. The version of the well-known myth of the Trojan War presented in *Helen* completely contradicts the better-known version on which *Trojan Women* and *Orestes* are based. Helen has not gone to Troy at all in this version, but an *eidolon* or phantom has gone in her place. This seems rather far-fetched to modern

audiences. Do you think the fifth-century Athenian audience would have been able to accept this version of the myth? Apart from providing a new setting for his play and a slightly different characterization of Helen, do you think Euripides had any other reason for using this device? Do you think there could be an underlying message that wars may be fought and lives lost in other circumstances, too, over misconceptions?

3. In *Trojan Women,* Helen blames everyone for the war, except herself. Despite Hecuba's rebuttals of these claims, Helen ultimately survives, despite being found guilty by Menelaus, and sails back home with him. This presentation contrasts with the Homeric Helen who is deeply contrite, accepting the blame for the war. Why do you think Euripides chose this particular portrayal of the heroine?

4. Describe the relationship between Helen and her husband Menelaus in each of the three plays and explain the differences.

5. In *Helen,* it is Helen who comes up with the escape plan and not Menelaus. Do you think that here (and in various other plays) Euripides is challenging the *status quo* whereby women are supposed to be capable only of managing domestic matters?

6. In *Orestes* Helen is depicted as being particularly insensitive towards Electra. Indeed, there do not seem to be any instances of Helen having a good relationship with a female character. Do you think that the lack of empathy towards other women may be an important part of Helen's characterization? Explain.

7. Helen and Clytemnestra's father, Tyndareus, makes an appearance in *Orestes.* He admits he knows that Helen is present but refuses to see her, asking only for Menelaus. Tyndareus' condemnation of both of his daughters, as well as of Electra and Orestes is absolute. Do you think this depiction of such a cold-hearted father and grandfather, could make audiences more sympathetic to Helen as well as to Orestes and Electra?

8. The three plays discussed in this chapter all present the idea that the gods have interfered or even meddled with the affairs of man. Helen is the daughter of a god, Zeus, and a mortal woman, Leda; Aphrodite offered Helen as a prize to Paris, if he judged a beauty contest in her favor; and finally, Hera intervened by sending Helen to Egypt instead of Troy. Is Euripides criticizing the actions of the gods? What could be the Athenian audience's reaction to such a criticism? Explain your answer.

CHAPTER 6
HECUBA

Mythic background

In myth, Hecuba was the wife of King Priam of Troy at the time of the Trojan War. Homer wrote of Hecuba as being the daughter of the King Dymas of Phrygia, but according to Euripides she was the daughter of the Thracian king Cisseus. Either way, she was of royal descent. She had 19 children, including Hector, Paris, Polydorus, Polyxena and Cassandra. Hector and Paris were warriors who featured in Homer's *Iliad*. According to both Stesichorus and Tzetzes, Hector and another son Troilus, were sons of Apollo and not of Priam. Stesichorus (*Sack of Troy*, frag. 109F; Pausanias 10.2.7.2 is the source) further added that Apollo took care of Hecuba after Troy's defeat by ensuring her safety in Lycia.[1] Hecuba appears in Books 6, 22 and 24 of the *Iliad*, where she meets her son Hector on his return to Troy (6.254–62); pleads with him not to fight Achilles (22.85–89); worries about Priam retrieving Hector's body after he had been killed by Achilles (24:201–16); and finally laments Hector's death (24:748–59).

Introduction

Hecuba appears in Euripides' *Hecuba, Trojan Women,* and fragments of *Alexander*—the first part of the trilogy in which *Trojan Women* is the third play (see Chapter 5, p. 140). She is a wife who has witnessed the murder of her husband (*TW* 481–83); a mother who has lost her sons during the Trojan War and buried her daughter Polyxena and youngest son Polydorus after Troy fell; and a grandmother who has buried her grandson Astyanax (*TW* 1123–250; *Hec.* 511–628, 1287–88). She has heard that her daughter Cassandra will be murdered as well (*Hec.*1275). She is the woman who has lost everything. In both *Hecuba* and *Trojan Women,* Euripides' plots reveal the marked antithesis between Hecuba's physical frailty and her formidable mind, expressed most powerfully through the potent rhetoric seen in *Trojan Women*. Hecuba is by far the most tragic of all extant tragic heroines.

* * *

Through his characterizations of Hecuba, Euripides presents his audiences with heart-breaking depictions of an elderly matriarch who has lost everything through war. While she may be considered the personification of female suffering, Hecuba is not a passive victim, with Euripides characterizing her as:

- a defeated matriarch, a queen taken into slavery, a grieving wife, mother, and grandmother;
- a woman who demands some reparation for all she has suffered, through the punishment of those she sees as responsible;
- a woman with considerable rhetorical skills which she uses to no avail;
- a woman who becomes so embittered by her fate that she appears to have lost all moral rectitude, being prepared to use deception and physical violence to the extent of arranging the murder of her enemy's young sons.

Euripides' *Trojan Women*

The play is set outside the ruins of Troy, soon after the fall of the city. Poseidon remembers how he and Apollo had started building the city long ago, and then recounts how the Argive forces had hidden their soldiers in the belly of a wooden horse, and so were taken inside the battlements, leading to Troy's destruction. Now the Greek ships, laden with plundered treasures, are waiting for a favorable wind, that will allow them to set sail. Poseidon is also about to leave Troy, with its forsaken groves and ruined temples. While the Greeks will be joyfully greeted by their wives and children, the Trojan men are dead, and the captive Trojan women screaming out as each one learns of her fate. Poseidon calls Hecuba "queen of misery"; her husband Priam and many of her sons are killed; her daughter Polyxena has been sacrificed at Achilles' tomb, and her surviving daughter Cassandra has been chosen to be Agamemnon's concubine.

Hecuba sings an emotional monody for herself and Troy, telling the Chorus of Trojan women that they will soon learn to whom they have been assigned as slaves. Talthybius, the Herald of the Greek army, announces the allocations, leaving Hecuba collapsed in grief. But then Talthybius returns and adds that Odysseus has convinced the Greek commanders that Astyanax, the toddler son of Hector and Andromache, must be thrown to his death from the ramparts of Troy.

After two thirds of the play Menelaus enters, announcing that he will take his wife Helen back to Greece for execution to punish her for her elopement with Alexandros to Troy. Hecuba immediately intercedes, appealing to Menelaus to slay Helen immediately, without looking at her, lest she may bewitch him. In the formal debate that ensues, Hecuba clearly defeats Helen's arguments. Menelaus agrees that Helen should be killed, but takes her away, against Hecuba's advice, to his own ship for the journey home. Talthybius returns with the corpse of Astyanax on Hector's shield, and the little boy is buried. The Greeks set fire to the city. Hecuba tries to throw herself into the flames but is held back by the soldiers. The play ends with Hecuba and the Trojan women lamenting the city as they are led away to their appointed Greek masters.

HECUBA IN *TROJAN WOMEN*

After Menelaus announces that he is taking Helen back to Sparta to be executed there, Helen asks for an opportunity to defend herself. Menelaus initially refuses. However, Hecuba who wants Menelaus to kill Helen on the spot, intercedes and asks Menelaus to hear Helen out. She proposes that she herself will rebut all of Helen's arguments, while Menelaus will be the judge. The two women engage in a formal debate (*agon*, see Box on Formal Debate, p. 45).

As has been shown in Chapter 5, Euripides casts Hecuba as a powerful rhetorician who successfully contests Helen's claims of innocence and dismantles each of Helen's arguments with logical and factual counter claims. She demythologizes and takes apart Helen's argument of divine compulsion for her abandoning of Menelaus, and thus strips Helen of her main claim that she is not responsible for her actions. She elaborates on Helen's infatuation with Paris, explaining that Helen was lured to Troy not only by Paris' good looks, but also by the rare opulence of his city.

In response to Helen's version that Paris dragged her away to Troy and that Deiphobus had forced her to stay there, Hecuba points out that neither the Spartan women around her nor her twin brothers heard Helen's cries while she was being abducted. Hecuba also aptly brings up Helen's Trojan sojourn, which Helen has conspicuously omitted from her own speech. She deliberately attempts to arouse Menelaus' wrath by describing Helen's behavior during the Greek siege of Troy: when Menelaus excelled in the battle field, Helen would praise him to distress Paris, but when the Trojans were successful, "Menelaus was nothing" to Helen (1007). She also casts doubt on whether Helen really attempted to escape from Troy by asking why Helen had refused Hecuba's offer of help to steal herself away to the Greeks' ships, and thus deliver both the Greeks and Trojans from the ongoing war.

To render Hecuba persuasive, Euripides affords her a more diverse and colorful style and syntactic structure than he gives to Helen. After demolishing Helen's claims of being a victim of the divine and the mortals alike with no personal responsibility, Hecuba crowns her assault by pointing out Helen's sumptuous attire. Hecuba states that she should have appeared before Menelaus dressed in rags, trembling in fear and with a shaven head showing modesty and repentance. While this was aimed at arousing Menelaus' ill will towards Helen, it also underscores for the viewers the difference between the cold-hearted Helen resplendent in her finery and Hecuba's degradation. No further words are needed to show who the victim is in this picture.

Having refuted Helen's self-defense, Hecuba turns to Menelaus, asking him to crown Greece with glory by killing Helen, and thereby establishing a law: "Death to her who betrays her husband" (1029–32). However, following her Homeric persona, who always failed in her attempts to convince her listeners in spite of being always right, Hecuba is not successful in convincing Menelaus to kill Helen on the spot.[2] He agrees with Hecuba that Helen left Sparta of her own accord, but is adamant that she must be executed only after they reach Sparta.

Euripides' *Hecuba*

The play is set on the Thracian Chersonese (Gallipoli peninsula) opposite Troy. The stage-building represents Agamemnon's tent, in which captive Trojan women are being held. The ghost of Polydorus, the youngest son of King Priam, appears (perhaps on the roof of the stage building, to show his separation from the world). He explains that during the Trojan War his father had sent him, along with a large amount of gold, to King Polymestor in Thrace to ensure his survival and, by extension, a future for the Trojans if their city fell. However, just before the time the play takes place, Polymestor killed the boy and flung his body into the sea; the ghost says that his body will be discovered in the surf, doubling the grief of his mother Hecuba, who is on the Chersonese with the other Trojan women, all of them now slaves. Meanwhile, the ghost of Achilles has appeared above his tomb, stopped the winds which would allow the Greek fleet to sail home and demanded the sacrifice of Hecuba's daughter Polyxena. Hecuba now appears, disturbed by frightening dreams about Polydorus and Polyxena. The Chorus of Trojan Women join her and tell her that the Greeks have decided to sacrifice her daughter, a decision in which Odysseus played the key part. Agamemnon opposed the decision out of his affection for Cassandra, but was overruled. When Polyxena comes on stage and hears what is to happen to her, her sorrow is for her mother, not herself. Odysseus enters to take Polyxena away. He is deaf to Hecuba's pleas, even though she reminds him she had saved his life when he entered Troy on a spying mission. With aristocratic courage Polyxena accepts her fate and goes off willingly to her death. Hecuba collapses. The aged messenger Talthybius describes to Hecuba the Greek army's admiration for Polyxena's heroic decorum before and during her sacrifice by Achilles' son Neoptolemus. Hecuba finds some consolation in her daughter's nobility. She sends the old Serving Woman to the shore to bring water to bathe her daughter's body. The Serving-Woman returns with a covered corpse which Hecuba assumes is the body of Polyxena being brought for burial, but the Serving Woman tells her it is Polydorus, whom she found on the shore. In her agony of grief Hecuba realizes that Polymestor was the perpetrator of the murder. When Agamemnon enters to hasten Hecuba's burial preparations for Polyxena, Hecuba tells him what has happened, asking him to assist her in her vengeance on Polymestor and reminding him of his passion for her daughter Cassandra. Agamemnon answers that while he cannot support her openly since the army considers the Thracian to be their friend, he will afford her the time she needs. Hecuba sends her Serving-Woman to summon Polymestor to come with his two sons, because she has information that is important for his sons to hear as well. Polymestor and his sons arrive. Playing on Polymestor's avarice, Hecuba leads him into the tent in pursuit of hidden valuables she brought from Troy. Here, as Polymestor later explains, his children are killed and he is blinded by the Trojan women. After Agamemnon has listened to Polymestor's account of these events and Hecuba's response, he takes Hecuba's side; Polymestor retaliates by foretelling the murders of Agamemnon and Cassandra by Agamemnon's wife, and Hecuba's transformation into a dog, giving the name Poor Bitch's Grave to her tomb, which will be a landmark for sailors. Agamemnon exiles him to a desert island. The winds blow. It is time for the Greeks to leave.

HECUBA IN *HECUBA*

Although the play precedes *Iphigenia at Aulis* by close to 20 years, it is a precursor for Euripides' later portrayal of the parting between a daughter slated for death and the mother powerless to help her. Euripides casts Hecuba first and foremost as a mother, a function that transgresses national boundaries and can thus arouse pity in Greeks, Trojans, and Thracians alike.[3] Hecuba's persona is depicted as both oppressed and driven at the same time. She comes out of the tent of the captive women supported by some of the Trojan women. Unable to walk by herself, she embodies deprivation, captivity, and helplessness. Her sole activity when the play opens is to bemoan her fate and the fate of her family. However, all the other characters affect, illuminate, and transform Hecuba, bringing out her strength and resistance. Odysseus, Agamemnon, and Polymestor are the main actors in this respect, but her children, Polyxena and the dead Polydorus, are the main motivators.[4] Despite being a captive, Hecuba manages to plan a savage revenge on Polymestor for murdering Polydorus.

Hecuba and Odysseus

As the plot evolves, Hecuba is portrayed not only as dejected but also physically frail. After the other women have helped her come out of the tent (59–67), the Chorus tell her that Odysseus' arguments in favor of human sacrifice have broken the impasse in the Greek assembly's deliberations on whether Polyxena should be sacrificed on Achilles' tomb: shortly he will come to take Polyxena from her. Despite her miserable condition as a slave at the mercy of the Greek host, Hecuba does not give up. She appeals to Odysseus on the basis of one of the values known to the spectators as a motivational force in the Homeric world: gratitude (*charis*, 251–95). Her speech is usually regarded as a notable rhetorical example of persuasive speech.[5] First, in a combative mode, she presents her view of Odysseus' motives: he is one of those political leaders who, in order to gratify the crowd, forgets the moral debt of gratitude. She is not afraid to start with an insult: as is typical of any demagogue, his self-interest is without conscience. She carefully proves that Polyxena, unlike Helen, has done no harm to Achilles. If Achilles deserves the most beautiful thing for his tomb, Helen is the ideal choice. Why would they choose Polyxena over Helen?

Hecuba presents the plea for gratitude: Odysseus owes her a favor. Hecuba spared his life when he came on a spying mission to Troy, disguised by ragged clothing and self-inflicted wounds. An emotional appeal follows the moral appeal, as Hecuba describes her desperate need of Polyxena: "... do not tear my child from my arms, do not kill her!.... She is a consolation to me for many things, she is my city, my nurse, my staff, my guide upon the road" (277–81). For Hecuba, her city lives on in her children, and it is children who take care of their parents. Taking Polyxena from her has both political and personal ramifications. However, distraught she is, Hecuba still manages to organize her speech with care and to orchestrate it appropriately for an emotional supplication-scene. Knowing that she has no power, she ends each part of her speech with statements of general value, instead of with threats, as is appropriate for an older person who has lived long enough to have seen the world in its bitter ugliness.

In spite of her powerlessness, her combative spirit informs the speech. The Greeks deceive themselves if they expect to avenge Achilles by sacrificing an innocent girl instead of an animal. Using herself as an example, she expresses the knowledge that power does not last forever: fortune changes, so those who have power should not exercise it wrongfully (282–84). Hecuba ends her speech by asking for pity (286–95). She bases her plea on an example, so it might be easier for Odysseus to react positively. The Greeks have already shown pity to women, she says, and they do not discriminate between a slave and a free man when it comes to pity, so he can show it to her although she is now a slave. Finally, she adds flattery to her request: Odysseus' reputation will be enough to persuade the Greeks to change their mind about Polyxena.

Hecuba obviously fails. Odysseus will not change his mind nor try to change anybody else's. To Hecuba's splendid appeal, Odysseus replies with a lawyer's masterpiece devoid of any emotion, shifting the subject from her personal pain to that of what the Greeks owe Achilles. Luschnig has already commented that "a successful speech cannot be made by a weaker party" in this play (1988: 100). Indeed, as we will see later, Hecuba's loss has already been foreordained by Homer.

In a scene that will later become an indelible image when it is paralleled in *Iphigenia at Aulis* (1115–21), Hecuba turns to Polyxena and tells her to plead for her life, adding a pragmatic remark, that Odysseus too has children (334–41). However, Polyxena, like Iphigenia in the later play, is intelligent and independent. Understanding that her fate is sealed, she accepts it sorrowfully yet boldly, and marches off with Odysseus. With an invincible sense of freedom and aristocratic integrity, she transforms her enforced death into an expression of her own free will. She does not want to live as a slave (357–58, 367–69). Hecuba later learns of the way Polyxena heroically offered her beautiful breast and neck to the sacrificial sword of Neoptolemus. Furthermore, even as her life was ebbing away, she took great care to fall in a seemly fashion so that no part of her body was revealed. Talthybius, the Greek herald, who is the only male in the play who is not despicable (543–70), describes to Hecuba the way that Polyxena took charge of her own sacrifice, insisting again on her freedom: no enemy hand, but only the sacrificial blade was to touch her. He also tells Hecuba that the gathered Argives were in awe of the young girl's nobility and courage. Talthybius aptly summarizes what he sees as Hecuba's luck:

"As I say these things about your dead daughter, I regard you as of all women the most blessed in your offspring as well as the unluckiest" (580–82). Unlike the later Clytemnestra in *Iphigenia at Aulis,* who is devastated by Iphigenia's death but can at least occupy herself with plans for revenge against Agamemnon, Hecuba has no such hope. After hearing Talthybius' account, Hecuba tries to temper her grief with general reflections that might give her some solace (585–628). She first yields to bewildered despair: sorrows surround her, competing for her attention. Her daughter's courage and nobility bring her some comfort, as she reflects that the human moral character is unchangeable from birth and does not depend on external circumstances, like the earth's yield. Moving away from these thoughts, she forms a fresh resolve. She tells Talthybius to announce that no soldier should touch Polyxena: soldiers are vicious and uncontrollable. She now turns to planning Polyxena's funeral in the best way that she can under the circumstances, musing again on the ruins of the once great Troy and on the vanity of all human pride.

Hecuba with Agamemnon and Polymestor

The spectators have now seen Hecuba as dejected but capable of gathering herself together to plead both emotionally and logically for the life of her daughter (although this plea was in vain). Euripides inherited from the *Iliad* the image of Hecuba as a caring or mourning mother whose wishes are always thwarted. The ferocity of her love for her children is manifested in the *Iliad* in her inconsolable mourning for her dead son Hector when she says that she wished she could fasten onto Achilles' liver and feed on it (*Il.* 24.212–13). We find in the epic other vaguer allusions to eating someone raw that add to the power of this image.[6] The play reflects the epic in a nuanced way. The first half of the play presents the traditional epic image of Hecuba whose legitimate concerns for her children are rebuffed: she appears as a mother whose powerful pleas for the life of her innocent daughter are cruelly rejected by Odysseus, and also by Polyxena herself, who refuses to plead for her life. The second half of the play offers a wounded Hecuba who achieves some vengeance. This is a Hecuba who transitions from desolation to unstoppable rage, the *Iliadic* mother ready to fasten on and devour Achilles' liver. Her passivity transforms into active vengeance. Thus Hecuba not only orchestrates the blinding of the treacherous Polymestor but also arranges the killing of his two sons.

The brief reprieve during which Hecuba recovers some of her spirits amidst her grief for Polyxena, is cruelly reversed when her Serving Woman, who had gone to the shore to fetch water to wash Polyxena's body, returns carrying a wrapped body. Euripides heightens the drama by surprising Hecuba with the wrapped body of Polydorus, which she expects to be Polyxena's body brought for burial (671–82). This grisly discovery fulfills her expectant sense of dread from her nightmare (702–8, cf. 68–70) and provokes a swift and violent accusation of Polymestor as the treacherous murderer (710–20, cf. 25–27). Euripides elevates her wrath and bereavement for the audience by letting her expressions of despair be sung by her. The Serving Woman aptly describes Hecuba's situation: "Mistress . . . you are lost: though you see the light of day you are dead, without a child, without a husband, without a city, utterly destroyed" (668–69). Hecuba is numb; she loses, as it were, all sense of moral identity. Nothing is left to live for but revenge on Polymestor. And what Homer did not allow Hecuba to do in revenge for Hector, Euripides gives her full rein to accomplish in exacting a bloody revenge on Polymestor.

As she denounces the avarice and cruelty of Polymestor, Agamemnon arrives to make sure that Hecuba completes Polyxena's funeral as quickly as possible (726–35). In the only full "aside" in extant Greek tragedy we watch Hecuba deliberating with herself how to proceed in front of Agamemnon, who clearly does not hear her words (736–51).[7] After this self-deliberation she decides to ask Agamemnon for help.[8] She, the once proud Queen of Troy, decides to grovel before the enemy in charge, because in him she sees the only means to her revenge. Hecuba takes control of the situation, as Polyxena did when she refused to live as a slave. She explains to Agamemnon who the dead body in front of them is and convinces him of the likely cause of Polydorus' death—Polymestor's greed for the gold.[9] Next, steeling herself as a slave who has to beg from her master, she pleads that he should punish Polymestor, give her the means to do so, or at least by passive complicity allow her to act (787–845). When she realizes that Agamemnon wants to turn away from her supplication, Hecuba does not shy away from reminding him of the pleasures he derives from having her daughter Cassandra as his bed-mate. Having already heard that it was due to his affection for Cassandra that he objected to Polyxena's sacrifice, she has reason to think he will be on her side this time as well (824–32, cf. 120–22).

Hecuba's plea meets with partial success. Agamemnon says he wants to help her but fears the opinion of the army. Polymestor is the Greeks' friend, while Polydorus was their enemy. He urges her to contrive some means by which she may help herself. Even in this dire impasse, Hecuba is able to see the bigger picture: "No mortal is free!" (864), she concludes: one is a slave either to money, fate, the public, or laws. She quickly finds a solution, lowering her demand from active help to complicity, and the preventing of any intervention. She is sure she will be successful even without his active help. When Agamemnon doubts the women's ability to get mastery over men, Hecuba exclaims: "In a mass they [women] are fearsome, and with the aid of cunning hard to combat" (Collard, 884, 870–85).

Hecuba's plan of revenge is flawless. She summons Polymestor with his sons to the tent of the captive women. First, she elicits from him the lie that Polydorus is still alive and well; then she lures him and his sons into the women's tent, suggesting she has important information to convey and pretending that this is where she is hiding the jewels she brought from Troy. She allays his fear that men might be in the tent who could pose a threat to him, by assuring him that only women are in the tent (1018–22). Polymestor will recount later to Agamemnon what happened in the tent. He was sitting in the middle of a couch, his legs bent in repose, surrounded by many Trojan women. Some were admiring the weaving of his clothes. Others, looking at his two Thracian javelins, stripped him of them. Those who were mothers admired his sons, passing them from one to another in order to separate them from him. Then all of a sudden, the women produced daggers from their clothing and stabbed the boys. The dense and numerous throng of the women prevented him from saving his boys, and held him by his arms and legs, eventually blinding him with their brooches (1150-73). Hecuba's claim that numbers matter is justified.

Agamemnon becomes the judge between Polymestor and Hecuba. The speeches of the two are presented as a formal debate (*agon*, see Box on Formal Debate, p. 45). Polymestor's main defense is that he killed Polydorus to help the Greeks. Hecuba rebuts Polymestor's claims. Hecuba's well-organized speech starts, as is her habit, with a general statement: words and deeds should match; false eloquence is ultimately self-defeating. Hecuba denies that Polymestor could have been acting in the Greeks' interest, claiming that friendship between Barbarians—like the Thracian Polymestor—and Greeks is not possible. Greed was Polymestor's actual driving force, a claim she proves with the argument that if it were in the Greeks' interest to kill Polydorus, Polymestor would have done it when Troy was still standing and turned the gold over to the Greeks. Even after killing Polydorus when Troy had been sacked, Polymestor is still keeping the gold for himself. She ends her speech by pointing out to Polymestor the advantages he would have gained had he kept Polydorus alive. If he, Polymestor, had ever been in trouble, Polydorus would have come to his aid. She ends her speech by cautioning Agamemnon that his own reputation is riding on the verdict. Agamemnon finds Polymestor guilty: he is banished to live in exile on a desert island.

However, Hecuba's woes are not over. Before leaving Polymestor delivers his parting blows, informing Hecuba of her fate. He tells her that she will change into a dog, jumping off the mast into the waves, and that her grave will receive the name of "the mound of the wretched bitch," which will be a sign for sailors (1259-73). He also tells her that her surviving daughter Cassandra will be murdered by Clytemnestra.[10] The spectators last see Hecuba going off to bury her two children, Polyxena and Polydorus, knowing that she is fated to become altogether childless. This woman, for whom her children were the essence of her life, now knows that whether still alive or already dead she will be bereft of every single one of them. She is fated to nothingness.

It is common to see, in the blinding of Polymestor and the savagery of murdering his innocent children (which she fails to justify in her speech) degradation in the morality of Hecuba.[11] But is it a degradation or an instance of volcanic eruption of the helplessness and rage that coincide in her all the time? For Hecuba, her children meant everything. As long as she thought that Polydorus was alive, she knew there was hope for her city and for her family. Once that hope was taken away from her, she is overcome by her wish for revenge. She wants to reduce Polymestor to the same state she is in.

Readers may, however, question whether this particular form of revenge would be congruent with the frame of mind of women who have recently lost their own children. Is Euripides casting a grim judgment on human nature, indicating that bloodthirsty determination to exact revenge may overcome our capacity for empathy? We may also question whether it is significant that women carry out this revenge. Does the scene indicate an underlying misogyny conflicting with the play's overall sympathy for women victims of war? Readers of this scene may consider that it reinforces the idea that Euripides may have shared with other Greeks that if women achieve power, they will lose any apparent restraint and behave with as much savagery as men or perhaps even outdo their male counterparts. On the other hand, Euripides may have emphasized the violence of the off-stage scene either for dramatic purposes or so as not to risk falling out of favor with those holding misogynistic views.

There is further significance in the revenge meted out by Hecuba to Polymestor. As her Serving Woman told her, although she still sees the light, i.e. is alive, for all intents and purposes she is dead. She has no male heirs, therefore no city or family. Her revenge is a *quid pro quo*: she takes the light from Polymestor and his children. Now they are even. A lot is made of "seeing" in this play: the apparition of Polydorus to Hecuba in her dreams prophesying his death; the apparition of Achilles on his mound demanding the death of Polyxena; and seeing and unseeing the light by Hecuba and Polymestor, who are metaphorically dead while physically alive. This is why the death Polymestor predicts for her has no meaning for Hecuba. In her own eyes she is already dead.

Conclusion

Euripides' *Hecuba* is particularly difficult for modern audiences to grapple with, as indeed is the persona of the Trojan Queen herself. In Hecuba's ancient aristocratic world, people made sense of their lives through interpreting actions either as being the will of the gods or as conforming to society's laws and conventions. Euripides did not introduce gods into *Hecuba*, leaving justice in the hands of men and women, who acted in line with their interpretations of the law. However, the setting of *Hecuba*, in a remote army camp, after the defeat of Troy gives a sense of detachment from the normal rules of society. Everything is in flux. The Greeks are waiting to leave Thrace and return home, while the Trojan women in general and Hecuba in particular are grieving for what they once had, and awaiting with trepidation their new lives as slaves. Hecuba herself goes through various transformations. She is the grieving mother, an eloquent rhetorician, and then a person of action. As a mother in turn fighting for, grieving over, and then avenging her children, Hecuba at first fulfills and then goes beyond the conventions for ancient Greek women. Both in her use of rhetoric and in her strategic ability in planning a swift and effective revenge, Hecuba proves her prowess in what are usually considered male preserves. Although as noted above, many critics considered the unity of *Hecuba* to be problematic, it would seem that the play as a whole does present a consistent persona for Hecuba, however much she evolves throughout the plot in response to the new situations she faces. Hecuba remains the consummate mother figure, who is prepared to fight for her children any way she can, both throughout their lives, and after their deaths.

DISCUSSION TOPICS

1. *Trojan Women* portrays Hecuba's encounters and conversations with her daughter Cassandra as well as with her daughter-in-law Andromache. Compare

Hecuba's relationship with her daughter and Andromache. Do you think that actors portraying Hecuba, Cassandra, and Andromache could have portrayed these differences on stage? How do you think this could have been achieved?

2. In *Trojan Women*, Hecuba frequently laments her fate and sees herself as dead, however, she advises Andromache to forget Hector and accept Neoptolemus to whom she was allotted as her new master without objection. Do you think this is related to the difference in ages of the two women? Do you think that Hecuba lacks empathy for Andromache, or just the opposite? Explain your answers.

3. Describe the differences in the portrayal of Hecuba in *Trojan Women* and in *Hecuba*? Do you find each portrayal equally believable? Explain your answers.

4. Euripides' *Hecuba* deals with the atrocities related to warfare, which, in this case, continue even after the fighting has ceased. The human sacrifice of Polyxena on Achilles' tomb, demanded by the ghost of Achilles, is the first of several horrifying episodes in the tragedy. Why do you think the poet chose to include this apparently meaningless murder in the play? Can you trace the impact of Polyxena's death on further events?

5. Hecuba is expecting to see the body of her daughter Polyxena, but instead finds the body of her son Polydorus, who has been brutally murdered with his body thrown out to sea. What does the loss of Polydorus signify to Hecuba?

6. Hecuba suffers multiple losses throughout *Hecuba*, each one sufficiently devastating to cause lasting grief and trauma. Do you think these are intended to justify her actions against Polymestor?

7. When Hecuba seeks revenge on Polymestor, she and the other Trojan women plot for Polymestor's sons to be murdered and for him to be blinded. The murder of young children by women who have lost their own family members seems a particularly repugnant act. Do you think that the play's message is that war reduces everyone to bestiality? Can you find any other themes?

8. When you have read Chapter 10, compare Hecuba's actions with those of Medea.

CHAPTER 7
ALCESTIS

Mythic background

There are few extant references to the story of Alcestis' agreeing to die for Admetus. The *Iliad* (2.713–15) briefly mentions Alcestis and Admetus as the parents of Eumelus who led the forces of Pherae and Iolcus in the Trojan War on the Greeks' side. The *Iliad* also singles out Alcestis for praise as "the most honorable of women" and "the most beautiful of the daughters of Pelias." The only known Greek dramatization of the story prior to Euripides was by Phrynichus (Snell 1986: vol.1: T 3.1), who was an older contemporary of Euripides, active from about 510 to 476 BCE. All that remains of Phrynichus' play is Hades' appearance on stage with a sword to cut a lock of Alcestis' hair (Snell 1986: vol. 1: F 3 and apparatus). None of the subsequent extant references mention the core story of Alcestis' sacrifice for her husband. The Chorus of Aeschylus' *Eumenides* (723–28), produced twenty years earlier, refer obliquely to the story when they accuse Apollo of getting the Fates drunk and inducing them to turn mortals in the house of Pheres (Admetus' father) into immortals. The second *hypothesis* (ancient summary of Alcestis' plot outline by an unknown author) alleges that neither Aeschylus nor Sophocles treated this story. The last known reference to the myth contemporaneous with Euripides is a drinking-song attributed to Praxilla (*c.* mid-fifth century): "Learn the story of Admetus, my friend, and seek the brave/ but keep off the cowards since there is little gratitude in them" (Page [ed.] 1962: 2).

Euripides' *Alcestis*

The action takes place in Pherae, outside Admetus' palace. Apollo recounts his time spent as a slave in Admetus' household, while being punished by Zeus for having killed the Cyclopes. Admetus showed exemplary hospitality and Apollo rewarded him by allowing Admetus to have a substitute die in his place when his time comes, which is this day. Admetus has asked each of his parents to die for him, but they have refused. His wife Alcestis is the only person willing to agree to this sacrifice. When Thanatos, the god regarded as the personification of Death, comes for Alcestis, Apollo pleads unsuccessfully for a reprieve for her. Although Apollo can't change Death's mind, he predicts that a man sent by Eurystheus (the King that Heracles serves, performing twelve labors) will take Alcestis from Death by force. After Alcestis' last hours are described by a Maidservant, Alcestis is brought out, supported by Admetus and her servants, to take one last look at the light of the sun, while the Chorus praise her as the best of wives. In her dying moments Alcestis elicits a promise from Admetus not to force a stepmother on their children by remarrying. When Heracles arrives at Admetus' home on his way to Thrace to fetch the horses of Diomedes (his eighth labor), Admetus does not reveal Alcestis' death and encourages his friend to revel in his palace. Meanwhile, Admetus' father Pheres comes with funeral gifts, which Admetus rejects. The two trade accusations, with Admetus blaming his father for not agreeing to die for him because of his wish for long life. Pheres rebuffs the claim by saying that he does not have to die for his son. After Admetus exits with the Chorus to bury Alcestis, the slave charged with taking care of Heracles enters, decries Heracles' unseemly merriment and reveals to him Alcestis' death. Heracles immediately sets off to rescue her. Returning with a veiled and silent woman, he convinces Admetus to take her in, without Admetus realizing at first that the woman is Alcestis. The *exodos* is cast as a recognition scene which unfolds in phases.

Introduction

Alcestis appears in *Alcestis* of 438 BCE, the earliest of Euripides' surviving plays. The play defies genre categorization. It is usually termed a pro-satyric play, due partly to its performance as the fourth play of the tetralogy, a position usually reserved for satyr plays (see Box on Satyr Plays, p. 181), and because it shares with satyr plays certain elements, such as its use of folktale motifs (e.g. personification of Death on stage), as well as sexual innuendos (especially when Heracles offers Admetus a woman to replace Alcestis), together with the many comic scenes seemingly more appropriate to a satyr play than tragedy. Much of the dialogue is ambiguous, or written in riddles, from the first scene between Apollo and Death right up to the exchanges between Admetus and Heracles at the very end of the play. Even the essence of the plot, which revolves around a deal with Death by which Admetus is to be spared if someone else agrees to die in his place seems more fitting to satyr drama than tragedy. On the other hand, various markers of satyr plays are not found in *Alcestis*. Apart from the short scene where Heracles drinks to excess, the play is free of the coarse bawdry of Euripides' extant satyr play, *Cyclops*. *Alcestis* also has moments of true sadness and revolves around man's mortality, courage, self-sacrifice, and the meaning of life, the predominant themes of classical tragedy. Moreover, Euripides wrote *Alcestis* using the high diction of tragedy, and follows tragic structural features, such as prologue, choral odes, formal debates, and recognition.

These inconsistencies fuel an ongoing scholarly debate over whether the play is more comic or tragic.[1] Comic elements include the reduction of Apollo to the servant of a human being and his coming on stage with a bow as if to threaten Death; the speed with which Admetus breaks his exaggerated vow to mourn Alcestis' death all his life; and

Satyr plays

Each contestant customarily entered four plays into the competition in the Great Dionysia festival in Athens: three tragedies and one satyr play. The satyr play is thought to bring some relief to the tense subjects of the three tragedies. The amusement was effected not so much by the action as by the relation of the chorus of satyrs to the action, which included coarse obscenity. The subject of satyr plays was lighter than that of the tragedies. The material for satyr drama was taken from epic or myth, and the claim is that an overall theme taken from the trilogy, or from one of the tragedies, was incorporated into the satyr play. Their main characteristic was a chorus of satyrs and Sileni, the companions of Dionysus. Only one satyr play has come down to us in entirety, the *Cyclops* by Euripides. The main features of satyr drama were brevity, defeat of some sort of ogre, hospitality (*xenia*, see Box on Hospitality, pp. 189–190), and its abuse, trickery and folkloric magic, often accompanied by sexual innuendoes.

Heracles' inebriation and wrestling with Death.[2] The ambiguity of the ending adds to the uncertainty. Other Euripidean tragedies, namely *Orestes, Iphigenia among the Taurians, Ion,* and *Helen,* also seem to end on a positive note, although not without the foreshadowing of some unwelcome consequences.[3] In this case, Heracles overcomes death and rescues Alcestis. However, while the initial catastrophe is reversed, one cannot help thinking back to Apollo's encounter with Death at the start of the play. If Alcestis has been spared, who will take her place?

* * *

Alcestis is another highly feminine heroine, depicted by Euripides as an almost completely submissive wife, yet she too has her moment of defiance. Her character traits include:

- "volunteering" to die in place of her husband, Admetus, although her awareness of the consequences of refusing to "volunteer" casts doubt on the extent of her volition in this decision;
- bewailing her rapidly approaching demise, and not stopping when this fails to elicit any acknowledgment of his culpability in Admetus;
- she uses a more creative avenue of invoking some sense of guilt in Admetus by extracting from him a promise that he will not remarry, a promise she knows Admetus cannot keep.

Views of Alcestis

Alcestis' character is gradually revealed throughout the first half of the play. Prior to her appearance on stage, she is praised repeatedly. Apollo tries to convince Death to postpone

Alcestis' death with the argument that if Alcestis is allowed to live to old age, Death's honor will be higher since her burial as an older person will be much richer (52–56). The Chorus laud her over and over: she is the best of wives (83–84, 200, 230, 241–42; after her death 418, 442, 460), the best wife under the sun, who will die with fame (*kleos*) for her sacrifice (150–51), a sentiment repeated by Alcestis' Maidservant (152). The Chorus even suggest that Admetus might consider committing suicide for losing such a wife (228–30), a suggestion which adds to the nonsensical undertone of the play.

What do we learn in this scene about the relationship between Alcestis and Admetus, or about why she offered to die for him? How does the Alcestis we hear about in the first episode compare to the onstage Alcestis in the second? We see Alcestis' last day at home through the Maidservant's eyes. Knowing that the day of her death has arrived, Alcestis has taken great care in her preparations. She "bathed her pale skin in flowing water" (159–60) and dressed herself in finery, ready for death to come. She has prayed to Hestia, the hearth goddess, that her children will live long and happy lives in their ancestral home (169), introducing one of the many problematic themes of the play: was Alcestis being a good mother when she chose to sacrifice herself so Admetus could continue living? Indeed, the emphasis on the children is apparent elsewhere in the play, especially in the lament of Alcestis' son over his dead mother, which must have been arresting both for its poignancy, and for the novelty of having a boy sing (as Torrance notes 2019: 53).[4] Ebeling highlights the importance Euripides places on the character of Alcestis in general, and as a mother in particular, positing that Phrynichus' earlier version had Alcestis' death occurring on her wedding day, necessarily precluding Admetus and Alcestis from having any children.[5] The question could be resolved by considering that Alcestis might have thought she had no choice. She might have feared that her weak, cowardly, self-centered husband could have stooped so low as to sacrifice one of their children if she had refused to die in his place. After all, he did ask his mother and father to die for him.

If this view of her husband's character is tenable, one element of the next scene supports it. The housemaid reports that Alcestis continued performing her duties as mistress of the house, praying at all of the altars. Then, entering the bedchamber, she wept at the sight of her marriage bed. In a bizarre scene, Alcestis takes leave not of her husband, but of the bed where she yielded up her virginity and which has now caused her death (177–79).[6] Next, she kisses her children farewell, caressing and comforting each one of them, and shaking hands with every slave, finding a good word for each (189–95). What stands out, however, is that there is not a word about her husband, other than her belief that another woman will now have the marriage bed, and the wish that her children will not die as prematurely as she does. Love or affection for a husband does not seem to be a prerequisite for this best of wives.

Finally, Alcestis appears on stage, supported by servants and Admetus. They are accompanied by their two children. The audience have not yet seen the main protagonists, but they have heard the Chorus acclaim Alcestis' bravery and wifely sacrifice and bewail the loneliness and misery that Admetus will soon face. The unremitting praise for Alcestis might have led to certain expectations of her behavior. If she does indeed display the best characteristics of wifely behavior, the audience might now expect to see some expressions of her devotion to her husband.[7] However, Euripides gives a far more realistic presentation of the situation. Here, as in his other plays, his women are characters of flesh and blood in spite of the mythic framework. The tone is set by the Chorus' ominous hint that marriage might not be joyous, and is developed in the couple's exchange (238–79). We hear Alcestis uttering almost delirious cries on her deathbed, calling upon the sun and her native land Iolcus, and maintaining that she sees Charon, who is hurrying her, and Hades himself. She is very clear about not dying gladly, instead pleading with the vision she sees of Hades: "What do you want? Let me go! Ah, what a journey it is that I, unhappiest of women, am making" (262–63). Admetus' behavior is selfish to a degree that it is almost incomprehensible. He has asked Alcestis to die for him. His cowardly choice to go on living at the expense of his wife has brought them to this point. Yet now, he selfishly and illogically urges her to continue living, demands that she not leave him and tells her to pray to the gods for deliverance, ignoring utterly his responsibility for her plight. He almost suggests that her death is her fault: "Rouse yourself up, poor woman, do not abandon me. Pray for pity to the gods who have you in their grasp" (250–51). It does not seem to occur to him that perhaps it is he who should be doing the praying, in an attempt to reverse the bargain and die in place of his wife. Alcestis for the most part ignores Admetus and talks at him rather than to him. Her disregard of him reaches its peak in the heartrending farewell addressed only to her children (270–72). In turn, Admetus' insensitivity reaches its highest point when he includes the children in his pleas: "I beg you by the gods, by the children you will orphan, do not have the hardness to desert me. Up, endure! For if you are gone, I live no more. Whether we live or not is in your power, for it is your love we hold in reverence" (275–79). The fact that he is the one depriving his children of their mother is not mentioned.

    The rift and cross-communication between the couple is underscored by the meter. While Alcestis sings in a variety of emotive lyrical meters, Euripides carefully ensured that Admetus' brief interjections into her delirious utterances are spoken in unemotional iambic trimeter characterized by conversational cadence, usually used when no poetic elevation is sought by the playwright (246–47, 250–51, 257–58, 264–65). When Admetus finally abandons his iambs after Alcestis' farewell to her children, his recitative anapests (273–79), midway between unemotional trimeter and lyric verse, accentuate his cold and unemotional character. Alcestis' lyric dactyls are evocative and symbolic, with the sun symbolizing life in the Greek mind as early as Homer and the racing clouds emblematic of Alcestis' imminent death. Admetus, however, picking up the image of the sun, does not answer Alcestis' anguished cry for life, but takes the opportunity to exculpate himself and complain of the gods' unfairness: "The sun god sees you and me, two unfortunates, who have done nothing to the gods to deserve your death" (246–47). Despite the continuing changes in the tone, substance, and rhythm of Alcestis' song, Admetus' responses remain tuneless and prosaic, emphasizing his failure to be moved by her pain and isolation, and underscoring his concentration on himself. The discrepancy would be further emphasized by the likelihood that Alcestis' singing was accompanied by a musical instrument, while Admetus' statements were not. Although adult males usually do not sing in Euripidean drama (the exceptions are Hippolytus and Theseus in *Hippolytus,* and the Phrygian slave in *Orestes*), here was an opportunity for Euripides to make Admetus more agitated, affectionate, and tender by allowing him to sing, but he foregoes the opportunity.[8] The cold, monotonic responses of Admetus contrast with Alcestis' loneliness and despair.

Alcestis Revived

As mentioned in the introduction to this book (pp. 5–6), many of the Tragic heroines make use of eloquent rhetoric. This is manifested in Alcestis' well-designed speech to Admetus. After her heartrending death throes, Alcestis recovers all of a sudden to give a lengthy, well-structured speech aimed at getting Admetus to promise what she knows he would be unable to do due to his disposition: never to remarry (280–325).[9] Her revival, resulting in a well-thought-out, lucid, and coherent speech is surprising, but characteristic of Euripides' penchant for baffling the audience and having the characters do the opposite of what one would expect. The sudden non-sequitur in both her manner of speaking and her physical stamina is combined with her contradictory expectations as she forbids Admetus to remarry, although in private she had seemed to consider a new marriage inevitable (181–82). Has his coldness during her painful last moments angered her to the point of seeking some kind of revenge? Has the approach of death brought home the brutal reality of her husband's demand? Euripides clearly emphasized the sequence of these scenes. If Alcestis' farewell to life had followed her contractual speech, the natural development of the two episodes would have been smooth, but the proleptic sequence is baffling, if not peculiarly humorous.

Alcestis launches now into spoken iambic trimeter, the meter that her husband used when interrupting her soul-stirring lyrics. The speech is not that of a loving, generous-hearted, or altruistic woman. She bluntly tells Admetus not only that she is sacrificing her life for him but also that had she wanted to, she could have had her pick of men after his death and lived on royally in their palace. She goes on to let him know that her motive was not love or concern for him, but rather her reluctance to make her children fatherless (288–89). She expresses deep bitterness towards Admetus' parents who refused die for their son. Mercilessly she points out that they had every reason to save Admetus because he is their only son. The result of their refusal is her premature death; otherwise Admetus and she would have been living the remainder of their lives together. A more honorable wife might have said that she forgives his parents, or failed to mention their refusal altogether instead of sowing future discord between the son and his parents. She must have known Admetus would harbor a deep grudge against his parents. Admetus' upcoming tirade against his father proves how well she knew her husband (614–738).

Alcestis' comments about the choices she had available to her had she opted to let Admetus die, and her mention of his parents, are the build-up for the demand she is about to make as a fair although insufficient *quid pro quo* for her momentous sacrifice. Nothing can equal life, she states (299–301). Casting the demand in terms of "gratitude," or "reciprocity" for her sacrifice (*charis*—an expected behavior between friends, guest-friends, and surely between spouses), she demands that he remain single to assure their children are the lords of the house.[10] Alcestis' demand becomes the fulcrum on which the plot is about to swing. Her lengthy expatiation on the malice of a stepmother reinforces the reasonableness of her expectation (305–10, 314–16). Concerns over a stepmother's potential cruelty to her children indicate Alcestis' maternal love but do not show any attendant compassion for Admetus. She is certain that Admetus will not honor this request, and will be in breach of the expected reciprocity for her sacrifice, of *charis*. As mentioned, she has indicated that she expects another woman to have the marriage bed (181–82), and at the start of her request to him she adds in an aside "if you are of sound mind" (303), hinting that she does not believe Admetus has the mental capacity to keep his word in this regard. We also hear from the Chorus after his speech that Admetus' mental competence is suspect in regard to remarrying: "Fear not (I do not hesitate to speak for him): he will do this [i.e. not remarry] *if he has any sense*" (326–27). Alcestis' doubts about Admetus' capacity to keep his word are also clear from the following address to her daughter:

What sort of stepmother will you get? May she not cast some disgraceful slur on your reputation and in the prime of your youth destroy your chance of marriage! (314–16)

Clearly Alcestis believes that Admetus will remarry. Thus, in return for his selfish behavior in agreeing that she dies in his place, she is condemning him to at least experience some remorse, not only for her death but also for his inability to live up to her wishes, and to the socially accepted value of gratitude. There is a good deal of anger and spite in her demand. Admetus' welfare after her death is of very little interest to Alcestis. Her mention of Admetus' parents' refusal to die is unnecessary and insidious, provoking his anger and ensuring that there will be no loving relationship between her husband and her parents-in-law. She also sows the seeds of a hostile relationship between the father and his children, when she turns to them after hearing Admetus' empty promises,[11] and says:

Children, you yourselves have heard your father promise never to put another woman over you, never to dishonour me. (371–73)

Being forced to go to an early death, Alcestis no longer cares whether her children will grow to hate their father, a reality that the Chorus voice when they add themselves to the number of those who will hate Admetus if he remarries. They sing:

And if your husband should take a new bride, he will be hateful in my eyes as in those of your children. (463–66)

Nor is Alcestis a humble woman. She knows the worth of her sacrifice, and she is sure that whoever Admetus will marry next will not be as virtuous as she is (182), probably less so (306). She is fully aware that she will receive fame upon her death as the best of wives and the best of mothers (324–25). She is not sacrificing her life in order to obtain fame, but fame will be a result of her sacrifice (445–54).

Why she agreed to die for Admetus is something of a mystery. As suggested earlier, knowing how egotistic and unscrupulous her husband is, a man who did not hesitate to ask his mother and father to die for him, and without hesitation turned to his wife, whom he professes to love, it might well be that Alcestis assumed that if she had refused, he might have turned next to one of his children. Perhaps rather than being an excellent wife, Alcestis was in fact an excellent mother, who gave her life to protect her children. This would explain her last-minute request from her husband. Instead of being a device to take revenge on Admetus, it may be considered that on her deathbed, with her last strength, Alcestis is fighting for the future of her children.

Alcestis Most Present in her Absence

Alcestis speaks her last word in the middle of line 391, bidding farewell to her husband, but seems more present in her absence than when she was on stage preparing to die, or later when she returns as a silent veiled figure. Euripides conveys the anguish associated with the untimely death of the young mother by having a young child, the son of Admetus and Alcestis, express his profound grief on stage. This breaks all conventions, being unique in extant plays, and must have been a powerful moment for the audience. The Chorus sing the praises of Alcestis while Admetus prepares her funeral. When Heracles arrives unexpectedly, Admetus makes light of his grief, wishing to honor the duty of hospitality. Although Heracles had been aware of Alcestis' pledge to die in place of Admetus, and although he asks whether it is Alcestis who has died, he does not guess the true meaning of Admetus' cryptic speech about the woman who died, when to his question whether the dead woman was 'related by blood' to Admetus, the answer was "not by blood, but she was in other ways closely connected to the family" (532–33).

Admetus' one positive trait in this play is his hospitality. However, this hospitality, overshadowed by Alcestis' death, now seems to be a perverse act, for which Heracles later reproaches him (1008–18). However, as often is the case in Euripides' writing, every act is multifaceted: Admetus' hospitality has many sides. When Heracles finally learns the truth behind his host's mourning, he immediately resolves to save Alcestis. Ironically, this is the one moment after her death which is more about Admetus than Alcestis. Heracles will act to save his friend from his grief due to Admetus' worthy hospitality, rather than rescuing Alcestis for her own virtues as "the best of wives."

Until the burial proper nothing can break through Admetus' surreal behavior, even his father's blunt words: "You live beyond your fated day by killing *her*" (695–96). Only after his return to the desolate palace, while continuing with his laments, does Admetus finally seem to focus on what he has lost, and on how valuable Alcestis was, "Now I understand," he says (*arti manthanō*, 940). It appears that the reality of what he has done finally dawns upon him, although he frames it in words of an imagined enemy who would say, "Look at this man who lives in disgrace! He did not have the courage to die, but in cowardice escaped death by giving his wife in his place" (955–57). Admetus' moment of clarity may be short lived, but it does seem that for this brief interlude he truly sees who Alcestis was, and recognizes what he has done. In response, the Chorus elevate Alcestis almost to the level of the gods, calling her "a blessed divinity" (995–1003). This sets the scene for Alcestis to return, completely unrecognized. What follows is similar in some ways to one of tragedy's many delayed recognition scenes, but with a twist. As we shall see, Alcestis herself remains silent, but is present in two ways: first as the veiled figure Heracles leads onto the stage, and second as the memory of the blessed wife who only moments earlier has been praised to the heavens. The irony of this final scene cannot be overstated.

Alcestis' Return

The audience learns that Heracles was true to his words. He went to Alcestis' grave, wrestled with Death and recovered Alcestis. How this actually occurred is quite vague. Admetus had prepared a funeral pyre, so presumably Alcestis was to be burnt on the pyre, following one of Greek customs of burial. Did Heracles rescue her before this, or did he somehow retrieve her soul and repersonify it? What would Death's reaction have been? The audience saw Death refusing Apollo earlier in the play when he asked him to give up a soul. It is not clear whether Heracles used his physical strength to persuade Death to change his mind altogether, or whether this is just a temporary reprieve.

One way or another, Heracles returns to the palace with Alcestis veiled and silent, and proceeds into a quasi-comical interchange with Admetus. The scene resembles something of a game of hide-and-seek, in which Heracles prevents Admetus from getting a full view of Alcestis while trying to convince Admetus to take the woman into his home. Admetus fails to recognize his own wife, even as he tries to get a better look at the enticing woman.[12]

The episode starts with Heracles' lie (1008–36) about how he came into the possession of this woman. He tells Admetus that he won in a competition "a herd of oxen and a woman followed in addition to the herds" (1031–32). Some of the spectators would recognize the echo of an incident in *Iliad* 23, where Diomedes, the pronounced winner of the chariot race in the games in honor of Patroclus, receives a prestigious double prize "a woman and an eared tripod" (23.262–65, 512–13). While the Homeric passage reflects the relative importance of the woman by mentioning her first, Heracles minimizes the woman's importance by mentioning her as an afterthought, either to mimic Admetus' diminishment of Alcestis' death by not admitting it, or in order not to arouse Admetus' suspicions regarding the woman.[13] There is no need for such subtlety, however, because Admetus is rather slow-witted, and falls for Heracles' lie, not recalling that he has just banned all entertainment in Pherae. He never inquires how Heracles could have found a competition so nearby. Instead of probing Heracles' story, he rejects Heracles' offer to take the mysterious woman into his house with a plethora of *figurae etymologicae* (see Glossary) packed in such close succession (1037–69) that they make his protestations of grief sound hollow. What makes this dialogue a piece of dark humor is that it is conducted in the presence of Alcestis, who is visible to the audience, and at least partially visible to Admetus and the Chorus. A basic source of the scene's possible humor lies not only in Admetus' failure to recognize the wife for whom he has professed so much love, but also in his intense desire to get a full view of her.

Why doesn't Admetus recognize the woman by her clothing? In all likelihood, she would still be wearing the magnificent clothes in which she was dressed at her funeral (1050). A great deal is made of that clothing. The Maidservant says that Alcestis has picked out the finery for her death (161–62), and that Admetus pointedly refuses to bury Alcestis in the clothing that Pheres brings for that purpose (631–32). It is also clear that Admetus can gauge that she is young by whatever he can notice of her clothing and general appearance. He is obviously ogling the woman: "Woman, whoever you are, know that *in shape* you are like Alcestis and resemble her *in appearance*" (1061–63). This failure to recognize his own wife, even if she is not fully visible to him, brings his obtuseness to new heights, and Alcestis is watching it all. His weaknesses are on full display as he intends to lead the woman to his house and subsequently to his bedroom, supporting Alcestis' earlier suspicion that he would remarry.

Dark humor is evident in Admetus' persistent self-deception, as he pretends not to want the strange woman while proceeding to convince himself that he has no choice but to take her into his personal space. Although he begins properly enough by urging Heracles to take the woman to another house, he is clearly thinking of accommodating her in his own. Heracles tells him that he brought her to work in Admetus' house as a servant (1024), which would suggest that she should be housed in the female servant-quarters, but Admetus strangely enough contemplates possible housing in the men's quarters or in Alcestis' bed. The only reason for all these inappropriate musings would be if he were immediately, in spite of all his protestations, thinking of taking her not as a servant, but as a mistress or new wife. The sexual turn of his thoughts is clear from the way that even without seeing her fully, he quickly ascertains and focuses on her youth; he is concerned that she is in danger of being raped if she is lodged in the men's quarters (1052), and suggests that the alternative is to take her to his wife's bed. Both possibilities are raised as rhetorical questions, in a manner supposedly meant to rule them out, and are followed by self-evident, inflated and self-righteous counterarguments, which are rendered even funnier by their superfluous nature. Not only is it obvious that neither alternative is remotely acceptable, but it is clear to the audience that these are not the only choices, and that Admetus studiously avoids mentioning the most obvious lodging for the woman: the female quarters, where she would not be exposed to any sexual impropriety. Admetus' intention towards the woman becomes clear when he addresses her directly in the vocative *gynai* (1061), which in Greek signifies both "woman" and "wife." Indeed, Admetus finally agrees to take the woman to his house, and obviously to Alcestis' bed. In short, he is anticipating remarrying, unbeknownst to him, the woman he has married before, and who has been watching his betrayal of his promise of gratitude for her dying for him.

After finally taking the woman from Heracles by his right hand, Heracles reveals the woman's face. At first Admetus disbelieves his eyes, but Heracles assures him that he sees his own wife; he also tells Admetus that she cannot speak for three days. Only then will she be purified in the sight of the gods below. Heracles urges Admetus to take his wife in and continue to be the exemplary host he is.

So is all well at the end of the play? Is this a happy reunion between a husband and wife? The view that *Alcestis* has a happy ending is based on Alcestis' resurrection from death and reunion with her husband. But it is impossible not to imagine that their marriage will now be rocky. The final scene mirrors the one at the beginning of the play in which Alcestis is poised between life and death. After seeing Charon and his boat, she suddenly revives to address her husband. Her revival speech (280–325) with its spite and impossible demands suggests that if there were an additional scene following her return from death, in which Alcestis were reempowered with speech, Admetus might have found that living with a woman who had died for his sake and then saw him apparently prepared to break his promise to her would be less than idyllic. The chances of Admetus and Alcestis living happily ever after are slim, even if Death further obliges Apollo and does not claim a body for the one just snatched from him.[14]

Conclusion

Alcestis is seen not only by Admetus, which would have been logical, but by the Chorus as well, as the perfect wife both before and after her death. In an ironic way, as a pro-satyric play might do, the message is that the only way a wife can be beneficial for a husband is to agree to die for him, as the Chorus sing:

> But you died in your prime, a young bride saving a young husband. Be it my fate to find such a dear wife, for this lot in life is rare! Truly, such a woman, living with me my whole life, would bring me no grief. (471–76)

The idea informing this sentiment is that women are no more than a plague to men (Hesiod, *Theogony* 561–612). Zeus has sent women as punishment to mankind to afflict them. The only woman, according to the Chorus, that might counter Zeus' purpose is the one who would die for her husband.

Hospitality

"Hospitality" translates the Greek term *xenia*. The Greek word *xenos* means "stranger" as well as "guest," "guest friend." The practice of hospitality was sanctioned by Zeus Xenios ("who protects strangers"). According to Herman 1987: 10, *xenia* suggests "a bond of solidarity manifesting itself in an exchange of goods and services between individuals" coming from different city-state communities. A *xenos*, stranger, was protected by Zeus Xenios upon his arrival to a new community, and expected to receive from his *xenos* (guest-friend) food and shelter. The relationship of *xenia* was largely personal, and was passed from one generation to another being practically indissoluble, although in practice the bond could fade away through disuse.

The theme of hospitality is crucial to the plot of *Alcestis*. Admetus can postpone his death as Apollo's token of gratitude for Admetus' generous hospitality to him. Admetus insists on hosting Heracles even when grieving of the dead Alcestis, so he does not lose his *xenos*. In exchange for this act of unusual act of hospitality, Heracles saves Alcestis from Death.[15]

DISCUSSION TOPICS

1. How would you summarize Alcestis' main character traits?
2. Do you feel that the character of Alcestis is less developed than some of Euripides' other heroines, such as Electra or Medea? Can you think of a reason why characterization may be less important in this play than in some of Euripides' other tragedies?
3. Would you describe Alcestis as being altruistic? Explain your answer.
4. *Alcestis* is named after the play's heroine, and the plot revolves around the events occurring as a result of her decision to die for her husband. However, she is absent from the stage for most of the play. Who do you think is the main character of the play, Alcestis or Admetus? Explain your answer.
5. If you were to stage a production of *Alcestis* would you choose to opt for a comic or tragic interpretation? Which scenes would you emphasize to support your choice?
6. Many of Euripides' heroines have a complex relationship with death. For example, Iphigenia (in *Iphigenia at Aulis*) seemed resigned to die in order to gain heroic status, but then, in one version, disappears from the altar where she is about to be sacrificed. How would you say Alcestis relates to death?
7. Throughout tragedy women kill themselves (Deianeira, Antigone, Phaedra), kill others (Clytemnestra, Electra, Medea), plot the deaths of others, (Creusa, Hecuba) or seem unmoved by deaths they have indirectly caused (Helen). Do you think that Athenian society placed different values on life and death than are accepted today?

8. Lamenting the dead was a very important aspect of both tragedy and of Athenian life. In *Alcestis*, Admetus essentially laments his wife's death while she is still alive. Later in *Alcestis* the heroine is literally snatched from the hands of death. By making death a character, and reversing the natural order of events (lamenting before death; having a funeral and returning to life) do you think Euripides might have been commenting on the place of death in Athenian society?

CHAPTER 8
DEIANEIRA

Mythic background

Heracles, the most iconic of all Greek heroes, born to Zeus and the mortal Alcmene, first demonstrated his great strength shortly after his birth. He strangled two snakes placed by the jealous Hera in the cradle he shared with his twin brother. As a young man, in Thebes he married Megara, Creon's eldest daughter eldest daughter. Hera, still determined to punish the son for the father's infidelity, struck Heracles with madness, which resulted in his killing Megara and their children. Belonging to the mythic age before the Trojan War, stories of his adventures abound in ancient myth, with the best known perhaps being the twelve labors he was sent to undertake for Eurystheus, in punishment for having murdered Megara. Other adventures include killing the eagle that had tormented Prometheus, freeing Theseus from Hades, and setting sail with the Argonauts. Heracles wrestled with the river god Achelous, to win his second wife, Deianeira, daughter of king Oeneus of Calydon. Soon after their marriage, his young bride was attacked by the centaur (half man and half horse) Nessus. Heracles shot and killed Nessus, using arrows poisoned by hydra's blood. The Centaur tricked Deianeira into thinking that his poisoned blood would work as a love charm on her husband. Deianeira eventually used the charm when she believed Heracles to be in love with Iole, daughter of Eurytus King of Oechalia, but instead of saving their marriage the poison killed Heracles.

Some of the story-elements on which *Women of Trachis* is based, were already part of the myths about Heracles in the time Sophocles. According to Easterling (1982: 15), the fragments of the epics the *Sack of Oechalia* (attributed to Homer or to Creophylus of Samos) and of *Heraclea by* Panyassis of Halicarnassus (epic poet of the fifth century BCE), as well as some fragments of Archilochus (a Greek lyric poet), show that Heracles' fighting Achelous to win Deianeira; Nessus' attempted rape of Deianeira; and the passive role of Iole (the girl Heracles took as a concubine after sacking Oechalia) in Heracles' death were part of the hero's saga received by Sophocles. Fragment 25.17-25 M-W from the *Catalogue of Women* attributed to Hesiod briefly tells the story of Deianeira sending the poisoned robe which destroys Heracles, but due to a lacuna (a gap) in the fragment Deianeira's motivation is unknown; that is, whether she believed she had used a love charm on the robe or she wanted to deliberately harm Heracles out of jealousy. In his 16th ode, Bacchylides (a lyric poet *c.* 518–*c.* 451 BCE) links Iole's existence and Deianeira's sending of the robe, but it is impossible to tell whether the poem predates or postdates the play. For Heracles' deathbed commands to his son Hyllus, there are no literary references that predate the play with any certainty, although the assumption is that those existed prior to *Women of Trachis* (Easterling 1982:16).

Sophocles' *Women of Trachis*

Deianeira's opening monologue sets the tone of Sophocles' tragedy: she has always known that her life would be marked by sorrow. She describes her terror when the monstrous river god Achelous asked her father for her hand in marriage. Even after Heracles defeated Achelous, her marriage to him has been filled with worry, as he is always away on some labor. Before leaving on his last venture, Heracles gave her a tablet stating that fifteen months after his departure he would either see the end of his labors or die in Euboea. The fifteen months have now gone by, and Deianeira, who has heard nothing of her husband's whereabouts or wellbeing, is experiencing extreme anxiety. Her Nurse convinces her to send her eldest son Hyllus to seek some news about his father. Hyllus tells his mother that Heracles is alive and well at Euboea. When Hyllus learns of the prophecy on the tablet relating to Euboea, he agrees to set off immediately to join his father. The Chorus and Deianeira continue discussing her suffering and her fears over Heracles' fate, until a Messenger arrives. He reports that Heracles has been successful in his latest endeavor, and will be returning to Trachis shortly. Before Heracles appears, his envoy Lichas enters, followed by a group of captive women, the most beautiful of whom is Iole, whom Heracles has ordered to be received in his household. Focusing on Iole, Deianeira questions Lichas about her. Lichas fails to disclose that the young captive is the daughter of Eurytus, king of Oechalia, and that she alone was the reason Heracles attacked Oechalia when she was denied him by her father. The Messenger, however, reveals the truth, and Lichas eventually admits his omission. Deianeira cannot bring herself to blame Iole for the situation or even to feel anger at her. However, although she accepts that Heracles has had numerous unions with other women during their marriage, she cannot accept a rival for her husband's affections living in her house and being invited into the marital bed.

Throughout her marriage Deianeira has kept hidden a gift from the centaur Nessus, which he claimed would act as a love charm, to prevent Heracles from loving another woman more than Deianeira. This charm was made from blood taken from Nessus' fatal wound after Heracles shot him with an arrow poisoned by the blood of the Hydra of Lerna. Despite her concerns about using this philtre, Deianeira decides that her situation might only be remedied by sending Heracles a gift of a robe smeared with the blood. Giving precise instructions that only Heracles may touch the robe, she sends it to him to wear while he makes celebratory sacrifices. She quickly becomes aware that her gift is dangerous, however: she tells the Chorus that the woolen swab she used to apply the blood to the robe disintegrated in a disturbing fashion when exposed to the sun, revealing the poisonous effect of the centaur's blood. Hyllus returns, reporting that Heracles is being tortured and destroyed by the robe, and assuming his mother intended to destroy Heracles, he curses her. Without responding, Deianeira exits to commit suicide. Heracles, already semi-conscious from pain, is carried on stage by litter-bearers. When told by Hyllus that Deianeira acted in error due to the machinations of the centaur Nessus, Heracles recalls an oracle that he would be killed by one of the dead. He forces Hyllus to promise to prepare his funeral pyre and marry Iole. The play ends with the characters leaving for Mount Oeta, and with Heracles' demise.

* * *

Sophocles' Deianeira has been frozen by fear as a young adult, worships her husband Heracles, and shuns taking action until the fear of losing him grows stronger than her fear of taking action. Thematic analysis reveals Deianeira displaying many traits considered to be highly feminine:

- she is a submissive wife, who is only moved to taking action when societal norms are broken, in that her husband seeks to bring his captive trophy bride into their home, and into their bed;
- on discovering that she has been deceived, Deianeira deceitfully sends Heracles what she wrongly presumes to have been a love philtre;
- Deianeira's feminine gullibility is almost beyond belief;
- her regard for honor and sense of shame are also highly dramatized;
- Deianeira always seeks counsel from others before making decisions, until she fatefully decides to send the robe daubed with potion to Heracles. On realizing the deadly consequences, she immediately decides to take her own life.

Introduction

Deianeira appears in Sophocles' *Women of Trachis* which is of uncertain date. She is Heracles' second wife and his unwitting murderer. The great concern and good intentions that motivate her throughout, but which nevertheless lead to a tragic outcome, make her unique among the tragic heroines. Helplessness and fear of losing Heracles to Iole, a younger woman, drive Deianeira to use Nessus' poisoned clotted blood, having been misled by the Centaur to believe that it was a philtre (a love potion). Winnington-Ingram refers to Deianeira as the "most appealing of Sophoclean women" (1980: 74). Indeed, in comparison to Sophocles' Electra, Antigone, or Aeschylus' Clytemnestra—all singleminded women on a mission, who are unable to compromise—Deianeira, whose tragedy arises from an attempt at compliance and the best intentions, is a much more likeable heroine. She is most similar to Ajax's wife, Tecmessa in Sophocles' *Ajax*. Both heroines lose their husbands in spite of their efforts to keep them alive and well.[1]

For the most part, Deianeira appears to be a fearful woman, almost overwhelmed by her anxieties. Her response to her fears is to avoid taking any initiative. She typically discusses each situation she faces with others, trying to think of every possible outcome. She also tries to give people the benefit of the doubt, excusing her husband for his many infidelities, and greeting a young captive girl with great sympathy. Even when she learns that her husband is obsessed with this girl, she does not blame the younger woman, but tries to employ a strategy that will win her husband back. Tragically the one time Deianeira acts without due caution, her deed leads to her own death as well as that of the husband she loves.

Fear, Loneliness, and Inaction

Sophocles opens the play in a unique fashion, as noted by Kitzinger (2012: 114): Deianeira's forty-eight-line opening monologue lacks an addressee, in spite of the fact that the Nurse accompanies her. This type of opening might create a special relationship between Deianeira and the audience, in which the spectators can view themselves as a "stage-audience," as Kitzinger sees it, but it could also highlight Deianeira's loneliness, which she will soon express as she tells the spectators how little time Heracles spends in Trachis. The audience see Deianeira describing herself as a young woman so paralyzed by fear that she could not even watch the suitors fighting for her hand. She recounts how she had been courted by the horrific river god Achelous, who appeared to her as a bull, a darting coiling serpent, and a bull-headed man. She was saved from a marriage worse than death by Heracles, who defeated Achelous in a fierce battle, which she was unable to watch, "sitting there numb with fear that my beauty might end by bringing me pain" (24–25, cf. 523–25). She did not run away, she did not scream, she did not express her fear, but silently sat and waited there piteously as a statue, the object of the strife (527–28). After her wedding to Heracles, as she was being carried by the centaur Nessus across the river Evenus, he tried to rape her in mid-stream. This time however she did cry out, and Heracles shot an arrow smeared with poisonous blood of the Lernaean hydra into Nessus' lungs, killing him.[2] As he was dying from the poison, Nessus told her to take his black clotted blood from the wound and keep it to use as a philtre if necessary (562–77).

Deianeira's subsequent married life is marked by anxious loneliness. Instead of Heracles, fear has become her constant companion. One night brings distress and another dispels it by bringing a fresh source of anxiety (29–30), with little to relieve her loneliness. She says they had children, but Heracles saw them only as a farmer sees a distant field, at seed-time and during harvest (31–35). Thus, her life with Heracles follows the pattern of the recurring seasons, he comes and goes, but does not tend to the fields in between. We might recall Clytemnestra's eloquent depiction of how it feels when a husband leaves a wife alone at home for years (Aesch. *Ag.* 858–94). Both women suffer this grinding experience, but while this mutilated life drives Clytemnestra to console herself with a lover, Deianeira longs for her husband to return, pierced with cruel pangs of apprehension not only for Heracles' safety, but also her own and that of her children, since they are inextricably intertwined (84–85).

At the time of the opening scene, Deianeira is overwrought with worry. Before leaving for his last labor, Heracles gave her a tablet inscribed with an oracle predicting his fate. He also gave her instructions on how to allocate his ancestral lands should he not return. He explained that once he has been absent for fifteen months, he is either fated to die or, surviving the moment of crisis, live a life free of pain. She tells the Nurse that the designated moment has arrived, and she is afraid that she is about to be robbed of "the noblest of all men" (177). However, she takes no steps to alleviate her consternation, as if fear has paralyzed her once again. It takes the Nurse to suggest she send her son Hyllus to look for his father.

Unfettered by the bewilderment that reigns over Deianeira's life, Hyllus knows that Heracles is alive and well, already released from the slavery to Omphale and is either about to attack Oechalia, the city of Eurytus, or has already done so (69–75). One might wonder why Deianeira does not react to the fact that while her son is fully informed about her husband's whereabouts, she has been left in the dark. Is this because the playwright means to portray Deianeira as the average female, who is uninformed about the outside world, the proverbial Bee Woman (see Box on Simonidean Bee Woman, p. 54) who is not prone to gossip and is entirely devoted solely to the concerns of her household and children? Whatever is the case, Hyllus imparts a crucial piece of information: Heracles is now in Eurytus' city, the very place where his fate is to be decided according to the oracle. Deianeira is once again consumed by anxiety. On hearing about the oracle, Hyllus decides to set off for Euboea immediately, leaving no time for discussion.

Overthinking and Confusion

From Deianeira's monologues it quickly becomes obvious that she overthinks everything she experiences, as Kitzinger points out "Deianeira reveals her character in a particularly intimate, extensive and self-reflective way" (2012: 114). Deianeira's anxieties about Heracles' wellbeing gain an additional dimension as she busily explores all possible outcomes in her mind. As stated by Catenaccio (2017: 5), "Deianeira ... consistently questions, analyses and explores the instability of human fortune ... yet ... consistently falls short of comprehending the web of destiny in which she is entangled." It might appear that the more she thinks, the less she understands. She seems unable to make sense of the world she lives in and find a safe path through it. When the Messenger announces that he has heard from Lichas that Heracles is alive and victorious (180–83), Deianeira's fears do not dissipate. She already seems to have some sixth sense that things are not as they should be. She asks: "But why is he himself not here, if indeed fortune favors him?" (192), a simple and straightforward, logical question. Why isn't Heracles at the door of his palace? Sophocles, however, makes the Messenger misunderstand her query: he thinks that by "he" Deianeira refers to Lichas, and he explains that Lichas is detained by the people who want to hear the news about Heracles. Her important question is sidelined, and she does not bring it up again. Despite having a mind keen enough to identify problems, Deianeira typically gets sidetracked when looking for a solution or finds an answer to a completely different problem. When Lichas arrives and announces that Heracles is alive and victorious (230–35) Deianeira responds with the interesting phrase that it is in the nature of those who judge well to fear for him who fares well (296–97). As we will see, this statement has significant implications for Deianeira's actions later on. While her motives remain good, reflecting her kind-hearted personality, her anxiety and her resultant confusion eventually seal her fate.

Naïveté to Clear-Sightedness

In the course of the play, Deianeira progressively moves from ignorance, mostly caused by her naïveté and kind spirit, to clear-sightedness. Her realizations occur slowly and painfully. According to Catenaccio (2017: 8), Deianeira – "occupies the space between knowledge and ignorance, between consciousness and unconsciousness ... without ever fully inhabiting either position." While this seems true for the most part, Deianeira does finally gain a clear insight into reality, but only when it is too late. Her tragedy derives from her gradual discoveries.[3] The slower her grasp of new reality, the more horrific the knowledge and its ramifications become.

Iole

Deianeira's attitude toward Iole both before and after realizing that the young woman poses a threat to her, reveals her character. She is kind; suspicion is not one of her traits. The moment Deianeira sets eyes on Iole, she is intrigued by the young captive and experiences an unexplained sense of affinity with her:[4]

> Lichas, who among human beings is the stranger?
> Who is her mother, and who is the father that gave her life?
> Tell me, because I pitied her most when I saw her,
> in as much as she alone can feel and understand. (310–13)

This could be due to the young woman's beauty. Because she is a princess, she might also have a noble demeanor which makes an impression on Deianeira even before she learns the girl's identity. Iole is a nebulous figure, in spite of her dramatic importance, with the text giving only two hints to her behavior: lines 312–13 ("because I pitied her most when I saw her") suggest that she stands out in some way from the other captives, and in lines 325–27, Lichas claims that she has been weeping ever since she left home. However,

Lichas does not hold much credence with the audience, considering his earlier blatant lies regarding Iole. As Easterling (1982: on 313) points out, editors differ widely in their interpretations: Jebb imagines that Iole is distinguished by her "sense of the calamity, while her companions are 'comparatively callous'"; Kamerbeek on the other hand prefers "an Iole whose self-control is contrasted with the unrestrained lamentations of her companions," a suggestion that contradicts Lichas' later claim of her weeping unceasingly. Easterling sums up by saying:

> All that is universally agreed is that she 'looks noble'; perhaps this is all that would have been actually rendered on the Greek stage. In a masked performance it is most unlikely that actors taking the part of silent bystanders mimed their reactions to the words that were being spoken. It is hard to convey subtle shades of feeling without facial expressions, and more important, the audience need to know who is speaking: elaborate action on the part of the actors who are *not* speaking is liable to lead to confusion. D.'s sympathetic reaction acts as a guide to our own: it is natural to share her pity for Iole.

Deianeira initially invites Iole into the palace with kindness and understanding, completely oblivious of the fact that she is welcoming a rival for her husband's affection. However, it is after the Messenger's revelation of her husband's obsession with this young woman, and the extreme actions he took to win her for himself that the extent of Deianeira's good nature is revealed. The Messenger warns Deianeira that Iole is not a mere slave, but Heracles' concubine or rather a wife (351–74, 428). He, together with many other men of Trachis, has overheard Lichas reporting that Heracles brought down the high towers of Oechalia, due to his infatuation with Iole, as Eros had bewitched him. Once Heracles failed to convince her father Eurytus to give him his daughter "to have as his secret love," he killed him and sacked the city. Upon hearing the brutal truth, Deianeira understands that she has taken "a disaster" into her house (376).

Deianeira typically is initially frozen into inactivity. Her good nature makes it impossible for her to be angry with Iole, who she realizes is not to blame for the situation. She also is sufficiently realistic to know that Heracles has taken many other mistresses, and this behavior is inherent in his nature (459–60). Only a fool would try and stand up to Eros, she claims, and she would be mad if she blamed Heracles for succumbing to this god. She continues that none of the many women Heracles has lain with incurred reproach from her. However, this situation has one crucial difference: Heracles has invited his mistress into his palace and into the marital bed. Deianeira has to take action, but cannot do so alone. She turns to the Chorus for advice: "What must I do, women? The story we have heard leaves me struck numb" (385–86).

Deianeira sees Iole as a victim of her beauty: "I pitied her most of all when my eyes lit on her, because her beauty had destroyed her life, and by no fault of hers, poor creature" (463–66). Does Iole's misfortunes, with Heracles killing her father and destroying her city remind Deianeira of her own sufferings as a young woman? She also had been an object of violent passion, fought over because of her beauty (24–25, 379, 523). Deianeira's sympathy for the subdued captive women results in her identification with them and internalization of their plight to the extent that she transports their predicament to the possible sufferings of her future generations and prays to Zeus that no similar fate would ever befall her children (303–06). Such self-reflection is the absolute antithesis to *hybris*, taking advantage of situational upper-hand which she could have applied as a mistress of the house.

The extent of Deianeira's amenability and her attempts at compliance are, however, quite bewildering. Is she so naïve that she does not grasp the implications of having a concubine in her own house? Once Lichas had admitted his lie, the expected reaction would have been that Deianeira, as the legitimate wife, would have erupted with rage. As has already been pointed out in the case of Clytemnestra, while it was societally permissible for a husband to have extra-marital liaisons (of which Deianeira is aware and forgiving, 459–60), bringing a concubine to cohabit with a wife was not acceptable.[5] Such an act threatened the wife, but Deianeira's first reaction to Lichas' revelation is devoid of any sign of jealousy or anger.[6] One interpretation of her response could be that she is in utter denial of this new reality, perhaps believing that she could secure the previous *status quo* through compliance. Another nuanced interpretation is that she is incapable of processing the anger and jealousy she should be experiencing. These emotions are entirely foreign to her. She goes to extreme lengths to see the situation from both Iole's and Heracles' point of view, almost negating her own rights within the marriage. Even when she finally realizes that she will have to share her husband with his concubine in her own household, she fails to express unqualified anger at her husband.

Although she rebukes him for bringing a concubine to take her place "as a reward" for her taking care of his household for years during his absence, and although she sarcastically refers to him as one who is *called* "loyal and noble" (541, my translation) rather than one "who *is* the 'noblest of men'" (177), as she referred to him previously, she still admits: "I do not know how to be angry with my husband now that he is suffering severely from this malady [i.e. Eros]" (543–44). However, it is clear to her that she cannot live with Iole under the same roof "sharing a marriage with the same man" (545–46). Indeed, what woman could? Many see this statement and the following despair at her understanding that she is getting older while Iole's youth continues to blossom (547–49) as expressions of jealousy, but are they?

Deianeira needs time to process her new situation. When she reappears on stage following the first choral ode when the Chorus are already on the *orchestra*, she has fully acknowledged Eros as ruler of gods, and she admits he rules her too. She asks: "how should he [Eros] not rule another woman like me?" (444). She empathizes with the beautiful young woman on whom Heracles imposes his affection, as she had experienced this in her youth. She exculpates both Heracles and Iole. Heracles cannot fight infatuation, and Iole cannot help being young and beautiful. At the same time, she is threatened by Iole: "I am afraid that Heracles may be called my husband, but the younger woman's man" (550–51). She adds a new fear, that Iole may steal her husband, to the list of fears she has already experienced: fear of Achelous, fear of Nessus, fear of Heracles dying and fear of her offspring being enslaved. We ought to believe her when she sums up her complaints and says: "But as I said it is not honorable for a woman of sense to be angry; and I shall tell you what means I have of remedying the pain" (552–54).

Nessus

How Deianeira perceives sending the robe smeared with blood from Nessus is her second transition from naïve ignorance to clear-sightedness. Her independent and rather reckless decision to use the charm is presented as stemming from despair. Until this moment, she is shown as the traditional Athenian submissive wife (Just 1989: 277), diffident and lacking in initiative to boot.

Deianeira details to the women of the Chorus the instructions the dying Nessus gave her for obtaining and storing the love potion. He told her to gather in her hands the coagulated blood from the wound made by Heracles' poisoned arrow. This blood, she was told, would serve as a charm to prevent Heracles from ever loving another woman instead of her (572–77). As pointed out by Scott (1997: 44), while this statement could be interpreted as meaning that after using the potion, Heracles would love Deianeira to the exclusion of all other women, it could also mean that the potion will irrevocably prevent Heracles from doing anything at all, i.e. that he will die. Considering the circumstances under which Nessus gave Deianeira the charm, a reasonable person might have suspected that Nessus was cunningly disguising the true result, that on being touched by the blood, Heracles would no longer be able to look at any other woman: he would be incapacitated through death. Deianeira was, through her own admission, still a child during these events (555–60). She may not have realized then the possible sinister interpretation of Nessus' words.[7] Scott (1997) proposes that Deianeira might unconsciously have wished to punish Heracles; however, she might also have simply turned a blind eye to the possibly devastating consequences of using the potion.[8]

Deianeira has kept the blood hidden for many years. In all this time, she has never used the potion, despite Heracles' many infidelities. We cannot know whether she had simply forgotten about the philtre's existence, did not see the need for it, or whether she had qualms about its true nature, suspecting that Nessus might not have had her best interests at heart. However, she needed to act quickly in response to the threat presented by Iole. We have seen that she is normally extremely hesitant, slow to work situations through. Either she had insufficient time to consider whether the philtre might in fact be poisonous, or she was so incapacitated by her own anxiety at the need to take decisive action quickly that she could not think clearly.

The playwright uses the following brief conversation between Deianeira and the women of the Chorus to remove any doubt about both the innocence and despair driving Deianeira to use the charm. She states she is normally loathe to use magic but sees no other way to "somehow overcome this girl" (582–85). The deed has been done, she says, but as if doubting her action she adds: "unless you [women of the Chorus] think that what I am doing is foolish! If so, I shall abandon it" (586–87). As is typical in Sophoclean plays, however, when great crises emerge, the Chorus keep a somewhat dispassionate aloofness and are non-committal. If there are grounds for confidence in what she is doing, she has not been ill-advised, they say (588–89). Her confidence in the charm extends so far that she believes it works, but she has never put it to test, Deianeira replies. The Chorus continue to qualify their approval: in order to be sure, they say, the charm needs to be put to the test (590–93). She sees Lichas approaching and concludes the conversation by asking the Chorus to keep to themselves her use of love charms, a choice likely to be thought shameful by the outside world. It might well be as Gellie points out, that "her shame begins in the very need for artfulness in her attempt to hold on to Heracles. To act at all is a piece of uncharacteristic self-assertion for Deianeira" (1972: 65). Her abhorrence at using love charms only underscores how desperate she is.

Modern readers might find it easy to see Deianeira's three attempts to get approval from the Chorus as some premonition on her part against using the coagulated blood of the Centaur. Whether the original audience felt the same, we will never know. This is the first time that we see her acting without a prompt from someone else, whether the Nurse, the Messenger, or the Chorus. It would be quite natural for her to feel insecure and in need of approval from the Chorus who are with her at all times. In short, she acts in character. Sophocles' greatness in shaping a character is shown by the way he prevents a black-and-white reading of Deianeira and enables varying interpretations through some vagueness and indeterminacy of motivation. Although the Choral responses are rather non-committal, we should not read them as discouragement to Deianeira, but simply expressions of caution. It is understandable that Deianeira, whose sole focus is to recover the former stability of her marriage and domestic situation, reads the Chorus' answers as encouragement to test the charm. And this she does. She dispatches Lichas with the robe and detailed instructions (mostly probably derived from Nessus), that the robe must not be exposed to light or heat before it is worn by Heracles. These Lichas promises to deliver reliably. How ardently Deianeira wants Heracles to think of her as a good wife, we learn from her bidding Lichas to inform Heracles of the kind welcome she offered to his concubine, quite a humiliating gesture for a wife.

The Truth About the "Philtre" is Revealed

Deianeira's final transition from naïve ignorance to a full grasp of her tragedy follows. Panicked, she comes out of the palace telling the Chorus that she might have done "great harm in the expectation of good" (667). She blames the awful mishap on acting in haste in matters of which she has no experience (669–70). She reports to the Chorus the terrifying event that has made her suspect that the charm might be lethal. The piece of wool with which she smeared the robe and then threw away, when exposed to the sun's rays, completely disintegrated and crumbled, resembling a powder, and in the place where it fell there were sinister clots of foam; the bluish-green color suggests to her poison (693–704). Her next sentence is most characteristic of her: "So I do not know, in my trouble, what decision to come to; and I see that I have done a terrible thing" (705–06). Deianeira is utterly helpless. What is the decision she is contemplating? Does she think she can still retrieve the gift? If so, why hasn't she already sent for Lichas to stop him from delivering the robe? Here the playwright comes to Deianeira's aid. As the plot evolves, it becomes clear that her watching the disintegration of the tuft of wool coincides with the burning and convulsions of Heracles enveloped in the bewitched robe. Deianeira knows she has to make some decision about what she has done, but is unable to formulate it. However, it is not her indecisiveness that is causing the current disaster. For once her desire to act, although commendable in itself, is useless. It is simply too late, as is her realization that Nessus had no good reason to help her, but used her to kill the man who shot him. Sophocles now has her utter one of the leading themes of the play, and her own main feature: "learning the truth too late" (710–11).

Learning the Truth too Late

This theme applies to Hyllus and Heracles as well as Deianeira. Hyllus learns too late that his mother has not killed his father on purpose. He has no opportunity to take back the blame and harsh words he directed at her. For a second and final time, Deianeira has acted too quickly and dies before Hyllus can reach her. Heracles also learns too late that Nessus is his real killer and that Deianeira has simply served as an agent of the oracles about his end, which are being fulfilled in real time. However, the processes Deianeira undergoes while learning the truth about her situation are different. Neither Hyllus nor Heracles had the full information they needed to begin with. Hyllus accused his mother erroneously because he simply did not know that she had sent the robe as a philtre. Heracles had no way of knowing of Nessus' manipulation because Deianeira had kept Nessus' advice secret. Deianeira, however, had all the pieces. She should have asked herself before using the charm whether Nessus had a reason to ensure Heracles' love for her. Deianeira had always been extremely cautious and anxious about Heracles' wellbeing. When she grasps the reality of the situation with Iole, this anxiety may have intensified to the extent of precluding rational thought. She had to find a remedy to allow herself to continue functioning. The one closest at hand, Nessus' philtre, was not in reality the answer to her problem. To accept it as such, Deianeira had to turn a blind eye to any possible harmful consequences. She moved from one extreme of hesitancy and diffidence, to the other extreme that we might call recklessness, motivated by her new fear, that of losing her status as a wife and mistress of her household.

Forcing herself to take action seems to have had a powerful impact on Deianeira. Once she realizes the probable effect of the poison, we see for the first time a Deianeira not only in full possession of certain knowledge, but also resolute: she states that if Heracles dies, she will die too. Albeit the two reasons that she gives for her decision are at odds with each other: she will die for name and reputation (721–22) and she will die because she believes she had acted wrongly:

> That is the kind of thing that a person who has no trouble of his own
> would say, but not the one to whom the evil belongs. (729–30)

The first consideration was known to motivate Homeric heroes whose main concerns were what *others* think of them, but also a consideration a woman could adopt out of wishing to be thought well of by others. The second explanation is given to the Chorus who tell her that allowances are made for innocent intentions, an allusion to what people will say of her. Deianeira wholeheartedly rejects the Chorus' attempt at consolation. The fact that she has caused Heracles' death unintentionally does not absolve her *to herself*. She "owns" Heracles' current torture. She similarly maintains her silence after hearing Hyllus' accusation against her (759–812), and leaves wordlessly when the Chorus admonish her that her silence might be construed as an admission to Hyllus' charge (813–14).

What motivates her suicide is no longer what others would think of her, but what she thinks of herself. Should we see this change in attitude as a transition in her grasp of reality? Maybe. She has taken a risk and failed. She has lost the thing in her life that matters most to her: Heracles. His upcoming death is the end of her domestic and married life. Her suicide tells us unequivocally that she considers herself guilty. At the same time that Heracles is tormented physically in his last moments, Deianeira is tormented mentally by guilt and shame. As she roams the house that has been the center of her existence, she sees and touches all the familiar objects for the last time, and weeps when she looks at the familiar faces of her attendants. Finally, she enters the bridal chamber, the center of her wedded life, and kills herself with a double-edged sword on the bed she shared with Heracles (899–931).

Conclusion

In Sophocles' play it is fear not jealousy that motivates Deianeira to send Heracles the charmed robe. As to previous treatments of the story of Deianeira and Heracles, the most promising fragment from the *Catalogue of Women*, attributed to Hesiod (frag. 25.17-25 M-W), briefly tells the story of Deianeira's sending of the robe, but the lacuna in the very spot in the text that describes Deianeira's motivation makes it unclear whether her act was an innocent mistake or deliberately malicious (Easterling 1982: 16). Earlier portrayals of Deianeira in vase paintings show her as a more active, even aggressive, figure, which might suggest that earlier versions of the character actively killed Heracles out of jealousy (March 1987: 49–57). We do not see, however, any trace of jealousy in Sophocles, nor is jealousy involved in Aeschylus' *Agamemnon*, the narrative pattern of which Sophocles is using. Clytemnestra is enraged at Agamemnon for bringing Cassandra and ordering her to accept her kindly in the palace, but Clytemnestra has decided long before this moment that she was going to kill Agamemnon. Sophocles inherited the name Deianeira which means in Greek "man-killer" or even "husband-killer," but by no means does he attribute jealousy or ill-will to her.[9] She sends the robe for the reason she states: she wants to win Heracles back. She realizes that she cannot offer him youth and beauty anymore, so she tries to seduce him back using what she excels in as an older woman: her handiwork. Indeed, she is by no means sure that she will win him over. As Winnington-Ingram rightly defines the play, it is a "tragedy of sex" (1980: 75, 86, 90), saying that "to have taken the sexuality of a normal woman and made it a motive force in tragedy could be one of the most original things Sophocles ever did" (1982: 240), and he gave Deianeira the saddest words as she sends Lichas off with her gift:

> What else could you [Lichas] say to him? For I am afraid you might be premature in saying how I long for him, before knowing if I am longed for there. (630–32)

Sadness has habituated Deianeira to expect the worst. Her painfully hesitant words to Lichas, spoken in a semi-aside[10] when he is on his way out with the robe smeared with what she thinks is a love potion, may be tame, but they nevertheless express the turmoil of habitual diffidence at odds with upwelling despair on the part of a woman, a wife, a mother, who for many years has overseen Heracles' household, taken care of his children and for last fifteen months awaited him in agonizing fear for his wellbeing; a woman who probably was no more than in her thirties, but "middle-aged'" in her culture; a woman who saw in him "the best of men" (177) in spite of knowing that he was unfaithful to her while away on his many labors and adventures (459–60). In spite of these extra-marital transgressions, she knew that he always would come back to her, to his family, and that their life as a husband and wife would resume even if only for brief periods of time. Introducing Iole into their household, while bidding her to welcome the young woman, has shattered the confidence Deianeira had in herself, in her marriage, in her ability to have Heracles physically as a husband. These are words of a woman past her prime that reflect her embarrassment, her hopes, and above all her fear of rejection.

For Winnington-Ingram it was all about the "one blanket" Deianeira saw herself sharing with Iole (539–40). If however we see Deianeira as slowly progressing from innocence to clear-sightedness in each aspect of her new reality, we should probably consider that eventually she realizes that she won't be sharing this blanket at all. It will all be Iole's. Although a victim of Nessus' deceit, sending the robe which she had woven herself in order to seduce Heracles to compensate for her passing youth, is trickery, even if well-intentioned. Deianeira's trickery is nothing more than an attempt at seduction, by which she wants to restore her position as a woman against the threat Iole poses to her. The use of magic and poison was thought to be a feminine art especially in affairs of erotic emotions (Just 1989: 268), and Deianeira's deceit combines the two. Her innocence and good intentions only buttress the traditional male suspicion of women and their simple, home-manufactured guiles, however well-meant, and Heracles' wish that she had died just proves it, see also, Euripides' frag 464: "Well, go and get married, get married, and then die either through poison or plot from your wife" (Kanniicht 2004: vol. 5.1; trans. Collard and Cropp).

The positive dramatic portrayal of Deianeira is emphasized by her very human womanliness, her dependence, and care for others, which is set against the superlative masculinity and super human force of her husband and his utter self-absorption. Did Sophocles intend dramatic irony when he had Heracles and Nessus killed by the same hydra-venom and for a similar sexual transgression: as Nessus could not resist the temptation to try to violate Deianeira, so Heracles could not check his desire for Iole? Is

Heracles' untoward and unintended agony during which he claims to be "unmanned" (he becomes "a womanish creature," 1075), as if his cries castrate him, meant to match his sexual crime? On the other hand, should Deianeira's suicide with the sword be seen as a "masculine" way to die, since women usually commit suicide by hanging themselves (Winnington-Ingram 1982: 240, cf. 1980: 75, 86, 90; Gould 1980: esp. 57)?

Deianeira is one of the more feminine heroines. She does not exhibit the gift of rhetoric although she is touchingly clear in her expressions of fear and calls for help, and she is a very good listener. Characteristic of her age, she does not jump to conclusions like the younger Electras and Antigone. She listens to what the Messenger has to say about Lichas' lies but does not scold Lichas, and acts only upon viewing the beauty of Iole herself. Deianeira is observant and empathetic, but there is some consuming fear, rooted in her experience with Nessus in her youth, that prevents her from decisive action. Her submissiveness and her usual lack of initiative borders on helplessness. *Mutatis mutandis*, she seems to be the forerunner of the "damsel in distress" prototype, but one who is not rescued by the hero. On the contrary, she causes the hero's demise. Like every heroine, she is marked by an attempt of deceit, but fails to execute her attempt successfully. Her only act of defiance is her suicide brought about by her love for Heracles and realization of her guilt. It is noteworthy that Sophocles gave her the masculine way of killing herself: by the sword, rather than by the noose, as if to rehabilitate her from all of her other feminine failing ways.

DISCUSSION TOPICS

1. Heracles had been victimized by Hera since birth, and is finally killed by a woman. Do you think that Deianeira is merely a pawn in the hands of the gods, or should we see her as acting independently?
2. From the well-known myths of Heracles, are you surprised at the way in which his wife, Deianeira, is characterized? Would you have expected him to have a more assertive bride?
3. Deianeira instantly singles out Iole from the other slave girls. What do you think Sophocles was indicating about both Deianeira and Iole in this scene?
4. Do you think that Sophocles' presentation of Deianeira's treatment of Iole rings true? Do you think that it fits the way that Deianeira is characterized throughout the play? Explain your answer.
5. Both Deianeira and Phaedra (Chapter 11) are motivated by love for a man. How do they compare? What are the dramatic devices used for the delineation of their characters?
6. Compare Deianeira's last moments to those of Alcestis as described by Alcestis' maid (Euripides, *Alcestis* 158–96). What is distinct in the portrayal of the two heroines as they face death?

7. How does Deianeira's use of a philtre compare to the actions of other rejected women in Greek tragedy, like Clytemnestra and Medea?
8. Considering the male dominated society, do you think that the male audience was more sympathetic to Deianeira than they would be, for example, to Clytemnestra, Medea, or Phaedra?
9. If you were categorizing the heroines into those who are more actively assertive and those who are submissive (their desires remain implicit, rather than being explicitly expressed), how would you classify Deianeira? Is there a group of heroines in which you would include her? Does she stand out from among the various heroines, or would you compare her to any one heroine in particular— and if so, which one?
10. What do you think that Deianeira's decision to kill herself says about her character? Do you think it indicates strength or weakness? Do you think that Sophocles is more interested in sending a message about a woman's role in society, or in making a comment on Deianeira, with this ending?

CHAPTER 9
MEDEA

Mythic background

Nephele, a cloud nymph, married the human King Athamas of Boeotia. They had twins: a son, Phrixus and a daughter, Helle. Athamas discarded Nephele for Ino, who hated her step-children and planned to have Phrixus killed. Before the plot was executed, Nephele had a flying ram with a golden fleece (note the magic component) sent to her children to carry them away from Greece to safety, with the stipulation that they were not to look down during the flight. Helle, however, did look down, fell into the sea and drowned. The sea was named after her: Hellespont, meaning "Sea of Helle". Phrixus was carried all the way to Colchis, on the eastern shore of the Black Sea, where King Aeetes treated him kindly and gave him his daughter Chalciope in marriage. After sacrificing the ram, Phrixus gave the golden fleece to Aeetes, who hung it in a giant oak tree, where a huge serpent guarded it.

Meanwhile in Thessaly, King Cretheus of Iolcus had fathered several children by his wife Tyro including Aeson, Pheres, and Amythaon. However, Tyro also had twin sons with Poseidon: Pelias and Neleus. After Aeson was made king, the power hungry Pelias deposed him. Pelias then received a prophecy that he would be killed by a man entering Iolcus wearing only one sandal. When Aeson's son Jason, returned to Iolcus wearing only one sandal, Pelias promised Jason the throne on the condition that Jason bring the Golden Fleece from Colchis. Having gathered a crew of heroes, the Argonauts, Jason set sail. When they arrived at Colchis, Aeetes promised to give the Golden Fleece to Jason if he could perform three tasks.

Noticing Jason's helplessness, Hera enlisted the aid of Aphrodite and her son Eros to make Medea, Aeetes' daughter, fall in love with Jason, so that she would aid him. Medea then helped Jason yoke fire-breathing bulls; sow dragon's teeth (which sprouted into an army of warriors); and finally put the fleece-guarding serpent to sleep. After acquiring the Golden Fleece, Medea and the Argonauts fled Colchis, with Aeetes in hot pursuit. To distract her father, Medea is said to have killed her brother Apsyrtus, cut his corpse into pieces and thrown them into the sea so that the fugitives would have time to escape while Aeetes stopped to gather the pieces. Another version says that Jason killed Apsyrtus after luring him into a trap, chopped off his fingers and toes, and buried the corpse. Zeus punished Medea for killing her brother by raising a storm. The Argo then spoke, advising the Argonauts to seek purification from Circe. After being cleansed, they continued their journey home.

Back in Iolcus, Medea convinced Pelias' daughters that she could make their father youthful by chopping him up into pieces and boiling the pieces in a cauldron of water. She demonstrated this remarkable feat with the oldest ram from the flock, adding magical herbs to the water: the ram leapt out of the cauldron as a lamb. The daughters then cut up their father and put him in the cauldron. Medea, however, had withheld from them the information about the herbs, and Pelias died. Pelias' son, Acastus, drove Jason and Medea into exile for the murder, and the couple settled in Corinth. It is at this point that the play begins.

In some versions, after Jason's betrayal and her terrible vengeance, Medea stopped off at Thebes on her way to Athens, and healed Heracles from a curse inflicted by Hera. After arriving at Athens, she married the king, Aegeus, and gave birth to a son. Aegeus had already fathered a son, Theseus. When Theseus arrived in Athens, Medea tried to kill him. She and her son were banished by Aegeus. She then either went to Persia (the locals becoming known as Medes after her), or returned to Colchis, where her uncle Perses had usurped the throne. In that version, Medea killed Perses and restored her father, Aeetes to the throne.

Family Trees

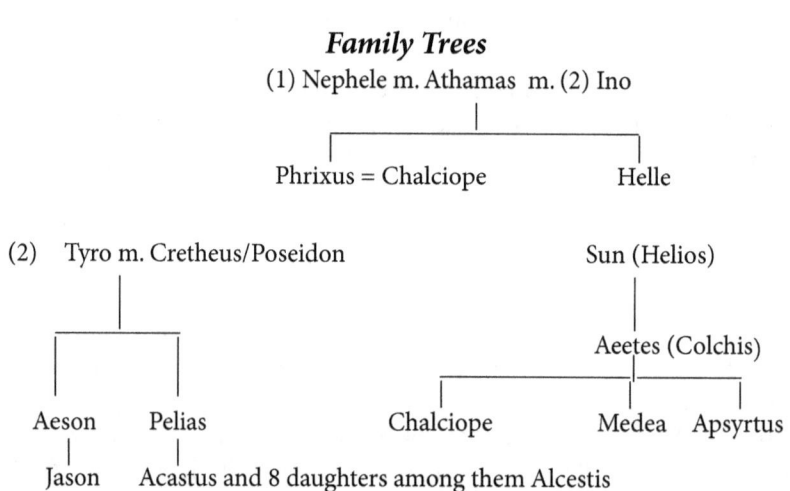

Euripides' *Medea*

In Corinth, Jason abandons Medea and in spite of being an exile and non-citizen, Jason has become engaged to the daughter of Creon, the king of Corinth, to strengthen his political ties in the city. Creon decides to exile Medea and her sons from Corinth while Jason refuses to intervene on their behalf. When Medea confronts Jason about the engagement and cites all the help she has given him, he retorts that it was not she, Medea, that he should thank, but Aphrodite, who made Medea fall in love with him. Aegeus, king of Athens, enters abruptly, complaining about his childlessness. When Medea promises to cure his childlessness and relates her own misfortunes, Aegeus offers her asylum in Athens. After he leaves, Medea announces her plan to kill her children and sends her Nurse to summon Jason. Incensed with Jason for breaking his oath of marriage, Medea takes her revenge by sending her sons to the princess with a poisoned dress as a wedding gift. Once the princess puts the dress on, it sticks to her body and burns her to death. When Creon tries to rescue his daughter, he burns to death as well. In her revenge spree, Medea then kills the two sons she bore to Jason, fearing that they would be murdered by the Corinthians as vengeance for her actions. She escapes Corinth for Athens in a dragon-drawn chariot, given to her by her grandfather, Helios (the sun god).

Introduction

Medea was first produced for the Great Dionysia in 431 BCE, coming third in competition with plays by Euphorion (Aeschylus' son) and Sophocles. At the start of the play Medea is despondent, but she gradually concocts a plan which, in her eyes, is suited to the grievous wrong her husband Jason has inflicted upon her.[1] She forms an allegiance with the Corinthian women of the Chorus, whom she decides she can trust to keep her plans secret. After Creon decrees that she is to be exiled in order to ensure his daughter's safety, Medea's wrath is focused not only on her husband, but also on the king and his daughter, Jason's new bride. She finds a crucial ally in King Aegeus, visiting from Athens, with whom she will take refuge. However, it is after her discussions with Aegeus, that Medea's plans take an appalling new direction. In order to punish Jason, she will not kill him, but will murder their two sons, leaving him without male heirs.

It is this last part of the plot that indelibly blights the character of Medea as a child murderer. However, as has been repeatedly pointed out, most recently by Luschnig,[2] it is likely that the early treatments of Medea's story did not have her kill her children, or not intentionally. One source also refers to Medea not as a refugee at Corinth as she is in Euripides, but a rightful Queen of Corinth, a position she inherited through her grandfather Helios. In this version she kills her and Jason's sons inadvertently when attempting to make them immortal (Pausanias 2.3.10–11). Another version has it that the children were killed by the Corinthian citizens avenging the murder of their king by Medea (the reason for Medea's act is not given. Scholia on *Medea* 264). Still another version, attributed by the same scholiast to the Alexandrian Parmeniscus, is that the boys were killed by the Corinthian women, rebelling against the rule of a foreign sorceress. It seems that the deliberate child-murder is Euripides' innovation.[3] In characterizing Medea in this way, Euripides must have aimed to shock the audience. While it is likely that the chaos created by her violence was intended as commentary on human nature, it is impossible to know whether Euripides was also commenting on any contemporary affairs affecting Athens. His choices are a mystery which will never be solved.[4]

* * *

Euripides' Medea almost defies conventional classification, as he emphasizes her otherness, and her volatility throughout. The contradictions in Medea's characterization form an integral part of the characterization of a highly volatile person:

- Medea's situation is largely feminine: a foreign wife, left without status or homeland, when she is cast off by a husband seeking to further his own position through a more advantageous marriage;
- yet Medea's reaction to her situation is perhaps best described as Machiavellian;
- she uses rhetoric to gain support from the local women, from Aegeus, and even, when it suits her purposes, from Jason;
- she resorts at first to what is considered a feminine means of taking revenge, a poisoned robe and coronet to kill Jason's new bride, but then commits a very masculine murder, using a sword to kill her own two sons.

In trying to understand Euripides' characterization of Medea it is first important to appreciate her background as presented in the play.

How Medea's Background is Reflected in Her Characterization

In Euripides' *Medea* Jason's abandoned wife is an *apolis*, a woman with no (*a-*) city (*polis*). She is a barbarian, and therefore forever a foreigner, with no rights either in Iolcus or in Corinth. While a Greek would be treated as a co-national in a Greek city where they might not be a citizen, for Medea this privilege does not exist, and she is painfully aware of her condition. As long as she had a Greek husband, Medea's barbarian identity was mitigated. However, after Jason abandons her, Medea is on her own. Although this social and political "otherness" is a recurrent theme or leitmotiv of Medea's story, she has learned enough about Greek behavioral codes such as fidelity, gratitude, and the honoring of oaths to castigate Jason for breaking them.

Medea's passionate love for Jason caused her to sunder all of her previous ties for his benefit. Now she is not only heartbroken but has no one to turn to for help. She must rely entirely on her own resources to extract herself from a situation which she regards as intolerable; and Medea has many resources. One element of Medea's foreignness is her familiarity with magic and the use of poisons. She has already demonstrated that she is capable of violent acts including murder. Her intelligence is obvious in every encounter with other characters in the play; she thinks quickly and executes her plans with little hesitation. Furthermore, her abilities to persuade and deceive are quite stunning.

One of the most significant character traits in Euripides' portrayal of Medea is her apparent volatility. She is shown to have rapid mood swings and to be capable of extreme behaviors. The Nurse has introduced Medea as a good wife, who fell in love with Jason and followed him from Colchis to Iolcus and then to Corinth, where she lives as a stranger in a foreign land for his sake. She emphasizes that Medea is well loved by the citizens of her new city. The Nurse also warns of Medea's uncontrollable spirit and hints at a darker side to her character. She ominously mentions that Medea hates her children—and immediately afterwards expresses her fear that Medea may plan acts of violence (36–43). However, the question must be asked, as to how much of this description relates to her foreign background. People coming from different backgrounds are often perceived as volatile, violent, unreliable, and unstable in tragedy, partly because their customs are unfamiliar and partly because they are facing stressful situations away from their homeland. Both apply to Medea.

Notwithstanding her foreignness, Euripides does emphasize Medea's rapidly changing nature. She is depicted as rising from the depths of despair to being able to make a coldly rational analysis of her situation, leading to the successful manipulation of others in a matter of moments. It is difficult to assess the true nature of Medea, as in addition to being highly temperamental, she also demonstrates extraordinary acting abilities, transitioning smoothly from one persona to another. These characteristics make Medea unpredictable, possibly even to herself. We may also ask ourselves whether the mercurial and unpredictable spirit, use of witchcraft, intelligence, rhetoric, deception, and resourcefulness in Euripides' portrayal of Medea are characteristics of her "foreignness" and "otherness" or of her being a woman. The playwright seems to leave these questions for the audience to answer.

Medea's Interactions With Other Characters—Sincerity and Insincerity

The complexity of Medea's personality casts a veil between Medea and her on-stage and off-stage audiences, who cannot be certain as to what Medea is thinking, and whether she is being sincere. Examining Medea's interactions with other characters, it becomes clear that Medea, whose situation seemed so desperate to start with, somehow emerges with the upper hand.

Medea's changes in mood and persona make it hard to assess exactly when Medea is being sincere, and when she is being deceptive. Medea herself often appears to struggle with inner battles, fuelled by her intense emotions; yet however impassioned she becomes, her intellect and capacity for analytic thought allow her to strategize. While emotionally devastated by Jason's callous abandonment, she remains capable of correctly assessing the most effective way of causing him harm. Removed from a context of social norms and from a moderating inner voice, empowered by her emotions and knowledge of magic and poisons, Medea's intelligence becomes a dangerous weapon.

Medea and the Chorus

The Nurse has described Medea at the start of the play as feeling dishonored and betrayed. She is suffering from the wrenching symptoms of unrequited love: refusing food, lying practically inert and crying incessantly. This wretchedness appears to express Medea's state of mind as being beyond reason. (We may compare her behavior with that of Phaedra, pp. 253–260, however, the lovesick Phaedra has never had an actual relationship with Hippolytus, the object of her love, while Medea has loved and lost.) However, when Medea comes outside and addresses the Chorus, she is the epitome of composure. This is the first time that the spectators witness the rapid changes in behavior which characterize Medea. These apparent mood swings make it hard to assess Medea's personality and her motivations. Could the anguish and passionate hatred the audience learned about moments earlier and the calm speech delivered to the Chorus both be authentic? Is Medea being sincere in her interactions with the Chorus, sharing with them her dire predicament and demonstrating admirable self-restraint, or is she masking her true nature and intentions and already planning to deceive them in order to gain their assistance? Either way, Medea now is evidently in complete control of her words and actions, having pulled herself out of the despair she was experiencing just a few moments earlier.

Medea's first speech to the Chorus is motivated by the "otherness" associated with being a foreigner. Many see this address to the Chorus as a manipulative step towards attaining the single goal mentioned at the end of the speech: "And so I shall ask this much from you as a favor: if I find any means or contrivance to punish my husband for the wrongs, keep my secret" (260–63). Some see Creon and his daughter even at this early stage as additional intended victims for punishment (262). However, at this point, Medea's focus for retaliation is Jason alone, and the Chorus agree that Jason deserves to be punished (267–68). Since Medea does not know that Creon has decided to banish her with her sons, she does not yet have any personal reason to punish Creon. Indeed, Creon's incidental death from his daughter's poisoned robe could be regarded as accidental. Scholars usually agree that Medea is not yet considering filicide, with that plan only being formed after the arrival of Aegeus.

Medea presents herself to the Chorus as a woman who is a vulnerable foreigner, seeking help from other women. Her formal address to them as "Women of Corinth" (214) (rather than the simple, common address of "Women" or "Friends") indicates how "alien" she feels (Mastronarde 2002: on 214). She does not want to appear haughty or indifferent to her neighbors (214–19). She starts by acknowledging that as a foreigner she needs to comply with the city's customs and demands (222). She needs to show the women that she means well to them, and by extension to Corinth. She also wants to be liked. Her plea to the women to keep a secret might be seen as a way for Medea to forge a friendship or alliance with the women by implying that she trusts them. The exact purpose of this alliance is not completely clear. As often seen in tragedy, the Chorus do not actively help or hinder the main protagonists; they merely express their opinions. Dramatically, however, Medea is able to outline her plans out loud, on the stage, in the presence of the Chorus.

Pointing out common ground and shared experiences is a useful rhetorical ploy for establishing friendships. Medea seeks solidarity with the Chorus by pointing out the unfairly inferior status of women, while being fully aware that their experiences are not necessarily shared. She manipulates the syntax (in Greek) of her statement about marriage, bending the structure of the sentence, so as to allow her own inclusion. She bitterly laments that women buy their husbands at an exorbitant price, referring most probably to the custom of dowry of which the off-stage audience knows well. In her own case she "bought" Jason by the services she rendered him in Colchis. Medea masks the differences between herself and the women by using oblique language. She does not say "we women have to buy a husband," but presents the idea in an impersonal statement: "First at an exorbitant price *it is necessary* that we must buy a husband" (232–33).[5] Throughout the play the precise use of words and syntax is important to Medea.[6] Here, she creates an oxymoron by saying that the woman purchases a "master" for herself. Normally, of course, the purchaser would be the person receiving a service, and not the person expected to provide a service, which is the woman's role in the marriage.

Her next point also unifies her with other women when she says that a bride needs to find the best way to live with the stranger who is now her husband and to adjust to the customs and practices of her husband's house. Although every bride adapts to a new home, Medea also needed to adjust to the unfamiliar mores or customs of a new country. Although she achieved this splendidly according to the Nurse (11–15), her success was to no avail. Medea echoes her Nurse's claim that a lack of antagonistic feelings is the secret to successful marriage, but while the Nurse speaks of the wife, Medea attributes the stipulation to the husband (14–15, 241–42). If the husband resents the marriage, death is preferable, she says (243). This is the third time the Chorus hear of her wish to die on account of her licentious husband (146–47, 225–29), and they do not approve of Medea's extreme grief (155–59). The Chorus see Jason's infidelity for what it is, a common transgression in married life. Medea's utter devastation and extreme reaction indicate the imbalanced emotions which will ultimately incite her towards the unspeakable.

Medea's last point focuses not only on the husband's freedom outside his home while the wife is confined to the household, but on his blaming the wife for enjoying the seclusion which he socially imposed on her. She concludes: "Men say that we live life free from danger at home while *they* fight with the spear. How wrong they are! I would rather stand three times with a shield in battle than give birth once" (248–51). There must be little doubt that this now famous adage of Medea must have secured for her the most solidarity with the Chorus. There is nothing that unites women more than having given birth. But what does Medea mean in this statement? Childbirth is characterized by pain. Aeschylean Clytemnestra refers to Iphigenia as "the darling offspring of my *pangs*" (Aesch. *Ag.* 1417–18); and Sophoclean Clytemnestra similarly states: "For this father of yours . . . alone of all the Greeks had the heart to sacrifice your sister . . . to the gods—he who, when he sired her, *didn't labor with the pain that I endured when I gave her birth*" (Soph. *El.* 530–33). Medea would readily exchange this tortuous physical suffering for the risk of death in hoplite (heavily-armed foot soldier) warfare. But there is more significance to Medea's statement. Women can do men's work, she says, but men cannot do what women are able to do by nature. Hoplite tactics are acquirable, not the province of the men alone, as potentially women could learn these martial arts. Only women can give birth. Medea tells the Chorus that they are not only equal to men, but *surpass* them.

She realigns conventional gender roles, giving women the upper hand. It is possible that while seeking empathy from the Chorus, Medea does to some extent set herself apart from the other women with this last assertion. While she has referred to women in general up until this point, she now emphasizes her own preference. While challenging traditional gender roles, these words may indicate the extent to which Medea personally rejects traditional limitations of female activities.

While Medea seemed determined to find common ground with the Chorus in spite of stark differences with them, at the very end of her speech she also emphasizes the differences in circumstances that separate them. Why? She enjoys none of a "normal" woman's prerogatives: city, paternal home, and daily enjoyment of life in the company of her family (252–58). Medea blames her situation on Jason, who has committed *hybris* against her. Strictly speaking, *hybris* involves taking advantage of a situational upper hand against someone, while the weaker party has no viable ability for defense (Hesiod, *Works and Days* 203–16). Taking advantage of Medea's infatuation with him, Jason "made her" do horrible things to her closest family. Medea is not misrepresenting the facts here: everyone knows that she committed outrages against her land, her father, and her brother, which she has already told the Chorus and the audience (166–67). Her point is that she did not act out of her own free will, but was charmed by the handsome alluring foreigner, who did not hesitate to use her for his own purposes. Jason, in his turn, submits that Medea acted out of her subjugation to Aphrodite (526–28); he refuses to accept any blame for the wrongdoing. Is Euripides questioning a person's responsibility for an act of passion? Should a man or a woman violating moral boundaries and norms when under the influence of love or sheer infatuation be held responsible for their acts? Medea obviously does not think so. She thinks that the person who benefits from those acts while not reciprocating the emotion is the responsible party.

In drawing attention to this difference between her and the Chorus, Medea is motivated by her wish to have the Chorus see Jason as the culprit, so they will acquiesce to whatever punishment she plans for him. There can be no doubt that Medea believes everything she has said to the Chorus up until this point, and likewise, that the Chorus is on her side.

Medea and Creon

The scene with Creon is brief but highly significant for the plot and for Medea's characterization. Two main themes are brought up here: paternal love for children and Medea's capabilities for quick thinking.

Medea's vulnerability as a foreigner by nationality, who is also alien by race and nature, becomes painfully clear with the arrival of Creon. In the previous scene Medea has forged an alliance with the Chorus, seeking some protection from the citizens that could possibly offset her status-less situation. However, Creon's edict to exile her eradicates any illusion of security she might have thought that friendship with the Chorus would grant her. Medea initially does her utmost to change Creon's mind. With Creon's refusal to rescind his edict Medea becomes doubly displaced: she has lost the land where she grew up and now, she also has lost the city where she has been living as a foreigner: "what city will receive me?" (386), she exclaims.

Creon's explanation of his motive for exiling Medea is chillingly insightful. He knows exactly what Medea is capable of and is taking preventive action to protect his family. He states that Medea, who is clever, skilled in evil arts, and angry at having lost Jason's love, has been threatening to harm him, his daughter and Jason. Medea's response is masterful. She responds only to his charge that she is "wise" (*sophē*), which is the least problematic accusation. Creon used the term in association with Medea's knowledge of evil arts, but she tries to take the sting out of it, by approaching the notion of wisdom in a much wider and less horrifying sense than Creon intended. She changes his meaning by discussing the advantages and disadvantages of wisdom in terms of intelligence, and while doing so oscillates between her case in particular and generalizations, trying to include herself in a crowd to dilute her singular danger. She claims that there are two pitfalls of being wise: one is to be thought stupid by people who do not understand new concepts, the second to be envied by those who pride themselves on their wisdom and are afraid of being eclipsed. She thus criticizes both the simple-minded masses and the élite. The success of this rhetorical strategy depends on Creon's view of himself.

The next section, where Medea questions why Creon is frightened of her, demonstrates her art of manipulation to the full. She starts with an outright lie by stating that she is not the type of person who commits crimes against kings (306–08). She has already committed major transgressions against two kings: her own father and Pelias. It should be hard for the audience to believe anything she says after this outrageous statement. Her claim that she thinks Creon has acted sensibly with regard to the marriage between Jason and his daughter foreshadows her later deception speech to Jason. While admitting that she hates Jason, something she could hardly deny, she states that she has nothing against Creon or his daughter, a remark that matches her emphasis on Jason alone when speaking to the Chorus. As far as the play is concerned, we do not yet hear her making any specific threats against Creon or the princess, although one might wonder how she planned to punish Jason without involving the princess. Indeed, anyone mentioned at this point should probably be extremely wary of Medea.

Unable to sway Creon, Medea asks for a single day's extension of her stay in Corinth. After an initial refusal, Creon yields to her supplications. How does she succeed in eliciting his pity? First, she has cleverly made her appeal seem a trivial request, asking for only one day's grace to prepare for her exile. More importantly, she asks Creon to pity her children. Medea has identified a weakness in Creon: his attachment to his daughter, when he exclaimed that his country is dearer to him than all else except for his children (329). She immediately capitalizes on it. "You too are a father" (340–45), she says. In retrospect it would seem that Medea is already planning to strike at Creon through his child.

As soon as her appeal for one day's respite is granted and Creon takes his leave, the audience, for the first time, are fully exposed to Medea's own admission of her insincere playacting, her duplicity and her savage capacity for destruction. Medea reveals to the Chorus exactly what just happened, making no attempt to hide the fact that she has just lied to Creon. She openly declares that she is set to murder Creon, his daughter, and Jason (374–75), an opportunity that has arisen from the innocence and kindness of Creon. As long as she thought that she could remain in the city long term, Medea restrained her emotions, but now she erupts. With an astonishing change in persona, Medea claims she would never have supplicated Creon, unless she had something to gain (368–69).

Despite Creon's instinctive fear of Medea, he and the Chorus failed to detect the deceptiveness of her speech and underestimated the swiftness with which she could exact revenge. Medea sneers at the feeling of reverence in Creon, and considers him stupid. She gloats over the different ways she might cause the death of her enemies: fire, or as the Nurse feared, creeping into their house where the marriage bed is laid out and killing them with a sword (40–41, 379–80). She dismisses the latter for strategic reasons: she will be caught. She chooses poison, of which she is knowledgeable, and plans ahead. As soon as she has a refuge, she will proceed with the murder. However, if circumstances force her into the open, she will use the sword even if she is sure to die for it. Her reasoning is cold and logical. It should be noted that she does not have a clear, detailed plan yet.

Masculinizing Medea

The self-address that ends her speech is a horrifying glimpse of the Medea we face now:

> Come, Medea, spare nothing of the arts you are mistress of as you plot and contrive! Into the fray! Now it is a contest of courage. Do you see what is being done to you? You must not *suffer mockery* from this Sisyphean [= Corinthian] marriage of Jason, you who are sprung from a noble father and have Helios for your grandsire. You understand how to proceed, and furthermore we are women, unable to perform noble deeds, but most skillful architects of every sort of harm. (401–09)

Although the fear of being mocked is not limited to men, as Mossman notes (2011: on 383), it is men who seek revenge to prevent the laughter of their enemies. Although Medea does emphasize her femininity in terms of giving birth (250–51), or as a woman who is the most skillful architect "of every sort of harm" (409), she is masculinized by the playwright as she describes arranging her own marriage through oaths and handshake (21–23), by seeking revenge out of fear of being mocked, and by her verbal dueling, as we shall see next. Six times she mentions her dread of being derided by her enemies (383, 404, 797, 1049, 1355, 1362). In each instance, her fear of mockery is associated with her motives for revenge.

Pitting her divine and noble descent from the Sun (Helios) against what she implies is the shameful descent of Creon and his daughter from the notorious trickster Sisyphus, once king of Corinth, is reminiscent of verbal duelling found in heroic narrative. In these verbal contests the adversaries name and abuse one another, comparing ancestries and accomplishments (e.g. Homer, *Il.* 5. 284–89, 13. 446–54).[7] Verbal duelling also includes vaunting over the vanquished one, once the direct combat is accomplished (e.g. Homer, *Il.* 13.374–82, 13.620–39).[8] Medea performs the latter as well in her retort to Jason when she is in the carriage of Helios with the bodies of her sons at the end of the play. She not only boasts of her revenge, but also enjoys preventing him from touching and kissing their bodies when he begs to do so (1351–414). This kind of war language, following her self-exhortation expressed in military language—"Now it is a *contest of courage*" (*agon eupsuchias,* 403)—furthers her masculinization, which is countered explicitly by her final words boasting of her femininity. A crossover between femininity and masculinity is also present in the two options for revenge Medea considered: killing with a sword or with poison. While the use of a sword points to the masculine, which Medea has already admired when she expressed her preference to fight as a hoplite rather than give birth, the poison she ultimately opts for is the female method.

In spite of Medea's threat of revenge, the Chorus take her side completely, sympathizing with her loneliness, her status as a foreigner in a strange land, and her loss of her husband's love. They blame Jason for the disappearance of oaths and shame from the world. Jason's faithlessness, they assert, is such that there is not only a break in the natural world order, causing the streams to flow backwards, but also it ensures the poor reputation of women will disappear (410–45).

Medea's Royal Status—Medea with Aegeus

Medea's interactions with Aegeus allow us a glimpse of how Medea must have been before her disastrous marriage with Jason. She behaves towards Aegeus as to a person of equal rank. When he promises to receive her in Athens, she demands an oath to ratify his promise. Her status among the elite is also suggested by the fact that Aegeus not only knows about her wisdom, *sophia*, but also sees it in a positive way. His willingness to exchange an oath with her and establish a tie of hospitality (*xenia*, see Box on hospitality, pp. 189–190) indicates that he considers her an equal. Medea's former status is being reestablished on the strength of her own position and capabilities, as an independent woman.

When Aegeus appears, Medea has a predicament similar to the one she was experiencing during her first encounter with the Chorus: at that point she was in need of the goodwill of the citizens of Corinth, now she is in need of a place that will accept her once exiled. She asks Aegeus for asylum. While she could only offer the women of the Chorus psychological support, here she can offer Aegeus magical services to cure his infertility in exchange for his help.

On the face of it, nothing deceptive, sinister or unprecedented occurs in this scene. On the contrary, when Aegeus denounces Jason's behavior, this reinforces Medea's claim to be the wronged party. Her desire for revenge would not be viewed as excessive. However, given a closer reading of the play as a whole, it becomes apparent that the plot development here mirrors the follow-up to Medea's supplication of Creon.[9] Immediately after Creon granted her a temporary reprieve, Medea revealed to the Chorus that her ardent pleading for a one-day extension was a ruse to gain time to plan her revenge on him through his daughter, having realized the extent to which his children are dear to him. After having received Aegeus' promise ratified by an oath, Medea will reveal to the Chorus her abominable decision to kill her children, having again witnessed the importance of children to another man. It seems that in the case of Creon, she knew that she was going to avenge herself on him when she asked for the one extra day. There are no grounds, however, to assume that Medea has decided on murdering her children prior to her dealings with Aegeus. There also seems to be no decisive evidence that Medea is being disingenuous here. Medea's mind works rapidly, and while she may not have hidden anything from Aegeus, immediately after assuring herself of a place to go, Medea plans her next move in its entirety. Dramatically, the relative calm of this scene underscores the storm that is about to come. The action will progress quickly from now on with increasing intensity.

Medea's Open Admissions

Once Aegeus has left, the audience see a completely candid Medea, who openly shares her plans and her deliberations with the Chorus. Her speech to the Chorus after her encounter with Aegeus is more purposeful than the one following her interactions with Creon. It is also more shocking. Medea is completely open about her plans. She has decided not only how she will kill the princess, but also how she will avenge herself on Jason. Creon has shown her how much he cares about his children. Jason made it clear that he considered his sons' benefit (not hers) when he decided on new marriage. Thoughts of his children run as a leitmotiv in his speeches to Medea (461, 550, 562–67). The lengths to which Aegeus is prepared to go in order to resolve his childlessness has not only cemented the idea that men care deeply about their progeny (721–22), but has also given Medea the inspiration that making Jason childless would be a better revenge than killing him.

The murder of her children is part of the overall design Medea unveils to the Chorus, coupled with the killing of the princess. She will speak softly to Jason, and by asking that the boys may remain, send the princess the lethal gifts that will cause her death. It is to the murder of the boys that she must be referring when she tells the Chorus that she has no intention of leaving the boys behind "on hostile soil for my enemies to insult" (782–83); she repeats this fear later as she encourages herself to go ahead with the murder: "I must not, by lingering, deliver my children for murder to a less kindly hand" (1238–39). The reason they are mentioned as a second item in her report to the Chorus is that she needs the boys to facilitate the murder of the princess. We should note that she never mentioned to Aegeus that she would bring the children to Athens. Did she already plan to kill them? Are the children thought to be simply an extension of the mother, that is to say, since she will come, the children will obviously come with her, or has her plan crystallized after the meeting with Aegeus? It seems that she decided on filicide only once she met with Aegeus, when it became clear to her that she cannot leave the children behind. Her grammar supports this interpretation: she uses the verb "groan" in the aorist tense: "*I groaned* at what a deed I must do next!" (791–92). The aorist is a past tense which can be used in its instantaneous function to expresses a response to something that has been just said (Lloyd 1999: 28),[10] in this case to her avowal that she would not leave the boys behind in Corinth in spite of claiming otherwise to Jason. The deed she must do next and which causes her to groan is the killing of the boys.

Medea's main motivation for her monstrous plan is to assure that no one will laugh at her or think her weak or passive. On the contrary, she wishes to seem harsh to her enemies and kindly to her friends (809); a motto of which any Athenian would approve. However, Medea is so blinded by her intense rage and determination to get revenge for Jason's maltreatment of her, that she does not see how far she is transgressing. She will indeed deal harshly with her enemies, but she will also harm her sons, who should be considered among her family, her *philoi,* and in doing so, she will deal herself a bitter blow. She forces herself to act coldly, suppressing the maternal love, which, as the plot comes to a conclusion, she indicates that she feels. The boys will simply be pawns in a means to an end, or in this case to two ends: killing the princess and causing the deepest possible pain to Jason. The Chorus' plea that she desist from killing the children falls on deaf ears. Their silence about the murder of their king's daughter makes the horror of Medea's decision about the children even greater.

Deception

Medea and Jason – Formal Debate

The spectators are treated to a formidable formal debate (*agon*) between Medea and Jason (see Box on Formal Debate p. 45), the function of which is mainly to characterize Jason and rehabilitate Medea after her earlier outburst.

As often happens in Euripides, the less favored party, in this case Jason, speaks first, followed by Medea's rebuttal. Neither side in this debate is able to sway the other, as they lack any moral or ethical basis for mutual understanding and mostly talk past each other. As Medea has already intimated to the Chorus, she sees Jason as culpable both for her actions in Colchis and for her current situation. Jason has convinced himself that Medea's current situation is her own fault.

The audience have been prepared to meet an unscrupulous Jason, and he does not disappoint. Instead of acknowledging any fault or wrongdoing on his part, Jason opens by attacking Medea's "fierce temper" (447). This must have added fuel to the fury of the woman who minutes earlier was planning his murder. Jason's haughty opening statement, in which he addresses her sarcastically as *gynai* (460) (which in Greek can mean both a generic "woman," as he means here, but also "wife") would only have rubbed salt into Medea's wounds. Jason's foolish arrogance is further underlined when, after not naming Medea, he does not shy away from mentioning his own name (452), in what Page calls "skillful self-announcement" (1961: on 452). This may have reminded the spectators too closely of Odysseus' self-naming in the *Odyssey* ("I am Odysseus, son of Laertes, known to all men for my stratagems, and my fame reaches the heavens" 9.19–20). Jason does not compare well to the Odyssean hero; all the stratagems Jason needed in order to obtain the Golden Fleece were supplied to him by Medea.

Medea's reply to Jason's rebuke is famous for the vigor of her invective and the use of various Greek rhetorical devices to underscore her complaints.[11] She calls him the worst of all men, accuses him of shamelessness for daring to appear before his family whom he wronged. She recounts all the favors she has done him: she helped him to yoke the fire-breathing bulls, to survive the sowing of the dragon's teeth, and to get the Golden Fleece by killing the giant snake that guarded it. In rendering him these favors she cut herself off from her closest family. After traveling with him to Iolcus, she did him the further service of disposing of Pelias by the hands of his own daughters and destroying Pelias' whole household. How has Jason repaid her for all the benefits he reaped from her? By abandoning her for a new marriage. Had he been childless, his desire for another marriage would have been understandable, but he is not.

Jason's disregard for the oaths they have exchanged and for his clasping of her right hand and knees, symbolizing the sanctity of these oaths, is Medea's next point. The lines, as Mossman (2011: on 492–98) points out, reiterate the complaints reported by the Nurse in the prologue (21–23), and echo the Chorus' words (412–13, 439). The exchange of oaths through which Medea gave herself as a spouse to Jason combined with her powerful rhetoric in this debate serve further to masculinize her, despite her own repeated avowals of her femininity.[12]

With biting sarcasm, Medea addresses Jason as a "friend near and dear"/ "belonging to the family", *philos* (499), ironically reprising Jason's insistence that they are still "family" (*philoi* 459) even though, in her eyes, he has treated her as an enemy. Medea poses a series of incisive questions: where can she turn? To her country that she betrayed? To Iolcus whose royal family she destroyed? She succinctly summarizes what has transpired: "to my own kin I have become an enemy, and by my services to you I have made foes of those I ought not to have harmed" (506–09). Taking a line from Sophoclean Tecmessa, who points out to Ajax that if he commits suicide, the lowly status befalling her and their son would reflect back on him (Soph. *Ajax* 501–02), Medea sarcastically points out how her exile with his beggared sons would reflect back on Jason. Medea thus destroys Jason on moral, ethical, and religious grounds: Jason is indifferent to the value of gratitude, to keeping one's oaths, and to any feelings of obligation to her or his children. She describes him as amoral.

Jason coldly dismisses Medea's claim to gratitude by saying she deserves nothing; whatever she did was under the influence of Aphrodite, the goddess of love and the personification of passion. We have already seen this transferal of responsibility from a human to a god (indeed specifically Aphrodite), in Helen's self-defense (*TW* 924–33), which is torn apart by Hecuba's rebuttal (see pp. 146–150). However, even if it was accepted that Aphrodite led Medea to fall in love with Jason, it was Medea who helped him, and who paid dearly for her actions. Jason backtracks a little from this outrageous statement by acknowledging Medea's subtle intelligence, but then only makes matters worse by his preposterous claim she has received more than she gave: has she not lived in Greece where she learned about justice and the use of laws that do not gratify strength? Is she not famous for her "wisdom" (*sophia*)? Who would have heard of her had she spent her life in Colchis? Although this sense of ethnic superiority can be found in other texts and reflects the dominant ideology of the audience, in this particular case Jason's claims are completely spurious. As a foreigner and barbarian Medea cannot bring him to justice, whatever she might have learned of it. As to fame, the spectators have heard Medea explaining earlier (292–305) the disadvantages of reputation and being believed to be wise/clever. Jason's preference of fame to wealth and poetic skill underscores further the lack of common ground between the wife and the husband. One can only imagine Medea's emotional devastation when she realizes that her passionate love and the turmoil of her heart kindles little more than apathy, or perhaps a mere shadow of anger in this cold-hearted, amoral man.

After this disgraceful and inappropriate reasoning, Jason changes tactics by depicting the benefits of the new marriage to him and the children. Jason will be close to the throne; they will not live in poverty and the children will have royal children as their siblings. He is not marrying the princess out of love or the wish to have more children, but for advantageous reasons only. He goes on to attack Medea by blaming her for sexual jealousy. If she was not galled by being deprived of having sex, she would have realized how good his plan was. He goes on to condemn all women for their lust, and wishes that men might beget children from some other source, an idea that three years later, Euripides' Hippolytus will expand on (*Hipp*. 618–24), words that would infuriate any women, let alone an abandoned wife.

Jason's plan for his new marriage is nauseatingly devious, but it does indicate his concern for a more secure future for their sons. Furthermore, the lack of emotion on his part toward the princess would have not necessarily be objectionable to the Athenian audience (for whom marriages were usually of convenience to both families involved), if not for the close parallel to the advantage he took of Medea. Even if he seeks by extension to benefit his old family, Jason's heartless selfishness appears no less negative than Medea's excessive emotion. As Grube states: "on Jason's side is moderation and wisdom without passion, on the other passion without prudence, unchecked and untamed" (1961: 156). The abyss separating Medea and Jason is impassable.

Medea and Jason: Deception Scene

There is no comparable scene in which Medea lies so blatantly. She shamelessly capitalizes on every aspect of Jason's conceit using her familiarity with her husband's character. We do not necessarily feel pity for Jason, who is reprehensible, but there are moments in which we cannot but recognize his deep love for his children.

She starts her speech by asserting their common background: the former love which obliges him to forgive her anger. Next, she launches into a conversation with herself to convince Jason that she has changed her mind. This rhetorical device is quite unique and evinces a particularly light, easy-to-follow tone which would guarantee that the content would not to be lost on Jason with his predisposition for simplicity. She adheres closely to Jason's own justification of the new marriage on the basis of expediency and admits that Jason had her interests and those of the children in mind (although he has never mentioned her as a direct beneficiary of this marriage). Jason's claim that she should not have been upset that he abandoned her bed because she has enough children was not lost on her, even though it was expressed by him in no more than six words (565). She reinforces this claim in five words (in Greek): "Do I not have the children?" (880).

The audience must have been startled at how calmly Medea can mention the children, knowing everything she has planned for them. Denigrating her own intelligence to Jason is so out of character for Medea that he should have realized something was wrong. She even calls herself "senseless," *aphron*, a word which also has connotations of madness (885). Her next words are so far-fetched that it is a wonder that even someone as insensitive as Jason does not recognize the sarcasm: she says she should have taken part in his plan to remarry by standing like a mother-in-law by the marriage-bed and being delighted in tending to his bride (886-88). She further adopts Jason's perspective when she criticizes women as a race: "Well, we women are, I will not say, bad creatures, but we are what we are" (889). By doing this she prevents him from potentially insulting women as a class as he seemed to enjoy doing in their previous encounter. She exhibits absolute self-control throughout her manipulation of him, until the point that she needs to involve the children. At this point she almost breaks down (see below).

By appealing to Jason's sense of superiority while wearing the guise of a weak female, Medea attempts to reverse the impression she made in their earlier altercation, before Medea's meeting with Aegeus. Echoing his perspective and playing up to his arrogance allow her to entrap him. Jason's reply shows he has learned nothing. Once again, he addresses her as *gynai* "woman/wife," never by her name, even though Medea has addressed him by his proper name (869). His warm address to his children and the sincere care he expresses for their future (914–21) must have drawn Medea's attention. Jason has shown Medea his weakest spot, guiding the aim of her vengeance. It is clear that the only genuine emotion Jason possesses is his love for his sons, and this is where she will strike.[13]

Medea's Revenge: Medea and Her Children

The audience have been made aware from the start of Medea's passionate nature: "Her heart smitten with love for Jason" (8), but maternal love is not part of it. On the contrary, the Nurse states that: "She loathes the children and takes no joy in looking at them" (36). While still in the depths of despair at the start of the play, Medea herself had cursed the boys and wished them dead along with their father (112–14). Unlike Jason, who never forgets his children (459–64, 620–22), Medea barely mentions them except as part of her current fate. She does talk about the pangs of labor, but not about her sons proper. She asks Creon for a one-day reprieve to prepare whatever is needed for their exile (340–42), she rebukes Jason for wishing to marry again even though he is not childless (490-91), and mentions them again when showing how mistreated she is by him (510-15). However, she never accuses Jason face to face of being a negligent father. In her encounter with Aegeus, she fails to mention her sons altogether, as if they were just an extension of her. The poignant irony of this omission is that Medea's recognition of Aegeus' concerns very probably sealed the boys' fate, as Medea realized what childlessness can mean to a man, knowledge that in turn propelled her to the abominable murder of her sons.

In spite of Medea's masterly self-control during her deception speech to Jason, and the fierce hatred which is driving her to the filicide, Medea breaks down when the subject of the children comes up. She tells the Chorus that she has decided to kill them so that no one insults them, and indicates her fear that someone else may murder them out of revenge for the murders she has already committed. Medea is not completely alienated from her children. Her passionate temperament led her to exclaim in despair that she hated her children, but many mothers have shouted such things at dark moments. Medea's sons are in some ways dear to her, but this only becomes apparent in the most strangely convoluted manner at the height of her plans to murder them. Now that their deaths are indeed imminent, Medea thinks of the children as her "dear sons" and recognizes that their murder is an "unholy deed" (795-96). Despite acknowledging the feelings she has for her children, Medea still finds that her wish for revenge is stronger. She has already admitted to the Chorus that killing her children "is the way to hurt my husband most" (817), and for her the end justifies the means. The sincerity of any maternal instincts Medea may have felt was already brought into question when she planned to use them to send her lethal gifts to the princess. When she imagines her life in exile without the boys, it is not their fate that she imagines, but her own, unlike Jason, who thinks of their future either as siblings to his future royal children, or of their well-being when in exile. Medea mourns not having the opportunity to take part in their wedding rituals; she complains that her labor pangs were in vain and regrets that her children won't be able to perform the needed rituals when she dies. The children's existence seems only to serve hers.

When the time for the abhorrent deed finally comes close, Medea almost falters. During one of the many instances when she addresses herself about the children she says:

> Come, put on your armour (*hoplizou*), my heart! Why do I put off doing the terrible deed that must be done? Come, my unhappy hand, take up the sword, up, walk towards the painful marker-post of life, and do not play the coward, and do not remember your children, *how very dear they are*, how you bore them, but forget your sons for this little day, and then lament; for even if you kill them, all the same, they are beloved; but I am an unhappy woman. (1242-50)

Medea is clearly conflicted, experiencing an inner turmoil that she has brought upon herself. She is guided by hatred and her wish for revenge, but the mother in her doesn't want to murder her own children. However, having murdered the princess and her father, Medea realizes that if she does not kill the children, others will, avenging the blood of their cherished ones. One issue that is not raised in the play is whether Medea could take the children with her to Athens. If this had been an option, it would frame the murder more narrowly, as directed solely towards hurting Jason.

Medea regains her focus on revenge and drives any thoughts of love for her children from her mind. Choosing to cause Jason pain, over saving the lives of her children, is an inhuman act. There have through the ages been mothers who have murdered their children, sometimes to protect them from some worse fate. Medea's obsession with revenge, which led her to contrive the murders of Creon and his daughter, may have brought her to this point of no return, where killing her children herself is better than any other alternative. However, it seems equally likely that Medea is now being driven solely by her hatred for Jason and her determination to hurt him, just as she too has been hurt. Either way, it now matters less whether Medea is being deceitful to others, than whether she is misleading herself.

Medea arms her heart in steel, as if she were the hoplite whose travails, she once claimed, would have been preferable to the pains of giving birth. She enters the house where the children are. While Medea is in the house, the Chorus pray, to no avail, to Earth and Helios to prevent her from killing her own flesh and blood, and sing of her cruel and bloody mind and of the price of spilling kindred blood. It is then, at the end of the song, that a cry is heard from inside the house. The audience hear one child asking what he can do to escape his mother's hands and the other answering that he cannot tell him. The Chorus consider going inside to defend the children from murder, but do not. One of the children poignantly cries out for help, which will not come. The cry presages their ending, trapped by their mother's sword. The murder of the children is dramatized in a less graphic and more succinct manner than that of the princess and her father. Yet it is also presented so as to arouse the maximum horror. Do any of the on-stage or off-stage audience feel pity for Medea as a mother?

With the children's deaths, sympathies now shift from Medea to Jason. Unaware that he has arrived too late, he focuses not on Medea, but on his sons: "But it is not so much about her that I am concerned as about the children. *She* will be punished by those she has wronged, but I have come to save the lives of the children, that no harm comes to them from the next of kin, avenging on them their mother's impious crime" (1301–05). Jason proves Medea right that if she had left the children in Corinth, harm might have come to them.

When told by the Chorus that his children are dead, Jason, who has seemed thus far devoid of emotion, is roused to a passion of rage. Reeling from the shock of discovering that his two boys have been murdered, Jason tries in vain to find their bodies. Instead he is taunted by Medea, who is up above him, out of reach in the winged chariot of her grandfather Helios, on the *mechanē* (a crane which could hoist an actor, an object, or both up to a raised structure atop the stage-building). Now Medea is shown not only as a human woman but as the supernatural descendant of a god. Helios had not responded to the Chorus' earlier plea to prevent Medea's murdering her children, but now makes his chariot available to rescue her from certain punishment in Corinth.[14] Does his assistance imply his approval of the vengeance in all its horror and lend divine endorsement to the revenge, or has Medea acquired it by her own charms? And does the play endorse it?

On seeing Medea with his sons' corpses in the chariot, Jason reaches a violence of speech and feeling comparable only to that of Medea (1323–50). He calls her a detestable creature hateful to him, to the gods, and to the entire human race. He decries all she has done to her family upon leaving Colchis, and once again names sex as her motivation, this time for the filicide. In his grief Jason seems to gain a rather belated insight into the acts Medea performed on his behalf, which he previously welcomed without criticism. As if suddenly understanding the true horror of everything that happened earlier in their relationship as well as the murder of his sons, Jason cries out: "No Greek woman would have dared to do this" (1339–40). He seems dazed that despite Medea's standing as barbarian and the violent acts she had committed, he had preferred Medea to any Greek woman. This, however, did not remain the case, as the audience knows. Since expedience is the rule of his life, Jason did eventually prefer a Greek woman over Medea. No Greek woman would have been able to do for him what Medea did at Colchis, but after that she was expendable.

This time it is Medea who is devoid of passion. Untouched by his insults and grimly triumphant with the dead children by her side, she simply rehearses to him his transgressions against her and the children. She gloats and rejoices that he shall not mock her. After all she has gone through, it appears that Medea's inability to bear the shame of being laughed at is still one of her dominant concerns (1362, 1380). She does admit to suffering pain at what she had to do to the children, but in her eyes the pain is justified by having pained him as well (1362, 1370). In their exchange of words, both she and Jason show themselves deficient. Medea reveals no more understanding of the heinous crime of her filicide than she had before she committed it. She reiterates her refusal to be laughed at and points out, yet again, Jason's lack of gratitude and violation of his oath. She will not allow him to bury the children, as he requests, or even to kiss them goodbye. Justifying her refusal of his request to bury them, she informs him that she plans to bury the children in Hera's temple and to establish an annual feast and sacrifice. Finally, her ascendance to the divine is reinforced by foretelling that Jason will die by being struck by a piece of wreckage from his own ship, the *Argo*.

Conclusion

Euripides' *Medea* is a particularly challenging play for readers and audiences alike, as Medea herself dauntlessly heads towards the horrific murder of her own two sons. The playwright's characterization of Medea is nothing short of genius. From the opening moments, it is clear that everything about Medea is larger than life. Her emotions are almost too powerful for her to bear. Being overwhelmed by her own passions and jealousies, Medea is only aware of her own sense of injustice and sees everything around her as a means towards her own primary goal—that of revenge. Yet, whilst in the throes of her powerful emotions, Medea remains clearheaded enough to plan this revenge to the last detail. In a play peopled by largely unsympathetic characters, Jason seems almost absurdly impaired in his understanding of everything about his wife. As in other plays, such as his *Electra*, Euripides seems to give the commoners the greatest insight. In this case the Nurse's expression of her fears in the first scene proved to be a chillingly accurate portent of things to come.

In Medea's case it would appear that being of divine descent has detracted from her human attributes of motherly love, compassion, and empathy as well as having given her supernatural powers. Medea's larger-than-life behavior, with her extreme adherence to a particular behavioral code, with no concern for the consequences, characterized not only the gods but also the Homeric heroes. Medea's fear of ridicule and her insistence on revenge blind her to her fundamental duties as a mother. Euripides thus highlights how excessive devotion to one cause or principle inevitably leads to abject human suffering in its pursuance. As Medea departs she has fully taken on her new "superhuman" status, for better or for worse. Not only is she the granddaughter of Helios, but also her dogged determination for seeking vengeance and her capacity for hate have taken on "superhuman" dimensions.

DISCUSSION TOPICS

1. Medea provides an in-depth study of a relationship between a husband and wife that has gone disastrously wrong. While it is clear from the text that Medea had loved Jason passionately, there is no indication that Jason was motivated by love either in marrying Medea or in leaving her for the princess. Do you think this may reflect either Euripides' outlook on life or that of Athenian males in general? Do you think it continues to be an accurate reflection on society? Explain.

2. Medea often expresses her thoughts out loud, to the Chorus, as a way of indirectly addressing the audience. Do you think that this allows a fuller characterization of the heroine? If Medea's behavior varies at different times and when addressing different people, do you think a full assessment can be made of her character and her motives? If not, do you think this is a strong point or a weak point of the play?

3. Many cases of infanticide occur in ancient Greek myth and in Athenian tragedy. How do you think Athenian audiences would have reacted to Medea killing her sons? Do you think their reaction would have been different from that of today's audiences?

4. Do you think that Medea is intended to portray predominantly feminine traits?

5. The arrival of Aegeus marks a turning point in the plot and in Medea's state of mind. Briefly describe the impact he has on Medea's situation and on her future plans.

6. Medea refers repeatedly to oaths and to marriage contracts. Do you think that Medea was surprised that Jason failed to keep his oaths? Do you think Jason saw anything reprehensible in his own behavior?
7. Is there any indication that Medea will be punished for murdering her children? How does this differ from the endings of other tragedies where family members are killed?
8. There is only one other character in Greek tragedy who has a similar monologue with himself prior to an act of extreme violence (in his case, suicide) as Medea has prior to the filicide. It is the Homeric Ajax, who cannot get over his damaged honor. (Soph. *Ajax* 646–83) Are there any traits common to these two protagonists?

CHAPTER 10
CREUSA

Mythic background

Creusa is the daughter of Erechtheus, an archaic king of Athens, and as such her history is tied to one of the most important myths of Athens. She is the mother of Ion, after whom the Ionian race is called. Ion's story, however, is hardly attested before Euripides. In the Ps. Hesiodic *Catalogue of Women* (frag. 9 M-W),\, Herodotus (7.94, 8.44.2), and Euripides' lost play *Wise Melanippe* (Kannnicht 2004: vol. 5.1 frag. 481.9-11) Ion is the son of Xuthus. There is no evidence for Apollo as Ion's father prior to Euripides' play. Sophocles wrote plays titled *Ion* and *Creusa*, but very little is known about these plays or their possible relationship to Euripides' *Ion*. Like Euripides, however, Plato (*Euthydemus* 302d) makes Apollo Ion's father. This version could be based on Athenian story-telling of which no other trace survives.

The myth of Erichthonius ("very earthy") is equally important in the play because of its emphasis on autochthony (Athenians considered themselves as autochthonous, born of the soil and having always lived in Attica). Erichthonius was born from the earth after Hephaestus' unsuccessful attempt to rape Athena (Apollodorus, *Library* 3.14.6). Erichthonius was born from the semen which fell unto earth after being spilled on Athena's leg. Athena decided to raise him secretly in a chest guarded by snakes. She entrusted the chest to the daughters of Cecrops, also born from the earth. Although she had forbidden them to do so, two of them looked inside the chest and became mad as a result. Then all three leaped to their death from the Acropolis (*Ion* 267-74). The ornamental golden snakes that Creusa left in Ion's basket upon his birth as tokens of recognition parallel the snakes that watched over Erichthonius.

Creusa's history is thus tied to one of the most important myths of Athens. Creusa's sisters died when their father sacrificed one of them to save Athens from Thracian invaders. The other sisters fulfilled a suicide pact they had made with the victim and killed themselves. Creusa escaped her sisters' fate because she was a babe in arms at the time (*Ion* 275-80). Erechtheus himself, while battling Poseidon's son Eumolpus, disappeared into the earth where the god's trident caused it to gape open. Since Erechtheus left no sons, it fell to Creusa to continue the royal lineage, a major preoccupation of the play.

Euripides' *Ion*

In his prologue Hermes gives the back-story: Apollo raped Creusa, who then bore and exposed their baby son. Without Creusa's knowledge, Apollo ordered Hermes to rescue the baby from the cave in which he was abandoned and bring him to Delphi, where the boy was raised unnamed as a servant to Apollo. On the day dramatized, Creusa and her husband Xuthus, who have no heirs, have come to Delphi seeking a remedy for their childlessness. Xuthus is a foreigner who as an ally helped the Athenians bring the war with Euboea to an end, for which Athens thanked him by giving him Creusa as a wife. Hermes himself has come to watch the fulfillment of Apollo's plan, which he says is to make Xuthus believe the boy is his own while keeping Creusa in the dark until all three are back in Athens. The boy will be called Ion and become the eponym of the Ionians. The plan Hermes expounds will be only partially followed.

Ion (still unnamed) enters and greets the new day with a work song, during which he performs menial chores while praising Apollo. The Chorus of Creusa's handmaidens arrive, followed by Creusa, who wants to ask the oracle about the child she says a friend of hers once bore to Apollo after being raped by him and exposed the baby, but Ion, scandalized at the sacrilege to Apollo, won't allow it. Xuthus arrives and enters the temple to ask about his and Creusa's childlessness. Creusa leaves after praying to Apollo's mother for good results. Xuthus embraces Ion (still nameless) for the oracle said the first person he meets on leaving the temple is his son. Ion is doubtful about accepting Xuthus as a father and worried about Creusa's potential reaction to having a stranger brought into her home. He is also concerned about the true nature of his identity, not happy at the possibility that his mother could have been a slave. Xuthus decides to have a feast in honor of Ion, after which he will take Ion to Athens as heir to his throne. He keeps both events secret from Creusa.

Creusa reenters with Old Man (her father's aged Tutor) and learns from the Chorus what has happened. The Old Man concocts a conspiracy theory, and Creusa bursts into tearful song, revealing for the first time the long-ago rape and its painful aftermath. She plots with the Old Man to poison Ion, partly in revenge and partly to prevent him from inheriting her household. The plot fails, and the Old Man reveals under torture that Creusa was complicit in the poisoning scheme. She is condemned to death by the Delphians. Ion pursues Creusa to the altar of Apollo, but is stopped from violating her sanctuary there by the entrance of Apollo's Pythian Priestess, who gives him the basket in which she found him as a baby to help him find his mother. Creusa recognizes it, and proves that she is Ion's mother by identifying its contents. Recognition of mother and son follows. Creusa divulges to Ion that Apollo not Xuthus is his father. Ion is hesitant to believe this, upon which Athena appears *ex machina* and confirms Creusa's story, but prohibits Ion and Creusa from divulging the true paternity of Ion to Xuthus.

Introduction

The date of *Ion*'s first production and its order in the competition are unknown. Metrical evidence supports a date between *c.* 418 and 413 BCE. The nature of gods and their involvement in human life is addressed in the play via Apollo's rape of a young maiden together with his subsequent cruelty in letting Creusa torture herself for years thinking that the baby she has exposed has died. Euripides was known for his critical attitude towards the Olympian gods, and most interpretations of the play focus on Apollo's disturbing violence. However, a handful of scholars present different views, suggesting that Apollo's behavior was designed to provide Creusa with a son and heir, when the time was right. Some even see in Creusa an ungrateful woman who, failing to realize the boon the god is conferring on her, presumes to upset the plans of Apollo.[1] *Ion* poses many questions as to the interrelation of oppression and culture, the latter normally symbolized by Apollo, with Ion and Creusa both prepared to resort to violence to protect what they deem vital to them. *Ion* may also be expressing the playwright's criticisms of the conventional power structure, which conflates the rights and freedoms of Athenian citizens with the suppression of others.[2] In a theme closely related to the political and military status of the Athenian elite, some consider that the play focuses on Ion's discovery of his complex genealogy, descending from the divine Apollo and the mortal Creusa, thought to be the last living descendent of the autochthonous Erichthonius and the founding dynastic family of Athens. Since Ion is the patriarch of the Ionians, this exceptional heritage may have been thought to lend legitimacy to Athens' empire building activities.[3] Whether the play is about the moral corruptibility of the gods, about violence and culture, or about civic identity, Creusa incorporates all these interpretations, although she might not stir strong emotions in the audience. As Loraux (1990: 168) states, "in the complicated plot of this tragedy ... everything ... leads to Creusa for in her all the threads are tied together."

* * *

Euripides' Creusa may be considered a particularly feminine heroine. Her characterization centers on her loyalty to her family and her husband and her yearning for motherhood as seen in the following:

- much of Creusa's speech revolves around her anguish at having exposed her infant son, and having no other children;
- despite deceiving her husband Xuthus, on various occasions, she never intends to harm him, remaining loyal to Xuthus throughout;
- Creusa has a highly developed sense of family and guarding her family's heritage; with this resulting in a blend of submission to the traditions limiting a woman's roles together with an active rebellion against anything that may endanger the continuity of her family's heritage;
- when Creusa decides to commit murder to protect her family's lineage on the Athenian throne, her plan of using a poison derived from a family heirloom may be considered to be in line with her feminine characterization.

The Rebellious Victim

Creusa's Narratives of Her Rape and of the Birth Of Ion

Creusa, Queen of Athens, is portrayed as a victim of the divine: she was raped by Apollo, who then withheld from her the fate of the son she bore and exposed, and, through Athena, prevented her from sharing the cause of her sorrow with her husband, Xuthus. Throughout the play Creusa is depicted as a victim of male (human and divine) oppression, with no right to decide what happens to her body, deprived of her son and without agency to seek comfort by sharing her trauma and her loss.[4]

However, Euripides chose to let Creusa give a multitextured narration of this story throughout the play, adding new dimensions with each repetition. The audience first hear the story through Hermes' rather matter-of-fact account of the rape in the prologue, an account noticeable for being devoid of any intensity. According to him, Phoebus compelled Creusa to be his lover, after which Creusa gave birth in the palace, undetected, and then exposed the newborn in the cave where she had lain with Apollo (10–20).[5] Hermes may have wanted to cast as little shame as possible on Apollo in his version of events. In this account, Creusa was able to give birth in the relative comfort of the palace, and was able to continue her life with no one around her knowing what had happened. However, immediately on Creusa's entrance Ion notices that she is crying, and Creusa reveals that an old memory and an injustice have brought her to tears (245–55), hinting to the spectators at the powerful emotions associated with the traumatic past that she has hidden for so many years.

Creusa's first admission as to what took place between her and Apollo comes in the guise of a story she tells Ion about a friend who was raped by Apollo, exposed her baby, and now wants to know the fate of the son she bore. Creusa has one reproach for the god, in that he did not share with the mother the fate of their son. If he had reared the child in secret and kept that pleasure to himself, that would be also wrong, she says (358). Ion and Creusa develop a growing empathy through this story, as the young man is also suffering from lack of knowledge about the whereabouts of his family members, and Creusa's sensitive telling of her story might have made it easier for Ion to hear it.

Creusa's second account of her story, told to the Old Man and the Chorus, after she has heard their (mis)interpretation of the oracle that Xuthus has acquired a son, while she is to remain childless, is far more emotional. She describes herself as a young, innocent girl picking flowers, calling out for her mother's help as Apollo drags her by the wrists to bed in a cave (889-94). There can be no doubt here about the terror Creusa experienced. However, it is only after the Old Man asks her to repeat her story that Creusa fills in more details. This time she hides nothing. She gave birth alone, in the cave where she had been defiled by Apollo (949). She wrapped the baby in her robes and left him, in the hope that the god would save his own son (955).

The last time Creusa narrates her story she is seeking sanctuary in the temple after she has sought to kill Ion, whom she does not yet know is her son. The priestess has, for the first time, given Ion the basket he was found in. Creusa now reveals that she left a piece of weaving in this very same basket decorated with the figure of a Gorgon in the center and fringed with serpents. She had also placed two gold serpents crafted into a necklace for the newborn, alongside a holy olive wreath (1416–36). Creusa also explains to Ion how Apollo became her secret lover. There is no mention of rape in this account, as befits a story told by a mother to her son.

Throughout her different accounts, Creusa, the rebellious victim, retains control over what information she gives to others. She shares her stories on her terms. The details she adds gradually build her image throughout the play. She knows that she has suffered an injustice at the hands of Apollo and recognizes that losing her son was her ultimate tragedy, and she blames the god for this. She also knows that he wrongly took advantage of a young innocent girl. It is, however, in the third telling that the audience learn how much she cared for the child whom she lost, and can appreciate the mature foresight of the young girl who carefully marked her child's identity. Finally, Creusa, the mother who has been united with her son, develops her narrative further, showing enough compassion to spare her son details that could harm him.

Dualities and Repetitions

There is a thematic binary structure to the play that needs to be taken into consideration when discussing Creusa because it gives further balance to her suffering. First, Creusa's rape and quest for her son is balanced by the distress of Ion, who, in spite of flourishing as the trusted keeper of Apollo's temple while enjoying a carefree life of happiness under the special protection of the god, also feels bereft without the knowledge of his parents' identities. His suspicion that he might be the son of a slave is especially troubling for him. Although the status of his birth parents has no practical effect on his life, Ion's anxiety about this issue mirrors Creusa's concern with continuing her autochthonous heritage, with both issues indicating that identity is an important theme of this play. Second, the diffidence concerning Ion's origin is paralleled by Creusa's gnawing uncertainty as to the fate of the baby boy she exposed right after his birth. She supposes he is dead (348, 388, 902–05), but the hope that he has survived has never left Creusa, allowing her some sense of identity as a mother. Thirdly, the plot has both Ion and Creusa relive the violence in Creusa's past as the two come close to killing one another.

There is also a binary construction regarding Creusa and Xuthus. Creusa keeps her rape and the fact that she has given birth to a son secret from Xuthus, the same way that Xuthus has refrained from telling Creusa about his casual premarital sex, although this would be a more acceptable "secret" than Creusa's being raped. Both of them live as if they are childless, although neither can be certain that this is the case. Finally, Creusa's attempt at a secret appeal to Apollo at the start of the play, while Xuthus is sacrificing to Trophonius in a different location, is echoed in Xuthus' secret feast in honor of Ion, to which Creusa is not invited.

Yet, in spite of this binary structure of the play, Creusa's ordeal is not minimized. It outbalances those of Ion and Xuthus. The vicissitudes of her story create a character with whom it is easy to identify. Almost five decades ago, Whitman stated that Creusa is "the fullest and loveliest portrait of a woman in all Euripides" (1974: 145). She is proud of her autochthonous ancestry and uniquely concerned to ensure that her ancestral line will have succession on the throne of Athens. Even in the hour of her complete despair, recognizing that she has no choice but to abandon her son, she does what she can to ensure that he will be recognized for who he is. Bringing with her not only the weavings of her maidenhood to be left in the basket but the apotropaic golden snakes that are part of the legend of Erichthonius, her autochthonous ancestor, she links the identity of the child to the founding myth of Athens.[6] Her independent spirit and her awareness of her grand lineage do not let her forget that her marriage to Xuthus was made under the pressure of misfortune (58–64), and that she was no more than a war-prize won by Xuthus' sword (298).

Victimhood Balanced By Rebellious Resistance

Creusa has inherited not only her mythic nobility from her autochthonous ancestor Erichthonius, through her father Erechtheus, but also a streak of rebelliousness also seen in her sisters, especially against male oppression. According to a fragment of Euripides' lost play *Erechtheus* (Collard and Cropp 2008: frag. 370.65–74), when her father Erechtheus designated one of her sisters to be sacrificed in order to save Athens from the Eleusinians and their ally Eumolpus, the son of Poseidon, her two remaining sisters committed suicide per a pact with their appointed sister.[7] Victimhood balanced by rebellious resistance to male oppression is thus interwoven in Creusa's heritage. The mythic background would be assumed to be known by the Athenian audience, who are familiar with their autochthonous tradition. Erechtheus takes no part in the plot beyond Hermes' mention that Erechtheus was not aware of his daughter's pregnancy (14–15, 340), and as Huys points out, the omission of "the external conflict between father and daughter permitted him [Euripides] to concentrate on the internal conflict in Kreousa's soul" (1995: 95). This approach has not only prevented Creusa from being expelled from the palace, but allowed her to follow her own inclinations regarding the newborn and at the same time to retain her status as a princess.

Creusa's first appearance on stage is carefully prepared by Euripides. It follows Hermes' prologue and a light-hearted song by Ion, portrayed as a youth without a care in the world, although the shadow of his distress at not knowing his parents' identity does color it as well. The song of the entering Chorus, consisting of Creusa's maidservants, is likewise in a light vein. If, however, the average spectator hoped for the continuation of this light-hearted tone, they must have been crushed by what Creusa's entry brings. Looking at her and declaring that she must be a wellborn woman, Ion also tells the audience that she is crying and wonders about that, because most visitors are glad to see Apollo's sanctuary (237–46). Creusa immediately recovers her composure and intimates that her tears come from reliving a past event. As her noble demeanor requires, her feelings are usually kept in bounds, but her rebellious free spirit and her resentment are unveiled upon her first entrance when she exclaims: "O unhappy women! O the criminal deeds of gods! What is to happen? To what tribunal can we appeal when we are being done to death by injustice of our masters?" (252–54).

As her encounter with Ion progresses and sympathy grows between them, Creusa unfolds her tale of misery, with a remarkable combination of victimhood and rebellion.[8]

Fully aware that she has suffered injustice, she is not abashed or restrained in criticizing Apollo at every opportunity. Like all women who have been through this horrific experience, Creusa has never fully recovered from the trauma of her rape, and now that she is in the temple of her attacker, her memory of the violence to her body is even more vivid. She is not inhibited in expressing displeasure with the god of the venerated religious institution she is visiting. She bristles at the mention of places close to the cave where she was ravished. When Ion mentions the Long Rocks (below which there are caves, in one of which Creusa was raped, 13), and the altar of Zeus Astrapaios ("of lightning") which Ion claimed Apollo "honored,"[9] Creusa mocks the idea that this place was "honored" and says "I wish I had never seen it!" (286). When Ion asks why she hates what Apollo loves, she answers: "I know of a disgraceful deed done in that cave" (288). As she tells her story to Ion, in a guise that it is the tale of another woman, the youth, who considers the god as his surrogate father (136–40), looks for excuses and ironically suggests that maybe Apollo has secretly saved the child. However, for Creusa, so conscious of her own suffering, even this would not exonerate the god. If this is true, she says, it is unjust of Apollo not to share his joy in raising his son with the boy's mother (357–58). She is so incensed that she proclaims that even if Apollo should repair his earlier mistakes, he could not become entirely her *philos*, her "near and dear" (425–28). In short, Apollo's callous silence compounded with raping her is unforgivable. If Euripides intended to undermine the morality of the Olympian gods, Creusa was the perfect choice for his goal. Creusa knows what Phaedra knew as well—"men hate us" (Euripides, *Hipp*. 406–07). She also knows that people tend to make wholesale judgments on all women and there is no escape from this (398–400).

As the conversation between Ion and Creusa progresses, Creusa continues to challenge the god without one good word about him. She wishes to ask Apollo about the baby boy that "her friend" has exposed. Still unaware that Creusa's story is about her and not a friend, Ion warns Creusa not to force upon Apollo a revelation that the god is clearly unwilling to make and refuses to allow her the proper ritual to force an answer (369–80). His protective attitude towards Apollo is a little inconsistent with both his former and upcoming criticisms of Apollo, who rapes virgins and fathers children whom he lets die (436–51). Whether he feels indignant at Apollo's alleged conduct, or has lingering doubts about Creusa's story, is up to the spectators to decide. Ion decides that although Apollo has committed a transgression, he must feel tremendous shame and must not be proven a sinner in his own temple. Creusa has no choice but to accept Ion's refusal to allow her to question the god, but she does not bow to it without a fight. With exemplary logic she states that Apollo should answer her query because this is his function as the god of prophesy: "Surely he will if he sits on the tripod all Hellas consult" (366). In other words, if he is open to questions by any Greek person, he should also answer questions about his own behavior. If beforehand she has denounced gods in general terms (252–54), now she criticizes Apollo directly and by name:

> O Phoebus, you are unjust both then and now to the absent woman whose plea is here. You did not save your child, as you should have done, and prophet though

you are you will give no answer to the mother's question, so that if he is dead, he may receive a burial, but if alive, may come to the sight of his mother. Well, I must let it pass since the god prevents my learning what I want. (384–91)

At this point Xuthus arrives with his retinue from the cave of Trophonius, and she cannot pursue her questioning further.

The play thus opens with an illustration of Creusa's agency as she operates within the limits imposed on women, even royal women. She could only travel to Delphi with her husband when both of them had a query for Apollo. Her initiative however emerges immediately upon their arrival. When she is left behind by Xuthus, who has gone to make sacrifices in the cavern of the hero Trophonius in Lebadaea about fifteen miles from Delphi, she secretly attempts to learn about her exposed child. She has to be very cautious lest her secret is exposed. When Xuthus returns unexpectedly, she keeps her wits about her, turning to Ion and begging: "Say nothing to him [Xuthus], stranger, about what I have said so that my secret errand may not bring me into disgrace and the stir reach other ears than I intended" (395–97), although in her distress she has almost betrayed herself to Ion by not qualifying that it is allegedly not *her* disgrace but her friend's.

Creusa's recalcitrant nature is borne out as she does not desist after her husband brings the news of the preliminary oracle from Trophonius that neither he nor his wife would leave Delphi childless. Xuthus asks Creusa to help him with prayers when he goes in to consult Apollo's oracle. Creusa, however, cannot bring herself to pray to Apollo, her rapist, directly. Instead she calls on Leto, Apollo's mother: "I pray that our coming may be propitious and that our previous relations with your son [Apollo] may take a turn for the better!" (410–12, cf. 725–34). Creusa proves herself quick-witted and obstinate at the same time. She is able to "redirect" her address, enlisting the help of Apollo's mother, while reminding her of her son's bad behavior. Her fighting spirit does not relent.

In her first appearance, Creusa has proven herself a woman of initiative, free spirit, rebelliousness, and quick thinking. She understands how rhetoric can make her answers to Ion nebulous, and how to use deceit when necessary, taking advantage of her husband's absence to further her own interests. She is as resolute in her criticism of the god who molested her as she is in her attempt to find out what has happened to her abandoned son. She is a mother who for all these years has not found a way to appease the gnawing disquietude about the fate of the infant she has exposed. All her capabilities will come to play in her second appearance, when she will use any means she can to defend the throne of her ancestors from being defiled by those she thinks of as foreign usurpers.

The Mother Motif

The Anguish of Childlessness—A Mother Who Has Lost Her Son

Creusa's anguish as a mother who has exposed her infant unwillingly makes motherhood a constant motif in the play. A two-fold unwillingness was involved in giving birth to Ion:

Apollo coerced her into a sexual liaison by sheer force, and she has exposed her newborn against her will (1459–60). That she had second thoughts about abandoning the infant is suggested by her returning to the cave to check on his fate, not finding him there anymore (350). Her explanation for exposing her newborn became controversial due to the ambiguity of the text. Literally the text states that she cast out the baby in the place where she was raped "with the fear of a mother" (898), which for some means that the abandonment of her child was caused by the fear of her (i.e. Creusa's) mother. However, as Huys points out (1995: 95–96), the traditional motif in exposure stories is the fear of the father rather than the mother. Indeed, we are told by Hermes that she hid her pregnancy from her father not from her mother. Huys (1995: 95–97) proposes to understand the word "mother" as Creusa speaking of herself: she exposed the baby "with a fear a mother feels when doing such a thing." There are other places in the play where Creusa speaks of herself as a mother (918, 1439, 1459, 1493 and 1489 with Paley's emendation to "of your mother"), so such self-reference is not at odds with her character. Creusa's mother does not feature enough in the play to have this kind of important function. She is mentioned only in the conventional picture of the mother who holds Creusa in her arms as a newborn infant (280) and in the standard exclamation by a girl at the moment of her rape (893). It is also noteworthy that Creusa does the opposite of what her mother did. Her mother saved Creusa as a baby by keeping her in her arms when her father sacrificed his older daughter (although she supported the sacrifice for patriotic reasons). Would Creusa's own mother then have been the type to want Creusa to expose the newborn and thus assure his death?

The theme of motherhood permeates Creusa's first encounter with Ion. The fact that she has not nursed her baby boy weighs heavily on her. Her deep anxiety about never having nursed her child comes up immediately when Ion tells her that he was brought to the temple as a baby. All she is interested in is knowing who nursed him (318–20). For the Greeks, the breast was the most powerful symbol of the bond between mother and child, as we learn from the fact that the baring of her breast in supplication was the most effective gesture of the suppliant. Indeed, in Aeschylus' *Libation Bearers* (896–99) Orestes almost relents from his revenge matricide when Clytemnestra bares her breast begging for her life. Creusa refused her newborn her breast, and the guilt has never left her.[10] She misses this motherly function tremendously (962–63, 1492–93 cf. 761–67). Her sympathy and identification with Ion is instantaneous: "poor boy!" she calls him (320), once he tells her about being abandoned as a baby. She sees herself in Ion's mother: "another woman suffered as your mother did" (330), she tells the youth.

Shame, secrecy, and fear color Creusa's behavior throughout the play and all three are related to her struggle with motherhood. The feeling of shame and the need for secrecy interlace closely. She is so ashamed of her illicit intercourse with Apollo that she refuses in the beginning to explain to Ion her emotional upheaval and tells Ion not to think of it any more (256–57). When asked by Ion if she is childless, she gives him a riddling answer that does not reveal the truth: "Apollo knows about my childlessness" (306). The theme of secrecy and shame reemerges when she asks for a "secret oracle" from Apollo (334). As Lee (1997: on line) points out there is "a striking confluence of Apollo's and K's purposes."

Creusa wants a secret oracle from Apollo about the child born from the intercourse which they both want to keep secret (72–73, 396, 1484, 1542–43). Her fear is an additional emotion that is tied up with her motherhood. We are not privy to watching Creusa's fear "in real time'" when she gave birth and exposed her child even though she was fearing he would die (348, 916–18, 1498–1500), but we do see her torment when she expresses her fears that her child might be dead.

Xuthus' Son

It is only when she is told about Xuthus' son that Creusa's despair and outrage dissolve her shame, and she divulges her secret, i.e. her rape and her childbirth (859–922). Her anguish leads to her most direct rebuke of Apollo after the Chorus reveal that Xuthus has found his son, and the Old Man, who in the past was the Tutor of Erechtheus and now a loyal slave in Creusa's household, weaves imaginary and conspiratorial scenarios of Xuthus' betrayal. Poetically her reaction to the news is most dramatic. She bursts into one of the most touching lyrical monodies found in extant Greek drama, accusing Apollo *viva voce* for her rape. However, it is important to notice that her revelation is dramatically orchestrated by agitating, by inexact, reports of what has happened between Xuthus and Ion. The Chorus prevaricate about what has occurred. All the women heard was that Apollo had told Xuthus that the first person he would encounter upon exiting the temple was his son (530–39). Creusa is not mentioned at all, which might be the reason that the Chorus conclude that Creusa will never have children, as they tell her. Their strong identification with Creusa's misery, heightened by the contrast with her husband's joy, may have made them only consider Creusa's perspective, and to verbalize it most piteously to a woman who yearns to have a baby, yet will never be a mother: "My lady, it cannot be that you will ever take children into your arms, or suckle them at your breast" (761–62). Through the Chorus' sympathy with the plight of childlessness, they invoke the two tender moments for which Creusa yearns hopelessly, having not done so with her abandoned baby (318, 962–63, 1454, cf. 270).

Imagining that the oracle has indeed uttered this prediction must make the women of the Chorus, as Lee (1997: on 761–62) points out, word their report in such a way that the Greek will sound: "as if they were reporting what the oracle actually said." Euripides has made this Chorus take a more active role than normally expected in Greek tragedies, with their report driving the plot mercilessly forwards. The playwright may have chosen to give these women more agency than normally would be expected, while balancing this liberty with the expected criticism warning against women taking on a more active role in public life as they may easily be influenced by unfounded gossip.

With no proof, but a large dose of harmful imagination, the Old Man adds his own ideas as to what Xuthus might have done. Assuming that Creusa cannot conceive, he surmises that Xuthus had a child by some slave woman, smuggled him to Delphi to be raised in the temple, and now wants to establish him as a ruler in Athens without further delay (808–31). The audience do not have any reason to believe these accusations. In fact, taking Creusa with him to Delphi to consult Apollo about their childlessness might be considered an indication that Xuthus had not given up on fathering children with Creusa. Furthermore, he is fully aware that his good fortune in finding his own son might cause grief to Creusa, as he tells Ion: "I do not want my own good fortune to cause my wife grief in her childlessness" (657–58), and he intends to alleviate it. He is not at all oblivious to the ramifications that his finding a son might have for Creusa. He is a caring and well-intentioned husband. The Chorus of course should know the Old Man's accusations are unfounded, but their compassion and identification with Creusa's misfortune are so intense that they fail to realize this. The Old Man's suggestion that Creusa murder her husband and the boy by "a womanly deed" (843): by means of a sword, some plot, or a poison, shows his emotional confusion as well. Murder by means of a sword is not thought to be a "womanly" choice. As Lee suggests (1997: on 844–46), his own preference for masculine frontal assault intrudes despite his previous statement, while "poison" specifies the type of plot. He is willing to kill the boy, so that Creusa only has to deal with Xuthus. The emotional turmoil of the Old Man stems from violently resenting the insult to Athens at the ascension of this foreigner (810–11, 813–15).

The emotional upheaval of the maidservants and the Old Man certainly influences Creusa's reaction to the news, further disturbing her already emotional state of mind. Why does the playwright have Creusa act on misleading and inexact reports? Could this be related to the situation whereby, as Fletcher (2009: 128) points out, the play counterpoises the "pragmatic reality of everyday life and the fantastical event of mythic fiction" with the fantastical versions often presented as the truth within the narrative of the play? The audience accept that Ion's mixed mortal and divine parentage is the true version of events, while what in other settings would be a far more likely set of circumstances, i.e. Ion being Xuthus' son fathered before his marriage, seems fantastical. Euripides may be playing mind games with the audience, as the more plausible explanation is a fabrication in terms of the plot. When realizing this to be the case, it becomes understandable that Creusa would naturally believe this story. Alternatively, is Euripides attempting to exonerate Creusa's behavior by telling us that her loss of composure is due to misstated and fabricated tales? It is possible that the identity he has created for Creusa, a noble queen who has maintained her composure for so long, demanded something unexpected and shocking to provoke her into seeking revenge. Euripides may be indicating that had she not been faced with this web of lies, Creusa would not have reacted in the way she does. Indeed, until this point, Creusa is heroically controlled except for the occasional sobs.

The new circumstances are a complete surprise to Creusa, who had previously assumed that the children Apollo has prophesied to Xuthus will be hers as well (728–29). After the initial shock, in a conventional Euripidean response to great suffering, she expresses the wish to escape far away from Greece (796–99). Then she broods in silence for 58 lines (799–858). She must be digesting the Chorus' news that she will not have another child (which actually was *not* foretold by Apollo), while Xuthus has been given a son, which makes the loss of her own son all the more intolerable. Feeling betrayed, although she was not actually betrayed by either the god or by her husband, Creusa finally loses her self-control under the influence of the misleading constructions of reality by the Chorus and by the Old Man. One might expect her now to take immediate action along the lines of the Old Man's suggestions. However, it is more urgent for Creusa to finally share the suffering caused by the god who she believes has betrayed her and has forsaken their child. For years, she managed the noble and valiant reticence of which she is very conscious (859, 868–69). Now she needs to unload her heavy secret, by way of a direct verbal assault against the god. She divulges now her sexual encounter with Apollo in very similar terms to the kidnapping of Demeter by Hades. Both maidens were plucking flowers; both called upon their mothers when kidnapped by the god:

> You came to me with your hair
> gold-gleaming as into the folds of my gown
> I was plucking flowers of saffron hue
> reflecting the golden light.
> Seizing me by my pale white wrists
> as I cried out "Mother!"
> into the cave that was your bed
> you took me, divine ravisher,
> without shame
> doing what gladdens Cypris' heart. (887–96, after Kovacs)

Creusa's portrayal of Apollo as attractive with his golden-gleaming hair (887–88) has become an interpretative crux. This kind of hymnal comment "yoked to such distasteful content creates tension and ambivalence" says Lee (1997: on 887–88). It becomes an interpretative crux, however, only for those who take the comment as a hint to Creusa's giving in to Apollo willingly because she became susceptible to his beauty; otherwise she would have omitted this description, the claim goes.[11] We could equally surmise, however, that she did not pass over this depiction because it was a vital element of Apollo's treacherous *modus operandi*. Creusa is *reliving the moment*: as a young girl: she was plucking flowers when she saw the beautiful god whose pleasant form prevented her from suspecting violence until he seized her by her wrists, ignored her pitiful cry "Mother," and dragged her to the cave where he raped her. Her scream for her mother establishes clearly that Apollo's romantic or sexual approach was unwelcome to Creusa. The god's attractiveness only masks his all-too-human brutality. There is *nothing* positive in his handsomeness: it is actually damning. From the description of her rape, Creusa moves to how (she believes) he left his child to be torn by vultures while he keeps singing joyful songs on his lyre:

> Ah me! And now he [our son] is gone, seized
> by creatures of the air for their feast, my son—
> and yours, hard-hearted one! Yet you <forever> with your lyre
> go on playing "O Paian"! (902–06)

She repeats her accusations in her final curse against the god (911–22).

Creusa's monody is usually thought to be the emotional and structural center of the play that mobilizes its second half. On the one hand, it makes the spectators understand why Creusa falls in with the Old Man's plot. It is not only the memory of the rape that incites her; it is the vision of her child a prey to wild beasts and birds that has haunted her in her secret agony for years (345–52, 902–03, 916–18). On the other hand, the Old Man is stirred to incite immediate action when he hears the abuse and disrespect of his queen's past. But he is so enraged and distraught that his suggestions for revenge are impractical if not foolish.[12]

Scholars also claim that the monody brings Creusa from the state of passive lamentations and self-pity to an active will for vengeance (Lee 1997: on 859–922). Does this monody signify a change in Creusa? Does she abandon her former passivity in order to perform an action that the plot requires? Hardly. Creusa was not passive before. She was as active as the circumstances and the social conventions allowed her to be. Creusa has abandoned her baby, which by itself demanded incredible willpower and resolution. Her decision was not made on the spot. As she finally reveals, she chose to give birth alone in the cave where she had been raped, as if to close a chapter. She had also planned ahead of time to expose the child, as is shown by bringing a basket with tokens of recognition before the birth took place. She has made these preparations in the hope that the identity of the child would be noticed and recognized by whoever finds him, should he be rescued as she hopes.

She has maintained a stubborn grudge against Apollo; for many years (let's say 16–18) she is consumed by the thought that her baby was devoured by wild animals or birds of prey. She cannot, however, initiate a journey to the Delphic oracle unless her husband brings it up and plans it. When finally at Delphi, she is astute enough to capitalize on her husband's brief absence to try and query the god. Furthermore, she is inventive enough to camouflage her personal tale by the pretence of a friend's story, and does not give up easily when prevented from addressing the god with her query. She is not a passive heroine but a woman doing as much as she could within the parameters allowed by the social and gender strictures of her time and place. Indeed, her verbal assaults on the god do not portray a passive, inactive character. The fact that upon hearing what has happened with Xuthus and Ion, she resorts to more than contemplative action, is not due to suddenly becoming an active character, but because the situation has changed. What is going to happen is a continuation of what has gone before, as new possibilities open up. Until now, guarding her secret, she could only act alone. Now, the alleged treachery that endangers the bloodline of her ancestors calls for cooperation with others.

She is not passive in the plotting phase either. First, she objects to burning down the temple, second to the murder of Xuthus. Her reasoning for the latter reveals her character: "The thought of our earlier marriage, when he was good, inhibits me" (977). She refuses to act on the spur of the moment. Although she might believe the fantasies of the Old Man regarding the sexual behavior of her husband, she is disinclined to give up the past. Their marriage was not unhappy. Although for simplicity's sake one would like to think that people are all of a piece, her decision to save her husband indicates that she realizes that people can be both good and bad, simple and complicated. She is sage and mature enough to realize, even at a moment when she is told that her husband is not what she would want him to be, that he is composed of disparate parts making a whole that she still appreciates. However, the Old Man's third proposal, to kill Ion, finds a willing listener. After all, as far as she knows, she has no relationship with him, and he is the real danger to the pure bloodline of her ancestors. She allows the Old Man to persuade her, because she wishes to see Ion gone. However, she sensibly rejects the Old Man's suggestion of an open attack on the youth at the banquet when he is surrounded by his and Xuthus' friends. By means of her three objections to the rather outlandish plans of the Old Man, the playwright illustrates her vivid, active, yet thoughtful mind (to the extent to which any murder can be thoughtful). He has her propose the plan that will actually be followed, and thus indicates not only that the responsibility is hers, but that she only agrees to the Old Man's suggestions where they coincide with her own desires. Her wish to see the boy perish as soon as possible is also the reason for allowing the Old Man to overrule her idea to wait and kill the boy in Athens (1027). Creusa is far from being manipulated by the Old Man when it comes to planning the murder. However, as in the first half of the play, her participation is verbal rather than physical. She is not a Clytemnestra.

Creusa has a special poison, two drops of venom from the Gorgon's snakes given to Erichthonius by Athena. One drop kills; the other wards off diseases and nourishes life. After she gives the Old Man direct instructions on the way to make sure that only Ion is poisoned, the Old Man sets off on his way (1029–38). He should go to the location where the feast for Ion is being held in secret from Creusa. Once they finish their meal and are about to pour libations, the Old Man should put the deadly drop in the young man's cup alone.

The third choral song follows, and once again, the Chorus divulge information which we have not heard before: if the plot fails, Creusa will kill herself (1061–73).

Happy Ending?

The plot to murder Ion fails, the Old Man confesses under torture, and Ion demands that the Delphians vote for the death of Creusa by stoning, which they do. The audience may know that Creusa will ultimately be safe, but because she is Ion's mother their mutual hatred is still in itself tragic and suspenseful. Creusa is portrayed throughout the play as a woman of initiative and a problem-solver. The only time she cannot figure out how to proceed is in the final scene, when she is pursued by Ion and his friends after being condemned to death: "Where shall I take refuge?" she asks the Chorus (1253), who tell her to take refuge at the altar of Apollo and sit on it. If her pursuers kill her there, they will be tainted by the blood of a suppliant (1255–60). Unlike Deianeira, who constantly asks others what to do, Creusa not only has not done so, but has rejected advice given to her by the Old Man. Her question here is uncharacteristic of her, but easily understood. Indeed, as her handmaidens suggest, Apollo's altar is the only safe refuge for her. We can surmise that this solution would have been the last she would have chosen, precisely because it was Apollo's altar, and this may have initially prevented her making this obvious choice. Why would she trust the god who raped her, and as far as she knows allowed their child to die?

Eventually recognition follows. Creusa is reunited with her son after Apollo's virgin Priestess produces the basket with the trinkets that were left with baby Ion, and Creusa describes and then recognizes them. Creusa has regained her son, and the bloodline of Erechtheus is assured (1463–67). But what about Xuthus? Ion is correct to wish to share his news about finding his mother with Xuthus, whom he assumes to be his father. Creusa tells him that Apollo is his father and that he gave Xuthus his son as a gift (1534–36). Creusa was not present when Xuthus gave his account of Apollo's oracle, but heard it secondhand from the Chorus, who told her three times that Apollo "gave" a child to her husband (774–75, 780–81, 788). Creusa must be extrapolating from this information, but because Ion's discriminating mind does not accept Creusa's explanation, Athena must confirm it *ex machina*. Athena, however, does more than corroborate Creusa's words. She also forbids Creusa and Ion from telling Xuthus about Apollo's fathering of Ion.

Conclusion

It is usually claimed that this play, like *Alcestis, Iphigenia among the Taurians* and *Helen*, has a happy ending, but in fact only *Helen*'s ending does not leave the characters anticipating some downfall. Neither *Alcestis* nor *Iphigenia among the Taurians* ends with an unqualified "happy ending" for the thinking spectator.[13] Only Xuthus will remain in blissful ignorance of the facts and will be happy, although he still thinks he will have to slowly break the news to Creusa, as he has explained to Ion, so he won't hurt her feelings. It has already been suggested that the god's treatment of Xuthus is ambivalent, and in order that this might not have an impact on the spectators, Xuthus never returns to the stage (Grube 1961: 277). In addition, Creusa and Ion are supposed to live the rest of their lives hiding the truth from Xuthus. Creusa has retrieved her son, which must override all else for her, so for the moment she is happy. She has never shared her past trauma with her husband, and now is spared from doing so. However, there is a subtle difference. She leaves the scene being instructed by a god to continue pretending Xuthus is the father of Ion, while she has no claim to her son. Could she be fully happy with this pretence? Or does the playwright wish to intimate that it is so easy and characteristic of the female gender to deceive that it will not cause her any difficulty?

Ion has found his mother, but he has never had to keep the truth from anyone in the past. Will he ever be able to treat Xuthus as his real father? While Creusa moves from illusion to truth, but is still burdened with maintaining a lie, and Ion moves from ignorance of his identity to a full and troubling discovery, it is only Xuthus who remains in blissful ignorance.

DISCUSSION TOPICS

1. On meeting Ion, Creusa immediately feels an affinity for the young man. Did you think it strange that she never pauses to consider he may be her long-lost son? Or do we only think that because we know the full story, which she is ignorant of?

2. Euripides chooses to share the information about Ion and Creusa through Hermes at the start of the play. Do you think this changes the way we perceive Creusa throughout the play? Why do you think he chose this structure for the play?

3. Why do you think Euripides lets Hermes present in the prologue a different version of Creusa's giving birth from that we learn later from Creusa? What differences do you see between the divine presentation by Aphrodite in *Hippolytus* (Chapter 11) and by Hermes in *Ion*?

4. Creusa seems happily married to Xuthus, and is not prepared to murder him when this is suggested to her. Nevertheless, in spite of the affinity she has felt for Ion and the affection she feels for Xuthus, she is prepared to see the young man, whom she believes to be the son of Xuthus, killed. What does this tell you about Creusa?

5. Creusa was spared as a baby when one of her sisters was sacrificed by her father and the other two committed suicide. How do you think this affected Creusa's attitudes to life, death, and motherhood?

6. Tragedy as a genre almost always deals with death. Although no one actually dies in *Ion*, the concept of death is never far away. How do you think Creusa was affected when she thought the death of her son was confirmed?

CHAPTER 11
PHAEDRA

Mythic background

Phaedra was the daughter of King Minos of Crete and his wife Pasiphae. Pasiphae had fallen in love with a white bull sent to Crete by the god Poseidon, and had given birth to the man-eating Minotaur. Minos constructed a gigantic labyrinth where the Minotaur lived, until he was killed by Theseus.

Theseus was a major figure of Greek myth and one of the founding heroes of Athens, attributed with heroic journeys and labors, culminating in the *synoikismos*—the political unification of Attica under Athens. He was born in Trozen, the son of Aethra, daughter of Pittheos, King of Trozen, who had slept with both the god Poseidon, and the mortal, Aegeus, King of Athens, on the same night, uniquely giving Theseus two fathers. During his travels, Theseus arrived in Athens, and was recognized by Medea, who had married Aegeus. According to one mythic version, Theseus and Heracles made an expedition against the Amazons, in the course of which Theseus carried off Antiope/Hippolyte, Queen of the Amazons. As a result of this abduction, the Amazons marched against Athens, and were defeated by Theseus and the Athenians. Hippolytus was born to Theseus and Antiope/Hippolyte.

Following the murder of his eldest son in Athens, Minos demanded that King Aegeus send seven maidens and seven youths to the labyrinth in Crete, to be devoured by the Minotaur. To put an end to this retribution, Theseus volunteered to enter the labyrinth in the hope of killing the Minotaur. Phaedra's sister Ariadne, who was in love with Theseus, helped him defeat the Minotaur and find his way out of the labyrinth. Theseus then escaped from Minos with Ariadne and Phaedra, but later abandoned Ariadne, and married Phaedra. When Theseus married Phaedra, Antiope/Hippolyte appeared at the wedding with other Amazons, but they were defeated again. Antiope/Hippolyte was killed in the ensuing battle, either by the guests of the wedding or by Theseus himself.

On his return to Athens from Crete, Theseus famously forgot to change his black sail to white, a signal that he had been victorious over the Minotaur. In his grief at seeing the black sail, Aegeus threw himself off the cliffs into the ocean, which became known as the Aegean. There do not seem to be any other extant myth accounts associated with Phaedra from before the fifth century.

Euripides' *Hippolytus*

Euripides' *Hippolytus* was first performed in 428 BCE at the city Dionysia in Athens as part of a trilogy which was awarded first prize in the competition. Aphrodite opens the play, revealing her plans to destroy Hippolytus to avenge his rejection of the erotic love she represents and his absolute devotion to the virgin goddess Artemis. She has caused Phaedra to fall in love with him. Aphrodite acknowledges that Phaedra will also die as a victim of her machinations. Hippolytus comes to lay a wreath for Artemis, declares his devotion to her and boasts of his *sophrosyne*, which denotes chastity, temperance, moderation, and restraint. There is evidence that Aphrodite's work seems to have started as the Chorus of the Women of Trozen sing of Phaedra's weakness, apathy, and loss of appetite, without knowing the cause of her malaise. Phaedra enters, so weak that she has to be supported. In response to the Nurse's worried prodding, Phaedra finally reveals her illicit love for Hippolytus, declaring that she has decided to commit suicide as she cannot master her passion. Although she is initially shocked, the Nurse persuades Phaedra to reconcile herself with her situation, and use a love potion on Hippolytus to alleviate her suffering. After the Chorus reflect on the destructive power of desire, Phaedra overhears the Nurse tell Hippolytus of her love, and concludes that she has no choice but to kill herself. Hippolytus, repelled by the Nurse's revelation, delivers a misogynistic tirade. Phaedra reproaches the Nurse and determines to die in a way that will both preserve her good name and harm Hippolytus. Phaedra's death by hanging is announced and her body taken down. Theseus, after returning from abroad, finds the tablet on which Phaedra accuses Hippolytus of rape, and asks his father Poseidon to kill his son. Deaf to Hippolytus' claims of innocence, he exiles him (see Box on Exile, p. 264). The Chorus sing of their dismay at the deeds of humans and the instability of fortune, and their sorrow at Hippolytus' exile. A Messenger arrives and describes Hippolytus' chariot wreck in gruesome detail. A bull emerging from the sea chases the chariot. While trying to control his panicked horses, Hippolytus was thrown out and entangled in their reins. Artemis rebukes Theseus for murdering his son and reveals Aphrodite's machinations and Phaedra's deception. Hippolytus, brought in on a stretcher, is reconciled with his father before he dies. Artemis promises to reward him for his devotion and kill a devotee of Aphrodite in return.

The story of Phaedra and Hippolytus was dramatized in three fifth-century tragedies: Sophocles' *Phaedra* and two plays by Euripides, *Hippolytus Veiled* and *Hippolytus Garlanded*, only the last of which has survived. Known now simply as *Hippolytus*, this play won the first prize in the Great Dionysia, one of the three first prizes that Euripides ever won (the other two were: one in 441 for a play unknown to us, and in 405 BCE posthumously for *Bacchae*).[1] It is believed that all three tragedies dramatized the same basic story: Phaedra, wife of Theseus, falls in love with her stepson Hippolytus. When he rebuffs her, she commits suicide leaving a calumnious letter in which she falsely accuses Hippolytus of rape, as a result of which Hippolytus is killed. The story of a married woman falling in love with a younger man, being rejected, fearing denunciation, and accusing him to her husband is found in folklore and in other Greek myths (e.g. Bellerophon and Stheneboea). The sources of the tragedians' plot, however, are not known; nor are the sources known for Hippolytus' devotion to Artemis.

Introduction

In his tragedy *Hippolytus*, Euripides characterized Phaedra as a woman afflicted by an unrequited sexual desire for a younger man, who happens to be her stepson. Euripides' complex characterization of this lovesick, feminine woman includes:

- she remains almost completely inactive physically throughout much of the play, bewailing her fate;
- she employs deceit first when convincing her Nurse to plead her case but more significantly when seeking retribution against Hippolytus;
- Phaedra seems entirely self-centered, with her love for Hippolytus quickly turning to spite once she is rejected and her love spurned;
- Phaedra is prepared to cast aside societal norms as long as she is not caught; once her love is spurned, she prefers suicide over confrontation with her husband.

There is more to the play and the study of Phaedra within it than meets the eye. Although we cannot be sure about audience reactions to the tragedies, and the few clues from a contemporary are from Aristophanes' comic writing, there has been much scholarly discussion on the topic. More than one critic has observed that at least some of Euripides' tragedies were directed to at least two audiences: the literal-minded, who would have taken whatever was said on stage at face value, and the more astute, who would have been able to grasp the subtlety of his words, the innuendos and covert meanings.[2] Vellacott (1975: 19) goes as far as to suggest that there were three audiences:

> Euripides presented his most telling truths in ways which carried illumination to the sympathetic instructed spirit, and roused anger in the shrewd and suspicious reactionary; but which made it easy for the average obtuse listener or reader to be unaware that anything harsh or disturbing had been said.

To make such a discriminatory impact, Euripides' plays would have to be comprehensible on more than one level, on what I term here the implicit as well as explicit levels. The aesthetic of the implicit had been favored by the ancients since Homer.[3] Ancient critics urged orators to adopt intentionally oblique and implicit styles and had very little use for *parrhesia*, "saying everything bluntly." Unlike the modern approach, which emphasizes a message to the audience by proclaiming it explicitly to the readers, ancient practice preferred artful and indirect statements to plain and forthright speech, favoring covert allusions which created a bond between the author and some of the spectators. The ancient writer engages his audience in dialectic and forces them to supply the answers to the questions he implicitly asks. Tragedy supplies such instances in abundance. Thus, for example in *Alcestis*, when Admetus reproves his father for not dying to save his own life, Pheres replies acerbically that he is unaware of any law that requires fathers to die for their sons (*Alc*. 629–705). While the exchange suggests explicitly that the relationship between this father and son is not all that might be, the audience is left to draw their own conclusions about the morality of each character's position. Some will see the aged Pheres as selfish, others will wonder at Admetus' egocentricity in asking his father to die for him, while others still may notice the resemblance between father and son, each clinging to his life, each being selfish. While this approach is not suitable for all the plays, in some plays, as in *Hippolytus*, it adds another layer of meaning that qualifies and adds to the straightforward information given. In *Hippolytus* one explicit reading presents the audience with an innocent, faithful Phaedra, victim of Aphrodite's machinations, so deranged by the situation within which she finds herself, that she not only takes her own life, but also causes the exile and death of Hippolytus, after falsely accusing him of rape. On the other hand, an implicit reading finds a devious Phaedra, who with skillful rhetoric attempts to manipulate those around her when trying to gratify her own lust, who, when her plan fails, maliciously accuses her stepson of foul deeds before taking her own life.

Although many implicit messages are encountered in Euripides' plays, including greatly differing interpretations of Alcestis' character (see Chapter 7), none of the other heroines we analyze yield quite such a double reading as Phaedra, partly because Euripides wrote two tragedies about her. It is generally believed that the heroine of the lost *Hippolytus Veiled* was an overtly lascivious woman who openly tried to seduce Hippolytus, or sent her Nurse with a proposition letter to him,[4] and that Euripides wrote the second version that survived in response to a hostile audience reaction. The question is how was his second attempt corrective of the first Phaedra. Interestingly, we do not know of any other case where a tragedian wrote two dramatic treatments of the very same myth. It is therefore safe to assume that something new was on offer. However, the idea that Euripides has simply gone to the other extreme in Phaedra's characterization and painted her as overly chaste and faithful, is rather simplistic and would be foreign to Euripides' overall subversive and subtle dramatic strategy.[5] We should therefore expect that a more refined and subtle characterization is at play. Indeed, while on the face of it, one can take Phaedra at her word and believe that she is the paradigm of purity and chastity, the implicit reading of her character paints a different picture. There seem to be two Phaedras, as there are two types of shame (*aidos*) according to her. One is shame grounded in an inherent self-respect and self-restraint, the other stems from social conformity and results only in keeping up appearances. These two types of shame, according to Phaedra, should not have had the same word describing them.

Phaedra and Her Critics

The plot evolves in two concentric circles: in the outer circle, Aphrodite and Artemis oppose each other, while in the inner circle the characters try to reconcile the two divine forces. The divine manipulation poses several questions about Phaedra's characterization. Is she a wife who tries at all costs to remain faithful to her husband, in spite of being seized by sexual desire, described in the play as a "disease" (*nosos*), for her stepson? Or, is she a lascivious woman who exploits her dramatic and rhetorical skills to manipulate her Nurse into accepting her illicit passion and trying to help her to fullfill it? That Phaedra's passionate obsession would end disastrously was obvious, but scholars are divided as to how the disaster comes about.

Broadly speaking, the critics have approached the question from varied related perspectives. One focuses on the play's view of the power of the gods over human actions, examining the role that Aphrodite claims in the protagonists' tragic ends. According to Knox (1952: 25–27), Aphrodite repeatedly confounds the human characters, and the play "demonstrates the non-existence of human free will and the futility of the moral choice" (1952: 6). This approach presents the gods' interventions in a particularly sinister light, as they are achieved through manipulations of the characters' thoughts and actions. In contrast, Winnington-Ingram (1960) argues that Aphrodite's explanation for the disaster is simplistic and that the play explores the personal and environmental factors—the protagonists' hereditary backgrounds, personalities and social situations—that bring about the disaster. Going further, Fitzgerald (1973) argues not only that everything that occurs happens through the personalities and actions of the human characters, but also that the gods are portrayed in a way that casts doubt on their reality. Luschnig maintains that "the characters and motivations of the persons of the drama, both human and divine, are so closely parallel that they form but a single frame of action within a dramatic structure" (1980: 89), i.e. they are two facets of the same entity.

Another perspective concerns the play's depiction of Phaedra and Hippolytus. The writings from this perspective tend to be judgmental, awarding blame or praise to either or both protagonists. Fitzgerald (1973) and Roisman (1999) divide culpability between the two. Fitzgerald views Phaedra as a hypocrite, who wants to give the impression of moral struggle where there is none, and Hippolytus as a fanatic. Roisman sees Phaedra as a clever rhetorician who uses her verbal skill to get the Nurse to act as her liaison with Hippolytus, and Hippolytus as morally innocent. According to Roisman, Hippolytus is not opposed to all sex but only to sex outside of marriage, so he should not be considered to be a fanatic; however he is absorbed with unconscious sexual thoughts. This interpretation of Phaedra follows Wilamowitz-Moelendorff who views her unsympathetically, as a woman who is unconcerned about committing adultery and afraid only of getting caught.[6] She is seen to be playing insincerely with the idea of suicide while lying to others and deceiving herself.

At the opposite pole are scholars who emphasize the characters' virtues. Michelini (1987: 277–320) presents Hippolytus as a Socratic hero who stands firmly by his moral principles and is willing to die for them, while Phaedra is genuinely concerned with "shame" (*aidos*) and is a representative of contemporary social values who inspires sympathy and respect. Gill (1990) reads both characters as striving to be virtuous and to be seen as virtuous. Both scholars attribute the disastrous ending, in a somewhat modern manner, to the protagonists' mutual miscommunication and misunderstanding.

The positive reading has the advantage of accounting for the audience's sympathetic identification with the characters that is essential both for the play's tragic effect (Michelini *ibid.*) and for its ability to rivet audiences for so many centuries. This reading works well with Hippolytus because he behaves with integrity, and his fanaticism and preoccupation with sex can be put down to his youth. Applying it unreservedly to Phaedra is more problematic. Aristophanes' *Frogs*, performed in 405 BCE, 23 years after the extant *Hippolytus*, refers to Phaedra (1043) as a *pornē* ("prostitute"), suggesting that she may not have been seen as a virtuous woman even after her "corrective" portrayal in this second play. One may conclude, then, that Phaedra probably did not redeem her respectability: whether entirely of her own volition or not, she is still a promiscuous woman.

It should also be noted that Phaedra, according to Aphrodite (29–32), after having seen Hippolytus and been smitten by him, has built a temple to Aphrodite somewhere on the southern slope of the Acropolis, from which one can see across the Saronic Gulf to the district around Trozen, where Hippolytus was. The act might be silent, in the sense that it is wordless, but it is hardly suffering *in secret*, as Aphrodite has said she does. It requires a rather vast and ostentatious building project, visible to the public. Indeed, it suggests that, far from being a helpless passive victim of Aphrodite's arrows, as the goddess claims her to be, Phaedra is an active woman who has the initiative and intellectual ability to plan, build, and dedicate a temple. Despite all the claims about Phaedra made by the misleading self-serving goddess in the prologue,[7] this act not only reveals the strength of Phaedra's obsession, but also the lengths to which she is prepared to go. Phaedra is no passive pawn in the game of the goddesses. She is a calculating woman, determined to take her fate into her own hands and to get the man she wants.

Moreover, some dubious moral acrobatics are required to justify Phaedra's treachery exhibited in her calumnious letter. Thus Kovacs (1980: 301), who argues that Phaedra acts so as to avoid both bad reputation and adultery, claims that "the bare fact that she causes the death of her enemy and the enemy of her good name would not in the fifth-century have been regarded, without further encouragement from the poet, as evidence of moral failure". Conacher (1967: 32–33, 41), who argues that Phaedra's confession speech dramatizes her struggle between passion and intellect and shows her moral integrity, concludes that Hippolytus is the culpable party because his tirade against Phaedra is what led her to write her suicide note, in short, Phaedra is justified morally.

Balanced readings are offered by Willink (1968) and Mills (2002). Willink both recognizes Hippolytus' integrity and refrains from demonizing Phaedra. In his detailed analysis of Phaedra's confession speech (373–430), he writes that even though she is shown to value virtue only so long as it does not spoil her pleasure, Euripides portrays her sympathetically, as morally confused and illogical rather than evil. Mills (2002: 50–51) contends that all four characters (Pheadra, Nurse, Hippolytus, and Theseus) can be viewed both "favorably and unfavorably" because, for all their virtues, they all contribute to the disaster.

When adopting the implicit interpretation of Hippolytus, Phaedra may be considered to be a clever rhetorician who uses her skill on the simple-minded Nurse for furthering her cause. More specifically, Phaedra does all she can to make the Nurse understand that she is in love with Hippolytus. According to this interpretation, in contrast to what may be understood from an explicit reading, Phaedra fully intends the nurse to reveal Phaedra's illicit passion to Hippolytus, and furthermore, hopes for reciprocity. Once one analyzes Phaedra's rhetoric it is difficult to accept the general view that the naïve and loving Nurse reveals Phaedra's passion of her own volition, in a misguided effort to save her suffering mistress from the consequences of her undisclosed love. The Nurse is being guided to do this by her mistress who miscalculated the youth's reaction. Phaedra plays on the Nurse's love and naïveté and when her plan fails miserably, Phaedra also tricks Theseus into believing her false accusation of Hippolytus. When accepting this implicit interpretation of Phaedra's character, these behaviors fall well within the parameters of her attributes. In the case of Phaedra, as in the cases of Clytemnestra and Medea, the traits of rhetorical skills and independent thought in a woman lead once again to violence and death.

Phaedra and the Nurse: Dialogue

A discussion between the women of Trozen and the Nurse precedes Phaedra's appearance. Scholarly view of the Nurse is not laudatory. She is usually seen as parody of the Sophists: pragmatic, cynical, and full of doubt. It is thought that Euripides depicted servants as manipulative, unscrupulous, and inconsistent, changing with the drift of their masters.[8] Yet, the Nurse in this scene seems anything but the clever, manipulative character described by modern scholars. On the contrary: from her opening speech, the Nurse seems to be rather obtuse. She is duly worried about Phaedra's restlessness and capriciousness:

> Your every word was to come here outside, now again
> you quickly hasten to go inside. You are quickly disappointed
> and find pleasure in nothing, what is at hand does not please
> you, and whatever you do not have you hold dearer.[9] (181–85)

The misery of Phaedra disturbs her, and she soon moves from her mistress' condition to her own incongruous contemplations that it is better to be sick than to tend the sick and, from this, to reflecting on life itself:

> Man's whole life is painful
> and there is no rest from toil.
> But whatever else there might be that is dearer than life,
> darkness enwraps it and conceals it in clouds.

> Of whatever it is that glitters here on earth
> we appear to be lovelorn,
> Through ignorance of any other life
> and because what is beneath the earth is not revealed,
> we are carried aimlessly on mere tales. (189–97)

Not only might this string of clichés characterize a simple woman, relying on platitudes, or the commonly held beliefs, without really thinking about what she is saying, but these are also strange thoughts to utter in front of someone who is trying to starve herself in order to die. If the words do not quite recommend suicide, the suggestion that the "other life" might contain things "dearer than life" certainly does not seem to be designed to dissuade anyone from putting an end to her life. While on one level, this opening speech may make the Nurse seem rather callous and certainly seems to justify the critics' reservations about her character, a more caring interpretation is possible. Indeed, as the play will show, the Nurse, in fact, proves her love and devotion to Phaedra. Her speech serves other important functions. It hints at the difference between appearance and reality that is at the heart of the play, and which the rest of the dialogue will develop. The "symptoms" Phaedra pretends—weakness, distraction, loss of appetite, etc.,—are stereotypical symptoms of unrequited love that the audience would have recognized. The problem is that the Nurse does not.[10] This may show that the Nurse, as a woman of somewhat limited intellect but with great devotion to her mistress, may easily allow herself to be "led down the garden path," i.e. to be willingly misled by Phaedra. And for the play's spectators, the Nurse's failure to relate to the seriousness of Phaedra's physical condition may be significant. No one knows Phaedra's general physical condition better than the Nurse. Is Phaedra really as weak and helpless as she claims? The Nurse doesn't seem to think so. She tells Phaedra to stop tossing about (203–04) and advises her to bear her illness with the calm and noble spirit appropriate to her highborn status.

Phaedra's first appearance on stage is in lines 176–266, in which she is allegedly delirious. Lying on her sickbed, she asks her Nurse and other servants to lift her up and to hold her head erect (198). Her limbs are slack (198–200), she complains, and she is so weak, she says, that even her headband is a burden and she wants it to be taken off—"spread my locks on my shoulders" (201–202). She needs her shoulders to support her hair.

Here we find Phaedra's first hint to her sexual desire: married woman's hair was usually veiled and covered; spread-out tresses are sexually alluring. The veil, as Llewellyn-Jones (2003: 18, cf. 264) claims, "acts as a barrier to contain female *miasma* [impurity], especially the pollution inherent in female sexuality." In a similar fashion to some current-day religious views, ancient cultures considered that women with uncontrolled free-flying hair pose the greatest sexual threat to men. This threat can be neutralized by veiling in any fashion, thus concealing the dangerously attractive locks of hair. Phaedra, however, wishes to attract and seduce Hippolytus and therefore asks her hair to be unbound. That she is aware of the impropriety of her wish and its purpose is proven when she asks to have her hair covered as soon as she appears to come out from her alleged delirium (243, 245). Furthermore, it has also been suggested by the scholiast (ancient commentator of the play) that Phaedra is not only uttering "delirious" words but most probably also acting them out, especially when she is speaking of her wish to ride horses.[11] If Phaedra's delivery is in fact intense and excited and accompanied by large gestures, her claims to weakness may have appeared dubious to the outer audience.[12] However some of the audience may also have experienced first-hand the excited, feverish state of illness or delirium. If her state was more serious, it could have represented the phenomenon of people suddenly rallying round when they are close to death, appearing excited and agitated, as if they suddenly have more energy than before—and then dying. Euripides, for example, depicts Alcestis as highly agitated with a last burst of strength before dying (*Alcestis* 280–325).

Phaedra's efforts to appear ill, and her exaggerated dramatics, which may be seen as manifestations of *eros* (sexual desire, lovesickness) and an actual delirium, may also be Phaedra's first step in the strategy of *psychagogia* that she adapts vis-à-vis the Nurse. *Psychagogia*, as Friedrich Solmsen has defined it, is "the cleverly calculated guidance of another mind toward the objective that the speaker desires but may not see fit to disclose."[13] The reason that Phaedra is not open with the Nurse and does not directly ask her to act as her go-between with Hippolytus, is that a blunt revelation of her illicit passion would be off-putting and cause the Nurse to recoil. Phaedra has to make it look like she's fighting her passion—in other words, that she herself is a virtuous woman—and that her disclosure is dragged out of her against her will.

The Chorus have already divined that her refusal of food hints at such a possibility (131–60), but the Nurse is too obtuse to figure it out. Indeed, as the dialogue continues, Phaedra will continue to let clues slip out that her malaise has something to do with sex or a woman's nature:

How I would like to draw a drink
of pure water from the dewy spring,
and take a rest lying down
in the tall grass of the meadow
under black poplars. (208–11)

In Greek lyric poetry, the meadow scene with tall grass was the landscape of lovers, a convention of which the audience would be aware. In addition, Phaedra expresses here a yearning for a type of scenery and ambiance of hunters that translates into Hippolytus' and Artemis' favorite countryside. Both the on-stage and off-stage audiences know that Artemis is closely connected with Hippolytus. But either the Nurse is deaf to the Artemisian innuendo or, catching the eroticism of the landscape Phaedra desires, she is merely concerned with her mistress' lack of propriety. The latter might be behind the Nurse's warning that Phaedra lower her voice so that she will not be overheard by the gossipy group of people nearby (212–14). In either case, in the Nurse's understanding, Phaedra is "raving" and her words "ride on madness" (214).

Undeterred, Phaedra goes on to provide further clues as to the object of her yearning. Ignoring the Nurse's warning, she continues to speak within the hearing of the Chorus.

She seems to think that if the Nurse fails to pick up her hints, perhaps the women of the Chorus will help. Picking up the notion of "riding" suggested by the Nurse, Phaedra now asks to be sent to the mountain, to the wood where bitch-hounds hunt spotted deer: "By the gods," she says, "I desire (*eramai*) to cry out to the dogs, to throw from beside my golden mane the Thessalian javelin, while holding in my hand the pointed spear" (219–22). This is even more suggestive of the hunter, Hippolytus, the object of her passions. Phaedra dwells on details: the deer is dappled, and one of the javelins is Thessalian while the other has a spearhead. Her use of the Greek verb *eramai*—"I desire" or "I have a passion for"—is especially pointed. The context does not warrant the use of the verb which is associated with *eros*. The proper vocabulary would be the neutral verb *pothein*, which means simply "I long for," which is used in an adaptation of this same passage by Plutarch (see Box on Plutarch, p. 264).[14] Notwithstanding these hints, the Nurse continues to be oblivious of the real cause behind Phaedra's malaise, but Phaedra persists. Ignoring the Nurse's question about her sudden interest in hunting and the suggestion that she drink from the spring near the city walls, Phaedra refers more openly to Artemis and Hippolytus by pointedly calling directly on Artemis, Hippolytus' goddess, rather than her own goddess Aphrodite:

Artemis, mistress of the lagoon by the sea
and of the exercise grounds resounding to
horses' hooves, I wish I were on your
grounds, breaking the Enetian colts. (228–31)

The coastal lagoon with its adjoining sandbar in the precinct of Artemis Saronia is where Hippolytus used to race his horses (1173). The Enetian colts are horses from northern shores of the Adriatic. Phaedra's ability to identify these details quite precisely goes well beyond the cognitive skills of a person in a delirium. Phaedra hopes that the Nurse will finally pick up the allusions to Hippolytus and his favorite horses and connect her ravings to the young man. Everyone in the palace knows not only about Hippolytus' devotion to Artemis, but also the specific type of horse he prefers, and the place where he hunts.

Phaedra's words also are typical of a lovesick person, who always brings every discussion round to the person they are infatuated with, bringing the object of their desire into every sentence. So, while Phaedra is clearly giving hints to the Nurse, she may be speaking like this because she is lovesick as well as manipulative. It may also be important to remember that as part of Theseus' hero status, he spent much of his time traveling. We have already seen the effect of a husband's long absences on other heroines: while Clytemnestra took a lover (see Chapter 1), Deianeira demonstrated incredible patience and understanding of her husband's absences and excused his philandering (see Chapter 8). Phaedra may have been more human than Deianeira. When Theseus left his young wife at home, it may not have been surprising that she was tempted by Hippolytus, who might have reminded her of the young Theseus, as the Senecan Phaedra notes (Seneca, *Phaedra* 646–58, see Box on Seneca, p. 265). That an absent husband risks losing his wife, we can learn from Helen's elopement with Paris, while Menelaus was away in

Crete, especially as machinations of goddesses were involved there too. The difference here, of course, is that Hippolytus is her husband's son. This adds to Phaedra's horror at her affliction, and to the Nurse's horror when she finally understands what lies at the bottom of Phaedra's affliction.

At this point, however, the Nurse has not yet fully realized what has happened to her mistress, though she does seem to come slightly closer to appreciating the point Phaedra is trying to make. She attributes her mistress' cravings to madness, which can be associated with love. She recognizes that Phaedra is given to desires: "A moment ago you were gone to the hills," she says, "you expressed your yearning to go after animals; now you *have a passion* (an *eros*), for young horses on waveless sands" (233–35). In spite of using a verb indicating sexual love (*erasai*) for Phaedra's desire, on the whole, the Nurse still misses the more specific implications of her mistress' language and imagery.

The ever-resourceful Phaedra changes tactics and capitalizes on the Nurse's perception of her madness. The logic seems to be that even if the Nurse does not yet grasp her allusions to Hippolytus, Phaedra might nonetheless be able to use the Nurse's concern for her mental health to elicit her help. Whether purely to manipulate the Nurse, or as a result of an obsession that goes far beyond logic, Phaedra continues giving hints to the Nurse. She exclaims:

> O, I am miserable! What have I done now?
> Where did I go astray from my sound judgment?
> I was mad, I fell into a delusion of a god.
> O me, O me, I am miserable.
> Nurse, cover once again my head,
> I am ashamed for the words I uttered.
> Keep covering; a tear comes down my face,
> and my gaze has turned to disgrace.
> To keep one's sound judgment is agony;
> madness is terrible; but it is best
> to perish unaware. (239–49)

Pretending to be waking up from a deranged dream, she declares that she was mad and afflicted by delusions, as the Nurse had believed her to be. This declaration moves Phaedra closer to her revelation, building on the ancient Greeks' view of love as a form of madness. She offers further hints of her illicit passion as she tells the Nurse that she is ashamed of her previous utterances. If her previous statements had not been sexual, and if she had not been fully cognizant of their sexual nature, she would have had nothing to be ashamed of.

Finally, she ends her speech with her first expressed hint that she may seek release from her troubles through suicide (cf. 135–40): "Madness is terrible," she says, "but it is best / to perish unaware." These lines are an incipient threat, hinting that Phaedra will die if she does not consummate her love. Their message is aimed at provoking the Nurse's concern for her life, much as her earlier show of weakness and delirium was intended to do. The statement is manipulative, playing on the Nurse's love and concern for her. Eventually, the threat will be a major consideration that moves the Nurse to reveal Phaedra's passion to Hippolytus.

In her next speech, the Nurse elaborates on *philia*, that is the love of friends and family, and advises moderation. She does not yet grasp that Phaedra is absorbed with sexual love: *eros*. This realization only comes when the Nurse finally decides to ferret out Phaedra's secret, shifting the initiative from Phaedra to the Nurse. This could not suit Phaedra's purposes better. Once the Nurse is committed to finding out what ails her, she will be more readily enlisted in remedying the problem.

Initially, Phaedra allows the Nurse to speak at length. As Phaedra listens, the Nurse moves between beseeching her to reveal what's bothering her and berating her for not doing it. Phaedra knows that the Nurse will not stop trying to help her and that she will eventually be able to speak her mind. Her first opportunity comes when the Nurse warns her that if she does not get hold of herself, she will die and that if this happens, her children will lose their inheritance in favor of Hippolytus, who will become their master (304–09).

Phaedra takes advantage of the opportunity presented by the Nurse mentioning Hippolytus. In the next 52 lines (310–61), she leads the Nurse to finally realize that it is Hippolytus who is the object of her desire. But the process is a protracted one, as Phaedra cannot risk forfeiting the Nurse's sympathy by abandoning her pose as a woman who does everything to avoid yielding to her illicit passion. Thus, she begins her response with the statement: "You have destroyed me, Nurse! By the gods I beg you forever to be silent about this man" (311–12). By implicating the Nurse in her unhappiness, as these words do, Phaedra intensifies her sympathy—and guilt. Phaedra's play on these emotions will eventually contribute to the Nurse's decision to become her go-between. By entreating the Nurse not to mention "this man" again, she perpetuates the facade, which she maintains to the very end, of being unwilling to reveal her love.

The remainder of the exchange, until line 352, consists of rapid, tense *stichomythia* (dialogue in one- or two-liners which indicates heightened excitement), in which the Nurse presses Phaedra more and more to reveal her secret, while Phaedra, professing intense suffering and guilt, leads the Nurse to guess it, as she plays on her pity and concern for all it is worth.

At the beginning of the exchange, Phaedra picks up on the Nurse's words to supply her with one piece of information after another, each piece leading closer to the identification of Hippolytus. When the Nurse warns her that her refusal to reveal what troubles her will not help her children (313–14), Phaedra moves the conversation to the "storm" inside her (315), that is to her own inner sufferings. When the Nurse voices concern that Phaedra has blood on her hands, Phaedra assures her that her hands are clean, but lets her know that the *miasma* (317) ("impurity") she suffers resides in her *phren*—that is, the seat of passion and affection. When the Nurse mistakenly assumes that Phaedra's suffering was brought on by some external agent, perhaps a foreign enemy (318), Phaedra reveals that, on the contrary, it is a relative, *philos*, who "is killing" her: "against my will and against his" (319).

This information brings the Nurse, who identifies the destructive "relative" (*philos*) with Theseus, a bit closer to the truth, yet still far from the mark. But while Phaedra assures her that Theseus is innocent, she refuses to name the guilty party, leaving the Nurse at a loss.

Phaedra's teasing, partial answers have the effect—and one could say the purpose—of heightening not only the Nurse's curiosity, but also her distress. The Nurse grasps her mistress' right arm, embraces her knees in supplication, and resists Phaedra's equally dramatic motions to shake her off (333–34, cf. 328).[15]

Why should Phaedra want to upset her devoted Nurse? Two reasons come to mind. One is that, being worked up, the ordinarily phlegmatic and commonsensical Nurse will be more susceptible to suggestion than she would ordinarily be. Thus, Phaedra chooses this point to once again hint that she is on the verge of suicide. Without revealing the cause of her plight, she tells the Nurse that the matter she refuses to divulge will bring her honor and that the evil she is devising will yield the best possible outcome (329–31). The matter she refuses to reveal in these lines is not her love for Hippolytus, as that would not bring her honor, but rather the "evil" of suicide. These lines are part of Phaedra's pose as a virtuous woman, who would not succumb to passionate temptation, willingly or otherwise. Phaedra's words play on the Nurse's love for her, the limitations of her understanding, and her relentless pragmatism and conviction that the disclosure of the secret will save Phaedra's life.

The other reason has to do with the place of supplication in ancient Athens. Supplication was a very powerful means for asking something specific, and although it should not be assumed that the request would be granted, it was very likely that it would be. Once the person supplicated granted the request, a pledge was implicitly formed between the supplicant and the supplicandus, which was not to be breached. Phaedra makes gestures to put an end to the Nurse's supplication by trying to disengage the Nurse's hand and asking her to leave. These actions have the natural effect of making the Nurse dig her heels in and refuse to leave until Phaedra tells her what she wants to know. If we have followed Phaedra's actions to this point as being a clever manipulation then we will understand that this is precisely what Phaedra wants. Having brought the Nurse to the point where she will not budge, Phaedra can finally capitulate, citing as her reason her reverence for the aged woman's supplication: "I will give it. For I revere the honor of your suppliant hand" (335).

Although Phaedra is now bound to divulge her secret, she still does not make the revelation, but continues to lead the Nurse to discover it for herself. First, she hints at her illicit passion by alluding to her mother Pasiphae's perverse love for a bull and her sister Ariadne's illicit love for Theseus, and links her own situation to theirs: "And I the third one, poor me, similarly am destroyed" (341). These references can be seen as Phaedra's way of further heightening the Nurse's sympathy, further clearing herself of responsibility for what she presents as her hereditary passion, and of re-introducing the idea, which the Nurse has not yet realized, that the source of her misery is love. Thus, Phaedra clearly states: "It was from this family that I became wretched, not recently" (343). When the Nurse reminds her that she, the Nurse, has not yet heard what she most wants to know,

Phaedra responds with the cue "Poor me! If only you could say the things I have to say!" (345). For those in the off-stage audience who did not see through the fabrication of the delirium scene, Phaedra now states almost explicitly what she had wanted all along: that the Nurse understand and verbalize her affliction for her. Not surprisingly, the Nurse who had taken Phaedra's previous delirium at face value, takes this exclamation in the same way, telling her mistress: "I am not a prophet to know the obscure things clearly" (346). This rejoinder borders on the comic because it is so unknowingly accurate.

To get the Nurse to verbalize her affliction for her, Phaedra brings the discussion back to love: this time to *eros*, sexual desire, not *philia*, affection for the near and dear. She asks: "What is meant when they say people are feeling *eros* / are in love [*eran*]?" (347). A philosophic discussion of love is obviously inappropriate at this juncture, and the aim of the question is to bring the Nurse yet a step closer to making the identification that Phaedra wants. Conveniently, the Nurse gives an answer we find often in Greek lyric poetry: "It is both the sweetest and a painful thing" (348). This reply enables Phaedra to make a partial confession, namely that she is "probably suffering from the latter," in other words, from the pain of love. Phaedra's reply in turn brings the Nurse to ask the crucial question, namely whether Phaedra is in love and with what man (350).

Phaedra identifies the man by his maternal lineage, telling the Nurse that he is the son of the Amazon (351). But it is the Nurse who finally names Hippolytus, only for Phaedra to answer, in a mixture of triumph and self-justification, "You hear it from yourself, not from me!" (352) i.e. "You have spoken his name, not I."

The Disclosure of Phaedra's Love to Hippolytus

After the Nurse and Chorus duly express their shock and their fear of imminent catastrophe, Phaedra continues to manipulate the Nurse in what is known as the confession speech (373–430). This speech is generally read by scholars as a "resolute speech" that sets forth the moral issues that confront Phaedra. Indeed, this is what Phaedra would like the Nurse and the Chorus to believe. She begins with the pious, but also self-serving, observation that people wind up doing wrong despite their best intentions, and then goes on to recount the efforts she made to avoid the shame attendant on her illicit passion. The first was to keep silent about it. When that wasn't enough, the second was to conquer her love with discretion and good sense. And when that too didn't work, the third was to commit suicide. Although most critics believe her, we don't necessarily have to. Let's consider her threat of suicide, repeated here for the third time in the play (401). At the end, she does commit suicide. But this is not only because Hippolytus rejected her, but also, and perhaps mainly, because she was found out. What she cannot bear, she tells in this speech, is the shame of her illicit passion being found out and revealed to all. Here, the threat of suicide is aimed, as it had been all along at getting the Nurse to help her secure Hippolytus, with the Chorus' silent complicity.

As she has already demonstrated, Phaedra is a woman well in command of her behavior. As attracted as she is to Hippolytus, she did not operate hastily, but in a logical, step by step fashion to attain her goal. This is a woman who takes initiative, a woman who was able to plan and supervise the building of a temple to Aphrodite (a project of years, no less). Such an act was bound to reveal her love rather than hide it. Would she really give in now?

Initially overwhelmed by the news that Phaedra is in love with Hippolytus, the Nurse breaks down "You have destroyed me!" (353), she exclaims. She curses the sun, contemplates throwing herself off a cliff, and curses Cypris, and at the same time she retains faith in Phaedra's chastity, and assumes that what has happened was against Phaedra's will (358–59). Then she changes her mind with her famous statement that turned proverbial: "second thoughts are perhaps wiser" (436). She excuses Phaedra's illicit passion on the grounds that most people fall in love, argues the futility of trying to resist love, and urges her to yield to what she cannot help and make her feelings known to Hippolytus. She then proceeds to assure Phaedra that she can betray her husband without her infidelity being revealed outside the house. She winds up her argument with the point that one must not be too morally exacting, as perfection, if it is even desirable, is not attainable. And she ends with the injunction to obey the god's will: "Dare to love; a god wished it" (476). This injunction relieves Phaedra of the responsibility for her illicit love and echoes Phaedra's own claim that human beings cannot help straying.

The problem now for both Phaedra and the Nurse is not so much whether Phaedra should try to seduce Hippolytus (as she might have done in Euripides' first treatment of the myth in the lost *Hippolytus Veiled*), as how. The discussion then moves to the question of how to seduce the savagely chaste Hippolytus. It is the Nurse who leads the discussion and who comes up with the solution of using a charm. In other words, Phaedra has succeeded not only in gaining her sympathy, but also in totally involving her in her plight.

But Phaedra cannot accept the Nurse's change of mind outright without revealing her own lack of virtue. Thus, continuing her pretence, she blames the Nurse for saying things pleasant to the ear but morally wrong. Suddenly it is the Nurse who is responsible for leading her down the path of infidelity. Phaedra, secure in the Nurse's devotion, protectiveness, and love, knows very well that the Nurse will react to the accusation—and, if pressed, might come up with a more specific strategy.

Just as Phaedra had gotten the Nurse to name Hippolytus, the Nurse now states explicitly what Phaedra had been hinting at: "It is not fine words you need, but the man" (490–91). Fearing the Chorus, who after the revelation, had urged her to commit suicide, Phaedra calls the Nurse's words "most vile" and tells the Nurse to shut up (498). The Nurse does not mince words any more and answers:

> Yes, vile words, but better than those fine words of yours.
> And the deed is better, if it will save your life,
> than the name for which you die so proudly. (500–02)

Phaedra reacts now as if it is the Nurse who is leading her to be unfaithful:

> O, no, in the name of gods—for you are speaking well, but
> the words are vile—do not go further. My soul is so completely

made ready by desire, if you continue to speak skillfully,
I shall be all spent on that which I am fleeing now! (503–06, after Barrett)

Scholars tend to see this response as "a last desperate appeal."[16] Now that the Nurse has described her passion for what it is, all that Phaedra can do to maintain her good name is to reassign the responsibility for her actions. In a rather self-contradictory assertion, she praises the Nurse for speaking well, but calls the words "vile" and says they will trap her into doing what she would not do on her own initiative.

In contrast to her earlier obtuseness, the Nurse immediately picks up Phaedra's hint here. Telling her mistress to "obey her," the Nurse lets Phaedra—and the Chorus—know that she is ready to take upon herself the responsibility for Phaedra's deeds, and that she will proceed to release her from her troubles (507–15). The problem for Phaedra is that the Nurse is rather unclear about precisely how she will go about it. She states that she will use "loving charms for/of desire" but assures her that they will cause "no shame or harm to your mind" (511–12).

Phaedra expresses her concern that the Nurse will do the unthinkable and "*divulge* anything to the offspring of Theseus" (520). Like her earlier statement about the uses of charms, this statement is also a plant. There is no indication that the Nurse was planning to approach Hippolytus directly or tell him anything. She was simply undecided as to what type of charm to use: a salve or a drink. Phaedra's suggestion relieves her of the need to make a decision and of the need to figure out how to administer the charm.

Up until this point, it has *not* dawned on the Nurse "to divulge" anything to anyone. If Phaedra had not wanted the Nurse to disclose her feelings to Hippolytus, she should have stopped her then and there. The Nurse makes her intentions plain enough. She is going to talk not with just anyone, but with *philoi*, those who are near and dear (524). This is the same term, *philos*, that Phaedra had earlier applied to Hippolytus (319).

The spectators can obviously contemplate the result of such scheming. The Nurse's talk with Hippolytus will lead to Phaedra's death. What started as a plan of a sure death for Hippolytus, if he refused to quench Phaedra's passion, ends with Phaedra's own doom, brought about by her own manipulations.

Hippolytus

The Nurse tells Phaedra that she will arrange everything and exits the stage. The next time we see Phaedra, she is standing at a doorway listening to Hippolytus, who is not only berating the Nurse and denouncing women, but also actually talking at the partially hidden Phaedra (575–76). There are various ways of staging the scene in which Hippolytus utters the most misogynistic speech in Greek literature.[17] The most convincing way borrows Aeschylus' strategy in *Agamemnon*'s Cassandra scene, in which there are three actors on stage but one is ignored and there is no three-way dialogue. For the audience, Phaedra's silent presence would be both striking and surprising, because a three-way dialogue was already standard in plays at this time. While Hippolytus' speech is addressed to the Nurse, it is also addressed to Phaedra, but he does not even grant her the honor of an acknowledgment.[18]

For Phaedra, Hippolytus' talking *at* her rather than *to* her must have been extremely painful. He does not even identify her by name but refers to her by talking to the Nurse about "your mistress" (662), with the words thrown in as though an afterthought while at the same time making sure that it is clear exactly to whom his poignant insult and scathing remarks are intended. They show that he ignores Phaedra not out of self-respect or shame, but because of his deep contempt for her. He intuits that it was Phaedra who led the Nurse to approach him, but he never bothers to check this assumption out with the Nurse. The assumption is, of course, speaking correctly but the contempt he demonstrates is not unlike that which Theseus will soon show for him in assuming, without bothering to ask, that he seduced Phaedra.

Hippolytus speaks Phaedra's language, being implicit and explicit at the same time. He is able to let Phaedra know what he thinks of her without addressing her. And he is able to intimate that he will make her life difficult without actually uttering a threat. Thus, he gives the Nurse his word that he will not reveal Phaedra's secret, but when the Nurse seeks reassurances, he answers her in a way that is anything but reassuring: "My tongue swore, my mind took no oath" (612). Somewhat later, he reaffirms the oath (657–58), boasting of his piety in the process, but again manages to leave doubt about what he intends to do. For the time being, he says, he will leave the palace, but he will return when his father does, then "I will watch how you face him, both you and your mistress" (661–62). The vagueness creates the menace. What conduct might make him keep his word and what conduct won't is unclear. The general critical assumption is that Phaedra writes her defamatory letter because she cannot be sure whether he will keep his oath of silence.

Even if Phaedra had been a speaking character in this scene, she could not have altered Hippolytus' opinion of her. We can imagine her standing by helpless and humiliated. The youth for whom she yearns ignores her, addressing not a word to her. Once Hippolytus completes his tirade, he rushes off the stage without hearing Phaedra's subsequent lament of her fate and plea for help or guidance—a heart-breaking litany.[19]

Although Phaedra ignores the Chorus' counsel to commit suicide (362–72) as long as she can, she is eventually forced to go through with the promise she had not initially intended to keep. Hippolytus' contempt, coming after the Chorus' cold distance, brings home for her the damage her words have wreaked. Her manipulation of the Nurse is clear to Hippolytus, even though he has not witnessed it. And the Chorus women are aware that she herself revealed a passion that, if kept secret, would not have hurt her name.

Speaking to the Chorus, she quotes Hippolytus calling the Nurse "the mischievous bawd" who panders to the wicked one who has betrayed her master's marriage bed (590). She understands that the Nurse did it for love of her, but intent on preserving her reputation for virtue, does not admit that she put her up to it (596–97). Phaedra banishes the Nurse from her sight, wrongly accusing her servant of something that Phaedra herself had actually initiated (706–09). This may be seen to foreshadow Phaedra's false accusation of Hippolytus.

Conclusion

Euripides' Phaedra has for many centuries won the admiration of readers, who see her as a chaste woman overcome and driven to suicide by a love of which she essentially disapproved. The calumnious note accusing the innocent Hippolytus of trying to violate her honor is usually ignored by readers taken with her self-reflective admission that she is fighting a losing battle with her infatuation. This elevated view of Phaedra relies on the explicit tenor of her words.

But Phaedra can be also seen as a master rhetorician, as a powerful woman who, through the manipulation of language, tricks the Nurse into trying to help her seduce the youth she desires. This interpretation relies on the claim that language is used as a tool of manipulation both by Euripides in his dialectic with the off-stage audience and by the characters in their interchanges with the inner audience of the play. Secondly, it is assumed that Euripides presupposes the existence of a broad pool of mythic material known to the ancient audience from other adaptations of the myth about Phaedra, Hippolytus, and Theseus, and that he attempts to modify, and even displace, former interpretations of the story, even his own in the failed *Hippolytus Veiled*. These methodological claims enable the analysis to look beyond the explicit meanings of the characters' words and to make sense of the disparities between what the characters say and do, which are usually ignored or discounted.

Whichever interpretation one chooses, Phaedra remains a fascinating heroine whom readers have admired throughout centuries.

Exile

Exile in ancient Greece was permanent or long-term removal from one's native place, usually as a punishment imposed by government or other superior power. In Greece it was from earliest times a standard consequence of homicide, and was as much a religious way of getting rid of a source of pollution as a punishment.

Plutarch

Plutarch was a Greek scholar who lived *c.* 46–120 CE. He was a biographer and essayist. In his work *Moralia*, roughly translated as "Matters relating to customs and mores (traditional moral values)," there are 78 essays and transcribed speeches that provide insights into both Roman and Greek life as well as timeless observations in their own right. Plutarch wrote about the life of Theseus, and how his grandfather on his mother's side founded Trozen where the play *Hippolytus* is set.

Seneca

Lucius Aennaeus Seneca (*c.* 4 BCE–65 CE), A Roman stoic philosopher and scholar as well as advisor to the emperor Nero. He also wrote tragedies based on Greek myths and plays by Greek tragedians (except for *Octavia* which is a pure Roman tragedy based on historical events and figures). His *Phaedra* closely follows Euripides' play.

DISCUSSION TOPICS

1. In *Hippolytus*, Phaedra is lovesick for her stepson. Why do you think Euripides needed to frame his story with Aphrodite's anger at Hippolytus for preferring Artemis over her? Do you think that the play could have worked equally well without any intervention of the goddesses?
2. Describe the relationship between Phaedra and her Nurse. Do you think Euripides was trying to make a point about the dangers of being too manipulative?
3. During Phaedra's lovesick speeches she never mentions Theseus. Do you get any idea of the relationship between Theseus and Phaedra when reading the play?
4. Phaedra also barely mentions her children during the play. Do you think this is an intentional part of her characterization?
5. Given the intervention of the goddesses, do you think that the deaths of both Phaedra and Hippolytus were inevitable?
6. Euripides' characterization of the Nurse is quite brilliant. She is shown to change her mind frequently, often within a single speech. Yet, Phaedra decides to accept this woman's help. Whether one accepts the implicit or explicit analysis of the play, it might seem extremely unwise to accept the council of someone who may be considered kind-hearted, yet foolish. Do you think that Euripides is criticizing women in general when he chooses to allow Phaedra to listen to the Nurse?
7. In other tragedies, Antigone and Deianeira also commit suicide. Antigone commits suicide after being condemned to death, and this results in the suicides of Haemon and Eurydice, without Antigone necessarily intending for this to happen. Deianeira acts out of grief and shame as a result of accidentally killing Heracles. Phaedra's suicide is unique, in that she acts out of shame, but intentionally uses her death as a weapon to cause the death of Hippolytus. Do you think that Euripides has any sympathy for Phaedra? Explain your answer.

8. How would you analyze the relationship between Theseus and Hippolytus? Do you think that if Theseus were to allow Hippolytus to explain what has happened, he would have believed him? Explain.

9. Do you think that Hippolytus' abstinence and chastity have to do with the image of Theseus as having many affairs? If Hippolytus chose on purpose a different way of life from that of his father, do you think that Theseus respected his choice?

CONCLUSION

Heroines in Tragedy

Most of the thirty-two extant tragedies place considerable focus on female protagonists. This might have also been true for the tragedies that did not come down to us, about half of which seem to be named after a female protagonist or a female Chorus. This is a rather high percentage considering the low status of women in every aspect of Athens' political and social life (with the possible exception of where they had religious responsibilities).

Why the tragedians chose to focus on women so often remains unknown. It is possible that portraying women's weaknesses was a convenient and surreptitious way of attracting attention to human weaknesses in general without having to challenge concepts of male moral superiority (see also Zeitlin 1996: 346–47). If indeed the audiences of the tragedies were predominantly male, as is assumed by scholars, it also could have made women an easy target. They could dramatically exploit the commonly believed stereotypes attributed to women without alienating the audience. On the one hand, the depiction of women as deceptive and murderous may have confirmed the Athenian males' conviction of their gender-related superiority, and enabled them to justify keeping women in an inferior position. Or conversely, the playwrights may have intended to show that women were unduly relegated to second place in society and that more would be attained if women's talents and skills were allowed to flourish (Moss 1988). The tragedians may well have been playing it both ways: flattering the male audience by showing females as wayward and often dangerous, while warning them that their expectations that women would continue to accept their inferior status were smug and unrealistic.

There is, of course, also a possibility that the ancient dramatists, as the modern ones, have recognized that women, their dilemmas, and the solutions they offered to their predicaments, were simply a good subject for dramatization just as focusing on the exploits of men for heroic epic literature.

Comparison Between the Heroines

In summarizing the characteristics of the heroines, we find that there is not one single common denominator shared by these women that can serve as a basis for a comparison. We can, however, draw parallels by age groups. There are younger and older heroines. The younger ones react to a situation brought upon them by male authorities who are their relatives, and which they oppose with every fibre in their body. They feature usually as intransigent and stubborn ready to die for their beliefs, or to exact their revenge executing it in the most hideous way possible. Antigone dies for burying her brother,

Electra has recourse to matricide with cruelty and deceit at its lowest level. Iphigenia is an exception by changing her mind from unwillingly going to her death to embracing the male ideal of heroism, or living a life of detachment sacrificing human beings and serving Artemis but never reaching her home or family, remaining the victim whether in death or life.

The older heroines do not become unfaithful or vengeful except when men prompt their actions by harming them or their family. Motherhood incites some of the older women: Clytemnestra, Hecuba, Creusa, Phaedra, and Alcestis, who are all willing either to kill or die in order to save their children. As wives some choose to take revenge on their husbands for their misdoings, as we see with Clytemnestra or Medea, while other heroines choose to stand by their husbands, despite what might be considered the outrageous behavior of their spouses. Deianeira, Alcestis, Phaedra, and to a lesser extent Creusa are generally depicted as traditional women who submit to the ruling authorities, who also usually happen to be their husbands. In cases where subversive reactions to a husband seem justified, the wife often incurs either pain or death, as are the cases of Clytemnestra and Medea, for example.

We may say that one commonality of the heroines, young and old, is that men created impossible situations for all of these women, in which the women could never have won. Each tragedian depicts his heroines within the dramatic plot he is concerned with, so we see a snapshot of their lives, framed within the particular set of circumstances they are reacting to. Any comparisons made between the heroines are unavoidably colored by their unique situations. We could, however, ask ourselves how each would fare in the place of another, and in that way test how robust an image each tragedian created by the ease in which we can imagine their behavior.

In four instances, those of Clytemnestra, Hecuba, Medea, and Electra, the heroines actively incite towards, or even commit, murder. The situations of each of these women are quite different, with the audiences' reactions to them probably varying accordingly. As we have seen, Clytemnestra appears as a mother of several young children in *Iphigenia at Aulis*, and as a mature woman, mother of grown children in Aeschylus' *Oresteia* and in Sophocles' and Euripides' *Electra* plays. At the height of her powers she kills Agamemnon, her husband, and his concubine, Cassandra. This action took place when she not only ruled the *oikos*, her household, but also the *polis*. Later on, with the physical circumstances of her condition unchanged, but her power waned either through guilt, age, or perhaps even the curse that plagued the house of Atreus, she is killed by her children, Orestes and Electra.

We may compare Clytemnestra's characterization with her Trojan parallel Hecuba, wife of the Trojan king Priam, mother of many sons and daughters. Hecuba's husband and most of their children have been killed as direct or indirect outcomes of Troy's defeat by the Greeks. As seen in *Trojan Women*, if Hecuba blames anyone for her loss it is Helen, rather than the generals who fought the war. In this depiction, Hecuba is still in the vicinity of her home town, but the city is going to be destroyed and burnt to a cinder. In Euripides' earlier play *Hecuba* she is displaced not only from power, but also from her homeland. Here she finds herself in the same horrendous situation that Clytemnestra faced in *Iphigenia at Aulis*: having her daughter sacrificed to satisfy the demand of the Greek army. Ironically, while Achilles attempted to save Clytemnestra's daughter Iphigenia, Hecuba's daughter Polyxena is sacrificed at the foot of Achilles' grave. While Hecuba was depicted as a noble grieving woman, if vindictive towards Helen, in *Trojan Women*, in *Hecuba* she is brutalized by the effects of the war. After being presented with the drowned body of her youngest son, Hecuba orchestrates the other captive Trojan women to blind his murderer, King Polymestor, and murder the king's sons.

Despite the many parallels, the characterizations of Clytemnestra and Hecuba remain dramatically distinct from one another. While Clytemnestra uses blatant lies to manipulate all around her, Hecuba remains entirely authentic throughout, except when enticing Polymestor into the captive women's tent. At the start of *Hecuba*, the vanquished queen casts herself down on the floor in her grief. Clytemnestra remains defiant even moments before her death. Clytemnestra and Hecuba both kill to avenge the deaths of their children, yet Clytemnestra is reviled by her children, from whom she is distant but Hecuba is depicted as a loving mother, even though she kills another man's sons. Both women use masterful rhetoric, but nothing Hecuba says or does alters her situation. She remains very much within the domain of women, with no real power over anything beyond her immediate surroundings. Clytemnestra is concerned with the affairs of the state and not just the *oikos*, and remaining unique in the stature she achieved as the ruler of the *polis*.

The third heroine to actively incite towards and help commit murder is Clytemnestra's daughter, the Sophoclean Electra. Like her mother, she too is a political figure, concerned (especially in Sophocles' play) with the events in the *polis*, but she does not seem to share her mother's aspirations for power. She wants the corrupt rulers of the *polis* removed, but does not concern herself with what should happen next. In Aeschylus and Sophocles, she remains in the vicinity of her home, but has lost most of the privileges of a royal daughter, whereas Euripides' Electra is far from home, living in a peasant's hut. Sophocles' Electra seeks revenge against her mother, whom she claims to hate, and Aegisthus, in vengeance for the murder of her father, Agamemnon. This Electra however prefers words to actions throughout. She waits for Orestes to arrive before starting to plan any active revenge. In Euripides' *Electra* and even more so in his *Orestes*, she has gained the ability for strategic thought and is also complicit in plotting not only the matricide but also the attempted murders of Helen and Hermione.

The fourth homicidal heroine, Medea, displaced from her home and from her marriage to Jason, not only kills those she holds to blame for her situation, but also kills her own children. Medea's murders seem closest to what could be called crimes of passion. It seemed she loved and hated with equal intensity, having brought about the deaths of others both to help Jason and then to harm him when he abandoned her.

While the four heroines are reacting to vastly differing circumstances, it is still possible to sense the core differences between them. Electra's passions were directed mainly at her mother. She does not have the element of "the other" emphasized in the characterization of Medea and has no magic powers to fall back on. Electra is comforted to some extent by her (half) immortal uncles the Dioscuri, but they only point her towards a safer, more fulfilling future rather than provide her with an escape route in the form of a flying chariot, as Helios gave his granddaughter Medea. Notwithstanding Electra's claims of hatred towards her mother, and however powerful Medea's rage is towards the loathsome Jason, and the depths of abject misery faced by Hecuba that bring her to kill out of grief, none of them entirely compare with the towering Machiavellian figure of the Aeschylean Clytemnestra.

The next four heroines we will compare in this summary all choose their own death as a way of confronting the situations in which they find themselves. Alcestis, Antigone, Deianeira, and Phaedra all saw no alternative solution to their predicaments. Alcestis is given very little choice in the matter, and ultimately is also brought back to life by Heracles. She is not dying to defend a principle like Antigone, or responding to a situation she perceives as so shameful that she must take her own life, as with Deianeira and Phaedra. Until being faced with this sudden demand that she die in place of her husband, her life would superficially appear devoid of major worries or trauma. Her characterization is the most phlegmatic of any of the heroines, as fits her circumstances, of agreeing to die in place of her husband. However, the audience must have been left wondering what marriage to a man who preferred to sacrifice the lives of any of his nearest and dearest, including his parents and his wife, rather than die at his own appointed time, could have been like. Despite widely differing interpretations of the relationship between Alcestis and Admetus, it would be hard to imagine any of the heroines given more passionate characterizations agreeing to die as placidly as Alcestis.

Antigone argued passionately for what she believed in, the right to give her brother a decent burial. The futility of her actions, and her senseless death, which also causes the deaths of her fiancé and his mother, highlight the harm caused by extreme passion and radical idealism. They have no connection to Alcestis' almost passive acceptance of her fate. In Deianeira's case, it was her one attempt to finally end her passive acceptance of her husband's behavior that inadvertently brought about his demise and her own. Deianeira's actions were not clearly guided by principles and passions, but rather by her misunderstanding of the world around her. One could imagine that had Heracles asked her to die in his place, as Admetus had asked Alcestis, she may well have complied. We could wonder, though, whether she might have had a last-minute change of heart and "accidentally" done something to kill her husband first!

Phaedra was caught up in the machinations of the goddess Aphrodite, who wanted to punish Hippolytus for preferring the pastoral pursuits and hunting associated with Artemis over the affairs of the heart that she presided over. The love-struck Phaedra attempted to manipulate her situation enough to attract Hippolytus' attention, but not with the outcome she had hoped for. In killing herself, she is not seeking to serve any higher ideology or to protect her husband; she dies of grief and shame and in hope to protect her sons' legitimacy in the court. Antigone was shown having very little concern for the living, prioritizing the burial of her dead brother over her living sister. Despite being engaged to Haemon, we get no sense of her being willing to consider him in her actions. On her part it would seem this may have been a marriage of convenience, a possibility which heightens the pathos of both Haemon's death, and that of Eurydice.

Phaedra did not seem to have much concern for her own life. Although she claimed to desire Hippolytus, this infatuation turned out to be completely self-centered, as she makes sure that he too will be destroyed after her own death. Alcestis laid down her life possibly to protect her children as well as to preserve the life of her husband, but not without naming a condition that would ensure that while her husband might live on, he would do so alone, and in misery. Of the four, it may appear that Deianeira was most genuinely kind and loving. While she caused the death of her husband and herself, she was devastated by her actions. Of all these women, it was only Antigone who tried to think of some bigger picture beyond that of her own life, but in doing so paid the price not only with her own life but that of Haemon, her fiancé, and Eurydice.

The final group of our heroines comprising Iphigenia, Creusa and Helen could be termed the survivors. While Iphigenia agreed to be sacrificed to serve the greater good of the Greek fleet, by allowing it to set sail for Troy, she is saved by the goddess Artemis, and sent to serve at the shrine of the goddess amongst the Taurians. Her role at the temple is to prepare strangers arriving at these shores for their sacrifice to the goddess, thus constantly reliving the trauma she herself had endured at Aulis. Yet Iphigenia somehow survives. She never gives up hope that one day she will be rescued, and when her brother finally does arrive, although each sibling is initially unaware of the other's identity, they do escape, together with the statue of the goddess. Creusa had suffered a different trauma as a young girl. Raped by Apollo, she exposed the baby boy she gave birth to, without sharing her ordeal with anyone around her. Once married, striving for motherhood, she arrives at the temple of Delphi where, unknown to her, her son has been sent by Apollo. When believing incorrectly that the young man is her husband's son, who will become heir of her kingdom, she is prepared to kill the lad with whom she previously sympathized strongly to prevent a stranger taking the throne. Ultimately Ion's identity is revealed to Creusa, with mother and son having an emotional reunion. Like her fellow survivor Iphigenia, Creusa is also skillful at strategy and agrees that it is in everyone's best interests for her husband to stay in the dark about Ion's true parentage and everything that has just happened.

Although tragedy does not dwell on this point, according to Greek myth, Helen too was abducted and raped as a young woman, by Theseus. In some versions at this time she gave birth to a daughter, Iphigenia, who was raised by Helen's sister Clytemnestra. The one thing that can be said about the Helen in tragedy is that there is very little consistency both in the story of her life and in her characterization beside her natural intelligence displayed in every one of her appearances. She is married to Menelaus, and either falls in love with Paris or is abducted by him; either arriving at Troy or being replaced by a phantom, who is her splitting image (*eidolon*) while she sits the war out in Egypt. Helen tenaciously clings to life, throughout everything that happens around her. In *Trojan Women* despite losing her formal debate (*agon*) with Hecuba, Helen knows she can persuade Menelaus to spare her life. Even when Orestes and Pylades think they have killed Helen in *Orestes*, her bloodied corpse disappears, and she has been taken up to the heavens by Zeus' will and appears at the side of the Dioscuri.

While Creusa cared enough about protecting her Erichthonian lineage to attempt to murder a stranger, and Iphigenia was, as a young girl, prepared to offer up her life to ensure the victory of the Greek fleet, it seems to be Helen who, above all, personifies the image of the ultimate survivor. Concerned with little beyond her own safety, in tragedy she is presented as getting away with outrageous behavior, while showing little or no remorse. All three women demonstrate great strength of endurance, even if Helen is portrayed as more self-centered than the other two. Would Iphigenia and Creusa have reacted any differently if abducted and carried to Troy? It is hard to say. Would Helen have murdered an unknown young man who would inherit her throne? It seems doubtful that Helen would have cared. She showed very little concern for her daughter, Hermione. How would Creusa and Helen have behaved in Iphigenia's place among the Taurians? It seems likely that Helen would have had King Thoas at her beck and call, while Creusa may just have used some of the potions at her service to extract herself from this unpleasant situation in a different way. In surmising these outcomes, it is fair to say, that Euripides' characterization of all three is sufficiently robust to extend beyond the circumstances portrayed in the plays in which they appear.

Heroines' Characterization

Throughout the discussions in this book, we have considered the individual heroines' characterizations. Thinking for a moment of the distinguishing features may enable a reader to summarize the characteristics of a particular heroine, we may return to the themes introduced at the beginning of this book: masculinity versus femininity, defiance and submission, deceit, and rhetorical skill. These themes may also be helpful markers for a dramatist intending to produce any of the tragedies. When considering the highly developed dramatic skills of the ancient tragedians, it is only natural that their heroines' personalities are complex and defy neat classifications, as with women in real life. The themes, however, provide points of reference.

Deceit is the prime marker of the feminine gender, and in one form or another is to be found in the depiction of all the heroines, mixed in with varying degrees of submission and defiance. As may be expected from the wife of the supremely masculine hero Heracles, Deianeira is presented as a highly feminine figure. She is devoted to her husband and family, and shows almost endless patience during Heracles' long, repeated absences. Deianeira may be considered to epitomize submission to the highest degree: not only is she passive and unaware of her husband's whereabouts, but she is also forgiving of his infidelities. Perhaps unsurprisingly when this wife and mother, who has never made a decision for herself, finally decides to take action, it all goes horrendously wrong. In accordance with her highly feminine depiction, Deianeira resorts to deceit, sending a robe secretly daubed with what she perceives to be a love philtre. On discovering that she has caused her husband's demise, Deianeira decides to kill herself. In this last act, however, Deianeira choses to act like a man and kills herself with a sword. Another highly feminine figure, Phaedra, whose main identifying feature initially seems to be suffering from lovesickness for her stepson, eventually elects to hang herself, which would have been the female way of committing suicide. Phaedra however, may be associated with a different kind of deceit to Deianeira, in that one may never be certain as to the truth of Phaedra's words. When thinking of dramatizing these two heroines, we might expect to see Deianeira as the more submissive figure, eventually pushed into taking action by intolerable circumstances. Phaedra by contrast, only appears to be subdued and submissive, while harboring powerful emotions and taking decisive action, both against herself and against Hippolytus.

That each heroine has her own differentiated characteristics may be clearly seen in another highly feminine heroine, Helen. In her various representations, deceit is not one of her major characteristics. She uses her intelligence and gift of rhetoric to defend her actions and in *Helen*, and displays impressive planning skills to devise an escape plan from Egypt. Helen's plan does include deceit but also assures the safe return of herself and Menelaus to Sparta. Her soundly balanced and appropriate plea to Theonoe also assures that Theolcymenus remains in the dark about the true identity of Menelaus. While Helen's femininity is most strongly associated with her beauty, in the tragedies a guideline to her portrayal may be her insensitivity to the suffering of others.

The younger heroines, Antigone, Electra, and Iphigenia are all shown to defy authority figures and social expectations. Antigone defies the ruler Creon, Sophoclean Electra defies King Aegisthus and Queen Clytemnestra, as well as the social and religious expectation of mourning her father for years rather than the usual thirty days. Iphigenia surprises everyone with her change of mind to go willingly to her death contradicting her mother's wishes.

Antigone's most prominent characteristics are her unshaken conviction that she is in the right; an impressive capacity for improvisation and her complete defiance not only of authority but also of her family and friends. These characteristics may be thought to be apt for any head-strong young person of strong character, male or female. While refusing to obey the ruler's edict prohibiting the burial of her brother, Antigone formulates her arguments on the spot as the situation demands when talking to Creon, the ruler, or to Ismene, her sister. She is particularly dismissive of Ismene and ignores her advice of following a more cautious approach. Antigone is not deceitful, although she is prepared to "bend the truth" when talking to Ismene. Ultimately it is not only Antigone who pays for her actions with her life, but also Haemon and Eurydice.

The Sophoclean Electra shares many of Antigone's traits. She too is certain of the righteousness of her cause, defying societal norms of only mourning for thirty days, and dismissing her sister's intervention as being based on cowardice rather than prudence. However, while Antigone takes action of her own accord, Electra awaits her brother. Both the Sophoclean and Euripidean Electras show no qualms at deceiving others and Euripides' Electra not only devises the revenge plan but also plays an active role in the matricide.

The two characterizations of Iphigeneia depict very different stages of her life, yet both may be thought of as being feminine heroines displaying certain male traits. By nature, they appear submissive yet they are prepared to take on more masculine roles when called upon to rise to the occasion. The younger Iphigenia casts herself in the role of a Homeric hero, prepared to sacrifice herself for the good of the country, in order to gain fame, while the older Iphigenia devises an escape plan to save herself, Orestes and Pylades. The older Iphigenia is also very circumspect rhetorically, divulging only scanty information about herself and thus avoids being recognized. She is implicated in deceit, but only as the last resort. The escape plan devised by Iphigenia bears some similarity to that thought up by Helen, the epitome of the "feminine" heroine.

Alcestis and Creusa are compliant wives who do not defy societal norms, although Alcestis in fact supersedes what is expected of a wife by agreeing to die instead of her husband. While not appearing at first to be powerful characters they both show impressive, steadfast natures. Both women, but especially Alcestis, are also able to formulate and present their thoughts in a biting way to the males they engage with. Creusa is given to Xuthus as a prize for his fighting for Athens, and engages in deceit only when she suspects that the throne of Athens might be given to a stranger. Alcestis courageously dies for her husband. And yet, she manages first to manipulate him, as women are usually blamed of doing, by making him make a promise of never re-marrying. A promise she knows he would not be able to keep, thus gaining a small moral victory before her death.

Clytemnestra and Medea show different elements of the mix of masculine and feminine. We may picture Aeschylus' Clytemnestra as an imposing monarchical figure; a woman with an admirable capacity for strategic thought, who refuses to submit to society's rules confining women to the home and hearth. She has a magnificent presence, with energies matching those of any man, while being endlessly proud of her femininity, showing intense love for her eldest daughter and feigning submission to her husband. Demonstrating superb rhetorical skills, Clytemnestra uses her wily intelligence and gifts of playacting to deceive her opponents. While Medea may initially be considered to be behaving like a typical lovesick woman, her volatility and intense jealousy, turn her into an indomitable force. While presenting herself as submissive to authority figures, Medea only submits to her own volition.

Hecuba is the only heroine who in spite of her rhetorical acumen, her use of deceit, and her understanding of societal expectations and the motivations that stir men, whether in the affairs of the heart or sheer greed, does not always win. She succeeds on avenging herself on Polymestor, but not on Helen. However, she is not shy to defy the Greek conquerors and never submits.

The Messages of Tragedy

Another aspect of any comparison between the heroines, is trying to understand what, if any, message the tragedians were trying to convey to the audiences by their characterizations and by their fate. It could be argued that the tragedians were simply telling fascinating stories based on myth, but art in general, and that which has enduring appeal in particular, often profoundly comments on human society, with this dialogue underlying the longevity of our fascination with the work.

Looking at the fates of our heroines, there often appears to be no logical connection between their deeds and their outcomes. Take for example, Sophocles' Antigone and

Electra who share certain characteristics. Both are zealous in following their principles, prioritizing their ideals over their own lives and over the lives of those near to them. However, Antigone ends up dying and inadvertently causing the deaths of her fiancé and his mother too, when all she had wanted to do was bury her brother, an act which in any other circumstances would have been deemed noble and praiseworthy. Electra on the other hand contrives towards the murder of her mother, even if she mostly "acts" through words rather than deeds, and ends up living almost "happily ever after" as far as we know. Similarly, Clytemnestra and Medea. Both are infuriated by their husbands. Clytemnestra kills her husband, possibly to avenge Iphigenia's death. Medea kills her sons who have done nothing wrong. Clytemnestra is murdered by her children and Medea goes off in Helios' chariot. Put Hecuba into the mix and we see a good wife and mother who suffers miserably, seeing everyone she loves meeting a terrible end. Helen on the other hand, causes havoc all around her and—at least in *Orestes*—is rewarded by being raised to the heavens.

Is tragedy's final word a more universal message to us all? Our enduring interest in these plays underscores not only how human nature remains fundamentally unchanged throughout the ages, but also how despite societies' apparent advances with time, we still experience the same human emotions, the same joys and sorrows, hopes and passions, jealousies, loves, and hatreds. Beyond the discussions of gender, human relationships and the role of the divinities in human fate, the tragedians appear to be reminding us time and again that anything can happen to anyone and there is little justice in the world.

NOTES

Introduction

1. See e.g. Dover 1974: 98–102; Walcot 1996: 91–102; Lefkowitz 1986: 61–79; Buxton 1994: 122–27 on representations of deceptive mythic heroines and their "feminine" crafts, especially weaving, for which see also Jenkins 1985: 112–20; for Homer see, e.g. Katz 1991: 24–119, 128–30; for tragedy, e.g. Zeitlin 1996 [1978] *passim*; Rabinowitz 1993: 132–41, 166–69.
2. For an excellent discussion, see Mossman 1995: 94–141.

Chapter 1 Clytemnestra

1. See Stanford 1937: 92: "a woman of irrational hopes combined with the deliberate and purposive resolution of a man."
2. W. Congreve 1697. *The Mourning Bride,* Act III, Scene 2.
3. R. Kipling 1911. The Female of the Species in *Rudyard Kipling's Verse: Inclusive Edition, 1885– 1918.* London: Hodder & Stoughton, 1919.
4. For further discussion of the stereotypical misjudgments of women in Greek Tragedy in terms of mental capacity, naïveté, susceptibility to gossip and rumor, incoherent thinking, and the like, see Moss 1988: 516; for the discussion of Clytemnestra see 519–24.
5. See Roisman 1986.
6. Hogan 1984: on lines 475ff explains this flip-flopping of the Chorus as a psychological phenomenon of someone who exhibits "natural ambivalence ... which desires the announced fall but from long and frustrated wait grows skeptical." Others (e.g. Dawe 1963) see in the reversal a psychological tool of frustrating the expectations of the audience.
7. For the preference of "loyal" over "faithful," see Roisman 1984: 99–103.
8. Verrall 1904 on line: "faithful to the revenge which she has meditated ever since."
9. The epithet appears only only six times in the *Iliad*, referring to four heroes: Patroclus (17.557, 18.235, 460), Stichius (15.331), Lycophron (15.430), and Podes (17.589). For discussion, see Roisman 1984 *passim.*
10. For discussion, see Roisman 1984: 105–06.
11. In Sophocles' *Electra* 234, the Chorus as a group refer to themselves metaphorically as a "loyal mother," implying that they, not Clytemnestra, had a mother's love and concern for her.
12. Ferguson 1972: 83 mentions this possibility but without any further elaboration. For a full discussion and grammatical ramifications of the use of *apistēn*, which is a compound adjective in an unusual female form in Greek (should have been *apiston)*, and of other *double entendres* mentioned here, see Roisman 2018b. For a similar intentional or unintentional manipulation of sound-play, see De Jong 2001: on *Od.* 18.306–43, where she discusses *erga gelasta* "the laughable deeds" that can be understood also as *erg' agelasta* "not laughable/grave deeds."

13. For further discussion of the concept of helping friends and harming enemies, see Blondell 1989: 31–59.
14. According to Raeburn & Thomas 2011: lxvi–lxviii, female dogs were thought to be "pre-eminently shameless." For further discussion of dog imagery and attributes see Franco 2014: 105–05, 125–26 (about this passage).
15. For discussion, see Roisman 2006: 13–14, 25–26, with bibliography.
16. Thomson 1966: on lines 611–12 suggests that "bronze" *(chalkos)* came over time to mean a metal in general.
17. For a brief summary of the various scholarly views on the phrase, see Hogan 1985: on line.
18. With Lattimore on line 854, Arnott 38–39, and Murray 1940: 216, Lloyd-Jones 1970: 62, on line 854 states her presence as a possibility; *pace* Taplin 1972: 93, 1977: 300–02.
19. Or maybe on another chariot, but within Clytemnestra's view, see Taplin 1977: 30.
20. See also Foley 2001: 210–11; McClure 1999: 77–80.
21. For an excellent summary and analysis of various scholarly views, see Easterling 1973: 12–17; cf. Bollack & Judet de La Combe 1981: 189–93, 197–98; Conacher 1987: 29–40. Fraenkel 1950, vol. II: 442 comments about Agamemnon's yielding to Clytemnestra: "It would be an understatement to call this a symbolic defeat. It is a real one." It leads to his decisive downfall; McClure 1999: 84–92; Mueller 2016: 48–60. The symbolism of tapestries created by weaving, the primary female economic activity within the household, is discussed at length by Bakola 2016.
22. Although scholars have traditionally associated it with the blood spilled in the Atreid household, see Goheen 1955: 115–26.
23. Let's hope no one still thinks that "The king … speaks with the gracious dignity of a great gentleman" (Fraenkel's claim 1950: on line).
24. Winnington-Ingram 1983: 106–07, sees this scene as an act of feminization of Agamemnon by Clytemnestra.
25. On this speech, see especially Easterling 1973: 13–14, Foley 2001: 209–10. Dawe's claim that Agamemnon's surrender has nothing to do with his characterization but rather "because it was dramatically necessary" (1963: 50) takes away enormously not only from the characterization of Agamemnon but also from Clytemnestra's powerful rhetorical intelligence and skill.
26. The text does not offer evidence for the view that Conacher (1987: 37–38) advances, that Agamemnon understands Clytemnestra to refer to Aulis, and he responds accordingly. That is to say, to quote Conacher: "'You say you won't do this deed, because it would offend the gods…? And yet (remembering Aulis and how you acted there), if you had been in a desperate plight which you could escape only by vowing to perform such an act as this, wouldn't you have so vowed—just as you paid Artemis *her* heinous price?'" And Agamemnon's reply, "Yes if one [like Calchas at Aulis] with full knowledge." There is no hint in the text here or in the rest of the *stichomythia* that the couple converses on another level than the explicit.
27. Fraenkel 1950: on 939f.
28. Cf. Bollack & Judet de La Combe 1981: 196.
29. McClure 1997, 1999: 80–92 reads lines *Ag.* 958–74 as magical incantation by which Clytemnestra wishes to exercize control over Agamemnon, who has just entered the palace.
30. The other occurrence is in choral song, *Ag.* 904.
31. 1035, 1039, 1049, 1053–54, 1059, 1070–71.
32. If Cassandra is not dancing, it would be unclear why she is given such excited meters, especially dochmiacs with resolution, in her song. These meters do not come through in

translation, but the original text is very clear about the excitement in Cassandra's song which would have been not suitable if she remained immobile. For the meters, see Fraenkel 1950: Vol. III on 1072-1177. On dancing see Schein 1982; Ley 2007: 28-32, 70-80, 92, 150: "The skene also awaits Cassandra, but the power of her vision is expressed fully in the playing space, in dance and song, and it contrasts strikingly with Clytemnestra's refusal to remain in the playing space." Cf. Easterling & Hall 2002: Chapter One, 3-38 *passim*.

33. Foley 2001: 89-90.
34. For taunting by vaunting, see Parks 1990: *passim*; Keith 1924; Kyriakou 2001.
35. 1462-67, 1475-80, 1497-1504, 1521-29, 1551-59, 1567-76. Hall 1999: 115; McClure 1999: 98-99 suggests that in this scene the lyric register of the Chorus vis-à-vis the recitative anapests of Clytemnestra and their silent departure at the end renders the Chorus feminized. For distinction between sung anapests and recitative anapest that are changed; see West 1982: 121-24.
36. I've found Taplin's (1977: 327-28) interpretation of this scene the most convincing. Conacher (1987: 55) sees an "uneasy truce" reached between Clytemnestra and the Chorus.
37. 1468-69, 1481-88; 1505-12.
38. Foley 2001: 203-04, 211-34.
39. ἐγώ (*egō*), "I", is rightly put in on the authority of the scholion. See Fraenkel 1950: on line.
40. In the *Odyssey* (4.512-37) Aegisthus is the dominant actor.
41. *LB* 133, 190-91, 240-41, 385, 514-39.
42. *LB* 430-33, 439-42, 444-49.
43. For a different view that sees Clytemnestra in *Libation Bearers* as very much the same as in *Agamemnon*, see McClure 1999: 102.
44. As Winnington-Ingram notes 1983: 117: "it is the circumstances that have changed, not the fibre of woman."
45. Lines *Ag.* 1423-24 where the verb *archein* "to rule" is mentioned are not clear enough after the lacuna of 1422.
46. For a different view, see Winnington-Ingram 1983: 117-18.
47. 1978: 13.
48. See Sale 1973: 8-9.
49. Burnett 1998: 137.
50. Gellie 1972: 114.
51. Cf. Goward 2004: 111-12.
52. Aristotle, *Nicomachean Ethics* viii.8.28-33, says that a mother's love is especially valuable because it does not derive from self-interest.
53. For further discussion see Roisman and Luschnig 2011: 28-32; Finglass 2007: 1-4.
54. The translations are mine, unless stated otherwise.
55. Roisman and Luschnig 2011: on lines 27-28.
56. Roisman and Luschnig 2011: on lines 86-87.
57. Roisman and Luschnig 2011: 253-59.
58. Clytemnestra's remarks on prejudice have something in common with another vengeful heroine, Medea (*Medea* 219-21, and also 292-305).

59. Her comment can be construed as what has been termed as internalized misogyny that reflects male patriarchal values (Chong-Gossard and Ng 2018). Nonetheless, Euripidean Clytemnestra does not give in to it, but rather challenges the misconception.
60. Roisman 2004.
61. Vellacott 1975: 238.
62. For further discussion see Roisman 2017.
63. This is the only "full" treatment of Iphigenia's sacrifice in extant tragedy.
64. For various echoes of *Agamemnon* in *Iphigenia at Aulis* see Radding 2015, who maintains that Euripides meant to rehabilitate Clytemnestra, similarly to his attempt at rehabilitation of Helen. He sees in *Iphigenia at Aulis* an intentional Euripidean response to the image of Clytemnestra in *Agamemnon*.
65. See also Lawrence 1988: 99.
66. For the issue of authenticity of this epilog, see Collard and Morwood with bibliography, 2017: on line.
67. See also Aélion 1983: I. 106.
68. For expansion and treatment of myth in this play, Eisner 1979; Sorum 1992; Michelini 1999–2000.

Chapter 2 Electra

1. Alexiou 2002: 5–6.
2. That the Chorus never criticize the revenge indicates to many scholars that Sophocles does not either. E.g. March 1996, 2001: 17–18.
3. For the Sophoclean methodology of having secondary characters reveal the intricacies of the major figures, partly by allowing them to explain their motivations, although the lesser roles themselves are not devoid of individual characterization, see Kirkwood 1994: 100–01; Bowra 1952: 79–82; Winnington-Ingram 1980: 232–42.
4. Electra's failure to mention her mother as a target of her planned revenge is explained in three ways: (1) Electra's omission is unconscious, and thus serves to deceive not only her sister but also herself as to exactly what she is proposing; (2) the omission is one of the many devices Sophocles uses to suppress all mention of matricide in the play; (3) Clytemnestra is not part of Electra's scheme of revenge. For bibliography, see Macleod 2001: 141 n. 7, who subscribes to the last view, as does March 2001: on 955–57. However, already in 582–83 and 603–04, Electra hints that her mother should be killed. Notice also the interplay between words and deeds. For discussion see Hartigan 1966: 85–88; Minadeo 1967; Woodard 1866.
5. That the Athenian audience would have recognized her words as referring to those who killed tyrants, see Juffras 1991.
6. Electra refers frequently to her mother's sexual betrayal, which highlights and contrasts with her own asexual existence (Soph. *El.* 97–98, 492–94, 561–62, 587–89). Aeschylus' Orestes also charges Clytemnestra with infidelity (*LB* 894–907).
7. For similarity between mother and daughter, see Segal 1966: 505–21, 525–26.
8. Winnington-Ingram 1980: 229; Roisman 2000: 190–99.
9. Cf. Sale 1093: 2–3.

10. Winnington-Ingram 1980: 228: "Electra is in fact conceived and drawn as both the victim and the agent of the Furies."
11. Electra: 276–79, 300–38, 771, 970–84, 1142–46, cf. 135–66; Chorus: 743–46, 876–79, 957–58, 1147–64, 1168–71.
12. For the relevant discussion and bibliography, see Roisman and Luschnig 2011: on line 140.
13. Eur. *El.* 229, 345, 1322.
14. For discussion of echoing other plays as well see e.g. Zeitlin 1980.
15. To some her attending to her brother seems "A little effusive and self-assertive," Mullens 1940: 153.

Chapter 3 Iphigenia

1. It is important to note that neither Aeschylus and certainly not Euripides say explicitly that Artemis "demanded" this sacrifice.
2. This much with some minor adjustments will be also maintained by the second Messenger in the chronologically later *Iphigenia at Aulis*.
3. Cf. Vellacott 1975: 238.
4. Reading with Wecklein *dystychesterois* (δυστυχεστέροις) "more miserable," in line 352. If the manuscript version of *eutychesterois* (εὐτυχεστέροις) "more fortunate" is kept, the sentence has no meaning, and one must admit even higher degree of confusion on Iphigenia's part.
5. See pp. 113–114.
6. Platnauer 1938: on 354.
7. Kovacs's translation ignores the conative force of the imperfect and suits more an aorist tense: "slit my throat" or "put me to the sword" (*ekainomēn xiphei*, ἐκαινόμην ξίφει, 27). Way's noncommittal translations in the former edition of the Loeb: "High raised was I, the sword in act to slay" (27) "and would have slain me" (359–60), are preferable.
8. Kyriakou 2006: on 515–16. For the transposition of lines 515–16 after 510 by Platnauer 1938, see Kyriakou.
9. In her analysis of the plot features, Edith Hall (2013 *passim*) offers excellent discussion of films, theatrical performances, operas and ballets that base themselves on this ancient drama, all of which feature a very fast-moving action as much as the genre permits.
10. Reams have been written on Iphigenia's change of mind; for discussion and summary of the various interpretations see Gibert 1995: 222–54; Michelakis 2006: 37–40. Luschnig 1988: 108–09: "The inconsistency of Iphigenia's character parallels the contradiction in the motivation of the Trojan War, and insists that only through an impossible reversal can the two opposites—the fight over Helen's body and a glorious campaign for national identity—coexist. Equally fine is Iphigenia's eloquence in begging for her life. And it makes sense." Bacalexi (2016) claims that Iphigenia's decision to die is a result of three interconnected motivations that should be examined simultaneously: her desire to live noble life, her love for her father, and love for Hellas.
11. See also Lawrence 1988: 100: "it is hard to believe that she would have insisted on voluntary self-sacrifice had an acceptable safe avenue of escape opened to her."
12. Stockert 1992: vol. 2, on l. 1394, notes the irony in this statement considering the qualities of the male characters in this drama.

Notes to pp. 114–133

13. Collard and Morwood state (2107: on 1389-90): "Her memorial and fame will replace her normal expectations from life."
14. Scholars still debate the date and authorship of the *Rhesus*. Opinions about its date range from around mid-fifth to fourth century BCE, while theories about its authorship include the belief that the *Rhesus* was one of Euripides' early plays and its attribution to an unknown author of the fifth or fourth century BCE. I believe that the *Rhesus* was composed by Euripides possibly as a pro-satyric play. For full discussion and bibliography please see Roisman 2018c. For the significance of *hapax*-words used in *Rhesus* in determining authorship see Roisman 2020: 220.

Chapter 4 Antigone

1. For a full discussion of the two sisters, see Roisman 2018a and bibliography. This chapter owes significantly to this discussion.
2. It is noteworthy than neither those who admire Antigone, e.g. Winnington-Ingram 1980: 117–149; Gellie 1972: 29–52, 117–149; Kitto 1961 (1954): 126–27; Kitto 1956: 149–78; Lesky 1979: 104–05; Whiteley's reply to Sourvinou-Inwood 1989, nor her critics, e.g. Agard 1937; Minadeo 1985; Sourvinou-Inwood 1989 (esp. 138–142) discuss this discrepancy between what Antigone has just relayed as having already happened to Eteocles' corpse, and Creon's proclamation to the elders about what he wants to see happening to the brothers' corpses in the future. For full discussion, see Roisman 2018a: 66–67.
3. The translations are by or follow Lloyd-Jones 1998.
4. Antigone uses the first person in lines 18, 19, 32, 46, 69, 72, 76, 81, 89, 91 x 2, 96, 443, 448, 452, 458, 460, 462 x 2, 467, 468 x 2, 469, 470, 497, 501.503, 505, 523, 539, 543, 547, 551, (555), 557, 839, 846, 848/49, 866, 868, 877, 892, 896, 897, 901, 902, 903, 904, 905, 907, 908, 910, 913, 914, 920, 924, 939, 942. Creon in lines: 165, 173, 183, 185, 188, 191, 192, 198, 293, 305, 477, (484), 490, 491. 495, 532, 561, 569, 571, 655, 657, 658, 660, (680), (726), 744, 774, 886, 935, 995, 1035, 1036, 1043, 1051, 1053. 1095, 1095, 1099, 1105, 1108, 1108 x 2, 1271, 1298, 1320, 1336, 1340, 1342, 1343. In the bracketed lines the usage is of the "royal we." These lines don't include other phraseology that points to the first person, e.g. "for me," "by me," etc.
5. Antigone: 71, 80, 458, 462, 463, 542, 547, 557, 866, 868, 900, 904, 913, 939; Creon: 164, 184, 191, 484, 498, 571, 668, 886, 1099, 1111, 1272, 1273, 1319, 1320.
6. Some explain her return as motivated by her sense of inadequacy arising from not having actually interred Polyneices (e.g. Knox 1966: 64), others by the dramatic effect of having two impacts from the burial (e.g. Kitto 1956: 152–58; Kirkwood 1994: 70).
7. E.g. Jean Anouilh's *Antigone* (1944), Athol Fugard's *The Islan* (1973); Femi Osofisan's *Tegonni: an African* Antigone (1999); Janusz Glowacki's *Antigone in New York* (1994); Seamus Heaney's *The Burial at Thebes: A version of Sophocles' Antigone* (2004) and Sophie Deraspe's film *Antigone* (2019).
8. For seeing Ismene in a more positive light than usual, see Roisman 2018a.
9. For the question of why did Ismene want to share in Antigone's blame, and whether Ismene is cowardly, as many scholars assume, or did she genuinely love her sister and tried in her pleadings with Antigone to save both their lives, see Roisman 2018a *passim*.
10. See also e.g. Heilbrun 1973: 1–16; Love 2005: 117–18, 123–28.
11. *Pace* Scodel 2018.
12. It is often assumed that this explanation has been adapted by Sophocles from Herodotus.

13. Griffith (1991: on 773-76) comments that "For unmarried women in particular, immurement has often seemed esp. appropriate, since it sheds no blood and leaves their bodies still hidden ... closed-off, and unviolated."
14. Gellie 1972: 30.

Chapter 5 Helen

1. Roisman 2006.
2. Ahl and Roisman 1996: 33-42.
3. Marshall 2014: 69-71.
4. I agree with Croally that Gorgias' piece predated the *Trojan Women*; Croally (1994: 157-62) assumes that Euripides has used Gorgias' *Encomium of Helen*. Contra: Lloyd 1992: 100-01. For bibliography and discussion see Sansone 2012: 127 with n. 17. For the significance of the presence of Gorgianic rhetoric in Helen's defense, see Croally 1994: 222-23 with n. 142.
5. Austin 1994: 8-9, 12 and *ibid*. G. Nagy in the Foreword, xii.
6. Wohl 1998: ii-xi.
7. Blondell 2013: 1-2. For discussions on beauty and the moral weight of the term *kalon* in Athenian culture see Konstan 2014; Konstan 2015: 372, 376-78; Kosman 2010.
8. While it has been rather usual to see in *Trojan Women* an intentional reference by Euripides to the destruction of Melos and the fate of its inhabitants, on the basis of chronology of both the destruction of Melos, the procedure of selecting the poets who were to compete at the Dionysian festival, and the span of time to write three plays, I would caution against viewing the play as a response the fate of the inhabitants of Melos, see Erp Taalman Kip 1987 with bibliography, cf. also Kovacs 2018: 258-59. Above all we need to consider not only how long it took to compose a play or a trilogy, but also how long it would have taken for the chorus and actors to learn and rehearse their whole repertoire. It would therefore appear likely that Euripides had started composing the trilogy before the destruction of Melos. On the other hand, Croally 1994: 232, n. 170 is correct in suggesting that it is not the date of composition that is the issue, but rather whether the audience saw in the play a response to Melos, which would have been theirs rather than Euripides'.
9. There are also extant 43 fragmentary lines of an adaptation of the play by the Roman poet Ennius.
10. The husband was forbidden from continuing to cohabit with his adulterous wife; he would face the penalty of *atimia* (a form of disenfranchisement) if he did; see Harrison 1998: vol. I, 35-36.
11. For formal debates see Collard 2014; for trial debates see especially 157-58.
12. Lloyd 1984: 304; 1992: 101, maintains that she speaks first because of dramatic logic: "she is so much on the defensive when the scene begins that a further prosecution would be superfluous."
13. For the effect of Euripides' formal debates on the immediate action, and the integration of this into the sequence of the play's events, see Lloyd 1992: 110-12; cf. Croally 1994: 134-36.
14. Harrison 1998: vol. I, 36.
15. Having Menelaus as a judge is reminiscent of the formal debate in *Hecuba* 1109-292, where Agamemnon serves as the judge in the formal debate between Polymestor and Hecuba. However, unlike Menelaus, Agamemnon has no personal involvement in what has transpired between the two opponents, and seemingly is not swayed by either of the adversaries. Cf. Euripides, *Phoenician Women* 446-637.

16. E.g. Kovacs 2018: 58–59.
17. See Papadodima 2014.
18. The tale about Hecuba's dream that she gave birth to a firebrand that burned Troy to the ground was told to the audience in the prologue of *Alexandros*, the first play of the trilogy in which *Trojan Women* constituted the third play. *Alexandros* dealt with Hecuba's and Priam's failure to do away with the ill-fated infant.
19. This must have been a known sophistic argument. A few years earlier (423 BCE), Aristophanes mocked it by putting it in the mouth of Worse Argument: "If you happen to get caught *in flagrante*, tell him this: that you have done nothing wrong. Then pass the buck to Zeus, on the grounds that even he is worsted by lust for women, so how can you, a mere mortal, be stronger than a god?" (*Clouds* 1079–82, trans. Henderson 1998).
20. For the different interpretations of *logos*, see Grimaldi 1980 ad loc. For a detailed discussion of the meaning of the psychological attitude of the listener and the character of the orator, and whether Aristotle means here the character of the auditor as well as of the orator, see Grimaldi 1988: 5–6 ad loc.
21. For the effectiveness of the implicit over the explicit, see Roisman 1999: xiii-xvi, 1–6, and *passim*; Ahl and Roisman 1996: 10–16; Ahl 1984.
22. It is noteworthy that Menelaus refuses to mention Paris by name, in spite of the polyonymity Helen used for her lover in 941–42. Cf. his reference to Helen as "the Spartan woman" (869–70, see above). Likewise, Hecuba does not refer to Clytemnestra by name but calls her "the Spartan wife" (250).
23. Helen's first point that Hecuba and Priam are responsible for what happened to her because of giving life to Paris and not making sure that the baby is dead was dealt in the first part of the trilogy, which includes the human factors of compassion that Helen chooses to gloss over; but they were in the mind of the spectators. Hecuba ignores the charge not only because it would be of no interest to Menelaus, but because there is no effective answer to it besides pointing out the futility of such a charge, which would distract from Hecuba's line of rebuttal.
24. The usual claim (e.g. Vellacott 1975: 145; Fitzgerald 1989: 219–20; Croally 1994: 147) is that the audience would know that Hecuba's argument is not true because of Athena's promise in the prologue to punish the Greeks for the violence done to Cassandra by Ajax, son of Oileus. She asks Poseidon to join her in giving them a grim voyage home (75–86). The punishment, although grievous, is an isolated case, a one-time reversal of fortune, not a complete destruction or subjugation to barbarians. The two issues are not comparable. See also J. Roisman 1997: 44 with n. 17.
25. For the importance of marriage in this play, especially as a theme in the various speeches of the female characters, see McCallum-Barry 2001; Mossman 2005: 358 and bibliography.
26. Sophistic debating often involves casting doubts upon myths. Mossman 2005:362 maintains that Hecuba has no rhetorical markers in her speech, despite her sophistic leanings. But Hecuba avails herself of myth when it serves her cause, as in saying that Castor and Pollux have not heard Helen's cries of abduction even though "they were not yet among the stars" (1000–1001, Barlow's translation). Hecuba's view of the divine can be gleaned from lines 884–88; see Lloyd 1992: 105–09.
27. Lee 2001 (1976): on lines 987–8; Meridor 2000:18–19.
28. I am following Kovacs 1999; there is no need to assume that Hecuba is distorting Helen's argument in 998–1001, although she does make it more dramatic. See however Scodel 1980: 143–144; Lloyd 1992: 100, 105.
29. Herodotus, 7.136; cf. Xenophon, *Anabasis* 3.2.13, Isocrates, *Panegyricus* 151.

30. Cf. Meridor: 2000 esp. 25; Easterling 2001: 127–28.
31. Croally 1994:144–60 with n. 74.
32. For the view that Helen dies, see Lloyd 1984: 303–04. There are of course scholars who believe that Helen will survive, see bibliography in Croally 1994: p. 158, n. 78, and more recently Marshall 2014: 74.
33. Roisman 2011.
34. For broad Odyssean echoes in the play see Eisner 1980.
35. Cf. a similar droll entrance of Apollo who although a god appears in the garments of the lowest class of free citizen (*thēs*) upon his entrance in Euripides' *Alcestis*, 1–76 ; see discussion in Luschnig and Roisman 2003: 169–72.
36. For comparison with *Odyssey*, Book Six see also Marshall 2014: 32–33.
37. Plautus, *Amphitruo*, esp. 439–62.
38. For Euripides laying the groundwork for some elements of New Comedy and analysis of some comic scenes in his plays, see Knox 1970.
39. See Ahl and Roisman 1996: 260–72.
40. Cf. Penelope's postponement of formally acknowledging Odysseus' identity, Ahl and Roisman 1996: 229–72.
41. Cf. Similar couching and ego-soothing by Clytemnestra to Agamemnon (Aesch. *Ag*. 895–902, 943), Chapter 1, p. 27; and by Tecmessa to Ajax, Roisman 2019: 105–09.
42. On a fifth-century vase in the British Museum (London E 447, ARV^2 1035), the Phrygian Midas sits on a throne with a female slave fanning him.
43. Could the golden sandals hint at Helen's barbarization while at Troy? There is some evidence that the Greeks recognized the erotic nature of women's beautiful ankles and of women's walk, as well as association between bare feet and having sex. Portraying Helen, the most sexual of women, gold - sandaled might hint to the spectators of her giving up to the Trojan mores. The Phrygian slave is also shod with slippers. See Levine 2005.
44. *Il*. 3.154–60. See discussion in Roisman 2006.

Chapter 6 Hecuba

1. Finglass 2017: 9.
2. Roisman 2011.
3. Scholars criticize the lack of unity of the play, failing to see the connection between the fates of Polyxena and Polydorus. For a helpful summary of views trying to find a unifying theme, see Conacher 1967: 152–55. However, the two parts are clearly unified by Hecuba's motherhood.
4. Collard 1991: 23–24.
5. For Hecuba as a great orator in *Hecuba* and her rhetorical encounter with Odysseus, see Mossman 1995: 103–117.
6. Richardson 1993: on lines–see also Mossman 1995: 37.
7. Damen 2014.
8. See also discussion, Mossman 1995: 123–31.
9. For Thracians' portrayal as greedy and cruel in Greek literature, see Mossman 1995: 185–87.

Chapter 7 Alcestis

1. Luschnig 1995: 1–4 and bibliography.
2. See discussion in Luschnig and Roisman 2003:108–72, 208–14.
3. Cf. Torrance 2019: 20–21.
4. It has been suggested by Parker 2007: 131, that it was a Euripidean innovation to give speaking and singing roles to children.
5. Ebeling 1898: 72, 78, 81–83.
6. Wife and husband choose inanimate objects to represent their spouse. Alcestis addresses her bed as the symbol of her marriage; later on, Admetus promises to fashion a statue of Alcestis to embrace at night instead of his wife (348–54).
7. This is in fact how later treatments of this myth portray the two, see Parker 2007: xxiv-xxxvi; Roisman 2014a; 2015, and how some scholars still seem to view this play's protagonists: e.g. Smith in Wilson 1968: 47; Dale 1954: xxv-xxvi notes that Alcestis dies out of love for Admetus.
8. Sophocles has more adult males singing, e.g. Philoctetes, Oedipus, Heracles, and Ajax. For a full discussion of the meter and its effect on the meaning of the scene see Roisman 2000.
9. The scene has drawn considerable scholarly attention. For discussion and bibliography see Luschnig and Roisman 2003: 182–86.
10. For discussion, see Battezzato 2014b.
11. For full discussion of Admetus' promises, see Luschnig and Roisman 2003: 186–226.
12. For the staging possibilities of this scene see Roisman 2014a: 343.
13. For a slightly different interpretation of Heracles' account see Luschnig and Roisman 2013: 208–09.
14. For the issue that this kind of a scenario is "beyond the scope of the play" (Aristotle, *Poetics* 1454b cf. 1453b); see discussion in Luschnig and Roisman 2003: 217–18.
15. For further discussion, see Battezzato 2014a,b.

Chapter 8 Deianeira

1. For Tecmessa see Roisman 2019.
2. Killing the Hydra of Lerna was Heracles' second labor.
3. Easterling 1982: 3; Davies 1991: xix.
4. For Deianeira's identification especially with Iole see also Scott 1995: 21; 1997. For similarities between Deianeira and Iole, see Winnington-Ingram 1980: 76–77.
5. Foley 2001: 89–90.
6. For the absence of anger on Deianeira's part as indicator of her ambivalence about her marriage to Heracles, see Scott 1997: 35–38.

Notes from previous section (pp. 175–200):

10. For Polymestor's predictions and their function, see Gregory 1999: xxxiii–xxxvi.
11. For summary of scholarly views over the centuries on the morality of the revenge Hecuba exacted on Polymestor, see Battezzato 2018: 14–18, with bibliography.

7. There is vast scholarly debate as to whether Deianeira is the loving wife who was innocently deceived by the Nessus, or guilty of collusion with the ill-meaning centaur. For a summary of views see Hester 1980: 3–4 with notes 4 and 7.
8. Scott 1997: 44, who subscribes to this interpretation maintains that Deianeria subconsciously did not want to understand the ambiguity in Nessus' words.
9. For the claim that jealousy was the motivator see Easterling 1982: on 531–632; contra: Goldhill 2003: 166–67. For the view that Deianeira subconsciously wishes to harm Heracles "even while consciously she sees herself as pursuing his love," see Scott 1995.
10. For asides in Greek tragedy see Damen 2014.

Chapter 9 Medea

1. Jason pledged himself to Medea after all the favors she had performed for him and they sealed the pledge by the clasping of right hands. Medea's self-made marriage by oaths and handshake is not the normal marriage ritual practiced in fifth-century Athens. The lack of her father's presence and consent would be particularly notable. However, the quasi-magical and heroic world which the play portrays is not a direct reflection of Athens' contemporary culture, and the spectators were aware of this. We should therefore not seek in Medea's and Jason's marriage or divorce an exact parallel to the fifth-century Athenian institution of marriage. In the world of the play, Medea and Jason were a married couple, and his abandonment of her constituted a divorce.
2. Luschnig 2014 with bibliography and references.
3. Some believe that the tragic poet Neophron anticipated Euripides in ascribing the child-murders to Medea and even that he was actually the author of Euripides' *Medea*. It cannot, however, be asserted with confidence that Neophron antedates Euripides and the fragments may be derived from Euripides' version rather than the other way around. See Luschnig 2014: 441. Whether or not Euripides was the first, he makes the most of Medea's filicide. Mastronarde 2002: 52–55 speculates that the killing of her sons was Euripides' innovation.
4. Mossman 2011: 4.
5. My translation.
6. See Boedeker 1991.
7. For discussion, see Parks 1990: *passim*.
8. See Keith 1924; Kyriakou 2001.
9. A fact that goes against Aristotle's criticism (*Poetics* 1461b19–21) of the scene as not organic to the plot. For other aspects of the centrality of the Aegeus scene see Sfyroeras 1994–95.
10. With Mossman 2011: on 791, *pace* Lloyd 1999: 28 and Mastronarde 2002: n 791 who see this aorist as "tragic" or "dramatic," i.e. expressing recognition that something is lamentable by a more controlled manner than actually groaning, and which is often translated in the present tense in English.
11. See both Mastronarde 2002 and Mossman 2011 on lines.
12. For masculinization see also Mastronarde 2002: on 27, *pace* Mossman 2011: on 20–23. Mossman is right that oaths are not only the male domain and that women also exchanged oaths with each other and with men; she does not however present an example in which marriage was exacted by an oath and clasp of right hands between the husband and wife to be.
13. For discussion of the play as a revenge play, see Roisman 2014b with bibliography.

14. For Helios as the punitive titan god who guarantees the firmness of oaths, see Burnett 1998: 221–24.

Chapter 10 Creusa

1. For this view see Burnett 1962, who sees Creusa as willfully setting herself against the providential scheme of the god, hurling blasphemies at him. For Creusa' opposition to Apollo see also Rosivach 1977. For further analysis of the relations between Creusa and Apollo see Rabinowitz 2011:10–12.
2. For discussion see Hoffer 1996.
3. See Kindt 2007; Loraux 1990; Zacharia 2003; Zeitlin 1996 [1989].
4. See Rabinowitz 2011:10–12 for further discussion.
5. Hermes does not have all the details correct (71–73). Creusa tells the Old Man that she gave birth in a cave (949) and that she exposed the baby on the same bed where she was raped (899–901). In spite of Lee's claim (1997 on 949 and 1596) that Creusa is a woman "whose memory of the past is set in a fluid impressions," women do remember where they give birth, and there is no reason to suspect Creusa's account.
6. The theme of autochthony involved in the Athens-motive is important throughout the play: 8–13, 29, 57–64, 74–75, 80–81; cf. 184, 260–82, 568, 589–92, 671–72, 719–24, 736–37, 810–15, 987–1017, 1058–60 1069–73, 1074–89, 1106, 1220, 1297–99. The study of autochthony, particularly from a feminist perspective, received great impetus from the work of Loraux (1990) and Zeitlin (1989, reprinted in Zeitlin 1996).
7. The account in 279–80 implies that all the sisters were sacrificed. The audience however would be familiar with the version of the myth whereby the sisters made an oath that the two surviving sisters would commit suicide to join their sacrificed sister. Whether Creusa is looking at the end result of having lost all of her sisters because of the sacrifice is unclear.
8. Her rebelliousness has been noted by Grube 1961: 261–79, but somehow he fails to connect it to her victimhood.
9. From this area on three days and nights of three months in the year lightning flashes were watched for in the direction of a place called Harma on Mt. Parnes, visible from Athens, and when seen, a sacred embassy was sent to Delphi.
10. Cf. Clytemnestra's comment in Sophocles' *Electra* (775–78), when she frames Orestes' "self-exile" as keeping away from the nurture of her breast.
11. The glittering hair brought about the rationalizing and demythologizing of the plot even in 1889, when a translation of the *Ion* by H. B. Lennard appeared. According to Owen 1957 [1939]: xxxii, Lennard claimed that Creusa was raped by some youth whom "she fancied to be Apollo because his yellow hair glittered in the sunshine. The sickness of the princess was noticed by the servants, and the gossip of the servants' hall reached the ears of the Athenian priests, who, anxious to safeguard the honor of the royal family, transferred the child to Delphi from the cave where he had been left." The rationalistic approach was followed by A. W. Verrall 1890: xvi-xlv, who bases his view on the ending of the play, when Ion himself doubts that Apollo is his father. Vellacott 1975: 121, the most recent, without any explanation assumes that Creusa was seduced by a human lover whom she took to be Apollo because the act took place at the "Long Rocks" near the Athenian Acropolis, where Apollo has a shrine of some kind (285). This kind of interpretation robs the eponymous hero of the Ionians of his divine ancestry. Bowing however

to such a possibility, the playwright, anticipating this suspicion, has it raised by Ion, giving Creusa the opportunity to deny it (1523-31).
12. E.g. Grube 1961: 269-70; Lee 1997: on 859-922.
13. About *Alcestis* see Luschnig and Roisman 2003: 160-61, 170, 186, 206, 217-26.

Chapter 11 Phaedra

1. Torrance 2019: 13.
2. Verrall 1967 [1895]: 82-99 is the proponent of the "two audiences" theory. However, he also sees a double reality of Euripides' plays: one "superficial" and one "real." While this study accepts the multiplicity of layers of the performances as being absorbed by different sets of audiences, it does not see any level of action as "real" or "superficial."
3. For further discussion of the implicit style along the lines presented here see Ahl and Roisman 1996: 10-16 where the methodology is fully discussed. For a fuller discussion of the implicit reading of Euripides *Hippolytus*, see Roisman 1999: *passim*.
4. For the view that her proposition was not only sexual but also political: she also suggested deposing Theseus, see Roisman 1999: 10-16.
5. For Euripides' subversiveness, see Papadodima 2014.
6. Roisman in 1999 follows Wilamowitz 1963 [1875]: 209-19; 1891: 48-50. Wilamowitz focuses primarily on Phaedra's pretense of observing mores she does not have. The Nurse knows her mistress well enough to pursue her mistress' wishes. The scholiast's (ancient commentator's) note on line 670 (Phaedra: "What craft we do have, what words, once we have stumbled, that can undo the noose?"): "We have not lost the hope we were looking forward to of persuading him [Hippolytus] to commit the wrong deed," might indicate that the scholiast anticipated Wilamowitz' interpretation. For an explanation of Wilamowitz's assessment of the personality of Phaedra, see Calder 1979: 225-36. See further Gilula 1981.
7. See Roisman 1999: 6-9.
8. E.g. Knox 1952 *passim*; Barrett 1964: on lines 170-66.
9. The translations from Euripides' *Hippolytus* are my own.
10. The presentation of *eros* (lovesickness) as a real disease in tragedy have been widely discussed: McNamara, 2008: 308-09; Kosak, 2004: 49-64.
11. See also Barrett 1964: on lines 228-31.
12. For a description of a true delirium, see *Orestes* 211-306, in which he truly cannot move on his own.
13. Solmsen 1975: 55-56.
14. Plutarch, *Moralia* 959B. In a different quotation of the passage, Plutarch gives Phaedra's words in lines 218-19 on the mouth of a flatterer who tries to ingratiate himself with an avid hunter (*Moralia* 52C). The lines, then, became proverbial for expressing an ardent desire to hunt but not necessarily a sincere interest in the pursuit of the sport.
15. See Naiden 2006 chapters 1-3. Naiden identified four necessary steps in a supplication: (1) an approach to an individual or place, (2) use of a distinctive gesture, (3) a definite request must be put; and then (4) the "supplicandus" must respond, and need not grant the request.
16. E.g. Barrett 1964: on lines 503-04.

17. See discussion, Roisman 1999: 98–100.
18. Avery 1968: 26.n.6 asks whether we could see the address "woman" in 656: "I tell you clearly, it is my piety that saves you woman" as a direct reference to Phaedra. If so, the address seems inadvertent and discloses Hippolytus' inner thoughts about the identity of the addressee in his tirade.
19. Lines 669–79 clearly belong to Phaedra not to the Nurse *pace* Kovacs 1995.

GLOSSARY OF NAMES AND TERMS

Achillles Son of Thetis and Peleus, the greatest Greek hero of the Trojan War
Aegeus King of Athens
Agamemnon Son of Aerope and Atreus
agon Formal Debate
Aigisthus Son of Thyestes and Thyestes' daughter Pelopia; Clytemnestra's lover
Andromache Hector's wife and widow, assigned to Achilles' son, Neoptolemus, as a concubine after Troy's fall
Antigone Daughter of Oedipus and Jocasta of Thebes
Astyanax Toddler son of Hector and Andromache, whom the Greeks threw from the walls of Troy to his death
Atreus Son of Pelops, father of Agamemnon and Menelaus
Aulis A Greek port-town in Boeotia in central Greece, at the Euripus strait, opposite the island of Euboea
Cassandra Daughter of Hecuba and Priam, a prophetess who is not believed; Agamemnon's concubine
Castor and Pollux/Polydeuces (Dioscuri) Brothers of Helen and Clytemnestra, sons of Zeus and Leda. In one version, Castor is a son of Tyndareus
Chrysothemis Daughter of Clytemnestra and Agamemnon; sister of Electra
Clytemnestra Daughter of Leda and Tyndareus; wife and widow of Agamemnon; wife of Aegisthus; sister of Helen; mother of Electra, Chrysothemis, and Orestes
Creon Ruler of Thebes in Sophocles' *Antigone,* uncle of Antigone; King of Corinth in Euripides' *Medea*
Creusa Queen of Athens, mother of Ion
daimon Evil Spirit
Deianeria Second wife of Heracles; mother of Hyllus
Deiphobus Prince of Troy, Paris' brother, and Helen's third husband
deus ex machina "God from the machine". A character, typically a god is brought by crane from behind the stage-building to appear on high above stage and the mortal characters.
Dioscuri See Castor and Pollux
ekkyklema ("thing rolled out") A scenic device, a wooden platform on wheels or a revolve, that was rolled from the stage-building and revealed the result of an action that had taken place offstage.
episode The part in the tragedy performed between choral songs
Erinyes Furies, ancient chthonic goddesses of retribution for kindred bloodshed
figura etymologica The use of two or more words from the same root in close proximity
Haemon Son of Creon and Eurydice of Thebes; cousin and fiancé of Antigone
Hecuba Queen of Troy, widow of Priam, mother of Paris, Cassandra, and Polyxena
Helen Daughter of Zeus and Leda; sister of Clytemnestra; wife of Menelaus, Paris, and Deiphobus; mother of Hermione
Hermione Daughter of Helen and Menelaus; future wife of Orestes
Hyllus Son of Deianeira and Heracles
Ion Son of Creusa and Apollo
Iphigenia Daughter of Clytemnestra and Agamemnon; sister of Electra and Orestes
Ismene Daughter of Oedipus and Jocasta of Thebes; sister of Antigone

Glossary of Names and Terms

Jason Prince of Iolcus, son of Aeson deposed King of Iolcus, former husband of Medea, an Argonaut
Leda Mother of Clytemnestra, Helen, and the Diioscuri
Lichas An attendant of Heracles
Medea Princess of Colchis; Jason's former wife; daughter of Aeetes; granddaughter of Helios
Menelaus Son of Aerope and Atreus
monody An ode sung by a single actor
Neoptolemus Son of Achilles and Deidamia
orchestra (literally, "dancing space") was normally circular level space where the chorus would dance, sing, and interact with the actors who were on the stage near the *skene*.
Orestes Son of Clytemnestra and Agamemnon
oxymoron Juxtaposition of apparently contradictory terms or words
Paris Son of Hecuba and Priam, Helen's second husband
Pelops Son of Tantalus, father of Atreus and Thyestes
philia Literally: friendship. A term that covered a complex web of personal, family, political, and business relationships
pithanon tini pithanon (Aristotle, *Rhetoric* 1365B) "what is persuasive is what persuades someone"
Phaedra Daughter of Minos and Pasiphae of Crete, wife of Theseus, stepmother of Hippolytus
Pollux/Polydeuces See Castor and Pollux
Polyxena Daughter of Hecuba and Priam; sister of Cassandra and Paris
Priam King of Troy
proskynesis Foreign bowing or prostrating oneself before a person of higher social rank
Pylades Son of Anaxibia and Strophius; cousin and friend of Orestes, ultimately husband of Electra
Pythia Priestess of Apollo at Delphi
Strophius Husband of Anaxibia, Agamemnon's sister, ruler of Phocis; father of Pylades
Talthybius Greeks' Herald in *Hecuba* and *Trojan Women*
Tantalus Son of Zeus, father of Pelops
Teucer Greek warrior from Salamis who participated in Trojan War
Thecolymenus King of Egypt, son of Proteus, brother of Theonoe
Thyestes Son of Tantalus, brother of Atreus
Theonoe A seer, daughter of Proteus, sister of Theoclymenus
Theseus King of Athens, husband of Phaedra, father of Hippolytus
Thoas King of the Taurians
Tyndareus Father of Clytemnestra and, according to one version, of Castor

BIBLIOGRAPHY

Abbott, H. Porter. 2008. *The Cambridge Introduction to Narrative*. Cambridge: Cambridge University Press.
Aélion, R. 1983. *Euripide héritier d'Eschyle*. Paris: Société d'Édition "Les Belles Lettres", 2 vols.
Agard, W. R. 1937. "Antigone 904–920." *Classical Philology* 32: 263–65.
Ahl, F. 1984. "The Art of Safe Criticism in Greece and Rome." *American Journal of Philology* 105: 174–208.
Ahl, F. and H. M. Roisman. 1996. *The Odyssey Re-Formed*. Ithaca, NY: Cornell University Press.
Alexiou, M. 2002. *The Ritual Lament in Greek Tradition*. 2nd ed. revised by D. Yatromanolakis and P. Roilos. Lanham, MD: Rowman & Littlefield.
Allan, W. 2008. *Euripides: Helen*. Cambridge: Cambridge University Press.
Arnott, P. 1962. *Greek Scenic Conventions in the Fifth Century B.C.* Oxford Clarendon University Press.
Austin, N. 1994. *Helen of Troy and her Shameless Phantom*. Ithaca and London: Cornell University Press.
Avery, H. C. 1968. "'My Tongue Swore, but my Mind is Unsworn.'" *Transactions of the American Philological Association* 99:19–35.
Bacalexi, D. 2016. "Personal, Paternal, Patriotic: The Threefold Sacrifice of Iphigenia in Euripides' *Iphigenia at Aulis*." *Humanitas* 68: 51–76.
Bakola, E., 2016. "Textile Symbolism and the 'Wealth of the Earth': Creation, Production and Destruction in the 'Tapestry Scene' of Aeschylus' *Oresteia* (Ag. 905–78)." In *Spinning Fates and the Song of the Loom: The Use of Textiles, Clothing and Cloth Production as Metaphor, Symbol and Narrative Device in Greek and Latin Literature*, eds. M. Harlow, M. L. Nosch and G. Fanfani. Ancient Textile Series, Vol. 24. Oxford: Oxbow: 115–36.
Barlow, S. 1986. *Euripides: Trojan Women*. Warminster, Wiltshire, England: Aris & Phillips
Barrett, W. S. 1964. *Euripides, Hippolytos*. Oxford: Clarendon Press.
Battezzato, L. 2014a. "Hospitality." In *Encyclopedia of Greek Tragedy*, ed. H. M. Roisman, Chichester, West Sussex, UK: Wiley-Blackwell. Vol. II: 698–99.
Battezzato, L. 2014b. "Gratitude/Ingratitude." In *Encyclopedia of Greek Tragedy*, ed. H. M. Roisman, Chichester, West Sussex, UK: Wiley-Blackwell. Vol. II: 587–90.
Battezzato, L. 2018. *Euripides: Hecuba*. Cambridge: Cambridge University Press.
Bayfield, M. A. 1960. *The Antigone of Sophokles*. London: Macmillan.
Betensky, A. 1978. "Aeschylus' *Oresteia*: The Power of Clytemnestra." *Ramus* 7:11–25.
Bierl, A. 2017. "*Melizein Pathe* or Tonal Dimension in Aeschylus' *Agamemnon*: Voice, Song, and *Choreia* as Leitmotifs and Metatragic Signals for Expressing Suffering." In *Voice and Voices in Antiquity*. Orality and Literacy in the Ancient World, ed. N. Slater, Leiden; Boston: Brill. Vol. 11: 166–207.
Blaiklock, E. M. 1952. *The Male Characters of Euripides: A Study in Realism*. Wellington: New Zealand University Press.
Blondell, R. 1989. *Helping Friends and Harming Enemies: A Study in Sophocles and Greek Ethics*. Cambridge: Cambridge University Press.
Blondell, R. 2013. *Helen of Troy: Beauty, Myth, Devastation*. Oxford, New York: Oxford University Press.
Boedeker, D. 1991. "Euripides' Medea and the Vanity of ΛΟΓΟΙ." *Classical Philology* 86.2: 95–112.
Bollack, J. & P. Judet de La Combe. 1981. *Agamemnon 2*. Lille: Presses Universitaires de Lille.

Bibliography

Bowra, C. M. 1952. *Sophoclean Tragedy*. Oxford: Clarendon Press.
Brown. A. 1987. *Sophocles. Antigone*. Warminster, England: Aris & Phillips.
Burian, P. H. 2007. *Euripides: Helen*. Oxford: Aris & Phillips.
Burnett, A. P. 1962. "Human Resistance and Divine Persuasion in Euripides' *Ion*." *Classical Philology* 57: 89–103.
Burnett, A. P. 1998. *Revenge in Attic and Later Tragedy*. Berkeley, CA: University of California Press.
Buxton, R. G. A. 1994. *Imaginary Greece: The Contexts of Mythology*. Cambridge: Cambridge University Press.
Cairns, D. (ed.) 2005. *Body and Language in the Greek and Roman Worlds*. Swansea: The Classical Press of Wales.
Calder, W. M. III. 1976. "Seneca's *Agamemnon*." *Classical Philology* 71:27–36.
Calder, W. M. III. 1979. "The Riddle of Wilamowitz's Phaidrabild." *Greek, Roman, and Byzantine Studies* 20: 219–36.
Cameron, A. 1968. *The Identity of Oedipus the King*. New York: New York University Press.
Campbell, D. A. 1982. *Greek Lyric I: Sappho and Alcaeus*. Cambridge, MA: Harvard University Press.
Catenaccio, C. 2017. "Sudden Song: The Musical Structure of Sophocles' *Trachiniae*." *Arethusa* 50: 1–33.
Cheuse, A. and R. Koffler (eds.) 1970. *A Rarer Action. Essays in Honor of Francis Fergusson*. New Brunswick, New Jersey: Rutgers University Press.
Chong-Gossard, J. H. K. O. and Lin Li Ng. 2018. "Euripidean Women and Internalized Misogyny. Agones in *Troades*, *Electra*, and *Andromache*." In *Engaging Classical Texts* in *Contemporary World. From Narratology to Reception*, eds. L. Pratt and C. M. Sampson. Ann Arbor: University of Michigan Press: 71–90.
Collard, C. 1991. *Euripides: Hecuba, with Introduction, Translation, and Commentary*. Warminster, England: Aris & Phillips.
Collard, C. 2002. *Aeschylus. Oresteia*. Oxford: Oxford University Press.
Collard, C. 2014. "Formal Debates." In *Encyclopedia of Greek Tragedy*, ed. H. M. Roisman. Chichester, West Sussex: Wiley-Blackwell. Vol. I: 534–36.
Collard C. and M. Cropp. 2008. *Fragments. Selection*. 2 vols. Cambridge, MA.: Harvard University Press (Loeb classical library).
Collard C. and J. Morwood. 2017. *Euripides. Iphigenia at Aulis*. Liverpool: Liverpool University Press. 2 vols.
Conacher, D. J. 1967. *Euripidean Drama; Myth, Theme and Structure*. Toronto: University of Toronto Press.
Conacher, D. J. 1987. *Aeschylus' Oresteia. A Literary Commentary*. Toronto; Buffalo; London: University of Toronto Press.
Cousland, J. R. C. and J. R. Hume (eds.) 2009. *The Play of Texts and Fragments: Essays in Honour of Martin Cropp*. Leiden; Boston: Brill.
Croally, N. T. 1994. *Euripidean Polemic: The Trojan Women and the Function of Tragedy*. Cambridge: Cambridge University Press.
Cropp, M. J. 2000. *Euripides. Iphigenia in Tauris*. Warminster, England: Aris & Phillips.
Dale, A. M. 1954. *Euripides. Alcestis*. Oxford: Oxford University Press.
Dale, A. M. 1967. *Euripides. Helen*. Oxford: Clarendon Press.
Damen, L. M. 2014. "Asides." In *Encyclopedia of Greek Tragedy*, ed. H. M. Roisman. Chichester, West Sussex, UK: Wiley-Blackwell. Vol. I: 151–53.
Davies, M. 1991. *Sophocles. Trachiniae*. Oxford: Clarendon Press.
Dawe, R. D. 1963. "Inconsistency of Plot and Character in Aeschylus." *Proceedings of the Cambridge Philological Society* n.s. 9: 21–62.
de Jong, I. J. F. 2001. *A Narratological Commentary on the Odyssey*. Cambridge: Cambridge University Press.

de May, P. 2003. *Aeschylus: Agamemnon*. Cambridge: Cambridge University Press.
Destrée, P. and P. Murray (eds.) 2015. Malden, MA: Wiley-Blackwell.
Diels H and W. Kranz. 1952. (D-K) *Die Fragmente der Vorsokratiker*. 6th edn. vol. 2, no. 82. Zurich/Berlin, Weidmann.
Dover, K. J. 1974 *Greek Popular Morality in the Time of Plato and Aristotle*. Oxford: Blackwell.
Dunn, F. D. (ed.) 1996. *Sophocles' "Electra" in Performance*. Stuttgart: M&P.
Easterling, P. E. 1973. "Presentation of Character in Aeschylus." *Greece and Rome* 20: 3–19.
Easterling, P. E. 1977. "Character in Sophocles." *Greece and Rome* 24: 121–29.
Easterling, P. E. 1982. *Sophocles. Trachiniae*. Cambridge: Cambridge University Press.
Easterling, P. E. 2001. "Euripides' Trojan Women." In *Trojan Women: A Collection of Essays*, eds. D. Stuttard and T. Shasha. York: aod publications: 123–31.
Easterling, P. E. 2005. "*Agamemnon* for the Ancients." In *Agamemnon in Performance 458 BC to AD 2004*, eds. F. Macintosh, P. Michelakis, E. Hall & O. Taplin. Oxford University Press: 23–36.
Easterling, P. E. & E. Hall (eds.) 2002. *Greek and Roman Actors: Aspects of Ancient Profession*. Cambridge: Cambridge University Press.
Ebeling, H. L. 1898. "The Admetus of Euripides Viewed in Relation to the Admetus of Tradition Author(s)." *Transactions of the American Philological Association* 29: 65–85.
Eisner, R. 1979. "Euripides' Use of Myth." *Arethusa* 12.2: 153–74.
Eisner, R. 1980. "Echoes of the *Odyssey* in Euripides' *Helen*." *Maia* 32: 31–37.
England, E. B. 1986 [1891]. *Iphigenia in Aulis of Euripides*. Salem, NH: Ayer.
Erbse, H. 1966. "Euripides' *Andromache*." *Hermes* 94: 276–97.
Erp Taalman Kip, A. M. 1987. "Euripides and Melos." *Mnemosyne* 40: 414–419.
Faraone, C. A. and L. K. McClure (eds.) 2006. *Prostitutes and Courtesans in the Ancient World*. Madison, WI: University of Wisconsin Press.
Ferguson, J. 1972 (reissued 2013). *A Companion to Greek Tragedy*. Austin & London: University of Texas Press.
Finglass, P. J. 2007. *Electra. Sophocles*. Cambridge, UK; New York: Cambridge University Press.
Finglass, P. J. 2017. "The Sack of Troy in Stesichorus and Apollodorus." *Quaderni Urbinati di Cultura Classica* 144(1): 11–19.
Finkelberg, M. (ed.) *The Homer Encyclopedia*. Chichester, West Sussex: Wiley-Blackwell.
Fitzgerald, G. 1989. "Euripides and Hecuba: Confounding the 'Mode.'" *Maia* 41: 217–22.
Fitzgerald, G. J. 1973. "Misconception, Hypocrisy, and Structure of Euripides' *Hippolytus*." *Ramus* 2: 20–40.
Fletcher, J. 2009. "Weaving Women's Tales in Euripides' *Ion*." In *The Play of Texts and Fragments: Essays in Honour of Martin Cropp*, eds. J. R. C. Cousland and J. R. Hume. Leiden and Boston: Brill: 127–39.
Foley, H. 2001. *Female Acts in Greek Tragedy*. Princeton: Princeton University Press.
Fraenkel, E. 1950. *Agamemnon; edited with a Commentary*. Oxford: Clarendon Press.
Franco, C. 2014. *Shameless: The Canine and the Feminine in Ancient Greece*. Berkeley: California University Press.
Fulkerson, L. 2013. *No Regrets. Remorse in Classical Antiquity*. Oxford: Oxford University Press.
Garvie, A. F. 1986. *Aeschylus. Choephori*. Oxford: Clarendon Press.
Gellie, G. H. 1972. *Sophocles: A Reading*. Melbourne: Melbourne University Press.
Gibert, J. 1995. *Change of Mind in Greek Tragedy*. Göttingen: Vandenhoeck & Ruprecht.
Gill, C. 1990. "The Articulation of Self in Euripides' *Hippolytos*." In *Euripides, Women, and Sexuality*, ed. A. Powell. New York: Routledge, Chapman and Hall: 76–107.
Gilula, D. 1981. "A Consideration of Phaedra's EUKLEIA." *Sileno* 7: 121–33.
Ginsberg, L. D. 2015. "Don't Stand So Close to Me: Antigone's *Pietas* in Seneca's *Phoenissae*." *Transactions of the American Philological Association* 145: 199–230.
Goheen, R. F. 1955. "Aspects of Dramatic Symbolism: Three Studies in the *Oresteia*." *American Journal of Philology* 76: 113–37.

Bibliography

Goldhill, S. 2003. "Tragic Emotions: The Pettiness of Envy and the Politics of Pitilessness." In *Envy, Spite and Jealousy. The Rivalrous Emotions in Ancient Greece*, eds. D. Konstan and N. Keith Rutter. Edinburgh: Edinburgh University Press: 165–80.

Goldhill, S. and R. Osborne (eds.) 1999. *Performance-Culture and Athenian Democracy*. Cambridge: Cambridge University Press.

Gould, J. 1980. "Law, Custom and Myth: Aspects of the Social Position of Women in Classical Athens." *Journal of Hellenic Studies* 100: 38–59.

Goward, B. 2004. *Telling Tragedy: Narrative Technique in Aeschylus, Sophocles, & Euripides*. London: Duckworth.

Gredley, B. 1975. Review of *A Companion to Greek Tragedy* by J. Ferguson. *Journal of Hellenic Studies* 95: 222–23.

Gregory, J. 1999. *Euripides: Hecuba. Introduction, Text, and Commentary*. Atlanta, GA: Scholars Press.

Gregory, J. (ed.) 2005. *Companion to Greek Tragedy*. Malden, MA; Oxford: Blackwell.

Griffin, J. 2001 "The *Trojan Women*." In *Trojan Women: A Collection of Essays*, eds. D. Stuttard and T. Shasha. York: aod Publications: 61–89.

Griffith, M. 1999. *Sophocles: Antigone*. Cambridge: Cambridge University Press.

Griffith. M. & D. Mastronarde (eds.) 1990. *Comparative Literature in Honor of Thomas G. Rosenmeyer*. Atlanta, GA: Scholars Press.

Grimaldi, William M. A., S.J. 1980. *Aristotle, Rhetoric I. A Commentary*. New York: Fordham University Press.

Grimaldi, William M.A., S.J. 1988. *Aristotle, Rhetoric II. A Commentary*. New York: Fordham University Press.

Halliwell, S. 1987. *The Poetics of Aristotle. Translation and Commentary*. Chapel Hill: The University of North Carolina Press.

Hall, E. 1999. "Actor's Song in Tragedy." In *Performance-Culture and Athenian Democracy*, eds. S. Goldhill and R. Osborne. Cambridge: Cambridge University Press: 96–124.

Hall, E. 2002. "The Singing Actors of Antiquity." In *Greek and Roman Actors*, eds. P. Easterling and E. Hall. Cambridge: Cambridge University Press: 3–38.

Hall, E. 2005. "Aeschylus' Clytemnestra versus her Senecan Tradition." In *Agamemnon in Performance 458 BC to AD 2004*, eds. F. Macintosh, P. Michelakis, E. Hall, & O. Taplin. Oxford: Oxford University Press: 53–75.

Hall, E. 2013. *Adventures with Iphigenia in Tauris: A Cultural History of Euripides' Black Sea Tragedy*. Oxford: Oxford University Press.

Harlow, M, M. L. Nosch, G. Fanfani (eds.) 2016. *Spinning Fates and the Song of the Loom: The Use of Textiles, Clothing and Cloth Production as Metaphor, Symbol and Narrative Device in Greek and Latin Literature*. Ancient Textile Series, Vol. 24. Oxford: Oxbow.

Harrison, A. R. W. 1998. *The Law of Athens: The Family and Property*. New edn. Foreword and bibliography by D. M. MacDowell. London: Duckworth; Indianapolis: Hackett.

Hartigan, K. 1996. "Resolution without Victory / Victory without Resolution: The Identification Scene in Sophocles' *Electra*. In *Sophocles' "Electra" in Performance*, ed. F. D. Dunn. Stuttgart: M & P: 82–92.

Hazel, R. 2001. "Women's Voices, Women's Hands." In *Trojan Women: A Collection of Essays*, eds. D. Stuttard and T. Shasha. York: aod Publications: 10–29.

Heilbrun, C.G. 1973. *Toward a Recognition of Androgyny*. New York: Harper Colophon.

Henderson, J. 1998. *Aristophanes. Clouds, Wasps, Peace*. Cambridge: MA: Harvard University Press.

Herman, G. 1987. *Ritualized Friendship and the Greek City*. Cambridge: Cambridge University Press.

Hesk, J. 2000. *Deception and Democracy in Classical Athens*. Cambridge, UK; New York, NY: Cambridge University Press.

Hester, D. A. 1980. "Deianeira's 'Deception Speech.'" *Antichthon* 14: 1–8.

Hoffer, S. E 1996. "Violence, Culture, and the Workings of Ideology in Euripides' *Ion*." *Classical Antiquity* 15:289–318.
Hogan, J.C. 1984. *A Commentary on the Complete Greek Tragedies*. Aeschylus. Chicago and London: University of Chicago Press.
Huys, M. 1995. *The Tale of the Hero who was Exposed at Birth in Euripidean Tragedy: A Study of Motifs*. Leuven, Belgium: Leuven University Press (Symbolae Facultatis Litterarum et Philosophiae Lovaniensis. Series A; v. 20.).
Jebb, R. C. 2004 [1892]. *Sophocles: Plays. Trachiniae*. Bristol Classical Press.
Jebb, R. C. 2004 [1900]. *Sophocles: Plays. Antigone*. Bristol Classical Press.
Jenkins, I. D. 1985. "The Ambiguity of Greek Textiles." *Arethusa* 18: 109–32.
Juffras, D. M. 1991. "Sophocles' Electra 973–85 and Tyrannicide." *Transactions of the American Philological Association* 12: 99–108.
Just, R. 1989. *Women in Athenian Law and Life*. London and New York: Routledge.
Kamerbeek, J. C. 1970. *The Plays of Sophocles. Commentaries. Part II. The Trachiniae*. Leiden: Brill.
Kannicht, R. 2004. *Tragicorum Graecorum Fragmenta (TrGF)*. Vols. 5.1 & 5.2 Göttingen: Vandenhoeck & Ruprecht.
Kannicht, R. and B. Snell. 1981. *Tragicorum Graecorum Fragmenta* Vol. 2. Göttingen: Vandenhoeck & Ruprecht.
Katz, M. A. 1991. *Penelope's Renown: Meaning and Indeterminacy in the Odyssey*. Princeton, NJ.: Princeton University Press.
Keck, Karl Heinrich. 1863. *Aeschylus. Agamemnon*. Leipzig: B.G Teubner.
Keith, A. L. 1924. "The Taunt in Homer and Vergil." *Classical Journal* 19: 554–60.
Kells, J. H. 1973. *Sophocles. Electra*. Cambridge: Cambridge University Press.
Kindt, J. 2007. "Apollo's Oracle in Euripides' *Ion*: Ambiguous Identities in Fifth Century Athens." *Ancient Narrative*. Vol. 6: 1–30.
Kirkwood, G. M. 1994. *A Study of Sophoclean Drama: With a new Preface and Enlarged Bibliographical Note*. Ithaca: Cornell University Press.
Kittelä, S.-I. 2009. "The Queen Ancient and Modern: Aeschylus' Clytemnestra." *New Voices in Classical Reception Studies* 4: 123–37.
Kitto, H. D. F. 1961 (1954). *Greek Tragedy: A Literary Study*. London: Methuen.
Kitto, H. D. F. 1956. *Form and Meaning in Drama: A Study of Six Greek Plays and of Hamlet*. London: Methuen.
Kitzinger M. R. 2012. "The Divided Worlds of Sophocles' Women of *Trachis*." In *A Companion to Sophocles*, ed. K. Ormand. Malden, MA: Wiley-Blackwell: 111–25.
Knox, B. M. W. 1952. "The *Hippolytus* of Euripides." *YCS* 13:3–31.
Knox, B. M. W. 1966. *The Heroic Temper: Studies in Sophoclean Tragedy*. Berkeley and Los Angeles: University of California Press.
Knox, B. M. W. 1970. "Euripidean Comedy." In *The Rarer Action. Essays in Honor of Francis Fergusson*, eds. A. Cheuse and R. Koffler. New Brunswick, New Jersey: Rutgers University Press: 68–96.
Konstan, D. 2014. *Beauty. The Fortunes of an Ancient Greek Idea*. Oxford: Oxford University Press.
Konstan, D. 2015. "Beauty." In *A Companion to Ancient Aesthetics*, eds. P. Destrée and P. Murray. Malden, MA: Wiley-Blackwell: 366–80.
Konstan, D. and N. Keith Rutter (eds.) 2003. *Envy, Spite and Jealousy. The Rivalrous Emotions in Ancient Greece*. Edinburgh: Edinburgh University Press.
Kosak, J. C. 2004. *Heroic Measures: Hippocratic Medicine in the Making of Euripidean Tragedy*. Leiden: Brill.
Kosman, A. 2010. "Beauty and the Good: Situating the *Kalon*." *Classical Philology* 105: 341–57.
Kovacs, D. 1980. "Shame, Pleasure, and Honor in Phaedra's Great Speech (Euripides, *Hippolytus* 375–87)." *American Journal of Philology* 101: 287–303.

Bibliography

Kovacs, D. 1994. *Euripides: Cyclops, Alcestis, Medea*. Cambridge, MA; London, England: Harvard University Press.
Kovacs, D. 1995. *Euripides: Children of Heracles, Hippolytus, Andromache, Hecuba*. Cambridge, MA; London: Harvard University Press.
Kovacs, D. 1998. *Euripides: Suppliant Women, Electra, Heracles*. Cambridge, MA; London: Harvard University Press.
Kovacs, D. 1999. *Euripides: Helen, Phoenician Women, Orestes*. Cambridge, MA, London, England: Harvard University Press.
Kovacs, D. 2014. *Euripides: Trojan Women, Iphigenia among the Taurians, Ion*. Cambridge, MA, London: Harvard University Press.
Kovacs, D. 2018. *Euripides. Troades*. Oxford: Oxford University Press.
Kyriakou, P. 2001. "Warrior Vaunts in the Iliad." *Rheinisches Museum für Philologie* 144: 250–77.
Kyriakou, P. 2006. *A Commentary on Euripides' Iphigenia in Tauris*. Berlin, New York: Walter de Gruyter.
Lardinois, A. and L. McClure (eds.) 2001 *Making Silence Speak: Women's Voices in Greek Literature and Society*. Princeton, NJ: Princeton University Press.
Lauriola, R. and K.N. Demetriou (eds.) 2015. *Brill's Companion to the Reception of Euripides*. Leiden: Brill.
Lawrence, S. E. 1988. "Iphigenia at Aulis: Characterization and Psychology in Euripides." *Ramus* 17: 91–109.
Lee, K. H. 2001 (1976). *Euripides. Troades*. London: Bristol Classical Press.
Lee, K. H. 1997. *Euripides. Ion*. Warminster, England: Aris & Phillips.
Lefkowitz, M. R. 1981. *Heroines and Hysterics*. London: Duckworth.
Lefkowitz, M. R. 1986. *Women in Greek Myth*. Johns Hopkins University Press.
Lesky, A. 1979. *Greek Tragedy*. 3rd edn. Transl. by H.A. Frankfort, with Foreword by E. G. Turner. London: E. Benn; New York: Barnes & Noble.
Levine, D.B. 2005. "*ERATON BAMA* ('her lovely footstep'): the Erotics of Feet in Ancient Greece." In *Body and Language in the Greek and Roman Worlds*, ed. C. Cairns. Swansea; The Classical Press of Wales: 55–72.
Lewis, V. 2015. "Gendered Speech in Sophocles' Electra." *Phoenix* 69: 217–41.
Ley, G, 2007. *The Theatricality of Greek Tragedy: Playing Space and Chorus*. Chicago, IL: University of Chicago Press.
Llewellyn-Jones, L. 2003. *Aphrodite's Tortoise: The Veiled Woman of Ancient Greece*. Swansea: Classical Press of Wales.
Lloyd, M. 1984. "The Helen Scene in Euripides' Troades." *Classical Quarterly* 34: 303–13.
Lloyd, M. 1992 *The Agon in Euripides*. Oxford: Clarendon Press.
Lloyd, M.A. 1999. "The Tragic Aorist." *Classical Quarterly* 49: 24–45.
Lloyd, W. 1889. "On the Electra and Antigone of Sophocles." *Journal of Hellenic Studies* 10: 134–46.
Lloyd-Jones, H. 1970. *Agamemnon by Aeschylus*. Englewood Cliffs, NJ: Prentice-Hall.
Lloyd-Jones, H. 1998. *Sophocles: Antigone; The Women of Trachis, Philoctetes, Oedipus at Colonus*. Cambridge, MA: Harvard University Press.
Loraux, N. 1990. "Kreousa the Autochthon. A Study of Euripides' Ion." In *Nothing to Do with Dionysos? Athenian Drama in Its Social Context*, eds. J. H. Winkler and F. Zeitlin. Princeton, NJ: Princeton University Press: 168–206.
Love, K. 2005. *Lies Before Our Eyes: The Denial of Gender from the Bible to Shakespeare and Beyond*. Bern: Peter Lang AG, European Academic Publishers.
Luschnig, C. A. E. 1980. "Men and Gods in Euripides' Hippolytus." *Ramus* 9: 89–100.
Luschnig, C. A. E. 1988. *Tragic Aporia: A Study of Euripides' Iphigenia at Aulis*. Berwick, Vic.: Aureal Publications.
Luschnig, C. A. E. 1995. *The Gorgon's Severed Head: Studies of Alcestis, Electra and Phoenissae*. Leiden, New York, Köln: Brill.

Luschnig, C. A. E. 2007. *Granddaughter of the Sun. A Study of Euripides'* Medea. Leiden; Boston: Brill.
Luschnig, C. A. E. 2014. "Euripides: *Iphigenia at Aulis.*" In *Encyclopedia of Greek Tragedy*, ed. H. M. Roisman. Chichester, West Sussex, UK: Wiley-Blackwell. Vol. 1: 434–435.
Luschnig, C. A. E. and H. M. Roisman. 2003. *Euripides' Alcestis: A Commentary*. Norman: University of Oklahoma Press (Oklahoma Series in Classical Culture, vol. 29).
Lyons, D. J. 1996. *Gender and Immortality: Heroines in Ancient Greek Myth and Cult.* Princeton, NJ: Princeton University Press.
Lyons, D. J. 2003 & 2012. *Dangerous Gifts: Gender and Exchange in Ancient Greece*. Austin, TX: University of Texas Press.
Macintosh, F. 2005. "Viewing Agamemnon in 19th Century Britain." In *Agamemnon in Performance 458 BC to AD 2004*, eds. F. Macintosh, P. Michelakis, E. Hall & O. Taplin. Oxford: Oxford University Press: 139–162.
Macintosh, F., P. Michelakis, E. Hall, & O. Taplin (eds.) 2005. *Agamemnon in Performance 458 BC to AD 2004*. Oxford: Oxford University Press.
Macleod, L. 2001. *Dolos and Dikē in Sophokles' Electra*. Leiden; Boston: Brill.
March, J. R. 1987. *The Creative Poet. Studies on the Treatment of Myths in Greek Poetry.* Bulletin Supplement 49: 47–77. University of London. Institute of Classical Studies.
March, J. 1996. "The Chorus in Sophocles' *Electra.*" In *Sophocles' "Electra" in Performance*, ed. F. D. Dunn. Stuttgart: M&P: 65–81.
March, J. 2001. *Sophocles: Electra*. Warminster: Aris & Phillips.
Marshall, C. W. 2014. *The Structure and Performance of Euripides' Helen*. Cambridge: Cambridge University Press.
Mastronarde, D. J. 2002. *Euripides. Medea*. Cambridge UK, New York: Cambridge University Press.
McAuslan, I. and P. Walcot (eds.) 1996. *Women in Antiquity*. Oxford: Oxford University Press.
McCallum-Barry, C. 2001. "*Trojan Women*: Sex and the City." In *Trojan Women: A Collection of Essays*, eds. D. Stuttard and T. Shasha. York: aod Publications: 74–89.
McClure, L. 1997. "Clytemnestra's Binding Spell (*Ag.* 958-974)." *Classical Journal* 92: 123–140.
McClure, L. 1999. *Spoken like a Woman: Speech and Gender in Athenian Drama*. Princeton, NJ: Princeton University Press.
McClure, L. (ed.) 2017. *A Companion to Euripides*. Chichester, West Sussex: Wiley.
McDonald M. 1992. *Ancient Sun, Modern Light: Greek Drama on the Modern Stage*. New York: Columbia University Press.
McNamara, L. 2015. "Hippocratic and Non-Hippocratic Approaches to Lovesickness" In *Ancient Concepts of the Hippocratic: Papers Presented at the XIIIth International Hippocratic Colloquium, Austin, Texas, August 2008*. Leiden; Boston: Brill: 308–27.
Méautis, G. 1936. *Éschyle et la trilogie*. Paris: B. Grasset.
Mee, E. B. and H. Foley (eds.) 2011. *Antigone on Contemporary World Stage* [electronic resource]. Oxford; New York: Oxford University Press.
Meridor, R. 2000. "Creative Rhetoric in Euripides' *Troades*: Some Notes on Hecuba's Speech." *Classical Quarterly* 50: 16–29.
Merkelbach, R. & M.L. West (eds.) 1967. *Fragmenta Hesiodea*. (M-W) Cambridge: Cambridge University Press.
Michelakis, P. 2006. *Euripides:* Iphigenia at Aulis. London: Duckworth.
Michelini, A. N. 1987. *Euripides and the Tragic Tradition*. Madison, WI: University of Wisconsin Press.
Michelini, A. N. 1999-2000. "The Expansion of Myth in Late Euripides: *Iphigenia at Aulis*." *Illinois Classical Studies* 24/25: 41–57.
Mills, S. 2002. *Euripides, Hippolytus*. London: Duckworth.
Minadeo, R. 1967. "Plot, Theme, and Meaning in Sophocles' *Electra*." *Classica et Mediaevalia* 28: 114–42.

Bibliography

Minadeo, R. W. 1985. "Characterization and Theme in the Antigone." *Arethusa* 18: 133–54.
Mitchell-Boyask, R. 2014. "Aeschylus: *Oresteia*." In *Encyclopedia of Greek Tragedy*, ed. H. M. Roisman. Chichester, West Sussex, UK: Wiley-Blackwell. Vol. 1: 43–46.
Mitsis, P. and C. Tsegalis (eds.) 2010. *Allusions, Authority, and Truth: Critical Perspectives on Greek Poetics and Rhetorical Praxis*. Berlin/New York: Walter de Gruyter.
Morford, M. P. O. and R. J. Lenardon. 1985. *Classical Mythology*. New York & London: Longman.
Morwood, A. C. 1982. *The Syntax of Sophocles*. Leiden: Brill.
Moss, Leonard. 1985. "The Critique of the Male Stereotype in Greek in Greek Tragedy." *Soundings: An Interdisciplinary Journal* 68.1: 106–30.
Moss, Leonard. 1988. "The Critique of the Female Stereotype in Greek in Greek Tragedy." *Soundings: An Interdisciplinary Journal* 71.4: 515–32.
Mossman, J. 1995. *Wild Justice: A Study of Euripides' Hecuba*. Oxford, New York: Oxford University Press.
Mossman, J. 1996. "Waiting for Neoptolemus: The Unity of Euripides' Andromache." *Greece and Rome* 43(2): 143–56.
Mossman, J. 2001. "Women's Speech in Greek Tragedy: The Case of Electra and Clytemnestra in Euripides' Electra." *Classical Quarterly* n.s. 51.2: 374–84.
Mossman, J. 2005. "Women's Voices." In *Companion to Greek Tragedy*, ed. J. Gregory. Malden, MA; Oxford: Blackwell: 352–65.
Mueller, M. 2016. *Objects as Actors: Props and Poetics of Performance in Greek Tragedy*. Chicago and London: University of Chicago Press.
Mullens, H. G. 1940. "The Meaning of Euripides' *Orestes*." *Classical Quarterly* 34: 153–58.
Murray, G. 1940. *Aeschylus, The Creator of Tragedy*. Oxford: Clarendon Press.
Naiden, F. S. 2006. *Ancient Supplication*. Oxford; New York: Oxford University Press.
Nikoloutsos, K. S. (ed.) 2013. *Ancient Women in Film*. Oxford: Oxford University Press.
Nooter, S. 2012. *When Heroes Sing. Sophocles and the Shifting Landscape of Tragedy*. Cambridge: Cambridge University Press.
O'Brien, J. V. 1978 *Guide to Sophocles' Antigone: A Student Edition with Commentary, Grammatical Notes, & Vocabulary*. Carbondale: Southern Illinois University.
Ormand, K. (ed.) 2012. *A Companion to Sophocles*. Malden, MA: Wiley-Blackwell.
Owen, A. S. 1957 [1939]. *Euripides. Ion*. Oxford: at the Clarendon Press.
Page, D. L. 1961. *Euripides. Medea*. Oxford: Clarendon Press.
Page, D. L. 1970. *Sappho and Alcaeus: An Introduction to the Study of Ancient Lesbian Poetry*. Oxford: Clarendon Press.
Page, D. L. (ed.) 1962. *Poetae Melici Graeci. (PMG)*. Oxford: Clarendon Press.
Papadodima. E. 1014. "Euripides and Subversiveness." In *Encyclopedia of Greek Tragedy*, ed. H. M. Roisman. Chichester, West Sussex, UK: Wiley-Blackwell. Vol. I: 483–85.
Parker, L. P. E. 2007. *Euripides. Alcestis*. Oxford: Oxford University Press.
Parker, L. P. E. 2016. *Euripides: Iphigenia at Tauris*. Oxford: Oxford University Press.
Parks, W. 1990. *Verbal Dueling in Heroic Narrative: The Homeric and Old English Traditions*. Princeton, NJ: Princeton University.
Pearson, L. 1962. *Popular Ethics in Ancient Greece*. Stanford, CA: Stanford University Press.
Platnauer, M. 1938. *Euripides. Iphigenia in Tauris*. Oxford: Clarendon Press.
Powell, A. (ed.) 1990. *Euripides, Women, and Sexuality*. New York: Routledge.
Pratt. L. and C. M. Sampson (eds.) 2018. *Engaging Classical Texts in Contemporary World From Narratology to Reception*. Ann Arbor: University of Michigan Press.
Pulleyn, S. 1997. "Erotic Undertones in the Language of Clytemnestra." *Classical Quarterly* 47: 565–67.
Rabinowitz, N. S. 1993. *Anxiety Veiled: Euripides and the Traffic in Women*. Ithaca, NY: Cornell University Press.

Rabinowitz, N. S. 2011. "Greek Tragedy: A Rape Culture." *EuGeStA: Journal on Gender Studies in Antiquity* 11:1–21.
Radding, J. 2015. "Clytemnestra at Aulis: Euripides and the Reconsideration of Tradition." *Greek, Roman, and Byzantine Studies* 55: 832–86.
Radt, S. 1971. *Tragicorum Graecorum Fragmenta*. Vol. 3 and 4. Göttingen: Vandenhoeck & Ruprecht.
Raeburn, D. and O. Thomas. 2011. *The Agamemnon of Aeschylus: A Commentary for Students*. Oxford: Oxford University Press.
Rich, F. 1992. "Les Astrides: Taking the Stage to Some of its Extremes," *New York Times* (6 October), http://www.nytimes.com/1992/10/06/theater/review-theater-les-atrides-taking-the-stage-to-some-of-its-extremes.html?pagewanted=all Accessed 2.15.18.
Richardson, B. 1997. "Beyond Poststructuralism: Theory of Character, the Personae of Modern Drama, and the Antinomies of Critical Theory." *Modern Drama* 40: 86–99.
Richardson, N. 1993. *The Iliad: A Commentary. Volume vi: books 21–24*. Cambridge: Cambridge University Press.
Ringer, M. 1996. "Reflections on an Empty Urn." In *Sophocles' "Electra" in Performance*, ed. F. D. Dunn. Stuttgart: M&P: 93–200.
Roisman, H. M. 1984. *Loyalty in Early Greek Epic and Tragedy*, Beiträge zur Klassischen Philologie. Konigstein: Hain.
Roisman, H. M. 1985. "Helen and Penelope." *Bamah* 101: 116–25 (in Hebrew).
Roisman, H. M. 1986. "Clytemnestra's Ominous Words, Aeschylus, *Agamemnon* 345–47." *ZPE* 66: 279–84.
Roisman, H. M. 1999. *Nothing Is As It Seems: The Tragedy of the Implicit in Euripides' Hippolytus*. Lanham; Boulder; New York; Oxford: Rowman & Littlefield.
Roisman, H. M. 2000. "Meter and Meaning." *New England Classical Journal* 27: 182–99.
Roisman, H.M. 2004. "Women's Free Speech in Greek Tragedy." In *Free Speech in Classical Antiquity*, eds. I. Sluiter and R. Rosen. Leiden: Brill: 91–114.
Roisman, H. M. 2005. "Nestor the Good Counselor." *Classical Quarterly* 55: 17–38.
Roisman, H. M. 2006. "Helen in the Iliad: Causa Belli and Victim of War: From Silent Weaver to Public Speaker." *American Journal of Philology* 127.1: 1–36.
Roisman, H. M. 2008. *Sophocles: Electra. Translation with notes, introduction, interpretative essay and afterlife*. Newburyport, MA: Focus Publishing, Hackett, 2nd printing 2017 (with updates).
Roisman, H. M. 2011. "Hecuba". In *The Homer Encyclopedia*, ed. M. Finkelberg. Chichester, West Sussex: Wiley-Blackwell: 334–35.
Roisman, H. M. 2014a. "Euripides: *Alcestis*." In *Encyclopedia of Greek Tragedy*, ed. H. M. Roisman. Chichester, West Sussex, UK: Wiley-Blackwell: 339–45.
Roisman, H. M. 2014b. "Medea's Vengeance." In *Looking at Medea*, ed. D. Stuttard. London: Bloomsbury: 111–22.
Roisman, H. M. 2015. "Alcestis." In *Brill's Companion to the Reception of Euripides*, eds. R. Lauriola and K. N. Demetriou. Leiden: Brill: 353–80.
Roisman, H. M. 2017. "Euripides: Electra." In *A Companion to Euripides*, ed. L. McClure. Chichester, West Sussex: Wiley: 166–81.
Roisman, H. M. 2018a. "The Two Sisters." In *Looking at Antigone*, ed. D. Stuttard. London: Bloomsbury: 63–77.
Roisman, H. M. 2018b. "Loyal Clytemnestra: γυναῖκα πιστήν (Aeschylus, *Agamemnon* 606)." *Giornale Italiano di Filologia* 70: 11–18.
Roisman, H. M. 2018c. "The *Rhesus*—A Prosatyric Play." *Hermes* 146: 432–46. For abstract see https://www.ingentaconnect.com/contentone/fsv/hermes/2015/00000143/00000001/art00001.
Roisman, H. M. 2019. "Tecmessa." In *Looking at Ajax*, ed. D. Stuttard. London: Bloomsbury Academic: 97–115.

Bibliography

Roisman, H. M. 2020. *Sophocles' Electra*. Oxford Greek and Latin College Commentaries. Oxford: Oxford University Press.

Roisman, H. M. (ed.) 2014. *Encyclopedia of Greek Tragedy*. Chichester, West Sussex, UK: Wiley-Blackwell: 3 vols.

Roisman, H. M. and C. A. E. Luschnig. 2011. *Euripides: Electra: A Commentary*. University of Oklahoma Press.

Roisman, J. 1997. "Contemporary Allusions in Euripides' *Trojan Women*." *Studi italiani di filologia classica* 15: 38–47.

Rose, H. J. 1958. *A Commentary on the Surviving Plays of Aeschylus*. Amsterdam: N.V. Nord-Hollandsche Uitgevers Maatschappij.

Rosivach, V. J. 1977. "Earthborns and Olympians: The Parados of the *Ion*." *Classical Quarterly* 27: 284–94.

Sale, W. 1973. *Electra by Sophocles*. Englewood Cliffs, NJ: Prentice-Hall.

Sansone, D. 1991. "Iphigenia Changes her Mind." *Illinois Classical Studies* 16: 161–72.

Sansone, D. 2012. *Greek Drama and the Invention of Rhetoric*. Chichester; Malden, MA: Wiley-Blackwell.

Schein, L.S. 1982. "The Cassandra Scene in Aeschylus' *Agamemnon*." *Greece and Rome* 29: 11–16.

Scodel, R. 1980. *The Trojan Trilogy of Euripides*. Göttingen: Vandenhoeck & Ruprecht.

Scodel, R. 1990. "Euripides and *apate*." In *Cabinet of the Muses: Essays on Classical and Comparative Literature in Honor of Thomas G. Rosenmeyer*, eds. M. Griffith & D. Mastronarde. Atlanta GA: Scholars Press: 75–87.

Scodel, R. 1998. "The Captive's Dilemma: Sexual Acquiescence in Euripides' *Hecuba* and *Troades*." *Harvard Studies in Classical Philology* 98: 137–54.

Scodel, R. 2018. "Antigone's Change of Heart." In *Looking at Antigone*, ed. D. Stuttard. London: Bloomsbury: 79–106.

Scott, M. 1995. "The Character of Deianeira in Sophocles' *Trachiniae*." *Acta Classica* 38: 17–27.

Scott, M. 1997. "The Character of Deianeira in Sophocles' *Trachiniae*." *Acta Classica* 40: 33–47.

Scott, W. C. 1996. *Musical Design in Sophoclean Theater*. Hanover: University Press of New England.

Segal, C. 1966. "The *Electra* of Sophocles." *Transactions of the American Philological Association* 97: 473–545.

Segal, C. 1986. *Interpreting Greek Tragedy. Myth, Poetry, Text*. Ithaca and London: Cornell University Press.

Sfyroeras, P. 1994–95. "The Ironies of Salvation: The Aigeus Scene in Euripides' *Medea*." *Classical Journal* 90: 125–42.

Shelton, J.-A. 1983. "Revenge and Resignation: Seneca's *Agamemnon*." *Ramus* 12: 159–83.

Slater, N. (ed.) 2017. *Voice and Voices in Antiquity*. Orality and Literacy in the Ancient World, Vol. 11. Leiden, Boston: Brill.

Sluiter, I. and R. Rosen (eds.) 2004. *Free Speech in Classical Antiquity*. Leiden: Brill.

Smith, W. 1960. "The Ironic Structure in *Alcestis*." *Phoenix* 14: 127–45. (reprinted in Wilson 1968: 37–56).

Snell, B. (ed.) 1986. *Tragicorum Graecorum Fragmenta. (TrGF)*. Vol. 1. Göttingen: Vandenhoeck & Ruprecht.

Solmsen, F. 1975. *Intellectual Experiments of the Greek Enlightenment*. Princeton, NJ: Princeton University Press.

Sommerstein, A. H. 2008. *Aeschylus. Oresteia: Agamemnon, Libation Bearers, Eumenides*. Cambridge, MA: Harvard University Press.

Sorum, C. E. 1992. "Myth, Choice, and Meaning in Euripides' *Iphigenia at Aulis*." *American Journal of Philology* 113: 527–42.

Sourvinou-Inwood, C. 1989. "Assumptions and the Creation of Meaning: Reading Sophocles' *Antigone*." *Journal of Hellenic Studies* 109: 134–48.

Stanford. W. B. 1937. "Γυναικὸς ἀνδρόβουλον ἐλπίζον κέαρ (*Agamemnon* line 11)." *Classical Quarterly* 31: 92–93.
Stanford, W. B. 1972 (1942). *Aeschylus in his Style*. Dublin: University Press.
Steiner, G. 1999. "Greek is the Word." Review of Ted Hughes' translation of the Oresteia. *The Guardian* (October 24).
Stevens, P. T. 1971. *Euripides. Andromache*. Oxford: Clarendon Press.
Stockert, W. 1992. *Euripides. Iphigenie in Aulis*. Vienna: Verlag der Österreichischen Akademie der Wissenschaften: 2 Vols.
Storey, I, 1989. "Domestic Disharmony in Euripides' *Andromache*." *Greece and Rome* 36: 16–27.
Stuttard, D. 2005. *An Introduction to Trojan Women: including an adaptation of the play*. Brighton: Company Dionysus.
Stuttard, D. (ed.) 2014. *Looking at Medea*. London: Bloomsbury.
Stuttard, D. (ed) 2018. *Looking at Antigone*. London: Bloomsbury Academic.
Stuttard, D. (ed.) 2019. *Looking at Ajax*. London: Bloosmsbury Academic.
Stuttard D. and T. Shasha (eds.) 2001. *Trojan Women: A Collection of Essays*. York: aod publications.
Synodinou, K. 2013, "Agamemnon's Change of Mind in Euripdies' Iphigenia at Aulis." *Logeion* 3: 52–65.
Taplin, O. 1972. "Aeschylean Silences and Silences in Aeschylus." *Harvard Studies in Classical Philology* 76: 57–97.
Taplin, O. 1977. *The Stagecraft of Aeschylus. The Dramatic Use of Exits and Entrances in Greek Tragedy*. Oxford: Clarendon Press.
Taplin, O. 2003. *Greek Tragedy in Action*. 2nd edn. Berkeley and Los Angeles: University of California Press.
Thomson, G. D. 1946. *Aeschylus and Athens: A Study in the Social Origins of Drama*. London: Lawrence & Wishart.
Thomson, G. D. 1966. *The Oresteia of Aeschylus* (new edn. rev. and enl. of Cambridge 1938). 2 vols. Amsterdam: A. M. Hakkert; Prague: Academia.
Torrance, I. 2019. *Euripides*. London, New York, Oxford, New Delhi, Sydney: I. B. Tauris.
Usher. S. 1993. *Greek Orators—V. Demosthenes: On the Crown*. Warminster: Aris & Phillips.
Vellacott, P. 1975. *Ironic Drama: A Study of Euripides' Method and Meaning*. London, New York: Cambridge University Press.
Verrall, A. W. 1890. *The Ion of Euripides*. Cambridge: Cambridge University Press.
Verrall, A. W. 1904. *The "Agamemnon" of Aeschylus*. London: Macmillan.
Verrall, A. W. 1967 [1895] *Euripides the Rationalist: A Study in the History of Art and Religion*. New York: Russell and Russell.
Walcot, P. 1996. "Greek Attitudes Towards Women: The Mythological Evidence." In *Women in Antiquity*, eds. I. McAuslan and P. Walcot. Oxford: Oxford University Press: 91–102.
Way, A. S. 1988 [1912]. *Euripides: Electra, Orestes, Iphigenia Taurica, Andromache, Cyclops*. Cambridge, MA: Harvard University Press, London: William Heinemann.
West, M. L. 1982. *Greek Meter*. Oxford: Clarendon Press.
Wheeler, G. 2003. "Gender and Transgression in Sophocles' *Electra*." *Classical Quarterly* 55.2: 377–88.
Whiteley, R. 1989. "Was Antigone Really A 'Bad' Woman? Christiane Sourvionou Inwood's Reading of Sophocles' *Antigone*," http://www.moyak.com/papers/sophocles-antigone.html.
Whitman, C. H. 1974. *Euripides and the Full Circle of Myth*. Cambridge, MA: Harvard University Press.
Wiersma, S. 1984. "Women in Sophocles." *Mnemosyne* 37.1/2: 25–55.
Wilamowitz-Moellendorff, U. von. 1963 [1875]. *Analecta Euripidea*. Hildesheim: Georg Olms.
Wilamowitz-Moellendorff, U. von. 1891. *Euripides. Hippolytus*. Berlin: Weidmann.
Willink, C. W. 1968. "Some Problems of Text and Interpretation in *Hippolytus*." *Classical Quarterly* 18: 11–43.

Bibliography

Willink, C. W. 1986. *Euripides. Orestes*. Oxford: Clarendon Press.
Wilson, J. R. 1968. *Twentieth Century Interpretations of Euripides' Alcestis*. Englewood Cliffs, NJ: Prentice-Hall.
Winkler, J.H. and F. Zeitlin (eds.) 1990. *Nothing to do with Dionysos? Athenian Drama in Its Social Context*. Princeton, NJ: Princeton University.
Winnington-Ingram, R. P. 1960. "*Hippolytus*: A study in Causation." In *Entretiens sur l'antiquité classique 6: Euripide*. Geneva: Fondation Hardt: 160–97.
Winnington-Ingram, R. P. 1980. *Sophocles: An Interpretation*. Cambridge: Cambridge University Press.
Winnington-Ingram, R. P. 1982. "Sophocles and Women." In *Sophocle. Entretiens sur l' antiquité classique*. Vandeouvre-Genève. Vol. 29.
Winnington-Ingram, R. P. 1983. *Studies in Aeschylus*. Cambridge: Cambridge University Press.
Wohl, V. 1998. *Intimate Commerce: Exchange, Gender, and Subjectivity in Greek Tragedy*. Austin, TX: University of Texas Press.
Woodard, T. 1966. "The Electra of Sophocles." In *Sophocles: A Collection of Essays*, ed. T. Woodard. Englewood Cliffs, NJ: Prentice-Hall: 125–45.
Woodard, T. (ed.) 1966. *Sophocles: A Collection of Essays*. Englewood, NJ: Prentice-Hall.
Yunis, H. 2001. *Demosthenes. On the Crown*. Cambridge: Cambridge University Press.
Zacharia, K. 2003. *Converging Truths: Euripides' Ion and the Athenian Quest for Self-Definition*. Leiden: Brill.
Zeitlin, F. I. 1965. "The Motif of Corrupted Sacrifice in Aeschylus' *Oresteia*." *Transactions of the American Philological Association* 96: 463–508.
Zeitlin, F. I. 1980. "The Closet of Masks: Role-Playing and Myth-Making in the *Orestes* of Euripides." *Ramus* 9: 51–77.
Zeitlin, F. I. 1996 [1989]. "Mysteries of Identity and Designs of the Self in Euripides' *Ion*." *Proceedings of the Cambridge Philological Society* 35: 144–97; repr. in *Playing the Other: Gender and Society in Classical Greek Literature*, ed. F. I. Zetilin. Chicago and London: University of Chicago Press: 285–338.
Zeitlin, F. I. 1996 [1978]. *Playing the Other: Gender and Society in Classical Greek Literature*. Chicago and London: University of Chicago Press.
Zeitlin, F. I. 2010. "The Lady Vanishes: Helen and Her Phantom in Euripidean Drama." In *Allusions, Authority, and Truth: Critical Perspectives on Greek Poetics and Rhetorical Praxis*, eds. P. Mitsis and C. Tsegalis. Berlin/New York: Walter de Gruyter: 263–82.

INDEX

abandonment 212–13, 224, 232, 236, 238–40, 243, 287 n.1
Achelous 193–4, 196, 200
Achilles 6, 10, 11, 26, 50–3, 93–4
   chapter 3 *passim*, 141, 143, 167–74, 269
Admetus 5, 11
   chapter 7 *passim*, 250
adultery 9, 17, 20, 23, 25, 37, 39, 42, 45–7, 66, 68, 72, 88, 113, 137, 139, 141, 144–5, 148, 150–4, 158, 69, 193–4, 197, 199, 201, 205
   chapter 9 *passim*, 251–2, 254, 256, 260, 263, 272, 280 n.6, 284 n.22
Aegeus 12
   chapter 9 *passim*, 247
Aegisthus 9, 15
   chapters 1, 2 *passim*
Aelian 59
   Varia Historia ii.8: 140
   On Animals 7.39: 116
Aeschylus 1–2, 9, 18, 21, 28–30, 33, 35, 3–39, 44–5, 49; 51, 55, 59–62, 65, 80–1, 84, 96–7, 140, 179, 210, 267–9, 274, 281 n.1
   Agamemnon chapter 1 *passim*, 110, 204, 262; lines 11: 18, 49, 89; 154–5, 205–58, 231–43: 96; 267: 21; 269: 22; 270–80: 62; 317–51, 483–7, 591–6: 22, 62; 606–12: 24, 51–2, 278 n.16; 793–8: 25; 800: 113; 841–5: 25, 36; 851–7: 25; 855–974: 21, 24–7, 197, 285 n.41; 1035: 28, 82, 278 n.31; 1039: 278 n.31; 1049: 278 n.31; 1053–4: 278 n.31: 1059: 82, 278 n.31; 1070–1: 278 n.31; 1072: 28; 1102–46: 29, 82; 1126–9: 29; 1261–3:29; 1280–1: 29; 1372–86: 29; 1401–6: 29, 35; 1417–18: 41, 215; 1422–4: 279 n.45; 1435–7: 31; 1440–8: 23, 31; 1462–9: 279 nn.35, 37; 1475–80: 279 n.35; 1481–8: 279 n.37; 1497–504: 31, 279 n.35; 1505–12: 279 n.37; 1521–9: 279 n.35; 1567–76: 31, 279 n.35; 1580–1: 31; 1625–6: 31, 32, 36; 1636: 32, 37; 1661: 32; 1672–3: 32
   Libation Bearers 16, 33–40, 42, 62–3, 65, 107; lines 6–7: 69; 168–210: 54; 279 n.41; 190–1: 279 n.41; 240–1: 279 n.41; 385: 279 n.41; 430–3: 279 n.42; 439–42: 279 n.42; 444–9: 279 n.42; 492: 35; 514–39: 36, 279 n.41; 626–30: 36; 667–8: 35; 672–3: 35–6; 696–7: 36; 707–16: 35–6; 735–41: 35; 749–65: 35;
764–5: 35; 844–6: 37; 850: 35; 885–930: 33, 36–7, 280 n.6; 896–9: 239; 920: 37; 924: 75; 928–9: 36
   Eumenides 16–17, 20, 33–40, 43, 47, 54, 95; lines 736: 38; 246–7: 75
   Seven against Thebes 120–1: lines 1037–8: 132
Agamemnon see Aeschylus
Agamemnon 1, 5–6, 9, 11
   chapters 1, 2, 3 *passim*, 141, 143, 147, 154, 160, 170–1, 173–5, 197, 204, 215, 262, 268–9
age chapter 8 *passim*, 210, 249, 267–8, 274
agon see Formal Debate
aidos see shame
Ajax see Sophocles
Ajax 124, 197, 222, 285 n.41, 286 n.8
Alcestis 1, 4, 5, 8, 11
   chapter 7 *passim*, 250, 255, 268, 270–1, 274
Alexandros see Paris
Amazon 247, 260
ambiguity 23, 26, 104, 114, 139, 156, 180–1,186, 202, 239, 252–3, 287 n.8
Andromache 5, 141–2
anger 98–9, 101, 110, 150, 159, 173, 175, 185–6, 194, 199–200, 221, 223, 226, 249, 270, 286 n.6
Antigone see Sophocles
Antigone 1, 4, 7–8, 10, 69–70, 75
   chapter 4 *passim*, 196, 206, 267, 270–1, 273–5
anxiety 194, 196, 198, 201, 203, 205, 235–6, 239
apathy 97, 99, 223
Aphrodite 1, 11, 93, 137, 147, 149, 151–2, 164, 209, 211, 216, 222, 242
   chapter 11 *passim*, 270
Apollo 11–12, 19, 20, 29, 34, 38–9, 41, 43, 54–5, 63, 68, 75, 82–4, 95, 107, 160–1, 167–8
   chapters 7, 10 *passim*, 271, 285 n.35
Apollodorus *Library* 3.14.6: 231
Areopagus 19, 34, 39–40, 55
Ariadne 247, 259
Argos 17, 28, 36, 39, 51–2, 59, 68, 74, 76, 78, 83–5, 94, 96, 99–109, 111, 116, 120, 142, 149, 159–60, 162–3
Aristophanes 249
   scholion on *Birds* 842: 140
   Clouds 1079–82: 284 n.19
   Frogs 1043: 252

Index

Aristotle 5–6, 22, 74, 148, 150, 284 n.10
    Poetics 1450a 9–25: 7; 1454a26–33: 112; 1461b19–21: 287 n.9
    Nicomachean Ethics viii.8.28–33
    Rhetoric 1355b-56a: 148; 1356b: 22; 1418b5–22: 149; 1453b: 286 n.14; 1454b: 286 n.14
Artemis 41, 50–1, 53, 59, 68, 93–4
    chapter 3 *passim*, 248–9, 251, 255–6, 268, 270–1, 278 nn.1, 24
aside 174, 205, 285 n.7, 287 n.10
Astyanax 141, 143, 148, 167–8
asylum 211, 220
Athena 20, 33–4, 38–40, 55, 95–6, 107, 141, 143, 147, 149, 151, 164, 231–2, 234, 244, 284 n.24
Athens/Athenians 12, 19, 23, 34, 38–9, 50, 55, 60, 69, 74, 84, 95, 107, 109, 113, 116, 122, 139, 140–2, 144–6, 149, 151, 165, 181, 210–12, 219–20, 226, 231–4, 236, 240–1, 244, 247–8, 267
Atreus 8–9, 15–17, 30, 81, 84, 96, 100, 104, 107, 119, 268, 280 n.5
Attica 107, 231
audience 1–3, 8, 13, 21, 26–8, 31–3, 35, 37–8, 40, 42–3, 45–8, 51, 59, 64, 66, 73, 77–9, 96, 98–9, 102, 104–6, 108, 111–14, 117, 130–1, 134, 140, 143–5, 148, 151, 153–4, 157, 160–3, 167, 173, 176, 182–4, 186–8, 196, 199, 202, 211, 213–17, 220–1, 223–4, 226–7, 234–6, 245, 249–50, 252, 254–5, 260, 262, 264, 267–8, 270, 274, 277 n.6, 280 n.5, 284 nn.18, 23, 24, 285 n.43, 287 n.1, 288 n.7, 289 n.2
Aulis 10, 16, 41, 50–1, 60, 93–117 *passim*, 271
Aulus Gellius *Attic Nights* 6.5: 74
autochthony 231, 233, 235–6, 243–4, 271, 274, 288 n.6

barbarian *see* foreigner
beauty 137–9, 147–52, 158, 163–5, 194, 198–200, 204, 206, 254, 273, 283 n.7, 285 n.43
betrayal 9, 111–12, 126, 188, 210, 213, 222, 240, 242
    see also treachery
bravery *see* courage
brother *see* siblings
burial 63, 66, 70, 74, 80, 84–5, 87, 105, 116
    chapter 4 *passim*, 141, 143, 152, 156–7, 160–1, 167–8, 170–1, 173–5, 180, 182, 187–8, 195, 227, 238, 267, 269–70, 273, 275

Calchas 50, 99, 101, 103, 105, 109, 115
calumny 249, 250, 252–3, 263–4
Cassandra 9, 17–33, 38–9, 47, 55, 141–3, 147, 167–8, 170–1, 174–5, 204, 262, 268, 278–9 n.32; 284 n.25
Castor *see* Dioscuri
Centaur 193–5, 202, 287 n.7

change of mind 53, 95, 98, 110–12, 123, 133–4, 144–5, 150, 172, 179–82, 187, 204, 216, 261, 268, 270, 273, 281 n.10
chariot race 30, 41, 59, 65, 107, 119, 126, 187
Charon 183, 189
chastity 248, 250, 255, 258–9, 261, 263–4
child exposure 232–40, 243, 271
childlessness 1, 39, 56, 75, 119, 175–6, 211, 219–20, 222, 225, 232–5, 238–41
children 2, 9, 11–13, 16–17, 19, 33, 35–7, 41–8, 50, 52–3, 55–6, 68, 81–2, 85, 103, 111, 114, 116, 119, 122–3, 131–4, 139, 141, 143–4, 148, 151, 160–2, 168, 170–4, 176, 179–80, 182–3, 186, 194, 196–7, 200, 204, 209–11 (and stepchildren), 213–14, 216–17, 220, 222–5, 227, 232, 234, 237, 240–2, 268–9, 271–2, 274, 284 n.23, 286 n.4
Children of Heracles see Euripides
Chorus 283 n.8;
    Aeschylus: *Agamemnon* 5, 18–33 *passim*, 36, 51, 53, 279 n.35; *Libation Bearers* 33–7, 61, 63–5; *Seven Against Thebes* 120
    Sophocles: *Electra* 40, 43, 66, 68–9, 75, 280 n.2
    Euripides: *Alcestis* 11, 180, 182–3, 185, 187, 189; *Electra* 45, 61, 67–9, 72, 76, 79, 81, 281 n.11; *Hecuba* 170–217; *Helen* 152, 156, 162; *Hippolytus* 253, 255, 256, 260, 261, 262, 263; *Ion* 232, 236, 240, 241, 244–5; *Iphigenia among the Taurians* 100, 102, 105, 108; *Iphigenia at Aulis* 115; *Medea* 12, 210, 214–19, 221–2, 225–6; *Orestes* 85, 87, 163; *Trojan Women* 141, 143, 147, 168
    Sophocles: *Antigone* 123, 125, 127, 130, 131–4, 273, 282 n.2; *Oedipus at Colonus* 121–2; *Women of Trachis* 194–5, 200–4
chronology 16–17, 54, 94, 98–9, 111, 117, 281 n.2
Chrysothemis 15, 41–3, 55, 62, 65–6, 69–73, 75, 93, 131
Cilissa 34–5, 37
circumlocution *see* periphrasis
clothes 78, 145, 148, 150, 152, 155, 161, 169, 172, 174, 182, 188, 193–5, 202–5, 212, 214, 272
Clytemnestra 1, 3, 5–6, 8–9
    chapters 1, 2, 3 *passim*, 124–5, 137, 139, 159–61, 173, 175, 197, 200, 204, 215, 253, 256, 268–71, 273–5, 284 n.22
Colchis 209–10, 213, 215, 221, 223, 227
compliance *see* obedience
complicity 87–8, 137, 174, 232, 260, 269
compromise 10, 31, 66–8, 125, 196
concubine 25–6, 28–9, 39, 46–7, 168, 174, 193–5, 198–200, 202–3, 268
convincing *see* persuasion
Corinth 12
    chapter 9 *passim*

Index

courage 2–3, 10, 28–9, 31, 33, 36–7, 44, 69–72, 95, 112, 113, 124, 128, 129, 147, 151, 156, 158, 162, 170, 173, 180, 182, 187, 204, 218
cowardice 9; 31, 32, 36, 52, 70, 79, 90, 126, 182, 187, 273, 282 n.9
Creon
    Euripides' *Medea* 5, 12; chapter 9 *passim*; *Phoenician Women* 121
    Sophocles' *Antigone* 8, 10; chapter 4 *passim*, 273
Creusa 1, 8, 12
    chapter 10 *passim*, 268, 271–2, 274
cruelty 9, 16, 44, 46, 51, 55, 72, 86, 87, 89–90, 97, 99–100, 102–4, 111, 113, 117, 135, 143, 173–5, 197, 217, 226, 233
culpability *see* responsibility
cunning *see* deceit
curse 15, 19, 20, 30, 59, 86, 89, 119–22, 132, 164, 195, 210, 224, 242, 260–1, 268
Cyclops/Cyclopes 179–81

daimon 15, 29–31, 32
dance 28, 278–9 n.32
death/Death chapter 7 *passim*, 196, 201–4, 206, 215, 218, 231, 236, 238–9, 242, 244, 250–5, 257, 262, 267, 269–71, 273–5, 287 n.7
deceit 4–5, 6, 11–12, 17–18, 20, 41, 50–2, 62, 65, 93, 96–7, 99, 101, 107–10, 150, 154, 158, 168, 174, 205–6, 212–14, 217–20, 225–6, 233, 238, 245, 251, 267, 269, 272, 280 n.4
defiance 4, 6, 10, 29, 33, 55, 73, 121–2, 124, 129, 131–2, 181, 206, 233, 235–8, 269, 272–4, 288 n.8
Deianeira 1, 3–9, 12
    chapter 8 *passim*, 244, 256, 268, 270–3
Deiphobus 143; 147, 151, 161
delirium 254–5, 257, 260, 289 n.12
Delphi 34, 63, 119, 232, 238, 240, 243–4, 271, 288 nn.9, 11
Demosthenes, Ps. 43.62: 63
deus ex machina 83, 153, 163, 165, 226, 232, 245
diffidence chapter 8 *passim*, 235
Diomedes (Homeric) 180, 187
Dioscuri 15–16, 46, 83, 109, 143, 153, 158, 253, 163, 269, 271, 284 n.26
dirge *see* lament
'disease' *see* sexual desire
disingenuity 77–8, 220
disobedience *see* obedience
double-entendre 21, 24, 26, 109, 113
dragon-drawn chariot 211, 270, 275
dream 10, 26, 34, 36, 41, 43, 55, 63–5, 97–100, 102, 105, 170, 173, 176
duality 11, 52, 138, 152–4, 156, 160, 164–5, 235, 252, 254
duplicity 26, 51, 87, 108, 217
    see also deceit

egocentricity 4
    chapter 7 *passim*, 205, 223, 271–3
Egypt 10
    chapter 5 *passim*
eidolon see phantom
Electra see Euripides, Sophocles
Electra 1
    Aeschylus' *Libation Bearers* 16, 33–4, 67
    Sophocles' and Euripides' *Electra*s 4–5, 8, 9, 16, 40–5 *passim*; chapter 2 *passim*, 59, 62, 107,124, 131, 156, 196, 206, 268–70, 273, 275; *Orestes* 62, 159–65 *passim*
Erechtheus 12, 231, 236, 240, 245
Erichthonius 231, 233, 236, 244
Erinyes *see* Furies
Eros/*eros* 199–200, 209, 256–8, 260
    see also lust
Eteocles 119–23, 128, 131, 282 n.2
Euboea 194, 197, 232
Eumenides see Aeschylus
Euripides 1–2, 9, 12, 45–9, 51, 53–5, 60, 62, 64, 77, 79–80, 83, 86–7, 89, 94, 97, 100–3, 105–6, 108–9, 111, 113–14, 117, 138, 144–6, 148, 149–51, 153–4, 156–8, 160, 162–5, 167, 169, 173–6, 179–80, 184, 211–13, 218, 221, 228, 231, 233, 236, 241, 245, 249–50, 253, 255, 264, 267–8, 272, 274, 281 n.1, 282 n.14, 283 nn.4, 8; 286 n.4, 289 n.11
    Alcestis 11, 245; lines 1–84: 182, 285 n.35; 150–1: 131, 182, 183; 177–9: 182; 181–2: 184, 185; 200–79: 182, 183; 280–327: 184, 185, 186, 255; 306: 186; 348–54: 286 n.6; 371–3: 185; 391: 186; 418: 182; 442: 182; 445–54: 131, 186; 460: 182; 463–6: 185; 471–6: 189; 532–3: 186; 614–738: 184, 186, 188; 940: 186; 955–7: 187; 995–1069: 187; 1008–18: 186; 1024: 188; 1052: 188; 1061–3: 188
    Children of Heracles 116
    Electra 6, 45, 52–3, 55, 59, 60, 62, 76, 85, 87, 90, 96, 107, 110, 228, 268; lines 27–30: 46; 32–3: 36; 58–9: 77; 60–3: 46, 77; 74–5: 77; 86–9: 47; 90–7: 36, 47, 69; 112–74: 77, 78, 281 n.11; 215–27: 156; 185–9: 78; 191–7: 78; 200: 78; 208–12: 78; 216–19: 79; 229: 81; 274–83: 79, 80, 281 n.11; 281: 46; 300–38: 77, 78, 281 n.11; 345: 81: 431:79; 508–46: 54, 64, 80; 641–3: 47; 647: 46, 80; 650–60: 47, 81; 699–746: 81, 281 n.11; 767: 81; 876–9: 281 n.11; 957–8: 281 n.11; 970–88: 281 n.11, 47; 1035–48: 48; 1071: 86; 1102–10: 48, 49, 52; 1114–15: 49; 1124–7:47; 1142–64: 55, 281 n.11; 1168–71: 281 n.11; 1182–4: 62; 1190–7: 82; 1224–5: 62; 1244–9: 62, 83; 1284–7: 62, 83; 1322: 81
    Erechtheus 236

Index

Hecuba 6, 11, 115–16, 140, 268, 269; lines 59–67: 171; 120–2: 174; 251–95: 171, 172; 285–95: 172; 334–41: 172; 357–8: 172: 172; 511–628: 167, 172 173, 671–82: 173; 702–51: 173, 174; 787–845: 174; 864–85: 174; 1018–22: 174;1109–292: 283 n.15; 1150–73: 175; 1259–73: 175; 1275–81: 167; 1287–8: 167

Helen 5, 10–11, 138, 245; chapter 5 *passim*, 181; lines 19–20: 160; 55–9: 160; 71–125: 160, 161, 284 n.24; 211: 143; 235: 143; 250: 284 n.22; 279–91: 147, 156, 288 n.7, 147; 301–2: 158; 353: 261; 357: 143; 372–99: 143; 413–17: 147;423–7: 155; 436: 261; 500–9: 156; 541–54: 156; 618–19: 158; 663: 161; 721–4: 147; 767–79: 144; 778–83: 156, 157; 791: 157; 830: 157; 840–59: 147; 862–70: 144, 284 n.22; 873–94: 144; 919–65: 147, 148; 932–7: 148, 959–86: 149; 998–1028: 149; 1029–32:150; 1036–41:148; 150; 1049: 157; 1073: 157; 1105: 161; 1666–9: 158

Hippolytus 12–13, 184, 264, 265; lines: 29–32: 252; 131– 60: 255; 176–266: 253, 254, 255, 257; 203–4: 254; 218–19: 289 n14; 228–31: 289 n.11; 304–19: 258, 262; 329–43: 259; 345–52: 260; 362–72: 263; 373–430: 252, 260; 490–8: 261; 500–74: 261, 262, 290 n.16; 590–7: 263; 612: 263; 618–24: 223; 656: 290 n.18; 661–2: 263; 669–79: 289 n.6, 290 n.19; 706–9: 263

Hippolytus Veiled 13, 250, 261, 264

Ion 12, 181, 231; lines: 8–20: 234, 236, 237, 288 n.6; 45–55: 234; 57–64: 236, 288 n.6; 67–81: 231, 240, 288 n.6; 71–3: 288 n.5; 136–40: 237; 184: 188 n.6; 237–46: 236; 252–7: 237, 239; 260–82: 239, 240, 288 n.6; 286: 237; 298: 236; 306: 239; 318–20: 239, 240; 330–4: 239; 345–58: 234, 237, 239, 243; 366–80: 237; 384–97: 238, 240; 398–400: 237; 410–12: 238; 425–8: 237; 436–51: 237; 530–9: 240; 568: 288 n.6; 589–92: 288 n.6; 657–8: 241; 671–2: 288 n.6; 719–34: 238, 241, 288 n.6; 736–7: 288 n.6; 761–7: 239, 240; 774–88: 245; 796–858: 241, 240, 241, 288 n.6; 859–922: 234, 239, 240, 242, 243; 949: 234, 288 n.5; 955: 234; 962–3: 239, 240; 987–1017: 288 n.6; 1027–83: 244; 1058–73: 244, 288 n.6; 1069–73: 288 n.6; 1106: 288 n.6; 1220: 288 n.6; 1253–60: 244; 1297–9: 288 n.6; 1416–39: 235, 239;1454–67: 239, 240, 245; 1484: 239, 240; 1492–3: 239; 1523–31: 289 n.11; 1542–3: 240; 1534–6: 245; 1596: 234

Iphigenia among the Taurians 10; chapter 3 *passim*, 157, 181, 245, 289 n.11; lines 4–9: 96, 101; 123–202: 100; 221–8: 100; 344–91: 100, 101, 102, 103, 281 n.4; 456–66: 102; 515–37: 103; 540–53: 104; 565–67: 105; 575–6: 105; 784–5: 101; 816–18: 100; 926: 104; 976–86: 107; 1023: 107; 1031–2: 108; 1115–21: 172; 1187: 107; 1177: 101; 1205: 108; 1298: 108; 1317–18: 112; 1431–4:108

Iphigenia at Aulis 5, 10, 16–17, 49–50, 52, 54–5; chapter 3 *passim*, 171, 173, 268, 269, 281 n.2; lines 27: 281 n.7; 359–60: 281 n.7; 515–16: 281 n.8; 539–41: 50; 564–4: 112; 594: 50; 634: 51; 638–9: 52; 691–2: 51; 718: 51; 725–6: 51; 732: 51; 736: 51; 739–41: 51–2; 917–18: 53; 1012: 52; 1024: 52; 1141: 53; 1148–52: 53; 1157–64: 52, 53; 1171–6: 53; 1180–2: 53; 1211: 111; 1219–52: 113; 1279–335:112;1345–68: 112; 1383–94: 113, 114; 1398–9: 114; 1456: 115; 1475–6: 115; 1510–12: 114, 115; 1540–612; 53; 1615–18; 53

Medea 12, 210; lines 8: 224; 11–15: 215; 20–3: 218, 222, 287 n.12; 27: 287 n.12; 36–43: 214, 224; 112–14: 224; 146–7: 215; 155–9: 215; 166–7: 216; 214: 214; 219–21: 279 n.58; 222: 214; 225–9: 215; 232–3: 215; 241–2: 215; 248–51: 215; 250–1: 218; 252–8: 216; 260–8: 214; 264: 211; 292–305: 279 n.58; 306–8: 217; 329: 217; 340–5: 217, 224; 383: 218; 386: 217; 401–25: 218, 219, 222; 439: 222; 452: 221, 222; 460: 221; 447: 221; 459–64: 220, 224; 490–8: 22, 224; 506–15: 222, 225; 526–8: 216; 550: 220; 562–7: 220, 224; 620–2: 224; 721–2: 220; 782–3: 220; 791–2: 221, 287 n.10; 795–7: 218, 225; 809: 221; 817: 225; 880–9: 224; 914–21: 224; 1049: 218; 1355: 218; 1352–414: 218, 219

Orestes 9, 11, 59, 83–5, 87, 89–90, 138, 181, 268, 271, 275; lines 1–315: 85, 86, 87, 89, 289n.12; 385: 86; 615–21: 88; 787–9: 88; 844–1352: 85, 86, 87, 88; 1126–70: 85, 162; 1204–6: 89; 1207–10: 89; 1235: 88; 1238–9: 220; 1242–50: 225; 1301–5: 162, 226; 1369–70: 162; 1395–473: 162; 1427–30:162; 1467–8: 162; 1658–9: 89

Phoenician Women 121; lines 446–637: 283 n.15

Rhesus 115, 282 n.14; lines 898–9: 115; 934–5: 115

*Trojan Women*10–11, 115; chapters 5, 6 *passim*, 271; lines 481–3: 167; 924–33: 222; 1007: 169; 1029–32: 169; 1123–250: 167

Erechtheus see Euripides
Eurydice 123, 270–1, 273, 275
Eurystheus 30, 179, 192, 193
evasiveness 103–4
exile 41–2, 44, 46, 65, 73, 77, 81–2, 84, 86, 88, 119, 121–2, 160, 175, 210, 214, 217, 219, 222, 224–5, 250, 264, 288 n.10
expediency 223–4, 227

Index

explicit *see* implicit/explicit
extreme behavior/passion 79, 81, 156, 212, 215, 223, 227–8, 269

faithfulness *see* loyalty
fame 71, 95, 110, 112–13, 115, 116, 126, 131, 150–1, 153, 156, 169, 172, 182, 185–6, 203, 219, 223, 262–3, 274
family 1, 12, 19, 24, 30–5, 38, 60–1, 64, 77, 84–6, 88–9, 98–105, 107, 111, 125, 127, 129, 131–3, 143, 161, 167, 171, 175–6, 186, 205, 216–17, 221–3, 227, 233, 259, 268, 273
  see also parents, siblings
father *see* parents, 272
fear 11–12, 26–7, 30, 36, 41, 43, 46, 49, 62, 65, 74, 85, 88, 99, 120, 130–1, 134, 139, 144, 147, 149, 161, 169, 174, 182, 185, 194–8, 200, 203–6, 211, 213, 217–18, 220, 225, 228, 239–40, 249, 251, 260–1
femaleness 2–6, 9, 11–12, 17–18, 20–7, 29–31, 32–3, 35–7, 39, 44, 48, 51–2, 55, 61–2, 71, 74–5, 81, 86–9, 95, 100, 108–9, 113–14, 131–2, 139, 151, 153, 157, 162, 167, 173–5, 179, 181, 187–8, 195, 200; 204–6, 212, 214–16, 219, 221–4, 233, 238, 240–1, 249, 254–5, 262, 267, 269, 272–4, 277 n.4, 279, n.35
femininity *see* femaleness
fidelity *see* loyalty
filicide 2, 211–12, 214, 219–21, 224–5, 227, 269, 275, 287 n.3
foreigner 1, 7, 12, 100, 137, 212–14, 216–17, 219, 223, 227, 232, 238, 241, 269, 271
  see also strangers, hospitality
formal debate 6, 40, 42, 43, 45, 47–9, 55, 65, 73, 82, 141, 145, 165, 169, 180, 271, 283 nn.11, 13, 15
fratricide *see* kindred bloodshed
free-will (or lack thereof) 143, 147–51, 169, 172, 181, 185, 216, 239, 242, 251–2, 261, 268, 270
Furies 17, 30, 34, 37, 38–9, 55, 62–3, 83–4, 95, 108, 122, 159

gender 3–4, 18, 20–2, 32–3, 39, 48, 61–2, 87–90, 105, 114, 125, 139, 216, 243, 245, 254, 267, 272, 275
gift 194–5, 202, 204, 209, 211, 225, 232, 245
glory *see* fame
gods 1, 12–13, 24–6, 39, 41, 43, 53, 78, 83–4, 86, 98–100, 102, 108, 117, 123–4, 130, 132–3, 137–9, 147, 149–51, 155, 163–4, 169, 176, 183, 187, 189, 222, 226–8, 233–4, 236–7, 252, 261, 275, 284 n.26
golden fleece 209, 222
Gorgias of Leontini *Encomium of Helen* 137–8, 146–7, 147–8, 153, 283 n.4
gossip 22, 26, 52, 197, 240, 255, 277 n.4, 288 n.11

gratitude 6, 88, 147, 170–2, 185, 187–8, 190, 200, 211–12, 222, 227, 233
greed chapter 6 *passim*, 209
Greek lyric poetry 137, 193, 255, 260
grief 9, 53, 66–9, 73, 78, 85, 104, 112, 115–16, 158, 168, 170, 172–3, 176, 186, 188, 190, 215, 227, 234, 241, 247, 270, 275
grudge 98–101, 184, 189, 194, 243
gullibility 195
  see also obtuseness

Hades 179, 183, 193, 275
Haemon chapter 4 *passim,* 270–1, 273
hair 63–4, 69, 80, 85–8, 99, 158, 161–3, 169, 179, 242, 254, 256–7, 288 n.11
hallucinations 85, 159
happy ending 181, 189, 245
hatred 10–11, 31, 43, 47–8, 62, 64, 70–1, 73, 82, 77, 85–6, 88, 90, 98, 101, 105, 107, 115, 131, 143, 148, 152, 160, 162, 185, 209, 213, 217, 227–8, 249, 269–70, 275
Hector 141, 143, 168, 174
Hecuba see Euripides
Hecuba 1, 3, 5–6, 8–11, 19, 116
  chapters 5, 6 *passim*, 268–71, 274–5
Helen see Euripides
Helen 1, 6–8, 10–11, 15–16, 24, 30, 47–8, 60, 62, 84–7, 89, 93, 101–2, 109, 111–12, 114
  chapters 5, 6 *passim*, 222, 256, 268–9, 271–5, 280 n.64, 281 n.10
Helios 211, 218, 219, 226, 228, 270, 288 n.14
helplessness 12, 111, 171–3, 175, 195–6, 202–3, 205, 209, 252, 254, 263, 269
Hera 10, 78, 141, 143, 147, 149, 151–2, 164, 193, 209, 227
Heracles 5, 8, 11, 116
  chapters 7, 8 *passim*, 247, 270, 272
Hermes 10, 151, 153–4, 165, 232, 234, 236
Hermione 16, 60, 62, 84–7, 89, 154, 157, 160–3, 269, 272
Herodotus 94, 282 n.12; books 2.115–20: 138; 3.119: 133; 7.94: 231; 7.136: 284 n.29; 8.44.2: 231
Hesiod 94
  Works and Days lines 203–16: 216
  Theogony lines 319: 39; 561–612: 189; 896: 39; 924: 38
  frags. 9 (M–W); 23a.13–15 (M–W): 59; 23a.12–18 (M–W): 94; 23b (M–W): 109; 25.17–25 (M–W): 193, 204, 231; 358 (M–W): 137
Hippodamia 16, 30, 59, 107
Hippolytus see Euripides
Hippolytus 184, 214, 223
  chapter 11 *passim*, 271, 273
Hippolytus Veiled see Euripides

309

Index

Homer 15, 23–4, 59, 64, 93, 101, 108–9, 140, 150, 158, 169, 174, 183, 249, 267
  Iliad 11, 137, 163, 167; lines 2.713–15: 179; 3.154–60: 285 n.44;3.180: 24; 5.284–9: 219; 6.254–62: 167; 6.344: 24; 9.145:15, 93: 59; 9.287: 59; 339: 113; 13; 446–54: 219; 15.331, 430: 277 n.9; 15.430: 277 n.9; 17.557: 177 n.9; 17.589: 177 n.9; 18.235, 460: 177 n.9; 22.85–9: 167; 23.262–5: 187; 23.512–13: 187; 24.201–16: 167, 173; 24.748–59: 167
  Odyssey 17, 64, 137, 150, 154, 157; lines 3.263–75; 4.512–37: 279 n.40; 5.264: 155; 5.313–50: 155; 6.128–9: 155; 9.364–7: 156; 9.507–12: 156; 11.409–10: 277 n.12; 11.421–56: 15, 24, 108; 12.403–25: 155; 14.121–3: 25; 18.259–70: 154; 306–43: 277 n.12
Homeric hero 6, 10, 93, 113–15, 131, 158, 203, 218, 227–8, 268, 273
honor 6,10, 112, 122, 130, 149, 151, 182, 186, 195
hospitality 15, 33, 36–7, 44, 79, 107, 117, 153, 179–81, 184, 189–90, 209
human sacrifice 10, 16–17, 20–1, 23, 25–6, 29, 33, 37, 40–1, 47–53, 55, 60, 62, 64–5, 82, 86
  chapter 3, *passim*, 170–2, 174, 176, 231, 236, 239, 268–9, 271, 278 n.27
humor 88–9, 155–6, 158, 184–8
hybris 200, 216
Hydra of Lerna 194, 196, 205, 286 n.2
Hyllus chapter 8 *passim*
hypothesis 179
hysteria *see* extreme behavior

Iliad see Homer
implausibility 105–7, 146, 149
implication *see* implicit/ explicit
implicit/explicit 101, 125–6, 134–5 144, 148, 153–4, 214, 219
  chapter 11 *passim*, 284 n.21, 289 n.3
improbability *see* implausibility
inaction *see* passivity
indecisiveness 206
  see also helplessness, passivity
instability 79, 81
insult 21, 26, 28, 30–2, 38, 76, 78, 126, 161–2, 171, 220, 224–5, 227, 241, 263
integrity 10, 124–5, 130, 172, 252
intelligence 9, 16, 33, 51, 55, 95, 109, 139, 147, 155, 157–8, 165, 167, 185, 187, 212–13, 216–17, 219, 223–4, 227–8, 238, 243, 252–3, 271, 273, 278 n.25
intransigence 9–10, 44, 66, 70–1, 82, 121, 124, 127, 133, 238, 267
Iolcus 183, 20, 210, 212–13, 222
Iole chapter 8 *passim*
Ion *see* Euripides

Ion 12
  chapter 10 *passim*, 271
Iphianassa 15, 42, 59, 75. 93
Iphigenia 1, 8, 10, 16, 19, 23, 29, 35–7, 40–1, 48–53, 55, 60, 62, 64–5, 82, 86
  chapter 3 *passim*, 137, 172, 215, 268, 271–5, 281 n.4
Iphigenia among the Taurians see Euripides
Iphigenia at Aulis see Euripides
Ismene 69, 75
  chapter 4 *passim*
Isocrates *Panegericus* 131: 284 n.29

Jason 6, 12
  chapter 9 *passim*, 269–70
jealousy 13, 15, 20, 26–7, 150, 200, 204, 217, 227, 274–5, 287 n.9

Kannicht *TrGF* 2004: vol. 5.1: frag. 36: 3; frag, 522: 4; frags vol. 5.1: 41a-63: 140; vol. 5.1: 3; vol. 5.1: frag. 464: 205; frags. 41a-63: 140; vol. 5.2: 52 frags. 578–90: 140; vol. 5.2: 62 frag. 673: 140; vol. 5.1 frag. 481.9–11; 231
kindred bloodshed 34, 38–40, 55, 120–2, 163, 226

lament 35, 41, 44–3, 46, 60–1, 63, 65, 67–8, 70, 74–6, 84–5, 88, 100, 110, 123, 127–8, 132–4, 141, 143–4, 152, 160–2, 167–8, 171, 182, 199, 205, 215, 263, 273
laughing at *see* mocking
Leda 15–16, 26, 137, 163–4
letter 106, 109–10, 249–50, 252, 263
libations 34, 36, 63–4, 68–9, 83, 85, 87, 98, 100, 128, 130, 132, 159, 161–2, 244
Libation Bearers see Aeschylus
Lichas 194, 197–202, 204–6
lie *see* trickery, deceit
logic/illogic *see* rationality/irrationality
love 2, 10, 12, 25, 41, 43, 48, 52, 73–4, 82, 85, 89–90, 94, 98, 102, 105, 108, 111, 124, 144, 157–8, 173, 181–2, 186, 188, 193, 196, 201, 203–5, 212–14, 216, 219, 221, 223–4, 226, 228, 235, 253–4, 258–60, 263, 269, 271, 274–5, 286 n.7, 287 n.7
love charm 193–6, 201–3, 205–6, 209, 261–2, 272
  see also magic
loyalty/fidelity 2, 10, 13, 15, 19, 23–4, 70, 108–9, 125–6, 131–2, 139, 153–4, 158, 212, 233, 240, 282 n.9
lust 42, 147, 149, 150, 170, 174, 188, 205, 223, 227, 284 n.19, 285 n.43

machinations *see* manipulation
madness 85, 88, 107–8, 140, 161, 193, 199, 224, 231, 255, 257

Index

magic 5, 8, 11, 12, 144, 155, 181, 202, 205, 209–13, 217, 269, 272, 278 n.29, 287 n.1
  see also love charm
maleness 2–4, 6, 8–10, 17–18, 20–4, 27, 29, 31, 33, 35, 36, 39, 44, 52, 54, 61, 71, 80, 89, 95, 124, 131–2, 139–40, 151, 172, 176, 18, 204–6, 212, 215, 218–19, 222, 234, 267–8, 272–4, 287 n.12; 289 n.12
manipulation 139, 203, 214–17, 220, 223–5, 241, 250–1, 253, 256, 258–0, 262–4, 269–70, 274
marriage 1–2, 15, 16–17, 19, 23, 25–6, 28–9, 36, 46, 49–54, 62, 66–8, 71, 75–6, 78–80, 83–5, 89, 94, 102, 109–10, 114–17, 119, 123–4, 131–5, 137, 139, 141, 143–5, 148–9, 152–3, 155–8, 160–2, 164, 167–9, 174
  chapters 7, 8, 9, 10, 11 *passim*, 268–71, 274–5
masculinity *see* maleness
matricide 9, 16, 33–4, 37, 40–1, 43–5, 49, 62–3, 65, 71, 75–6, 79–84, 87–90, 96, 104, 108, 123–4, 159–61, 239, 268–9, 273, 275, 280 n.4
Medea see Euripides
Medea 1, 3, 5–8, 12, 124–5, 131
  chapter 9 *passim*, 247, 253, 270, 274–5
men *see* maleness
Menelaus 5, 10–11, 15–16, 41, 48, 50, 53, 83–7, 89, 93, 100–2, 110–12, 115
  chapters 5, 6 *passim*, 256, 271, 273
meter 66, 74, 133, 183–4, 223, 278–9 n.32
misogyny 114, 117, 175–6, 248, 262–3
mockery 35, 54, 73–4, 80, 132, 149, 157, 218, 227–8, 237
mother *see* motherhood, parents
mother–daughter relationship 9, 36, 42–4, 47–8, 55, 61, 64–5, 72–3, 81–2, 94, 98, 115, 171, 185, 273–4
motherhood 1, 9, 12, 16–17, 25, 32–3, 35–9, 41–50, 52–3, 55, 94, 115–16, 154, 167–8, 170–1, 173, 175–6, 180, 182, 185–6, 221, 224, 226, 228, 232, 234–5, 238–40, 268–9, 271, 285 n.3
mourning *see* lament
Mycenae 15, 30, 76, 85, 107
Motherliness *see* motherhood

naïveté 117, 198, 200–2, 253, 277 nn.4, 40
Neoptolemus 116, 141, 143, 170
Nessus 12, 193–4, 196, 200–3, 205–6, 287n n.7, 8
news 21–2, 25, 34–5, 37, 43, 46, 76, 79, 81, 86, 96, 100, 103–4, 108, 112–13, 122–3, 143–4, 194, 197–8, 238, 240–1, 245, 253, 261
nightmare *see* dream
nosos see sexual desire
Nurse chapters 8, 9, 11 *passim*

oath 12, 212, 218–20, 222, 227, 263, 287 n.12, 288 n.14

obedience 96–9, 117, 125, 129, 131–2, 134, 196, 200, 262, 274
obstinacy *see* intransigence
obtuseness 253, 255–7, 259, 262, 270
Odysseus 5, 15, 24, 93, 97, 99, 101, 103, 105, 108, 115, 140–1, 143–4, 147, 154–6, 168, 285 n.5
Oechalia 193, 197
Oedipus chapter 4 *passim* 286 n.8
Oenomaus 16, 30, 59
oracle 34, 41, 65, 116, 119, 122, 195, 197, 203, 232, 234, 238, 239–40, 243, 245
orchestra 21, 134
Oresteia chapter 1 *passim*
Orestes 9–10, 15–17, 19, 33–4, 36–8, 41–2, 44–9, 52, 55
  chapters 2, 3 *passim*, 156–65 *passim*, 268, 271, 274
orphans 183–4
otherness 1, 212–14
  see also foreigner
oxymoron 143, 215

Palamedes 5, 140
parents 11, 33–4, 38, 40–1, 44, 61, 65–8, 70, 72, 74–5, 78–9, 81–2, 84, 86, 88, 90, 93, 96, 1012, 104–6, 110–15, 122, 129, 132–4, 139, 141, 144, 151–2, 155, 160, 162, 170, 172, 179–80, 184–6, 194, 199, 203, 209–10, 216–18, 220, 224–5, 232, 234–5, 237, 250, 270
Paris 15–16, 93, 98, 111–12
  chapter 5 *passim*, 167, 169, 196, 256, 271
parrhesia 48, 250
Pasiphae 247, 259
passion *see* lust
passivity (or lack thereof) 195–6, 201, 206, 243, 249, 252, 261, 270
pathos 148, 150
Pausanias 94, 109; 22.3.10–11: 211;10.2.7.2:167
Pelias 179, 209–10, 217, 222
Pelops 16, 30, 59, 86, 107, 119
Penelope 153–4, 156, 158, 285 n.40
performance 23, 73–4, 104
periphrasis 103–4
persuasion 27, 148–50, 172, 180–1, 187–8, 212, 244, 271
Phaedra 1, 5, 8, 12–13, 125, 214
  chapter 11 *passim*, 268, 270–3
phantom 138, 152–3, 156, 163–4, 271
Pherae 179, 187
Pheres 179–80, 188, 209, 250
philia 23–4, 258–60, 262
Philoctetes see Sophocles
Philoctetes 4, 5, 124, 286 n.8
Phocis 34, 41, 46, 62–3, 65, 76, 83–4, 119
Phoenician Women see Euripides
Phrynichus 179, 282

311

Index

plausibility *see* implausibility
Plautus *Amphitruo* 155, 159
Plato *Euthydemus* 302d: 231
Plutarch 264; *Moralia* 52C, 959B: 291 n.14; Solon 21: 63;
Poison 4, 5, 8, 12, 193–203, 205, 212–14, 218–19, 232–3, 241, 244
pollution 96, 107, 119, 123, 134, 209, 254, 258, 264
Pollux *see* Dioscuri
Polydeuces *see* Dioscuri
Polydorus 168, 170–1, 173–5, 269, 285 n.3
Polymestor 6, 11
    chapters 5, 6 *passim*, 269, 274
Polyneices 119–23, 125–34
Polyxena 11, 110, 141, 143, 168, 170–5, 269, 285 n.3
Poseidon 141–3, 155, 164, 168, 209, 231, 247, 284 n.24
post-traumatic stress disorder (PTSD) 97–8
potions *see* magic
powerlessness *see* helplessness
prayer 27, 43, 63–4, 69, 75, 107, 183, 226, 238
prejudice 47, 279 n.58
Priam 11, 15, 19, 93, 141, 147–8, 163, 167–8, 170, 268, 284 nn.18, 23
pro-satyric 180, 189
promise 6, 10, 12, 30, 59, 105, 107–8, 111, 122–3, 145, 149, 180–5, 188–9, 195, 202, 204, 209, 211, 219–20, 263, 274, 284 n.24, 286 nn.6, 11
propriety 47, 79, 81, 86, 116, 170, 179, 182–3, 188, 223, 225–55
Proteus 151, 156
Pylades 10, 34, 36, 41, 46, 62–3, 65, 75–6, 79, 81, 83–9, 95–7, 102–3, 105, 107–8, 159–65 *passim*, 271, 274

rage *see* anger
rape 119, 188, 196, 205, 231, 233–5, 237–40, 242–3, 249–50, 270–1, 284 n.24, 288 n.11
rationality/irrationality 67, 74, 80, 100–1, 129, 133, 146–7, 150, 169, 183, 189, 203, 218, 257
reality *see* realism
realism (and lack thereof) 71, 74–5, 79–80, 82, 90, 157–8, 180–6, 198–9, 200, 203–5, 212–13, 267
rebelliousness *see* defiance
recognition 41, 54, 63, 65, 73–4, 76, 78–82, 96, 103, 106, 108, 153–4, 156–7, 180, 187–8, 224, 231–6, 243–5, 267, 271, 274
regret *see* remorse
remorse 9, 16, 25, 45, 49, 55, 62, 76, 81–2, 86–7, 132–3, 165, 169, 185, 272
reputation *see* fame
resourcefulness 5, 10, 154, 157, 165, 213, 257
respect 6, 46, 67–8, 73, 76, 78, 80, 119, 130, 134, 164, 259, 263

responsibility 10, 29–33, 35, 37, 44, 47–9, 55, 123, 125, 132, 135, 137–8, 140–3, 151, 154, 160, 165, 168–9, 181, 216, 221–2, 235, 259–62
revenge 2, 5–6, 9, 12, 15, 17, 21, 23, 28, 32–3, 35, 36, 38, 40, 42–4, 46, 48–0, 54–5, 59–64, 66–8, 71, 74–6, 78, 83–4, 86–8, 90, 99–101, 104, 107, 114; 124, 131, 143–4, 146–7, 148, 150, 160–2, 168, 170–1, 173–6, 184, 186, 210–14, 216–20, 224–8, 239, 241, 243, 251, 267–9, 270, 273–5, 280 nn.2, 4, 286 n.11, 287 n.13
reverence *see* respect
Rhesus see Euripides
Rhesus 115–16
rhetoric 2, 3, 5–6, 9, 11, 13, 19–20, 22, 24, 28–9, 33, 37, 42, 51–2, 55, 88, 125, 129, 137–8, 141, 144–9, 167–9, 172–3, 175–6, 184, 206, 212–13, 215, 217, 222–3, 238, 250–1, 253, 264, 269, 272–4, 284 n.26, 285 n.4
robe *see* clothes
rumor 25, 86, 152, 159, 277 n.4
ruse *see* deceit

sarcasm 102–3, 149, 159, 200, 222, 224
satyr play 180–1
savagery *see* cruelty
secrecy 194, 203, 214–15, 220, 232, 234–5, 237, 239–40, 242–5, 252–3, 258–60, 262–3, 271
self-sacrifice chapter 7 *passim*, 249
Semonidean Bee Woman 11, 52, 54
Seneca 265; *Phaedra* 646–58: 256
Seven against Thebes see Aeschylus
sexual desire 11–13, 42, 44, 54, 205, 249, 251–62, 263–4, 270–1, 289 n.10
    see also eros
shame 7, 46, 85, 90, 160–1, 195, 202, 204, 218–19, 227, 234, 237–40, 250, 252, 257, 260, 262–3, 270, 278 n.14
siblings 1, 10, 26, 60, 63–5, 70–6, 79–81, 83–7, 90, 95–108, 110
    chapter 4 *passim*, 152, 160–1, 162, 231, 236, 267, 270–1, 273, 275, 282 nn.1, 2, 288 n.7
silence 28, 43, 66, 75, 80, 131, 180, 186–7, 189, 204, 221, 237, 241–2, 262
sincerity chapter 9 *passim*
sister *see* siblings
Snell *TrGF* 1986: vol. 1: T 3.1: 178; vol. 1: F 3 and apparatus: 179
song 28, 31, 74–5, 100, 102, 111, 115, 121, 123, 132–3, 168, 173, 179, 182–3, 226, 232, 242–4, 278 n.32
Sophists 146–7, 253, 284 nn.19, 26
Sophocles 1–2, 9, 40, 42, 44–5, 47, 49, 60–2, 65, 68, 76, 81, 84, 86–8, 97,120, 125, 127, 131, 134–5, 179, 193, 196, 198, 201–2, 204, 206, 210, 235, 267–9, 286 n.8, 280 n.4, 282 n.12
    Ajax 196

Index

Antigone 10; chapter 4 *passim*; lines 1–6: 132; 7–8: 12, 130; 10: 131; 13: 127; 18–19 282 n.4; 21–2: 127; 32–4: 129, 282 n.4; 39–99: 70, 125, 127, 128, 129, 130, 131, 134; 46: 281 nn.4, 5; 164–98: 282 nn.4, 5; 220: 130; 250–1: 129; 253–4: 128; 293: 282 n.4; 381–2: 130; 410–12: 134; 423–5: 128; 443–97: 130, 131m 282 nn. 4,5; 447–9: 130; 460–4: 134; 477–98: 132, 282 n.4, 5; 503: 125; 504–8: 130; 523: 131; 532–71: 126, 131, 282 nn.4, 5; 558: 127; 591–6: 282 n.4; 501–57: 282 n,4; 599–600: 127; 655–80: 132, 282 nn.4, 5; 697–8: 134; 726–6: 132, 282 n.4. 283 n.13; 806–90: 132; 839–97: 127, 130, 282 nn.4, 5; 901–42: 127, 282 nn.4, 5; 944–87: 134; 995: 282 n.4; 1035–99: 128, 134, 282 n.4, 5; 1105–8: 282 n.4; 1111: 282 n.5; 1198: 134; 1220–5: 134; 1271–98: 282 nn.4, 5; 1319–43: 282 nn.4

Electra 6. 45–9 *passim*, 55, 60, 65, 90, 96, 107, 110, 268; lines 77–85: 66; 97–9: 40, 71–2, 280 n.6; 103–6: 69; 123: 66; 125–6: 40; 132–3: 69; 140–2: 67; 145–6: 68; 147–52: 68–9; 177–8: 67; 195–7: 40; 205–6: 71; 215–21: 67–8; 223–8: 69; 231–2: 69; 234: 43, 277 n.11; 236–50: 67–8; 256–9: 67–8; 266–81: 62; 271–4: 40, 43, 68; 277–83: 40, 66, 68; 287–98: 40, 72; 291–8: 67, 72; 304: 66; 308–9: 68; 314–15: 69; 331: 69; 335: 70; 338–9: 72; 352–65: 70; 378–82, 387: 67; 420–3: 43; 431–71: 40, 70; 484–5: 40; 492–4: 280 n.6; 516–633: 40–2, 71, 73, 215; 554–5: 48; 561–2: 280 n.6; 582–3: 280 n.4; 587–9: 280 n.6; 603–4: 280 n.4; 618–21: 73; 653–4: 43; 657–8: 43; 391: 70; 739–40: 52; 766–71: 43; 775–8: 44, 288 n.10; 791: 44; 801–943: 133; 800–2: 44; 807: 73; 819: 66; 835–6: 66; 891–928: 69, 133; 921–43: 133; 954–7: 71, 280 n.4; 970–2: 71; 978–85: 71; 996–1008: 62, 71; 1017–20: 71; 1043: 71; 1058–97: 72; 1098–231: 74, 126; 1130: 74; 1145–8: 74; 1153–4: 74; 1170: 74; 1181: 66; 1192: 73; 1196: 73; 1236: 74; 1238: 74; 1251–2: 74; 1257: 74; 1259: 74; 1271–2: 74; 1288–95: 74; 1301–3: 75; 1310: 75; 1405–26: 73, 75; 1430–5: 76; 1451–65: 62; 1483–7: 76

Philoctetes 5

Women of Trachis 11, chapter 8 *passim*; lines 24–5: 196, 199; 29–30: 196; 31–5: 196; 69–75: 197; 84–5: 197; 177: 197, 200, 205; 180–3: 197; 192: 198; 3056: 200; 310–13: 198; 325–7: 198; 351–79: 199; 385–6: 199; 428: 199; 459–60: 199, 200, 205; 523–5: 196, 199; 444: 200; 527–8: 196; 541: 200; 543–60: 200, 201, 205; 572–7: 201; 582–93: 201; 630–2: 205; 667–706: 202; 710–11: 203; 721–2: 203; 729–30: 203; 759–814: 204; 899–931: 204; 1075: 205

sorrow *see* grief
Sparta 15, 137, 143–5, 147, 152–3, 158, 164, 169, 273, 284 n.22
spectators *see* audience
stepmother 180, 185
stepson 12, 250–1, 257, 272
Stesichorus
  Oresteia 59, 64, 108
  Palinode 153–4, 158; frag. 192–3, Page *PMG* 104–6: 137–8; Sack of Troy Fr. 109F: 167;
stichomythia 45, 258, 278 n.26
strangers 97, 101–3, 106–8, 148, 188
  see also foreigners, hospitality
Strophius 25, 84
stubbornness *see* intransigence
submissiveness 181, 195, 201, 206, 233, 268, 272–4
subversiveness 109, 116, 138, 250, 268
suffering 11, 48, 55, 67, 72–4, 78, 81, 84, 117, 129, 137, 141, 143–4. 151, 155, 157, 161, 164, 167–8, 194, 197, 199, 206, 213, 228, 233, 235, 237, 241–3, 25?–3, 258, 271–2, 275
suicide 8, 25, 81, 84–6, 119, 123, 132, 134, 141, 152, 154, 158, 160–1, 182, 195, 204–5, 222, 231, 243, 247, 249–52, 254, 257, 259–61, 264, 270, 272, 288 n.7, 289 n.5
supplication 111–12, 117, 122, 150, 155, 162, 172, 217–19, 239, 259, 289 n.15
suspicion 79, 81, 107, 163, 187–8, 198

Talthybius 141, 143, 147, 167, 170, 172–3
Tantalus 16, 30, 59, 86
tapestries 18, 26–7, 278 n.21
Taurians 10, 93
  chapter 3 *passim*, 27
Tecmessa 196, 222, 285 n.41, 286 n.1
Teiresias 123, 128, 134
Thanatos *see* death/Death
Thebes 119–23, 127, 132, 159 193, 210
Theoclymenus 5, 152–3, 155, 157, 173
Theonoe 152, 173
Theseus 12–13, 109, 137, 184, 193, 210
  chapter 11 *passim*, 271
Thoas 10, 96, 100, 107–8, 117, 272
Thrace 170, 175–6, 180, 231, 285 n.9
Thucidydes 2.45: 113
Thyestes 15–17, 30, 107
tomb *see* burial
Trachis chapter 8 *passim*
transgender 114
  see also gender
treachery 40, 47, 49, 50, 101, 108–10, 173, 243
  see also betrayal
trickery 6, 10–1, 38, 46–7, 49, 55, 70, 81–4, 95, 98, 181, 187, 193, 201, 210, 217–18, 223, 253, 264

313

Index

Trojan War 10, 17, 21, 23–4, 26, 32, 50, 53, 60, 67–8, 97, 103, 110, 112, 114–15, 137–8, 140, 143, 146, 152, 154, 158, 162, 164–5, 168, 179, 268, 281 n.10
Troy 9–11, 15–19, 21–4, 26, 31, 32, 51, 53, 82, 85–6, 93, 110, 115
  chapters 5, 6 *passim*, 270–2
Trojan Women see Euripides
Tyndareus 15–16, 84, 86–9, 137, 152, 160, 162, 164

veil 186–7, 254
vengeance *see* revenge
violence 5–6, 31, 50, 97–8, 134, 165, 168, 173, 176, 199, 211–13, 227, 233, 235, 237, 253
virginity 60, 85–6, 116, 121, 149, 160, 182, 237, 283 n.13
volatility 79, 98, 212–14, 253, 274

war 1, 9, 12, 50, 113–15, 138, 140, 143, 151
wedding *see* marriage
wisdom *see* intelligence
women *see* femininity
Women of Trachis see Sophocles
word & deed 62, 66–7, 70–2, 75, 88–90, 273, 275, 280 n.4
word-play 23–4, 146, 256
worry *see* anxiety

xenia see hospitality
Xenophon *Anabasis* 3.2.13: 284 n.29
Xuthus 12
  chapter 10 *passim*

Zeus 15–16, 27; 29–31, 38, 64, 78, 84, 101, 122, 137, 139, 147, 151–2, 155, 159–60, 163–4, 179, 189–90, 193, 199, 209, 237, 271, 284 n.19

www.ingramcontent.com/pod-product-compliance
Lightning Source LLC
Chambersburg PA
CBHW050335230426
43663CB00010B/1871